Praise for *So You Want to Sing Cabaret*

"Such important information and a must-read for all singers and teachers. I was fascinated."—Chita Rivera, Tony Award–winning actress

"A remarkable combination of instruction, inspiration, reminiscence, and just plain good sense. David Sabella and Sue Matsuki's book is a wonderfully readable bible for those interested in the world of cabaret, professionally or just out of curiosity."—John Kander, Tony Award–winning composer (*Cabaret, Chicago, Kiss of the Spider Woman*)
"*So You Want to Sing Cabaret* is full of history, anecdotes, and practical knowledge from the legends who have dedicated their lives to this art form. It is an absolutely invaluable resource whether one wants to put together an entire act or simply learn to mine the depths of a song and really make it their own. If you are an aspiring performer or simply an appreciator of the genre, there are life lessons to be learned here that can honestly be applied to many different disciplines —singers, actors, directors, musicians, and anyone else with a thirst for knowledge, a curious mind, and a desire to connect with an audience by telling a thoughtful story through song."—Brian Stokes Mitchell, Tony Award–winning singer and actor

"David Sabella and Sue Matsuki have compiled and curated a comprehensive guide for anyone interested in performing or researching cabaret, including writings and interviews from the most prominent practitioners. It covers the history of cabaret from the beginnings to modern day with all of its marvelous incarnations along the way. A truly delightful and enlightening guide to this sorely neglected but eminently worthy vocal art form."—Lori McCann, Montclair State University, NATS Eastern Region governor and NYC board of directors and past president

"One of my favorite quotes from David Sabella and Sue Matsuki's wonderful, comprehensive book about cabaret is this: 'Cabaret is first and foremost a lyric-driven experience.' The book goes on to tell you everything you will need to know or ever consider about the art form, including interviews with some of the best artists in the business. An amazing accomplishment!"—Betty Buckley, Tony Award–winning actress and singer

"David Sabella and Sue Matsuki have compiled a treasure trove of information relating to every aspect of cabaret performance. Aspiring cabaret singers and devotees of the genre, this book is for you. In their unabashed celebration of a wonderful art form, the authors do their part in keeping it alive."—Mary Saunders Barton, professor emeritus, Penn State University

"What is cabaret? Many have asked but few have answered it in a more precise manner than David Sabella and Sue Matsuki do in *So You Want to Sing Cabaret*. It is just this kind of detail that makes this book required reading for performers and audiences alike. You couldn't ask for better guidance than that from some of cabaret's most respected artists featured in this book."—Frank Dain, editor-in-chief, *Cabaret Scenes* magazine

"The complete works of cabaret—this book is a banquet of history, inspiration, resources, and invaluable singing technique."—Julie Boyd, director, Fordham University Summer Musical Theatre Intensive

"This book needs to be a part of academic curricula and in every voice teacher's and singer's library. As a historical document and a vibrant exploration of cabaret and its evolution, this is a must-read, over and over again!"—Susan Eichhorn-Young, voice teacher, singer, actor, and writer

"*So You Want to Sing Cabaret* is a magnificent read for all solo cabaret artists. David Sabella and Sue Matsuki's beautifully crafted book will be our guide for cabaret development."—Ann Morrison, artistic director, SaraSolo Productions

"The quintessential text on everything cabaret! *So You Want to Sing Cabaret* should be required reading for every performer and teacher who wants to delve into this art form and industry. An absolutely invaluable resource!"—Regina Zona, singer and voice teacher

SO YOU
WANT TO
SING CABARET

So You Want to Sing

Guides for Performers and Professionals

A Project of the National Association of Teachers of Singing

So You Want to Sing: Guides for Performers and Professionals is a series of works devoted to providing a complete survey of what it means to sing within a particular genre. Each contribution functions as a touchstone work not only for professional singers but also for students and teachers of singing. Titles in the series offer a common set of topics so readers can navigate easily the various genres addressed in each volume. This series is produced under the direction of the National Association of Teachers of Singing, the leading professional organization devoted to the science and art of singing.

SO YOU WANT TO SING CABARET

A Guide for Performers

David Sabella
Sue Matsuki

With Michael Feinstein
Foreword by Lorna Luft

Allen Henderson
Executive Editor, NATS

Matthew Hoch
Series Editor

A Project of the National Association of
Teachers of Singing

ROWMAN & LITTLEFIELD
Lanham • Boulder • New York • London

Published by Rowman & Littlefield
An imprint of The Rowman & Littlefield Publishing Group, Inc.
4501 Forbes Boulevard, Suite 200, Lanham, Maryland 20706
www.rowman.com

6 Tinworth Street, London, SE11 5AL, United Kingdom

British Library Cataloguing in Publication Information Available

Library of Congress Cataloging-in-Publication Data

Names: Sabella, David, author. | Matsuki, Sue, 1958– author. | Feinstein, Michael | Luft, Lorna
Title: So you want to sing cabaret : a guide for performers / David Sabella, Sue Matsuki, with Michael Feinstein ; foreword by Lorna Luft.
Description: Lanham : Rowman & Littlefield, 2020. | Series: So you want to sing | Includes bibliographical references and index. | Summary: "So You Want to Sing Cabaret is the first book to examine, in detail, the unique vocal and non-vocal requirements for this genre of music. Sabella and Matsuki provide teachers and singers with never before documented industry knowledge and the experience of venerated professionals and stars of cabaret."—Provided by publisher.
Identifiers: LCCN 2019059372 (print) | LCCN 2019059373 (ebook) | ISBN 9781538124048 (paperback) | ISBN 9781538124055 (epub)
Subjects: LCSH: Singing—Instruction and study. | Music-halls (Variety-theaters, cabarets, etc.)
Classification: LCC MT855 .S2 2020 (print) | LCC MT855 (ebook) | DDC 782.42/143—dc23
LC record available at https://lccn.loc.gov/2019059372
LC ebook record available at https://lccn.loc.gov/2019059373

♾️™ The paper used in this publication meets the minimum requirements of American National Standard for Information Sciences—Permanence of Paper for Printed Library Materials, ANSI/NISO Z39.48-1992.

CONTENTS

FIGURES AND TABLES

FIGURES

TABLES

SERIES EDITOR'S FOREWORD

So You Want to Sing Cabaret: A Guide for Performers is the twentieth and final book in the NATS/Rowman & Littlefield So You Want to Sing series. And what a wonderful journey it has been! Collectively, these twenty volumes present a solid phalanx of reference and pedagogical wisdom on a host of genres, some of which we would have never dreamed of when the series was first conceived. We are indebted to Allen Henderson for his idea and vision that has now—seven years later—become fully realized. In sum, this series has engaged a grand total of ninety-nine distinct authors, all accomplished performers, scholars, and pedagogues from across the nation and the globe. Here are the genres that have been covered: music theater, rock 'n' roll, jazz, gospel, country, Gregorian chant, sacred choral traditions, contemporary Christian music, folk, barbershop, light opera (in all of its many forms, including zarzuela), CCM, blues, chamber music, early music, spirituals, Native American music, mariachi, Brazilian popular music (with all of its subgenres), traditional Irish music, Celtic pop, Lithuanian sutartinės, Georgian polyphonic singing, Egyptian vocal music, Persian *āvāz*, South African choral singing, Hindustani vocal music, Peking opera, overtone singing, and—last but not least—cabaret!

Cabaret is a genre that both Allen and I have wanted to cover since early on in the series. However, as the years went on, the right author never seemed to emerge. (There is a reason this is the twentieth book in the series.) One day, however, I realized that the perfect person to write *So You Want to Sing Cabaret* was right in front of my nose the entire time. David Sabella is not only a fine performer and writer (and superb pedagogue) but also a good friend. I have known David since 2007, first meeting him when I enrolled in Scott McCoy's vocal anatomy and physiology class, which was offered through the New York Singing Teachers' Association (NYSTA). David moderated the sessions, and— after I got to know David over the course of that semester—he invited me to serve under his leadership on the NYSTA board of directors. The rest, as they say according to the cliché, is history. David has had a career that is both extraordinary and unique. He started out as a classi- cal countertenor, winning prestigious competitions such as the Luciano Pavarotti International Competition and the New York Oratorio Society Solo Competition. Later, he was cast in the role of Mary Sunshine in the Broadway revival of *Chicago*, performing the role in New York and Las Vegas over the course of the next ten years. And now (post-opera and post-Broadway) he is flourishing as a cabaret artist in the greater New York City area. With connections to everyone in the business and a contagious energy and passion for the genre, David is the ideal author of *So You Want to Sing Cabaret*.

About midway through the writing process, David enlisted a coauthor. Sue Matsuki has been a major presence in the New York cabaret scene for more than thirty years, working as a performer, a writer, a teacher, and a producer. She has performed in all of New York's major cabaret venues and has especially been a fixture at the legendary club Don't Tell Mama at 343 West Forty-Sixth Street. Sue literally knows everyone in the cabaret world, and her insights and experience have made for a much richer book. *So You Want to Sing Cabaret* is the third book in the So You Want to Sing series that has been coauthored by a woman and a man, and all three books have benefited from this dual perspective.[1]

The journey that David and Sue will take you on as you make your way through this volume will be an edifying adventure . . . and a lot of fun! You will learn about the history of cabaret, meet the greatest stars and legends of the cabaret world, explore the ever-expanding Great

American Songbook, and—most important—learn how to perform this unique genre, which is much, much more involved and complex than singing "music theater in the crook of a piano." In music theater, you are playing a character. In cabaret, you are you. You are laying your soul bare and telling your story in a vulnerable way before a small audience in an intimate space. David and Sue bring more than fifty years of combined experience doing this, and they will show you how to truly connect with the lyric and your audience. Important practical matters—such as producing your show and working with your "team" (your musical director and director)—will also be discussed.

Like other books in the So You Want to Sing series, several "common chapters" are included as well. These chapters include a chapter on voice science by Scott McCoy, one on vocal health by Wendy LeBorgne, and one on audio enhancement technology by Matthew Edwards. These chapters help to bind the series together, ensuring consistency of fact when it comes to the most essential matters of voice production and microphone technique. Legendary cabaret singer Lorna Luft has graciously contributed the foreword.

The collected volumes of the So You Want to Sing series offer a valuable opportunity for performers and teachers of singing to explore new styles and important pedagogies. I am confident that voice specialists, both amateur and professional, will benefit from David and Sue's important resource. It has been a privilege to work with them on this project, just as it has been the opportunity of a lifetime to work with all of the So You Want to Sing authors over the past five years. *So You Want to Sing Cabaret* is a fitting final number and a perfect way to conclude our show. That's all, folks!

Matthew Hoch
Series Editor

NOTE

1. The other two coauthored books are *So You Want to Sing Barbershop* (2017) by Diane M. Clark and Billy J. Biffle and *So You Want to Sing Music by Women* (2019) by Matthew Hoch and Linda Lister.

FOREWORD

I started my career in cabaret in the 1970s when these intimate spaces were plentiful in almost every city in America. There was Mr. Kelly's in Chicago, the Back Lot in Los Angeles, and—in New York—Upstairs at the Downstairs, Reno Sweeney, Café Carlyle, the Algonquin, and the Bon Soir in Greenwich Village, among many others. Sadly, most of these iconic places no longer exist, but now there are places like Michael Feinstein's wonderful clubs in New York City, Los Angeles, and San Francisco, the Green Room 42, the Laurie Beechman, Pangea, the Beach, the legendary Don't Tell Mama, and Birdland, which now opens its doors to both cabaret and jazz. Through these venues, performers of cabaret can still hone their craft and gain experience in this tricky but rewarding field.

I have always been interested in the origins of the small entertainment rooms that have been variously called cabaret rooms, nightclubs, lounges, showrooms, jazz clubs, and saloons. What makes them different from one another? Is it the space? Is it the artist that is appearing there? Is it the music the artist is performing at the time? Is it the people who attend? Or is it all of the above?

I found out along the way how incredibly challenging this form of entertainment is to do well. You are stripped of any place to hide on stage. It is only you, the musicians behind you, your patter, and the song. There is no hiding behind a character or performing a script written by someone else. Your personality and your ability to communicate to the audience and your talent to make them laugh, cry, and feel you are singing directly to them requires courage, honesty, vulnerability, and openness. Learning how to look directly at their faces and not above their heads, making them feel as if you are in their living room, and never becoming self-indulgent with your material is a journey that many have tried yet few have succeeded.

Over the years I have talked with numerous actors who have appeared in film and on stage and television. Many have told me they could never do a club show because it is such a vulnerable, selfless, and terrifying idea to be on a stage as "themselves." It took me many years to learn my craft, trust myself, and realize I was up there on the stage without any trappings. In other words, it is like being on a flying trapeze without a net. But the rewards of being your true self in front of an audience can be freeing and thrilling.

Of course, I had a great deal of help along the way. Growing up in my family, our home was always filled with brilliant writers, directors, musicians, composers, lyricists, and amazing singers who shared their extraordinary talents with me and who showed me just how this art form, if done correctly, can be so fulfilling. My mother knew and worked with some of the best composers and lyricists of the Great American Songbook on her movies and television series—musical icons like Harold Arlen, Johnny Mercer, Ira Gershwin, Irving Berlin, Cole Porter, and Hugh Martin. I was able to learn this craft through a direct, person-to-person exchange by listening to and watching the best singers of that era interpret a song lyric. These included singers like Frank Sinatra, Sammy Davis Jr., Rosemary Clooney, and the brilliant Peggy Lee, whom I saw at the Empire Room at the Waldorf Astoria in New York. I have been lucky enough to see many great cabaret performers over the years, including wonderful singers like Steve Ross, Bobby Short, Ann Hampton Callaway, and Mabel Mercer at the St. Regis. The incomparable Marilyn Maye, who is still performing as of the publication of this book, is an inspiration to me and to every artist who has ever wanted to sing this type of music, and of course so is Michael Feinstein, who is single-handedly responsible for keeping the Great American Songbook relevant, alive, and thriving in the twenty-first century. ♪

Growing up with my mother, hearing, and later singing, her songs afforded me an education and insight into the art of cabaret that was both astonishing and rare, an education that was simply not available anywhere else. There was no formal education in cabaret singing. There was no analysis of craft. Nothing was written down. It was simply an art form that was passed down from generation to generation. The only way to learn the craft was directly from the great singers who were out there doing it.

Many people have made assumptions about what it takes to do cabaret well, and in doing so they have turned this beautiful art form, this intimate expression of song, into nothing more than a parody of its former self. Luckily now, David Sabella and Sue Matsuki have provided this wonderful book, which is a fabulous guide for all artists about every aspect of the art form that is cabaret. The rich historical insights about the development of this genre and the never-before-published "craft" and "business" sections are alone worth the price of admission. And there's more, including personal insights offered by some of the biggest names in cabaret, many of whom are dear friends. Whether you are an aspiring cabaret singer who is just starting out or an older, more established performer who wants to hone your craft, the valuable resources compiled here make this book a must-have for anyone considering performing in this wonderful and intimate art form.

Lorna Luft

Lorna Luft is a cabaret icon, having performed in nightclubs, supper clubs, and concert halls around the globe for most of her life. The daughter of legendary singer and actress Judy Garland and producer Sid Luft, Lorna Luft represents a link that harkens back to the golden age of singing. Luft made her show business debut at the age of eleven on the Christmas episode of her mother's television series, The Judy Garland Show. *She went on to make her Broadway debut in 1971 in the musical* Promises, Promises *at the Shubert Theatre. Other early Broadway and theater credits include* They're Playing Our Song, Grease

Figure F.I. Lorna Luft. Photo by Chris Davis.

2, Snoopy! The Musical, *and Extremities (with Farrah Fawcett). In the 1990s, Luft starred as Miss Adelaide in the American and world-touring revival of* Guys and Dolls. *She has also starred as* Mama Rose in Gypsy *and continues to tour the United States and United Kingdom in productions of Irving Berlin's* White Christmas. *Luft has brought new shows to iconic venues such as Feinstein's/54 Below, Birdland, and the Crazy Coqs in London and has also appeared in the London Palladium, Carnegie Hall, and the Hollywood Bowl. Her recording discography includes nine hit singles, nine cast albums, nineteen film and television appearances, and her highly acclaimed solo album* Songs My Mother Taught Me. ♪

In addition to her performance career, Luft is also an accomplished author, having written two bestselling books: Me and My Shadows: A Family Memoir *and* A Star Is Born: Judy Garland and the Film That Got Away.

ACKNOWLEDGMENTS

There are so many people to thank for all their help in bringing this book to fruition and none more so than series editor Matthew Hoch. During the process of writing and editing this book, Matt's steady guidance led me, like a shepherd, through what was a very difficult time of my life. Unimaginable family complications and tragedies arose. Months, and deadlines, flew by as I and my family dealt with a one-two punch that life had struck. And throughout all this, Matt remained my champion, calmly reassuring me that "everything is OK" and that "we have plenty of time to finish." Having the daunting task of writing this book was indeed a focus for me during this very trying time, and Matt's friendship and understanding are as much responsible for this book's existence as is his amazing "official" work as series editor. Thank you, Matt, for everything!

Sue Matsuki was first introduced to me by a mutual friend and wonderful cabaret performer, Richard Skipper. Richard has a wonderful way of "putting his hand in there," and by introducing me to Sue he single-handedly changed the nature of this book and made it better. Thank you, Richard.

Now, about Sue Matsuki: This remarkable woman, artist, teacher, and cabaret godmother is now one of my closest friends, and indeed my "sister-in-art." As soon as I met Sue, I knew I needed her. She agreed to collaborate with me and contribute "some information" to the book, and we began working together. Sue proved herself to be a great help, and one of the smartest women in this industry, having already built a substantial cabaret curriculum and having developed important personal contacts over the course of her thirty-five years of performing in every cabaret venue in Manhattan. However, when my personal life became insistent, that's when Sue became invaluable. She rallied to my aid and helped me in every conceivable way, including cooking meals for my family. With all that was going on, it became apparent that I would not make the publisher's deadline without substantial help, and so I asked her if she would consider the responsibility of becoming a full-fledged coauthor. Thank God she did, or else this book might not have happened at all. Her tireless work allowed me to take the time to navigate my kids through a difficult family situation and know that my other "baby" was in good hands. Sue Matsuki, thank God for you!

I first met Roy Sander at the behest of Sherry Eaker, the president of bistroawards.com and producer of the annual Bistro Awards ceremony. Roy is her lead reviewer and the editor of bistroawards.com and—as you will come to know as you read this book—one of the most learned men and prolific writers in the cabaret industry. Sherry asked if I would consider reviewing for bistroawards.com, with the caveat that I had to first "pass muster" with Roy. I guess I did pass muster, for I have been privileged to work with and learn from this wonderful man who has become my writing mentor and friend. Roy has written on the art of cabaret for many decades. He is a walking encyclopedia, history lesson, and grammar and spell-check program, all in one person. Not only did he contribute a chapter to this book, but he offered several articles for our online resource page and is the subject of one of our most compelling interviews. Roy also lent his editorial eye to several chapters of the book and helped us procure some of the images we use as well. Thank you, Roy, for your hard work, friendship, mentorship, and guidance. And thank you, Sherry Eaker, not only for agreeing to be an industry proofreader for the book but also for your forethought, for your invitation to review, and for introducing me to my writing guru.

I must give a special mention to my friend and client Patty Fricke, who graciously offered to "help out" by proofreading the book (not at all knowing just exactly how big it was). Her keen editorial eye—and hours of dedication to this cause—helped shape this textbook into a wonderful and concise tool. Thank you, Patty.

Frank Dain and Marilyn Lester were incredibly helpful in so many ways. Frank, editor of *Cabaret Scenes* magazine, helped to procure several of the images used in the book, and both he and Marilyn, executive director of the American Songbook Association (which publishes *Cabaret Scenes*), offered their international listing of cabaret clubs and training programs. Both Frank and Marilyn also volunteered as industry proofreaders for us, ensuring both accuracy of content and grammatic delivery. Thank you, Frank and Marilyn.

Three other contributors unique to this book must be acknowledged as well: the late Erv Raible for his wonderful chapter "A Brief History of Cabaret," Rosalyn Coleman Williams for her article on "The Cabaret Singer and Social Media," and Betsyann Faiella for "Hiring a Public Relations Professional." Each of these contributions is informative and a necessary component of the larger work as a whole. Thank you Erv, Rosalyn, and Betsyann.

Thank you to of all our interview subjects. Your words of wisdom and creative advice are the foundation of this work. You pass on a legacy of knowledge that simply cannot be taught anywhere else. And a special thank-you to my friend, the incomparable Lorna Luft, who agreed without hesitation to write the foreword.

Most of the subject interviews took place at the West Bank Café, home of the Laurie Beechman Theatre. My deepest appreciation to Steve Olsen, owner and proprietor of the West Bank Café, for always making me, and my interview subject, feel like the most important people in the restaurant. And many thanks to Sidney Myer at Don't Tell Mama, along with Kenny Bell and Michael Kirk Lane at the Laurie Beechman Theatre, who were among the first club managers to welcome me with open arms as a book writer and as a reviewer for both the Bistro Awards and Cabaret Hotspot! Thank you, gentlemen.

In addition to those mentioned above, I would like to thank the photographers who supplied us with all the wonderful photos for the book: Helane Blumfield, Natasha Castillo, Jeremy Daniel, Sadie Foster, Audrey Foto, Takako Harkness, Eric Stephen Jacobs, Rick Jensen, Maryann Lopinto, Paloma Marugan, Marc Meyerbroker, Stephen Mosher,

JP Perreaux, Daniel Reichert, Susan Stripling, Heather Sullivan, Stacy Sullivan, Rob Sutton, Steve Ullathorne, An-Khang Vu-Cong, Russ Weatherford, Bill Westmoreland, Elizabeth Wiseman, Matthew Wolf, and of course Seth Walters for his magnificent cover photo of cabaret star Jeff Harnar.

The production staff at Rowman & Littlefield, including Michael Tan and Natalie Mandziuk, must also be commended, not only for their work in bringing this book to press but also for the entire series of So You Want to Sing books, which sheds light on never-before-discussed genres and subcultures of vocal performance. The series is the only one of its kind, culminating with this, the twentieth (and last) book, and is a wholly worthwhile investment for any music library.

Thank you to the National Association of Teachers of Singing and executive director Allen Henderson for sponsoring the production of this entire series and for considering the vocal performance genre of cabaret worthy of in-depth analysis. Both Sue and I hope to live up to your expectations and the incredible standard that has already been set by the previous books in this series.

My most special and heartfelt thanks must go to my family: to my brother Ernie Sabella for all of his support during this process, and to my children Iraina and Faith, who this year suffered not only the physical loss of one of their parents but also the virtual loss of the other as I locked myself in my room, typing away at all hours of the day and night (or out of the house interviewing subjects and seeing and reviewing shows). You, my darlings, are the strongest young women I know. Thank you for being there for each other, and for me. Your contribution to this book cannot be measured, but without you, without your strength and compassion, this book could not have happened. Love always, Dad.

—David Sabella

* * *

I too would like to thank series editor Matthew Hoch for his enthusiasm, incredible patience, and knowledge in producing and editing this book, and for his joy in bringing the genre of cabaret into the So You Want to Sing family.

To coauthor David Sabella, I could write a whole book on how you have affected my life. I too hold that first day dear to my heart and will be forever grateful to Richard Skipper for changing my life with a simple introduction. Who knew when we met over dinner at your table and started to talk that I would welcome a new brother into my life (and have two gorgeous nieces), that I would once again be teaching and reviewing, through Cabaret Hotspot!, and that I would become your coauthor? I really didn't expect our friendship to coincide with a writing project. Writing a book about cabaret has long been a "bucket list" idea that has now been crossed off . . . and all because of you! Requesting from the editor and publisher that I become the coauthor (because you felt I earned it) is not what most people would do. There was no ego; there was only the idea of what would be best for the book. I am honored. Personally, you have shown me a new way of looking at myself, as well as my talent, intellect, worth, and strength. We have just given birth to our "baby," making us family for life. Thank you.

Thank you to Roy Sander for your first review and for being there for us during the writing of this book. You are a champion of all talent and of cabaret. I am grateful to all the people named above in David's acknowledgments and especially to those associated with the production of this book for their help and guidance. I wouldn't be where I am today without Gregory Toroian, my music director for the past twenty-five years whose collaboration, love, and friendship are beyond my ability to express in words. Thank you.

There is a long list of additional people I need to thank, everyone that helped me to become the singer and teacher that I am today, including every piano bar pianist I have ever played with; every music director and musician that I have had the honor of doing a show with; every open mic I have ever attended, with a special thanks to Birdland's "cast party" team—Jim Caruso, Billy Stritch, Steve Doyle, Daniel Glass, and owner Gianni Valenti—and Tanya Moberly and Mark Janas at the Salon; every booking agent and club that has ever booked me, every director that was a part of "Team Matsuki" (Helen Baldassare, Gerry Geddes, Jay Rogers, and Lina Koutrakos); all of the technical directors who made art with me; all of the hardworking waitstaff and bartenders (with a special shout to my girl, Randy Cohen Lester); all the songwriters that graced me with their music, including Dan and Michelle Page,

Gregory Toroian, Saadi Zain, and Paul Stephan; my photographer and makeup artist Eric Stephen Jacobs and the fantastic graphic artists, all of whom helped me create my "brand" with their artistic eye; the loving sisterhood formed by Meg Flather; Edd Clark and Paul Stephan, two of the most supportive friends that I have, for a joyous ten-year run of *Sue and Edd's Fabulous Christmas*; Joan Crowe, Laurie Krauz, Ellen Lawrence, Sarah Rice, Bryon Sommer, Tracy Stark, Deborah Stone, and Russ Woolley; the MAC membership and president Lennie Watts; and, finally, to my students at OLLI, the Theater Barn, the Canadian School of Performing Arts, MAC to School, and Cabaret Hotspot! who attended my classes, thus teaching me how to become a better teacher and, ultimately, write this book.

I would be remiss if I didn't mention Sidney Myer, because this cabaret "journey"—yes, I said it!—all started the day that I auditioned for him in 1986. Being one of those people on the other side of the now famous "Sidney talk" (see chapter 5), I can say that no one has affected my career more than Sidney Myer. If you come to New York, stop by Don't Tell Mama, sing at the piano bar, and ask to meet Sidney. Tell him that Sue Matsuki sent you. Maybe he'll even sign your copy of *So You Want to Sing Cabaret*!

Finally, to my sweet husband of thirty-five years, Kenro Matsuki, who has had to share me with so many producing projects, rehearsals, shows, and the writing of this book, thank you for your belief in me, your support, and for your never-ending and unconditional love.

To all the people above . . . you taught my heart to sing. Thank you!

—Sue Matsuki

* * *

Both David and Sue would like to thank the industry support professionals who cater to this art form and its community of performers: the club owners, booking managers, public relations reps, feature and reviewing press, and photographers/videographers. These individuals include Scott Barbarino (Iridium Jazz Club/NiteLife Exchange); Jim Caruso (Birdland/Birdland Theater); Daniel Dunlow (Green Room 42); Dan Fortune (Fortune Creative); Steve Frankel (Feinstein's/54 Below); Dave Goodside (Beach Café); Stephen Hanks (Cabaret Life Productions); Thomas Honeck (The Duplex); Beck Lee (Blitz Media LLC); Peter Martin (The Triad); Sidney Myer and Tanya Moberly (Don't Tell Mama); Steve Olsen, Kenny Bell, and Michael Kirk Lane (Laurie Beechman Theatre); Stephen Shanagan (Pangea); and Richard Skipper (Richard Skipper Celebrates). These people were especially gracious to us, welcoming us into their clubs, their work, and their lives, so that we could bring you the most comprehensive book on this subject possible. These names represent only a few of the many people who work diligently to secure the future of live small-venue entertainment for generations to come.

A special thank-you to the rarest of all breeds, the cabaret investors and producers. These people put their money where our mouths are, supporting this art form in a vital capacity: Charles Bullock (chairman of the board, Mabel Mercer Foundation); Adela and Larry Elow (the Donald F. Smith Award and the MMF annual high school American Songbook Competition); Peter and Linda Hanson (the Mabel Mercer Julie Wilson Award and the MAC Hanson Award); Peter Leavy and Frank Dain (*Cabaret Scenes*); Kitty Skrobela (Miranda Music); Tom Toce (Urban Stages); and the effervescent Russ Woolley (Russ Woolley Productions).

And last, the biggest thank-you to the wonderful singers who share their time, talent, and treasure in this art form, and whose performances and artistic excellence continue to inspire us. You are the backbone of the cabaret industry. You, the performers—often thought of and even referred to as the "cabaret community"—are actually the investors in this multi-million-dollar industry. Without you no club stays in business, no stories are told, and no songs are sung. In the words of Oscar Hammerstein II, "The song is you!" Thank you!

A SPECIAL ACKNOWLEDGMENT

Julie Wilson (1924–2015)

Sue Matsuki

No book on cabaret would be complete without acknowledging the Grand Dame of Cabaret, Miss Julie Wilson! When asked to write this tribute to her, I felt both honored and qualified. Qualified, because I was the very first Julie Wilson Award recipient, chosen by Julie herself, in 2004; and honored, because Julie was also my dear friend and mentor for eighteen years.

Julie Wilson was born in Omaha, Nebraska, the daughter of Emily and Russell Wilson. She first found her artistic outlet in her teenage years with a local musical group called Hank's Hepcats. After briefly attending Omaha University, she won the title of Miss Nebraska and would have competed in the Miss America pageant until it was discovered that she was just under the required minimum age of eighteen. She headed to New York City during World War II and found work in two of Manhattan's leading nightclubs, the Latin Quarter and the Copacabana.

She made her Broadway stage debut in the 1946 revue *Three to Make Ready*. In 1951, she moved to London to star in the West End production of *Kiss Me, Kate* and remained there for four years, appearing in shows such as *South Pacific* and *Bells Are Ringing* while studying at the Royal Academy of Dramatic Arts. Additional Broadway credits include *The Pajama Game* (1954), *Jimmy* (1969), *Park* (1970), and *Legs Diamond*

(1988), for which she received a Tony Award nomination as Best Featured Actress in a Musical. She also toured in *Show Boat, Panama Hattie, Silk Stockings, Follies, Company,* and *A Little Night Music.* ♪

In addition to her various theater credits, Julie also had a film and television career, as well as a solo recording career. With more than fifteen albums to her credit, she recorded the works of many of the Great American Songbook's greatest composers: Cy Coleman, Harold Arlen, the Gershwins, Bart Howard, Cole Porter, Kurt Weill, and Stephen

Figure A.I. Julie Wilson. *Courtesy of Roy Sander's collection.*

Sondheim, as well as many original cast recordings and "Live from . . ." events. ♪

However, rather than write about Julie Wilson's incredible professional history in movies, theater, recordings, and of course the New York cabaret industry, I'd like to write more personally and introduce you to the Julie Wilson that I knew, the person, the mentor, and my friend.

Although we both lived and performed in New York, I traveled to Fairbanks, Alaska, in 1997 to study with Julie at the Fairbanks Summer Arts Festival. We instantly bonded over our many similar likes and dislikes and became good friends. Julie became good friends with everyone.

While always considered beautiful, even in her advanced age her physical beauty was only a small part of what drew you toward her presence. She cared about everyone she knew on a very deep level. When speaking with someone, she was fully present, gazing at them with her intensely blue eyes. Although most often cast as the "vamp," Julie was nobody's fool. She had a keen sense of a person and their sincerity, onstage and off. She was always polite, but could also be a steel magnolia!

As a teacher, she was tough. She got right to the point and was always truthful. She was the best teacher I've ever had. And once you proved yourself, she was the most loving and supportive advocate of your work. She told me once to "compete with no one else except the performer that you were the last time you stepped on stage." She also said, "Raise the bar on your own performance a little each time."

I will never forget seeing her perform with her longtime music director, William Roy, at Joe's Pub in New York. It was her birthday show, so I made her a Julie Wilson teddy bear, complete with false eyelashes, a black gown, a red boa, and of course the signature gardenia in her hair. The bear came in a little box that also looked like a bear. I gave it to her before the show, but she came out with it and proudly announced to her audience that I made it for her and that it even came in a "little bear coffin"! Then she laughed that deep, robust laugh.

She saw dozens of shows every week, right up until the time of her passing. Generous to a fault in her guidance, if a performer onstage was talking too much or was not loud enough, Julie would often be heard as a voice in the darkened audience, coaching from her seat, saying, "Stop talking and sing!" or "I can't hear you . . . enunciate!" Diction was a big thing for her! Advice from Julie at any time, even during your performance, was considered "sage" and was received with the love with which it was intended. She was a cabaret icon, cherished by all, and it was considered an honor just to have her in your audience.

She used to call me her "Diva Sister." We would get all dolled up (Julie insisted that we always looked our best in public because "that's what stars do"), and we'd have what she called our "chicks' night out." This entailed seeing a cabaret show (or two) and ending up at Joe Allen's on Restaurant Row (Forty-Sixth Street) eating a burger at 11:00 at night.

Julie loved being a mom and adored her sons, one of whom passed at a young age and the other who became a famous actor, Holt McCallany. She took time off from her thriving career to raise her sons, and in return, Holt took incredible care of his mom and allowed all of us who loved her to be a part of her life.

When Julie had her first stroke, I was one of three people allowed to visit her. When I walked into the room, there she was, without a stitch of makeup on, looking more gorgeous than possible, sitting up cracking wise with Baby Jane Dexter (another wonderful performer) and her son Holt, who was telling an outrageous story and making his mom laugh again in that joyous and fabulously low voice. She was one of the strongest women I have ever met.

Little-known facts: Julie loved and owned pit bulls. She would often be all glammed up onstage in a Bob Mackie dress, but underneath she'd have bunny slippers on her feet. Her favorite color was purple, and she wore that iconic gardenia in her hair in tribute to Billie Holiday, whom she met by standing outside the stage door. Ms. Holiday was so taken with young Julie's beauty and sweetness, she invited her home and cooked for her. Julie's tribute show to Billie was incredible and one of my favorite shows ever.

This is who Julie Wilson was to me, and I miss her terribly every single day. I think of her every time I take the stage and smile. I have a picture of her on my desk and can still hear and feel her in my audience, cheering me on and beaming like a proud mama. She often sang "I'm Gonna Live Till I Die," and boy, did she! Julie left us six months short of her ninety-first birthday. What a life, what an artist, what a teacher . . . and what an extraordinary friend. ♪

INTRODUCTION

David Sabella

Thank you, reader, for picking up this book, and for your interest in this unique, often misunderstood, and very artistic genre of vocal performance.

How this book came to be, and its place within the So You Want to Sing series of books, is as unique as the genre of cabaret itself. In the winter of 2018, I realized I needed to make a change. My life was packed full with a very predictable schedule of teaching voice, both privately and as a faculty member at two universities (Montclair State and Fordham University), and parenting my two young daughters. What once had been a thriving career in classical music and on Broadway had turned into a life of security (if teaching can be called that) and family, which, make no mistake about it, I aimed for with great precision.

Newly divorced, however, I was determined to return to my performing career, and in order to do that I had to "clear the decks," and my schedule, to make room for "something else" to happen. I needed room in my life for something new to come in. I thought that "something" would be a return to professional singing. Instead it turned out to be *So You Want to Sing Cabaret*. Just seven days after I left Montclair State University in May 2018, series editor Matthew Hoch approached me about writing this book.

I had known Matt for several years. During my two-term presidency of the New York Singing Teachers' Association (from 2008 to 2014), Matt served as the editor of our own publication *VOICEPrints*, and later went on to become president of the New York Singing Teachers' Association (NYSTA) himself. He knew I had performed in cabaret venues during my tenure with the Broadway show *Chicago* and that I had recently (in 2016) begun to perform again within this genre, reengaging my own singing career after having raised my children, who were now teenagers. I had also contributed a chapter to another book within this series, *So You Want to Sing CCM*. These points of contact, as well as my long-standing membership in the National Association of Teachers of Singing and my reputation as a pedagogue in this field, led him to ask me if I would consider being the author of this book.

While incredibly flattered, my initial instinct was to say no, but I had specifically made room in my life for "something." I asked for something new to come in, and this is what showed up. The irony of my reengaging my performance career in cabaret and at the same time being asked to write a book on cabaret did not escape me either. However, in its own unique way, this scenario is compatible with the experience had by many singers in cabaret, who return to performance after some time away, from either raising children or another career. With this in mind—after some serious thought—I said yes! I assured Matt that I was in no way an expert in the field of cabaret but that I could get to the experts and deliver a book "straight from the horse's mouth," with interviews and insights from some of the most highly respected cabaret professionals in the country. Luckily, he and Rowman & Littlefield agreed, and *So You Want to Sing Cabaret* was born.

One of the first people I met with after agreeing to write the book was Sue Matsuki. Sue is an award-winning cabaret performer and just recently celebrated her thirty-third year of performing at New York's legendary Don't Tell Mama. She is also an esteemed teacher and mentor in this field. We immediately bonded, and, realizing she possessed such a wealth of knowledge, I asked her if she would contribute her expertise to the book. Luckily, she said yes. That "contribution" soon turned into full-fledged coauthorship, as Sue's knowledge and expertise (and kind spirit) became fully apparent to me.

One of the first things I realized was that cabaret was not what I thought it was! Even though I had performed for some time in cabaret venues, I had not really used what, through our research, we have come to identify as a "cabaret performance technique." What is a cabaret performance technique? That and many other surprising questions (and answers) lie within the book itself.

Concurrently, while researching for the book and interviewing its subjects, Sue and I developed a website, CabaretHotspot.com, which was modeled after the late Stu Hamtra's now defunct Cabaret Hotline Online, for which Sue had previously reviewed and written a well-received blog, *Sue's Views*. Cabaret Hotspot! was immediately embraced by the cabaret industry, the clubs, and community of performers, and thus allowed us access to both the performers and shows, without which this book could not have been written. CabaretHotspot.com also acts as an educational platform, offering classes on the art, craft, and business of cabaret; news, reviews, interviews, and feature articles; and its "Find-a-Pro" directory, where singers can find the teachers and other support professionals they need to help realize their artistic goals. This website, along with the online resource page on the National Association of Teachers of Singing (NATS) website, complements the contents of this book, and we encourage readers to explore these supplemental resources.

Although the genres of performance seen in cabaret venues are all-inclusive, including musical revue, showcase, emcee/interview show, spoken word, and characterization/impersonation, the scope of this book, as per the title, is necessarily quite narrow: the singing and requisite performance training needed for that singing. Unfortunately, this narrow focus disallowed us from including the many other multifaceted performances seen in cabaret clubs. The authors encourage each reader to experience the art of live cabaret entertainment with all of its unique subcategories.

While there are cabaret venues across the country and indeed around the world, we have, in large part, limited the scope of our inquiry to the performers and teachers that primarily work and reside within New York City. These artists and teachers may in fact bring their performances and classes to other cities, but no other city on the planet has as many small-venue cabaret clubs and training programs for cabaret performance as does New York City, which is considered the worldwide epicenter of small-venue performance.

Further, we decided early on to limit our investigation to those singers and teachers who have spent a lifetime within this genre as their primary source of artistic expression. There are many performers in other genres of singing (classical, music theater, jazz, etc.), and even other genres of performance (television and film), who occasionally perform within a cabaret venue, some to great success. These performers may also use a cabaret performance technique in some or all of their material. However, their appearance in cabaret is only temporary, as they make the bulk of their living in their primary genre and only visit the world of cabaret as a means of fulfilling other artistic needs, retaining public awareness of their celebrity, or publicizing their next primary production. Instead, we wanted to focus attention on those artists who live their lives within this genre and have specifically chosen small-venue performance as their primary means of artistic expression or income. The one caveat to this is our interview with Broadway and cabaret star Karen Mason, who has, throughout her career, performed equally in both genres to great success. Hence, her title as the "Countess of Crossover."

In addition to our interview with Karen Mason, we are honored to have been able to speak with some of the cabaret industry's greatest stars, including the "Queen of Cabaret" Andrea Marcovicci, the "Crown Prince" Steve Ross, award-winning singer-songwriter Ann Hampton Callaway, and—the "Ambassador of the Great American Songbook"—Michael Feinstein. Indeed, all the artists we've spoken to (singers, teachers, music and stage directors, and other support professionals) each bring a unique perspective to, and about, this style of singing. And with chapters devoted to the art, craft, training, business, and history of cabaret, we hope this book will illuminate, educate, and inspire the reader to explore this unique genre of vocal performance and artistic expression.

This book's target audience is both the aspiring cabaret singer and their teacher. Its goal is to dispel myths and misconceptions surrounding the genre, and even negative connotations regarding the use of the word "cabaret," and to create understanding as to the nature (the art, craft, and business) of cabaret performance. While employing the primary directive of communicating with a national and international community of teachers, it is also our goal that this book become a vital resource to all singers seeking to enter the world of cabaret concert performance.

In the words of lyricist Fred Ebb, "willkommen, bienvenue, welcome" to the world of cabaret!

ONLINE SUPPLEMENT

So *You Want to Sing Cabaret* features an online supplement courtesy of the National Association of Teachers of Singing. Visit the link below to discover additional exercises and examples, as well as links to recordings of the songs referenced in this book.

http://www.nats.org/So_You_Want_To_Sing_Book_Series.html

A musical note symbol ♪ in this book will mark every instance of corresponding online supplement material.

For more information and additional online resources, please visit www.cabarethotspot.com.

1

CABARET 101

❶

A BRIEF HISTORY OF CABARET

Erv Raible

In the mid-1970s, it seemed that New York cabaret was doomed to succumb to the same fate as that of vaudeville. However, a revival was about to occur. It wasn't long until Erv Raible (1946–2014) and his partner Rob Hoskins (1938–1984) took ownership of several cabaret rooms in Manhattan: Don't Tell Mama, Eighty Eight's, Brandy's Piano Bar, and the Duplex. Together, the two men not only revitalized the New York cabaret scene but also gave voice to a generation of performers still admired today, including Linda Lavin (b. 1937), Bonnie Franklin (1944–2013), and Harvey Fierstein (b. 1954). Raible was also the cofounder and president of the Manhattan Association of Cabarets (MAC), the first cabaret trade organization of its kind. He was the executive/artistic director of the International Cabaret Conference at Yale University and produced and directed cabaret internationally, presenting more than four thousand artists. He was an avid historian and beloved teacher within this genre. This opening chapter is Raible's account of the history of cabaret, from its earliest days in seventeenth-century Paris to the thriving New York cabaret culture of the present day, a scene that Raible and Hoskins played a significant part in revitalizing. ♪

Figure 1.1. Erv Raible. *Photo by Maryann Lopinto.*

THE EARLY YEARS

Cabaret originally inherited its name from the wine cellars and taverns of Paris in the 1600s, evolving as performance locales either because of tipsy patrons spontaneously joining in singsong or because enterprising hosts wanting to attract more customers—some things never change!—allowed the premises to be used by strolling players, balladeers, jugglers, and the complete retinue of out-of-season carnival personalities, and who centuries earlier would have included wandering minstrels and other chroniclers, recording history through their epic tales, which were often sung. These tales ranged from Homer's *Iliad* to *Beowulf*; let's not forget that even historians like Josephus (37–100) were merely storytellers, setting down early events in history as stories. These went on to become legend, and many of them ultimately became fact.

The earliest record of "cabaret-esque" space and performances was at the eighteenth-century Café des Aveugles in the cellar of the Palais Royal featuring an orchestra, a singer, and a ventriloquist. Remember, the Comédie Française is also located at the Palais Royal—could this also be the first record of a performer "moonlighting" to make a few extra sous? Around 1800, the Café des Estrangers was celebrated for its concerts. And during the Directory and First Empire periods, the "Jardin des Plaisirs" became popular, resembling their English prototypes and being the forerunners of the American amusement parks. They were outdoors, with swings and merry-go-rounds, fireworks, dancing,

Figure 1.2. **An artist's rendering of the Café Aveugle in 1771.** *Creative Commons (CC BY-SA 4.0).*

singing, and orchestras playing, while refreshments of all types were being served at small tables scattered throughout the gardens. Particularly in Paris, most of the big music halls of the boulevards had outdoor spaces during the summer in the park bordering the Champs-Élysées.

SINGING LEADS THE WAY

By the latter half of the nineteenth century, the song became the principal form of entertainment provided by French cafés and bistros. Imagine the powerful impact of the song as a medium of public communication in the days before radio and television. The songs evoked not only love but also other moods and emotions of a sociopolitical significance—recording daily history and voicing reaction to contemporary events. Songs were an artistic version of the newspaper—a satirical weapon for criticizing and protest. These performance freedoms were to later die, their worst death to date, under the Third Reich during the leadership of Adolf Hitler (1889–1945).

Eventually these bistros took on grand proportions growing into the café chantants, frequently involving orchestras and variety acts with costumes, sets, and props. The first of these grand spectacles included establishments like the Moulin Rouge, Lido, Paradis Latin, and the Folies-Bergère.[1] In 1848, the first of these, the Estaminet Lyrique, was opened in the Passage Jouffroy, a covered arcade on the Boulevard Montmartre. It produced the first real male cabaret vocal star: Darcier (1819–1883). It is worth noting—and quite interesting—that the first known major cabaret performer was male in what has always been a female-dominated genre. In the 1860s the appearance of the great Thérésa (1837–1913) marked the next step forward. Through the mastery of their craft, Thérésa and Darcier brought the café chantant into the era of the café concert.

THE EVOLUTION OF THE CAFÉ CONCERT

It was directly from these café concerts that cabaret as we know it today began to evolve. Known as the artistic cabaret, it by necessity became more intellectual and deliberately artistic, propelled by laughter and entertainment value. In 1881, Rodolphe Salis (1851–1897) took a far-reaching step in opening the first artistic cabaret—Montmartre's Le Chat Noir at 84 Boulevard Rochechouart. Its birth sparked by the Hydropathes of Emile Goudeau (1849–1906), a weekly literary society meeting, allowed its poets and writers, who included Anatole France (1844–1924), Jean Richepin (1849–1926), Catulle Mendès (1841–1909), Guy de Maupassant (1850–1893), Paul Verlaine (1844–1896), the artists Jean-Louis Forain (1842–1931) and Théophile Steinlen (1859–1923), the musicians Erik Satie (1866–1925) and Claude Debussy (1862–1918), and their only female member actress Sarah Bernhardt (1844–1923), to perform their poetry, sung lyrics, monologues, and short sketches— these often performed in and around popular protest and satirical songs of the streets.

Cabaret became the tightrope walker between the legitimate theater and the variety show, now defining an independent territory for itself;

Figure 1.3. *The Cabaret des Assassins* **by Raphaël Toussaint (b. 1937). Cre-*ative Commons (CC BY-SA 4.0).*

rolling with the punches of the times without ever losing its rebel-
lious wit, dissidence, or innovative nature. By 1884, Aristide Bruant
(1851–1925)—a champion of the underdog—who wrote poetry, songs,
and monologues became a patron and performer at Le Chat Noir, his
aggressive manner usually shocking the "regulars." He came to prominence in his own establishment, Le Mirliton, which replaced Le Chat
Noir in 1885 after it relocated to larger premises on the Rue Laval.

The Cabaret des Assassins, which opened in 1886 and still exists today
as the Lapin Agile in Montmartre, is a curious holdover of this period.
The performers for the evening begin by sitting around a table in the
middle of the room and singing the old street songs of Paris before
retreating backstage to then do their short solo turns for the audience.
Some are actual singers, but the majority of the acts tend to be more
what one would have expected of vaudeville. The last time I was there it
had a bit of a Barnum and Bailey sideshow atmosphere going on as well.
Cabaret can be anything musical or comedic as long as the performer
can figure out how to make it work for an audience's entertainment.

A STRUCTURE EMERGES

As the nineteenth century came to an end, the café-concert performers
began to formulate structural elements of cabaret performance—particularly—an intimate performance technique. Cabaret has often mistakenly been defined by the size (intimacy) of its performance space.
However, it is not the space that makes the performance intimate but
rather the actual performance technique developed by the café-concert
performers and still used by leading artists today. Otherwise, how can
you explain Liza Minnelli (b. 1946) at Radio City Music Hall, Bette
Midler (b. 1945) at Mandalay Bay, or Barbra Streisand (b. 1942) at Madison Square Garden? These are all cabaret performances at their best!

Indeed, a hallmark of a great cabaret performance is the intimate
relationship between the performer and the audience, both individually and collectively. The cabaret performer plays directly to his or her
audience and deliberately breaks down the illusionary "fourth wall" of
traditional theater. There is never any pretense made of an identity existing between actor and role. The performer sets up a dialogue with the

audience expecting a response in the form of laughter, tears, and body language—and—of course—applause. As Julie Wilson (1924–2015), who was widely regarded as the reigning queen of cabaret during her lifetime, once said, "Cabaret performance is one-on-one, heart-to-heart!" And the legendary Broadway and cabaret performer Betty Buckley (b. 1947) is famously quoted as saying, "Cabaret is a form of communication that is a cycle of: I know that you know, that I know, that you know, that I know."

CARVING OUT A NICHE

The evolvement of the artistic café-concert performances reached its pinnacle with the performer Yvette Guilbert (1865–1944) at the celebrated cabaret Le Divan du Monde, also known as the Divan Japonais, in 1891. It too still survives in its original location at 75 Rue des Martyrs in Montmartre, today known as Madame Arthur. The proprietor/proprietress Madame Arthur—a female impersonator—actually does a section of his/her show as Yvette Guilbert, who historically is thought to be the first person to incorporate gestures into her performances.

It was at this time, also, that the idea of using the cabaret stage to create yourself, and re-create yourself if need be, developed. Performers realized to "make it" they had to be different—unique. It was fine to be a good singer or a comic, but what could you do to distinguish yourself from the crowd? Stephen Sondheim (b. 1930) said it all in *Gypsy* (1959) with, "You Gotta Get a Gimmick" if you want to get ahead . . . and boy did they have some gimmicks in the 1890s!

There were several famous performers during this era, including Cicelia Loftus (1876–1943), the Englishwoman who did male drag performances; May Belfort (1872–1929), who dressed as a little girl and sang in a high-pitched, lisping, childlike voice; and the Machinson Sisters, five lovely English girls who did very risqué and sexual double entendre material—"I have a little cat, I'm very fond of that" while cradling black kittens in their aprons! In addition, there was my favorite, Le Pétomane—the *fartiste* or *farteur*, which translates of course to "farter." (Yes, you read that right!) Years of practice made him a master of this unconventional accomplishment: He could, and did, vary the tone

Figure 1.4. 1892 poster for the Divan Japonais by Henri de Toulouse-Lautrec (1864–1901). *Creative Commons (CC BY-SA 4.0).*

of his blasts at will in imitation of a wide range of musical sounds from sonorous bass to shrill soprano. He appeared nightly in the Elephant, the outdoor, more cabaret-esque stage of the Moulin Rouge. He was the eight o'clock show and at the height of his career pulled in fourteen thousand francs a week, the highest-paid performer in France, considerably more than Sarah Bernhardt.

Unfortunately, today the likes of Barbra Streisand, Bette Midler, and Liza Minnelli are a dying breed. Performers are going back to more shocking ways of making themselves stand out and be more unique on the New York stage, where literally anything goes under the "umbrella" of cabaret. Paul Newman (1925–2008), the great American actor and an avid cabaret goer, summed it up quite eloquently when he said, "Everyone is running around trying to be different or unique, when just being good is different enough!"

KABARETT IN GERMANY

In 1896, there was a record 274 café concert cabarets carried on the formal registers of Paris. The popularity of cabaret began to spread across the border into Germany, where by 1915, Kabarett was booming. The cabarets of the period were typified in the movie *The Blue Angel* (1930) with Marlene Dietrich (1901–1992). The first Kabarett venue was actually not in Germany but in France: Le Chat Noir was founded in 1881 by Rodolphe Salis (1851–1897). The first Kabarett venues in Germany and Austria were the Überbrettl in Berlin and the "ung-Wiener Theater zum lieben Augustin" in Vienna, both established in 1901.

By the 1920s, sociopolitical satire had evolved into the satirical revue. More often performed in theatrical spaces, the series of satirical sketches and monologues frequently took precedence over the song. German cabaret, unlike its French counterpart, was always governed by strict laws concerning freedom of speech and was continually censored. The *conferencier*, or emcee, was a "warm-up" type of act that got the audience excited, provoked, and involved and set up the sketches that were to follow. Often the conferencier was the owner, writer, and visionary for not only the cabaret but also sociopolitical direction of the times in general. However, they all became, shall we say, the far uglier

Figure 1.5. Überbrettl, Germany's first Kabarett. *Creative Commons (CC BY-SA 4.0).*

stepchildren of Aristide Bruant, taking his social commentary beyond anything that he could have ever envisioned.

One of the most prominent cabarets of the period was Elf Scharfrichter or the Eleven Executioners—"executing" nightly the social evils of the period. All major sociopolitical voices of the period performed under pseudonyms. The troupe famously included singer Marya Delvard (1874–1965), yet the conferenciers and performers are frequently less known outside Germany than their French and American counterparts.

Many writers and composers also made their mark in Kabarett, including Erika (1905–1969) and Klaus Mann (1906–1949), Kurt Tucholsky (1890–1935), Bertolt Brecht (1898–1956), Kurt Weill (1900–1950), and Hans Eisler (1898–1962). The most famous singers—in addition to Delvard—were Dietrich and Lotte Lenya (1898–1981). Delvard became widely known for her visual image, epitomizing the vamp look that is still so craved in cabaret today. Case in point: Julie Wilson. ♪

THE GREAT CABARET MIGRATION TO AMERICA

In the United States in the 1910s, the American innovation of the "floor show" was introduced. Out of the necessity for clubs to avoid theater taxation for a stage, the "stageless" performance space was born. At first this was a good solution, as it further broke down the formal barriers between performers and the audience by allowing them to move freely among the patrons. Reception was enthusiastic, but this resurgence of cabaret popularity was not to last.

During the 1920s vaudeville was declining, and singers began moonlighting. Cabarets were often referred to as saloons, and the performers were dubbed "saloon singers." A later generation of saloon singers included the likes of Tony Bennett (b. 1926), Julie Wilson (1924–2015), Frank Sinatra (1915–1998), Dorothy Loudon (1925–2003), and Sylvia Syms (1917–1992). Although the revue format also gained popularity during this period, the more prominent show used an overall theme that connected the individual acts.

THE GAY AESTHETIC

During Prohibition, many club owners sought outlandish acts to lure patrons into their now alcohol-free environments. In what would prove later to be in diametric opposition to Nazi Germany, gay-oriented shows for gay audiences known as "pansy shows" began in Greenwich Village. Due to their popularity, they soon spread to the Times Square–area nightspots, attracting heterosexual tourists and gay locals who were intrigued by homosexual exotica. The transgressive aura of homosexuality was seen as acceptable in the netherworld of the speakeasy. Many of the performers were heterosexual and performed the gender equivalent of vaudeville's blackface, delivering what they perceived to be low camp and effeminacy that epitomized the gay male. As for the gay audiences, they have always patronized cabaret entertainment.

FLEEING PROHIBITION

In the 1920s, cabaret was once again on the rise in Paris, and the jazz era had arrived in the United States. The rise of Parisian cabaret, however, was partially sparked by an influx of American cabaret performers and nightclub habitués who had lost their cabaret homes because of Prohibition; there were no longer any American saloons to sing in. In particular, black performers migrated to Paris. The most famous African American cabaret performer was the incomparable Josephine Baker (1906–1975), who had been called to Paris in 1927 by her friend Ada "Bricktop" Smith (1894–1984) because there was work available. At Bricktop's club, the American-born hostess greeted nightly the likes of Baker, Mable Mercer (1900–1984), Alberta Hunter (1895–1984), Cole (1891–1964) and Linda Porter (1883–1954), Duke Ellington (1899–1974), and Fats Waller (1904–1943). By the early 1930s, a glittering society also attended Bricktop's club, including the American socialite interior designer Elsie de Wolfe (1865–1950)—also known as Lady Mendl—and the American socialite Wallis Warfield Simpson (1896–1986) alongside Edward, Prince of Wales (1894–1972). These two were later to become the objects of the greatest love story of the twentieth century: the Duke and Duchess of Windsor. ♪

FLEEING THE NAZIS

Parisian cabaret came to a screeching halt in the late 1930s with the onslaught of the Nazis and the eventual occupation of Paris. Lady Mendl and the Duchess of Windsor put Bricktop on the last liner leaving for America before the Windsors themselves fled—or shall we say exiled—to the Bahamas. Josephine Baker chose to stay in France, where she became a decorated national heroine as part of the French underground.

By the late 1930s in Germany—and later in all Nazi-occupied countries—performers were severely censored in their performances in film, on radio, and in theaters, particularly in the satirical cabarets that flourished. The movie *Cabaret* (1974) with Liza Minnelli and Joel Grey (b. 1932) pretty well summed up the situation as it truly existed. Many of Germany's most accomplished cabaret performers and writers (mentioned above) fled altogether. During the twelve years of the Third Reich, more than six thousand performers were sentenced, by a kangaroo court, to death for performing anti-Nazi material.

YIDDISH CABARET

Along with the music halls of France and England and America's vaudeville, there was an eastern European counterpart that needs to be mentioned: Yiddish theater and cabaret. This Yiddish entertainment, however, was by no means confined entirely to Eastern Europe. The Jewish diaspora has spread the influence of Yiddish entertainment globally. Initially there were Jewish theaters and cabarets in major European cities, including Berlin, Vienna, Vilna, Warsaw, and Amsterdam. However, as the Third Reich regime strengthened, much of the genius of the Jews was transported to ghettos and ultimately to concentration camps. Hundreds of songs—cabaret story songs—have come out of the ghettos and camps from the period of the Holocaust. A vast body of comedic work has survived as well, giving a whole new meaning to the phrase "gallows humor." We read of the famous writers, singers, comics, directors, composers, lyricists, set and costume designers, and graphic artists who continued to work to produce cabarets, concerts, plays, musicals, and operas right up until the time of their murder. To this day, many of these songs continue to be part of the Jewish musical repertoire.

A NEW YORK RENAISSANCE

In the 1940s and 1950s, Bricktop opened clubs in Rome on the Via Veneto and later in Mexico City. However, the real international cabaret scene after the war emerged in New York City, specifically in the jazz clubs of Fifty-Second Street, up in Harlem, on Broadway, and down in Greenwich Village. In places like Small's Paradise, Minton's, and Café Society, you could see the likes of Billie Holiday (1915–1959), Charlie Parker (1920–1955), Miles Davis (1926–1991), Thelonious Monk (1917–1982), and Art Tatum (1909–1956). In the Broadway and midtown Manhattan area, the Copacabana and the Latin Quarter hosted floor shows and big bands; the Le Reuban Bleu featured Kaye Ballard (1925–2019), Carol Burnett (b. 1933), and Dorothy Loudon; and Hildegarde (1906–2005) sang in the Persian Room and later Plaza 9, both run by Julius Monk (1912–1995) at the Plaza Hotel. Other venues included the St. Regis Hotel, which featured Mabel Mercer (1900–1984), and the prolific Upstairs at the Downstairs that brought to our attention many top-flight cabaret performers, including Bette Midler, Madeline Kahn (1942–1999), Lily Tomlin (b. 1939), Joan Rivers (1933–2014), Fanny Flagg (b. 1944), Tammy Grimes (1934–2016), Marcia Lewis (1938–2010), Barry Manilow (b. 1943), Bill Cosby (b. 1937), Dixie Carter (1939–2010), and songwriting teams like Schmidt and Jones and Maltby and Shire.[2] ♪

Greenwich Village was the home of several clubs, including the Bon Soir with Pearl Bailey (1918–1990), Bobby Short (1924–2005), and Yul Brynner (1920–1985); this venue was also where Barbra Streisand's career was launched. The Village Vanguard hosted the likes of Eartha Kitt (1927–2008) and Judy Holliday (1921–1965). Upstairs at the Duplex opened in 1948 with Sylvia Syms (1917–1992), later followed by Hal Holbrook (b. 1925) and his Mark Twain sketches, and even later by Joan Rivers (1933–2014), Woody Allen (b. 1935), Dick Cavett (b. 1936), the husband-and-wife team Jerry Stiller (b. 1927) and Anne Meara (1929–2015), Richard Pryor (1940–2005), Linda Lavin, Totie Fields (1930–1978), and Rodney Dangerfield (1921–2004). During this prolific time, it became clear cabaret does not produce chorus members—cabaret produces stars! ♪

During the Vietnam War era of the 1960s, there was a revival of the century-old tradition of sociopolitical protest and patriotic songs, which were sung by folk singers in the coffeehouses of New York and across America. Sadly, until recently, it seemed that political satire had become politically incorrect. With the onslaught of rock music in the 1970s, places like Reno Sweeney, the Ballroom, Brothers and Sisters, and Jan Wallman's stood alone as the bastions of American popular music of the past, present, and future.

By the late 1970s and early 1980s, the Reno Sweeney nightclub, the Ballroom, and Jan Wallman's continued to stay open, along with the Duplex, Don't Tell Mama, Danny's Skylight Room, the Village Vanguard, the Village Gate, Mickey's, Marty's, Freddy's, Panache, Michael's Pub, Les Mouches, Grand Finale, the Café Carlyle, the Algonquin, Palsson's Supper Club, and comedy and variety rooms like Caroline's, the Improv, Catch a Rising Star, and Mostly Magic.

A NATIONAL RESURGENCE

For decades, most major cities across America had venues that featured solo singers and instrumentalists. These venues included country clubs, party and hotel circuits, comedy clubs, and piano bars. By the late 1980s and into the 1990s, however, actual cabaret rooms began to crop up nationally. These included Cite, Metropole, Gentry, Gold Star Sardine Bar, Palette's, Toulouse, Yvette, Yvette Winter Garden, and Davenport's in Chicago; the Gardenia, Hollywood Roosevelt Hotel's Cinegrill, and the Jazz Bakery in Los Angeles; the Club Cabaret and Sculler's in Boston; the Plush Room, Fanny's, Trinity Place, and Josie's Juice Bar in San Francisco; and numerous venues in Miami's revitalized South Beach. Other venues included Upstairs at Carol's in Cincinnati, Libby's in Atlanta, Le Chat Noir in New Orleans, and the Royal Room in Palm Beach. More and more rooms in New York City also opened: Rainbow & Stars, Tavern on the Green, the Russian Tea Room, and the legendary Eighty Eight's that brought us more recently established names. These performers included Nancy LaMott (1951–1995), Karen Mason (b. 1977), Sharon McNight (b. 1957), Tom Andersen (b. 1962), Jeff Harnar (b. 1959), KT Sullivan (b. 1953), Baby Jane Dexter (1946–2019), Natalie Douglas (b. 1968), Billy Stritch (b. 1962), Pamela Myers (b. 1947), Sally Mayes (b. 1959), Phillip Officer (b. 1956), Tovah Feldshuh (b. 1952), David Campbell (b. 1973), Brian Lane Green (b. 1962), Roslyn Kind (b. 1951), Judy Kuhn (b. 1958), Michele Pawk (b. 1961), Vicki Sue Robinson (1954–2000), Lina Koutrakos (b. 1960), Linda Purl (b. 1955), Harvey Fierstein (b. 1954), Marilyn Sokol (b. 1944), Julie Halston (b. 1954), Quentin Crisp (1908–1999), Varla Jean Merman (a.k.a. Jeff Roberson; b. 1969), Miss Coco Peru (b. 1965), and the duo Kiki and Herb.[3] ♪

Off-Broadway productions written in the cabaret tradition include *Closer than Ever* (1989) by Richard Maltby Jr. (b. 1937) and David Shire (b. 1937); *Hey, Love* (1993) by Mary Rodgers (1931–2014); *Cut the Ribbons* by Mildred Kayden (1922–2017), Nancy Ford (b. 1935), Mae Richards (1921–2010), and Cheryl Hardwick (b. 1944); Martin Charnin's *Loose Lips* (1995) by Kurt Andersen (b. 1954) and Lisa Birnbach (b. 1957); *Songs for a New World* (1995) by Jason Robert Brown (b. 1970); and *Pictures in the Hall* (1991) by Craig Carnelia (b.

1949), Richard Rodney Bennett (1936–2012), Julie Gold (b. 1956), and Carol Hall (1936–2018). Examples of regional cabaret venues include Odette's in Bucks County, Pennsylvania, and the Bradstan Country Inn in White Lake, New York. Overseas, clubs in London and Amsterdam and a newly flourishing community in far off Australia are exciting new developments. ♪

Along with the influx of cabarets, organizations and services catering to the cabaret performer and cabaret-going audience had arrived on the scene. The Manhattan Association of Cabarets (MAC) with its annual MAC Awards and the institution of March as National Cabaret Month were two of the most high-profile initiatives. Other organizations include Los Angeles's Cabaret West, the Boston Association of Cabaret Artists (BACA), the Cabaret Network in Washington, D.C., and Chicago Cabaret Professionals. There are also events such as the annual Bistro Awards, the BroadwayWorld Cabaret Awards, the Mabel Mercer Foundation's annual Cabaret Convention, and master classes that have been taught by cabaret luminaries such as Barbara Cook (1927–2017), Andrea Marcovicci (b. 1948), Karen Morrow (b. 1936), Sally Mayes, Ann Hampton Callaway (b. 1958), Tovah Feldshuh, Karen Akers (b. 1945), Margaret Whiting (1924–2011), and Julie Wilson, among others. There are also publications and websites devoted solely to cabaret, including Cabaret.Org, *Cabaret Scenes* magazine, NiteLife Exchange, and Theater Pizzazz. In addition, there are independent recording labels dedicated to cabaret artists, and cabaret departments being added to larger labels. ♪

FINAL THOUGHTS

Although cabaret is indigenous to New York, its move across America is now complete. Cabaret has survived because there has always been, and always will be, a steady stream of incredibly talented people who continue to seek out cabaret rooms in which to make their mark. Sometimes the stream is wide, sometimes it's just a trickle, but it is consistent! Babies continue to be born every day in all of the provinces of the world. In twenty years or so, they will be knocking on our doors for a chance to be part of the continuing, unique, and wonderful tradition that is cabaret.

NOTES

In 2010, Erv Raible wrote a comprehensive essay on the history of cabaret, which first appeared on January 9, 2012, on Stu Hamstra's blog *Cabaret Hotline Online*. The essay was preserved by *Cabaret Hotline Online* interviewer (and book coauthor) Sue Matsuki, who offers it here. It is with a great sense of respect and gratitude that the authors have chosen to present a lightly edited version of Erv's keen historical perspective (and dry wit) as the opening chapter of this book. Thank you, Erv.

1. Although the Folies-Bergère has fallen on hard times, it is currently rentable space in Paris.

2. The songwriting team of Schmidt and Jones consisted of composer Harvey Schmidt (1929–2018) and lyricist Tom Jones (b. 1929); the team of Maltby and Shire is made up of lyricist Richard Maltby Jr. (b. 1937) and composer David Shire (b. 1937).

3. Kiki and Herb are stage names for Justin Bond (b. 1963) and Kenny Mellman (b. ca. 1960). Jeff Roberson's alter ego, Varla Jean Merman, a fictional and ageless character, is said to be the illegitimate offspring of Ethel Merman (1908–1984) and Ernest Borgnine (1917–2012).

2

FROM BOUNTY
TO BUST TO BLOSSOM

Roy Sander

The article below is based on a piece published in the fortieth anniversary issue of *Backstage* newspaper on December 15, 2000, and
again sixteen years later on BistroAwards.com. Except for certain stylistic changes made by the series editor to conform to house and series
convention—and to retain consistency alongside other chapters—this
article has been reprinted as it appeared in 2000. Some of the clubs that
are discussed in the present tense are no longer open for business, and
some of today's most vital cabarets are not mentioned. Nevertheless,
the comments made in the final section of this chapter—"Trends and
Observations"—are fundamentally still valid today.[1]

CABARET: 1960–2000

It's Thursday, December 31, 1959, in New York City. The eve of a new
decade. How will you celebrate? You might opt to see the Will Mastin
Trio starring Sammy Davis Jr. at the Copacabana, Sarah Vaughan at the
Empire Room in the Waldorf Astoria, or Jane Froman at the Persian
Room at the Plaza. The Pierre's Cotillion Room is offering Carol Bruce
and Wilbur Evans, and Vicky Autier is singing at the Maisonette at the
St. Regis. ♪

If you're in the mood for a more intimate setting, how about Kaye Ballard at the Bon Soir, Gigi Durston at One Fifth Avenue, the Julius Monk revue *Pieces of Eight* (1959) at Upstairs at the Downstairs, or Rose Murphy at Downstairs at the Upstairs? Bobby Short and Barbara Carroll are both performing at Arpeggio, and Mabel Mercer is holding forth in the King Arthur Room at the Roundtable. ♪

Jazz? Lionel Hampton is at Basin Street East, and the Count Basie Band, with vocalist Joe Williams, is at Birdland (don't head for West Forty-Forth Street—it's at Fifty-Second and Broadway, you know). The Hickory House has the Billy Taylor Trio, and Lambert, Hendricks & Ross are at the Village Vanguard.

There's more. Lots more. You see, the calendar may be about to say 1960, but the scene is still very much the 1950s, when New York experienced a burgeoning of niteries, and in many ways still the 1940s, when the only way to see one's favorite artists perform was to go to a club. And that's exactly what people did—routinely and in large numbers. In addition to the independent rooms, nearly every hotel in town—from the posh Sheraton East (formerly the Ambassador) on Park Avenue to the less rarefied New Yorker on Eighth—offered live entertainment. Vincent Lopez and his orchestra were at the Taft, and you could swing and

Figure 2.1.   Roy Sander at the Bistro Awards. *Photo by Maryann Lopinto.*

sway with Sammy Kaye at the Roosevelt Grill. The Hotel Lexington was famous for its Hawaiian revue, and the Drake gave two options: dinner, supper, and dancing at Mon Plaisir, or relaxing with Cy Walter at the piano in the Drake Room. Indeed, when the Americana Hotel (now the Sheraton New York) opened in 1962, it naturally boasted a showroom, the Royal Box, which, just as naturally, offered dinner, dancing, and headline acts.[2]

The Party's Over

But this bounty was not to continue long. During the 1960s, the amount of live music in New York diminished greatly. Hotel orchestras became a thing of the past, and while a few of the bigger venues made it into the next decade, the smaller rooms were hit very hard.

The Blue Angel, perhaps the quintessential New York supper club of the period (they weren't commonly called cabarets back then), closed in 1964. Among the people who had begun their careers there prior to 1960 were Mike Nichols and Elaine May, Carol Burnett, Johnny Mathis, Pearl Bailey, and Harry Belafonte. In the 1960s, you could catch return engagements of Dorothy Loudon, Kaye Ballard, and Phyllis Diller, as well as such newcomers as Dick Gregory, Barbra Streisand, Lenny Bruce, Jerry Stiller, Anne Meara, and the Smothers Brothers.

The Showplace, which in 1958 had launched the career of Jerry Herman with his revue *Nightcap at the Showplace* (1958), also shut its doors in 1964. Appearing there in its final few years were Linda Lavin, Mark Murphy, and the revue *Stewed Prunes* (1960). John Wallowitch played the piano downstairs, as did Warren Beatty . . . that Warren Beatty; checking coats was Cass Elliot, yup, Mama Cass.

Another casualty of the mid-1960s was the Little Club, which had opened in the 1940s—its first solo act was Doris Day. Before it closed, you could enjoy Murray Grand at the piano and listen to singer Jane Harvey. Then in 1967, the Bon Soir left us after nearly twenty years, presenting in the 1960s such talents as Barbra Streisand (who alternated between the Blue Angel and the Bon Soir), Woody Allen, Mabel Mercer, and Felicia Sanders. ♪

Figure 2.2.   The Bon Soir. *Creative Commons (CC BY-SA 4.0)*.

In fact, seeing the handwriting on the wall, the Village Vanguard—which had previously hired acts like the Revuers—Judy Holliday, Betty Comden, and Adolph Green—Eartha Kitt, Pat Carroll, and Wally Cox—switched to an all-jazz policy as early as 1957. (Throughout this forty-year period, jazz has stayed relatively resistant to the vicissitudes affecting cabaret.)[3] ♪

How Could It Happen?

Two factors are usually cited to explain this decline: television and the change in musical tastes. The people that patronized clubs in the 1940s and 1950s could now see their kind of entertainment on television, while younger audiences were interested in a different type of music. That's true enough, but to understand the depth and magnitude of the challenges facing cabaret—now as well as then—it is necessary to examine this second point more closely and grasp its fundamental nature—and the nature of cabaret.

The type of music embraced by much of the then-younger generation reflected the central philosophical trend of the period: a rejection of reason. The flower-power/peace-and-love movement, while superficially appearing to have nonviolence as its motive, was in fact an exhortation to suspend judgment and embrace nature uncritically. Reason was either totally discredited or deemed inferior to feelings.

This gave rise to various musical styles, most notably Motown, disco, soft rock, and hard rock—the first three benign but vapid; the fourth equally lacking in content but cynical and nihilistic and often so cacophonous that its listeners were obliged to function on a subrational, preconceptual level. There was no room in any of it for songs that explored human experiences with intelligence, sensitivity, and wit. (This anti-reason trend was fueled by the same philosophical influences that decades earlier had made their mark on the more "serious" arts—examples include aleatory and atonal music, nonrepresentational painting, and stream-of-consciousness literature.)

Some contemporary music lay well outside this mold and could have found a home in cabaret—for example, the songs of Joni Mitchell, Dory Previn, Jimmy Webb, John Lennon and Paul McCartney, and—later—Randy Newman. However, there was another aspect of the anti-reason syndrome that conspired against cabaret. Many young people (as well as the fashionable set, wannabes, and others with disposable income) were resolutely determined not to use their minds when they went out. The noise level at discos—which by the late 1960s abounded—made contemplation and conversation nigh unto impossible. What's more, for many, getting stoned was the evening's prime objective. ♪

This could not have been more inimical to cabaret. Even at its most emotionally intense or frivolously comical, cabaret demands focus: One must tune in in order to turn on. Its effectiveness rests on communication between the performer and the audience; this will not work if the audience has checked its collective brain at the door. Indeed, cabaret is a bastion of reason and a playground for the mind. That is the source of its power to move, enthrall, or delight us. Therein lies its glory.[4]

A Few Rays of Light

Some good things did happen in and to cabaret in the 1960s. Early in the decade, the Duplex earned an enviable record for discovering new talent and launching careers. Alumni of the period include Jo Anne Worley, Joan Rivers, Rodney Dangerfield, Dick Cavett, Claiborne Cary,

Figure 2.3.   The Duplex Cabaret Room (2019). *Creative Commons (CC BY-SA 4.0).*

and Woody Allen. Often performers would try out material here before heading off to the Bon Soir or the Blue Angel. ♪

Julius Monk continued his series of bright and bubbly musical revues featuring original songs and sketches that commented wittily on the current scene. In 1962, he took them with him from Upstairs at the Downstairs to Plaza 9, located downstairs at the Plaza Hotel, where he continued for several years. William Roy was musical director and one of the contributors, and the casts included Mary Louise Wilson, Ronny Graham, Ellen Hanley, and Ruth Buzzi. (In the late 1960s, Plaza 9 switched to jazz before becoming an off-Broadway theater and then a cinema.) ♪

Meanwhile, Upstairs at the Downstairs and its sister room, Downstairs at the Upstairs, continued presenting revues in the Monk tradition under the helm of various producer/directors. Though the success rate varied, the club stayed open until 1974; among the cast members were Madeline Kahn, Marian Mercer, Fannie Flagg, and Marcia Lewis. Nonrevue entertainment, which prior to 1960 had included Portia Nelson, the nightclub debut of Tammy Grimes, and the double act of Annie Ross and Blossom Dearie, continued with such names as Joan Rivers, Mabel Mercer, Jackie Vernon, Dixie Carter, and Bette Midler. It was here that Midler first met Barry Manilow, who was entertaining at the piano between shows. ♪

From the mid-1960s into the 1970s, the Rainbow Grill on the sixty-fifth floor of the RCA Building (not to be confused with any other rooms bearing the name Rainbow) functioned as a jazz club, with artists like Jonah Jones, Red Norvo, Chris Connor, Stan Getz, Billy Eckstine, and Cleo Laine. The room went nonjazz on at least one occasion when Jule Styne presented a program of his songs in the mid-1970s. And in 1968, Bobby Short opened at the Café Carlyle. That must have been one hell of a contract.[5] ♪

Figure 2.4.   Café Carlyle. *Photo by Rosewood Hotel Resorts LLC.*

The Renaissance

Nonetheless, despite a few bright spots, the situation in the early 1970s was pretty bleak. To emerge again, cabaret would have to rediscover and reinvent itself. And that's what happened. In the mid-1970s, four clubs opened that revitalized the New York nightlife scene.

These clubs were Reno Sweeney, Brothers and Sisters, Grand Finale, and the Ballroom, and their arrival was exhilarating. Compared with earlier ventures, these rooms were more informal, more democratic, and more lighthearted. They attracted a younger audience—an audience that exhibited none of the smug self-satisfaction that can come from doing something one knows has been labeled smart. "Isn't this fun?" replaced "Aren't we sophisticated?" And not many people bothered to stay in the closet. I believe that these clubs set the tone and laid the groundwork for the cabaret world we know today. ♪

On West Thirteenth Street, Reno Sweeney had it all. It was festive and slightly funky, but it operated very professionally. It could be packed, yet the staff remained friendly and cheerful. Despite its medium-large size, few seats felt like Siberia, and from the active bar, you could get at least a sideways view of the show. The wildly eclectic lineup included Peter Allen, Maxene Andrews of the Andrews Sisters, Barbara Cook, Ellen Greene, Michael Moriarty, Cybill Shepherd, Holly Woodlawn, the trio of Weeden, Finkle, and Fay, Robby Benson, Nancy LaMott, Cissy Houston (mother of Whitney Houston), Judy Kaye, Marta Sanders, André De Shields, and a radiant and very exciting Andrea Marcovicci. ♪

The cabaret room at Brothers and Sisters, on Forty-Sixth Street between Eighth and Ninth Avenues, was very small and very plain—although as I recall the plywood walls had been given a coat of dark paint and perhaps some cloth covering. It was also very wonderful. The club specialized in presenting great and legendary ladies—Hildegarde, Dolores Gray, Portia Nelson, Greta Keller, Penny Fuller, and Karen Morrow. Julie Wilson appeared there several times, including one memorable engagement, *Julie Lets Her Hair Down* (ca. 1976), in which she forwent her signature chignon and gardenia. It is also where Barbara Cook began her cabaret and concert career. Carleton Carpenter and Larry Kert were among the handful of men represented. The piano café upstairs was very popular with show "kids"—many of whom actually had jobs on Broadway! For one year, the room was presided over by Tom Babbitt (dates unknown), a singer-pianist whose simple but eloquent renditions still rank today, decades later, as models of the art of song interpretation. Among the people who took over after he left was the supremely entertaining Danny Apolinar.

Of the four clubs, the Grand Finale on Seventy-First Street near Broadway was closest to what one thinks of as a nightclub. Its stage was large enough to accommodate choreography, and the tables were arranged in two tiers in a truncated *U*. The bar, located immediately behind the last row of tables, afforded a great view of the show. The roster included Bernadette Peters, Dorothy Collins, Margaret Whiting, Ann Reinking, Chita Rivera, Rita Moreno, puppeteer/ventriloquist Wayland Flowers and his puppet alter-ego "Madame," and Gotham—perhaps the first openly gay group to cross over to a more general audience. ♪

The Ballroom—the original one, that is, on West Broadway in Soho—was a small, cheerful, white restaurant with a stage not quite in the center of the room. Of the four clubs of the cabaret renaissance, the Ballroom was the most innovative, with an uncommonly perceptive eye for picking talent from among unknown as well as familiar names. Its lineup included Jane Olivor, Marilyn Sokol, Baby Jane Dexter, John Monteith and Suzanne Rand, Jo Sullivan Loesser, Margery Cohen, Betty Jane Rhodes, Pamela Myers, Dean Pitchford, Alan Menken, Audrey Lavine, Estelle Parsons, Al Carmines, Martha Schlamme, Alvin Epstein, Tony Azito, Lee Horwin, and Hildegarde, who closed the room in May 1979. In addition, the club ran a songwriter series in which you could see Sheldon Harnick, Carolyn Leigh, and Harold Rome perform their own works, and you could have been there in 1977 when Andrew Lloyd Webber and Tim Rice told their audience that they were hopeful of having *Evita* produced on the stage. The musical had its first production in London in 1978.[6]

Meanwhile . . .

A number of other venues came on the cabaret scene around the same time. Throughout the 1970s and into the 1980s, the Cookery presented a roster of mainly—but not exclusively—jazz and blues artists, including Susannah McCorkle, Marlene VerPlanck, Adelaide Hall, Gretchen Cryer and Nancy Ford, and Alberta Hunter in an extended engagement. Michael's Pub opened in 1973 and stayed for a long time on East Fifty-Fifth Street before making return appearances in other locations around town.

On Forty-Sixth Street between Eighth and Ninth Avenues—the site is currently Swing 46—Barbarann had an active entertainment schedule in its main cabaret room, including the off-Broadway production of the Richard Maltby Jr. and David Shire revue *Starting Here, Starting Now* (1977). Farther downtown and on the East Side, Once upon a Stove had its cabaret patrons walk through the restaurant, past the kitchen, up a metal staircase, and across a catwalk to get to the enchanting Valentine Room, where they could catch Anne Francine, Julie Wilson, Taina Elg, Denise Lor—or a revue put on by the staff. ♪

There was Cleo's on Broadway near Lincoln Center, where lucky audiences could see Mabel Mercer or Albert Hague and Renee Orrin. Before moving uptown a decade later, Jan Wallman's on Cornelia Street presented such artists as Judy Kreston, Barbara Lea, Daryl Sherman, Loria Parker, and Ronny Whyte in a warm and intimate setting. And don't forget Tramps, where you could see Pat Benatar, Cathy Chamberlain and her Rag 'n' Roll Revue (1976), and Stormin' Norman and Suzy; Yellow Brick Road on Tenth Street (remember Desmond Child and Rouge?), which years later would become Eighty Eight's; and on West Seventy-Third Street, the Bushes of CPW, which became Jason's at the Park Royal. ♪

It would be wrong to leave out the cabaret series presented for several years by the Manhattan Theatre Club in its homey East Seventy-Third Street facility. So many splendid offerings—John Kander and Fred Ebb, Charles Strouse, and Betty Comden and Adolph Green revues; "songs of" evenings—Dorothy Fields, Arthur Schwartz, Harold Arlen, and Martin Charnin; the joint show of Victor Garber and Don Scardino; Margery Cohen and Jonathan Hadary; Craig Carnelia; Jim Wann; and Dory Previn . . . the list goes on and on. And two of the revues made it big: *Theatre Songs of Maltby/Shire* (1976) became *Starting Here, Starting Now*, and a little number called *Ain't Misbehavin'* (1978) transferred to Broadway and won the Tony Award for Best Musical.

Finally, though it was a restaurant, not a cabaret, Backstage, owned by Ted Hook, was such an important part of the city's nightlife during the second half of the 1970s that it must be included—even if only because it was here that Steve Ross, its principal pianist-singer, came to prominence. Stars from the past and celebrities of the present made it

their home, and it was unpredictable when one of them might walk over
to the piano and do a number . . . or an hour. It was a special place.[7]

The Story Goes On

In 1981, the Ballroom reopened in a much larger space in Chelsea,
where for many years it continued to offer an impressive level and
variety of talent. Although the three other seminal clubs were gone by
then, the momentum they helped generate has continued through to
the present day, with new clubs appearing all the time. Some of these
ventures merely dabbled in live entertainment, while others made more
serious commitments. Some came and went quickly, some made more
lasting impressions, and several are alive and well.

There have been so many that an exhaustive list would be exhaust-
ing—and impossible. Besides, the more recent the establishment, the
more likely it is that you know all about it. So, in very rough chronological order, following is a partial list of clubs and developments, arbitrarily
limited to pre-1990 openings. You might enjoy playing "How many of
these do you remember?"

For over two decades now, the West Bank Café (now the Laurie
Beechman Theatre) has been presenting a mix of cabaret, theater, and
comedy, including Marcia Lewis in 1979, Susannah McCorkle in 1982,
and—in 1987—a group of young Canadian upstarts called the Kids in
the Hall. Shaped like a miniature 737, Mickey's on West Fifty-Fourth
Street was the performing home base for Karen Akers before she graduated to larger venues. For a few years, the King Cole Bar in the St. Regis offered a high-profile series of musical revues, while for five years
Blue Skies, a cozy Italian restaurant located in a cellar on Tenth Street
near Seventh Avenue, presented an extraordinary lineup of singers. A
couple of dance clubs tried their hand at cabaret: Hippopotamus—with
Julie Kurnitz, Juliette Koka, and Karen Akers—and Les Mouches, with
Donna McKechnie, Patti LuPone, Terri Klausner, and Liliane Montevecchi. ♪

Ted Hook took over what had been Barbarann and created OnStage,
an endearingly glitzy club with tables arranged in tiers and cigarette
girls in uniform; it was a joy. In 1982, the club became Van Buren's,
before metamorphosing into JoAnn's Silver Lining and then Red Blazer

Figure 2.5. The Laurie Beechman Theatre. *Creative Commons (CC BY-SA 4.0).*

Too. Another classic supper club was Freddy's on East Forty-Ninth Street, which in the first half of the 1980s presented the likes of Tammy Grimes, Phyllis Newman, Dixie Carter, Kay Starr, Keely Smith, Ronny Whyte, Carol Fredette, Daryl Sherman, Andrea McCardle, Maureen McGovern, and Margaret Whiting.

For the past two decades, Palsson's (later Steve McGraw's, now the Triad) has specialized in open-ended revues—most notably *Forbidden Broadway* (1982) and *Forever Plaid* (1989)—interspersed with a cornucopia of more limited-run cabaret offerings and special events. Spanning most of the 1980s were three incarnations of Panache, the last of which, Panache Encore, was located in the back room of Encore, Encore, one of the successors to Ted Hook's Backstage.

Early in the 1980s, two events of enduring significance took place. Live music, in the person and talent of Steve Ross, was reintroduced to the Oak Room at the Algonquin, which rapidly became one of New York's premier venues. Today the Oak Room is distinguished not only for the stars that perform there but also for its more creative programming, such as the "Cavalcade of Cabaret," which gives less-famous

Figure 2.6. Andrea Marcovicci at the Oak Room. *Courtesy of Creative Commons.*

performers a chance to play the Algonquin and the International Festival of Cabaret. And Don't Tell Mama opened. What can one say about a club that for two decades has been home to some of the freshest, brightest, most exciting talent anywhere, a club that sets no limits on the creative imagination of the artists who play there? It is the center and soul of New York cabaret.

In the mid-1980s we had Park Ten, at Park Avenue and Thirty-Fourth Street, where you could have seen Mel Tormé, Sylvia Syms, or Joshua Logan presenting a musical recollection of his career. There was Broadway Baby, which brought the spirit of the midtown cabaret scene to the Upper West Side, and—more Upper and more West—the marvelous J's, which for many years offered jazz in a spacious, comfortable, and friendly setting. A bit later, Jan Wallman's (subsequently to become Judy's) moved to Forty-Fourth Street, increasing its visibility and roster of performers. We also got Danny's Skylight Room and Chez Beauvais at Tenth Avenue and Fifty-Sixth Street.

The 1980s ended with the opening of two clubs whose passing a decade later was deeply mourned by the cabaret world. In 1988, Eighty Eight's arrived and immediately established its special niche. Beautiful but informal, it nurtured and encouraged hundreds of newcomers and at the same time was home to stars as luminous as Sylvia Syms. When it closed, we lost a member of the family. The year 1989 saw the birth of Rainbow & Stars, a sparkling gem that proved that glamour and elegance need not exist only in movies. From brilliant headliners to exceptional musical revues, the club gave us some of the greatest evenings in cabaret history.[8]

Trends and Observations

The blossoming of cabaret has not stopped—though to be sure, the growth has not always taken an uninterrupted or straight course. Freddy's may be long gone, but we now have the lovely Arci's Place. If we can't go to the Ballroom anymore, we can head down to Joe's Pub. The Russian Tea Room no longer presents cabaret, but the FireBird Café does, and while we miss Rainbow & Stars, now there is Feinstein's at the Regency. The Duplex moved and expanded across the avenue, making room for Rose's Turn; Judy's relocated its apostrophe and itself and now resides in larger, sumptuous quarters in Chelsea; and Don't Tell Mama added a second cabaret room and broadened its schedule, becoming a veritable cabaret Disneyland.

But cabaret is clearly still not mainstream and therefore needs to be nurtured. In the 1980s, two organizations were created to do just that. The Mabel Mercer Foundation has been working tirelessly to increase cabaret's visibility, most notably through the New York Cabaret Convention, the foundation's hugely successful annual series of cabaret concerts. The Manhattan Association of Cabarets—known as the MAC—serves club owners and artists alike through its series of seminars and showcases. The annual MAC Awards ceremony aims not only to recognize excellence but also to bring cabaret to the attention of a broader public.

* * *

Over the decades, the economics of cabaret have changed. In many rooms, instead of being "hired" for a salary, you are now "booked" and work for the cover charge; it is a lot easier to get booked than it was to get hired. Also, more often than not, performers are scheduled for scattered evenings, rather than for whole-week engagements. As a result, the cabaret door has been opened to many amateurs and people who are merely kidding or indulging themselves—people who may have a burning desire to perform but are blessed with less-than-persuasive talent. This is an inescapable fact. However, these same conditions have made it possible for artists to develop and grow over time; many fine talents have emerged as a result of this process.

Indeed, the array of talent that can be seen on today's cabaret stages is thrilling not only in quality but also in form and creativity. Partly because of the difficulties of working or producing in theater, shows can be found in cabaret that would have been unthinkable years ago—from traditional book musicals to highly individual forms of expression, such as a multimedia musical piece on the subject of voyeurism, a program of original songs and poems about the indignities of riding the New York transit system, a musical fantasia set in a fishing lodge in Finland in 1919, and an expanded anecdote with songs about one man's battle to reclaim money he overpaid his landlord.

Finally, even in cabaret's more traditional forms, artists today ask more of themselves than many did years ago. They understand that especially because cabaret is not in the mainstream, they must give audiences a reason for seeing their show instead of choosing a more conventional form of entertainment—or staying home listening to a CD. In recognition of this need, the Cabaret and Performance Conference at the O'Neill Theater Center was formed in the late 1980s to train people in the demanding art of cabaret performing. Many singers today enlist the services of a director—not only to assist in structuring their show but also to help them bring greater dimension to their performance. Instead of being presented an "act," audiences are taken on a journey. As a result, cabaret today can deliver a uniquely rich experience.

FINAL THOUGHTS

Although the supper club, with its midcentury sophistication, was inevitably replaced as the premier intimate entertainment venue by the more democratic cabaret club of today, the live entertainment performed in these intimate clubs continues to enthrall audiences.[9] Many clubs have appeared and disappeared from New York nightlife since Roy Sander's article was first published. And while some of the artists mentioned in this article who rose to prominence in this era are still performing today, still many others have emerged to reinvigorate the cabaret scene into the twenty-first century. Sander's keen observations regarding the development of the genre, the move toward "booking" instead of "hiring," and the demands placed upon individual artists to deliver a unique and authentic performance product bring us to the very reason for this book to exist. Cabaret and cabaret performance has evolved from its midcentury predecessor. Understanding the art, craft, and business of cabaret is now the responsibility of individual artists. They are the ones who must bring their performance vision to fruition. With only a handful of private classes and seminars available—and even then, only in major cities—and no university training of this genre, this book hopes to illuminate the craft, business, and history of this unique vocal performance style for generations to carry on into the future.

For more information on the history of New York nightlife and small-venue performance, we refer you to James Gavin's wonderful book *Intimate Nights: The Golden Age of New York Cabaret* (2006).

NOTES

1. Since there are so many figures listed in this chapter, birth and death dates will appear in endnotes according to section.

2. Dates of figures for the "Cabaret: 1960–2000" introductory section are as follows: Sammy Davis Jr. (1925–1990), Sarah Vaughan (1924–1990), Jane Froman (1907–1980), Carol Bruce (1909–2007), Wilbur Evans (1905–1987), Vicky Autier (b. 1924), Kaye Ballard (1925–2019), Gigi Durston (b. 1927), Julius Monk (1912–1995), Rose Murphy (1913–1989), Bobby Short (1924–2005), Barbara Carroll (1925–2017), Mabel Mercer (1900–1984), Lionel Hampton (1908–2002), Joe Williams (1918–1999), Vincent Lopez (1895–1975), Sammy Kaye (1910–1987), and Cy Walter (1915–1968). The Billy Taylor Trio consists of Billy Taylor (1921–2010), Earl Ray (1927–2008), and Charlie Smith (1927–1966), and Dave Lambert (1917–1966), John Hendricks (1921–2017), and Annie Ross (b. 1930) made up the trio of Lambert, Hendricks & Ross.

3. Date of figures for "The Party's Over" section are as follows: Mike Nichols (1931–2014), Elaine May (b. 1932), Carol Burnett (b. 1933), Johnny Mathis (b. 1935), Pearl Bailey (1918–1990), Harry Belafonte (b. 1927), Dorothy Loudon (1925–2003), Kaye Ballard (1925–2019), Phyllis Diller (1917–2012), Dick Gregory (1932–2017), Barbra Streisand (b. 1942), Lenny Bruce (1925–1966), Jerry Stiller (b. 1927), Anne Meara (1929–2015), Jerry Herman (b. 1931), Linda Lavin (b. 1937), Mark Murphy (1932–2015), John Wallowitch (1926–2007), Warren Beatty (b. 1937), Cass Elliot (1941–1974), Doris Day (1922–2019), Murray Grand (1919–2007), Jane Harvey (1925–2013), Woody Allen (b. 1935), Felicia Sanders (1922–1975), Judy Holliday (1921–1965), Betty Comden (1917–2006), Adolph Green (1914–2002), Eartha Kitt (1927–2008), Pat Carroll (b. 1927), and Wally Cox (1924–1973). The Smothers Brothers are Thomas ("Tom") Smothers (b. 1937) and Richard ("Dick") Smothers (b. 1939).

4. Date of figures for the "How Could It Happen?" section are as follows: Joni Mitchell (b. 1943), Dory Previn (1925–2012), Jimmy Webb (b. 1946), John Lennon (1940–1980), Paul McCartney (b. 1942), and Randy Newman (b. 1943).

5. Date of figures for the "A Few Rays of Light" section are as follows: Jo Anne Worley (b. 1937), Joan Rivers (1933–2014), Rodney Dangerfield (1921–2004), Dick Cavett (b. 1936), Claiborne Cary (1932–2010), William Roy (1928–2003), Mary Louise Wilson (b. 1931), Ronny Graham (1919–1999), Ellen Hanley (1926–2007), Ruth Buzzi (b. 1936), Madeline Kahn (1942–1999), Marian Mercer (1935–2011), Fannie Flagg (b. 1944), Marcia Lewis (1938–2010), Portia Nelson (1920–2001), Tammy Grimes (1934–2016), Annie Ross (b. 1930), Blossom Dearie (1924–2009), Jackie Vernon (1924–1987), Dixie Carter (1939–2010), Bette Midler (b. 1945), Barry Manilow (b. 1943), Jonah Jones (1909–2000), Red Norvo (1908–1999), Chris Connor (1927–2009), Stan Getz (1927–1991), Billy Eckstine (1914–1993), Cleo Laine (b. 1927), Jule Styne (1905–1994), and Bobby Short (1924–1995).

6. Date of figures for "The Renaissance" section are as follows: Peter Allen (1944–1992), Maxene Andrews (1916–1995), Barbara Cook (1927–2017), Ellen Greene (b. 1951), Michael Moriarty (b. 1941), Cybill Shepherd (b. 1950), Holly Woodlawn (1946–2015), Bill Weeden (b. 1940), David Finkle (b. 1940), Sally Fay (b. 1950), Robby Benson (b. 1956), Nancy LaMott (1951–1995), Cissy Houston (b. 1933), Whitney Houston (1963–2012), Judy Kaye (b. 1948), Marta Sanders (b. 1950), André De Shields (b. 1946), Andrea Marcovicci (b. 1948), Hildegarde (1906–2005), Dolores Gray (1924–2002), Portia Nelson (1920–2001), Greta Keller (1903–1977), Penny Fuller (b. 1940), Karen Morrow (b. 1936), Carleton Carpenter (b. 1926), Larry Kert (1930–1991), Danny Apolinar (1934–1995), Bernadette Peters (b. 1948), Dorothy Collins (1926–

1994), Margaret Whiting (1924–2011), Ann Reinking (b. 1949), Chita Rivera (b. 1933), Rita Moreno (b. 1931), Wayland Flowers (1939–1988), Jane Olivor (b. 1947), Marilyn Sokol (b. 1944), Baby Jane Dexter (1946–2019), John Monteith (1948–2018), Suzanne Rand (b. 1949), Jo Sullivan Loesser (1927–2019), Margery Cohen (b. 1947), Betty Jane Rhodes (1921–2011), Pamela Myers (b. 1947), Dean Pitchford (b. 1951), Alan Menken (b. 1949), Audrey Lavine (b. 1950), Estelle Parsons (b. 1927), Al Carmines (1936–2005), Martha Schlamme (1923–1985), Alvin Epstein (1925–2018), Tony Azito (1948–1995), Lee Horwin (b. ca. 1948), Hildegarde (1906–2005), Sheldon Harnick (b. 1924), Carolyn Leigh (1926–1983), Harold Rome (1908–1993), Andrew Lloyd Webber (b. 1948), and Tim Rice (b. 1944). Tom Babbitt's dates are unknown.

7. Date of figures for the "Meanwhile . . ." section are as follows: Susannah McCorkle (1946–2001), Marlene VerPlanck (1933–2018), Adelaide Hall (1901–1993), Gretchen Cryer (b. 1935), Nancy Ford (b. 1935), Alberta Hunter (1895–1984), Richard Maltby Jr. (b. 1937), David Shire (b. 1937), Anne Francine (1917–1999), Taina Elg (b. 1930), Denise Lor (1929–2015), Albert Hague (1920–2001), Renee Orrin (1926–2000), Judy Kreston (1933–2009), Barbara Lea (1929–2011), Daryl Sherman (b. 1949), Ronny Whyte (b. 1937), Pat Benatar (b. 1953), Norman Zamcheck (b. 1947), Suzy Williams (b. 1953), Desmond Child (b. 1953), John Kander (b. 1927), Fred Ebb (1928–2004), Charles Strouse (b. 1928), Dorothy Fields (1904–1974), Arthur Schwartz (1900–1984), Harold Arlen (1905–1986), Martin Charnin (1934–2019), Victor Garber (b. 1949), Don Scardino (b. 1949), Jonathan Hadary (b. 1948), Craig Carnelia (b. 1949), Jim Wann (b. 1948), Dory Previn (1925–2012), Ted Hook (1930–1995), and Steve Ross (b. 1938). The dates for Cathy Chamberlain and Loria Parker are unknown.

8. Date of figures for "The Story Goes On" section are as follows: Marcia Lewis (1938–2010), Susannah McCorkle (1946–2001), Karen Akers (b. 1945), Julie Kurnitz (b. 1942), Juliette Koka (1930–2011), Donna McKechnie (b. 1942), Patti LuPone (b. 1949), Liliane Montevecchi (1932–2018), Tammy Grimes (1934–2016), Phyllis Newman (b. 1933), Dixie Carter (1939–2010), Kay Starr (1922–2016), Keely Smith (1928–2017), Ronny Whyte (b. 1937), Daryl Sherman (b. 1949), Andrea McCardle (b. 1963), Maureen McGovern (b. 1949), Margaret Whiting (1924–2011), Mel Tormé (1925–1999), Sylvia Syms (1917–1992), and Joshua Logan (1908–1988). The dates for Terri Klausner and Carol Fredette are unknown.

9. The "Final Thoughts" paragraph was written by author David Sabella.

③

WHAT IS CABARET?

Legendary cabaret singer Nancy LaMott (1951–1995) once said, "Cabaret is an art that is as individual as the people that are doing it. So, it can be very difficult sometimes to find a specific definition for it."[1] Indeed, the word "cabaret" can mean different things to different people, even among the elite professionals in this field. While conducting research and interviews for this book, it was suggested more than once that the title be changed for fear that the word "cabaret" would have negative connotations, conjuring up images of a seedy nightclub or smoke-filled burlesque akin to the Kit Kat Klub in Kander and Ebb's 1966 Broadway musical (and 1972 film) *Cabaret*.[2] This treatise will attempt to define cabaret in spite of the complexities and multifaceted nature of the genre.

DEFINING CABARET

Some of the confusion over the definition of cabaret stems from the fact that the word "cabaret" is used to describe both an intimate performance venue and an artistic performance technique. To make matters more confusing, those two definitions are not at all mutually exclusive. Many different styles of performance—and singing—can take place in a cabaret venue. And conversely, the artistic performance technique of cabaret, which requires an authentic personal intimacy from the performer, can take place in a venue of any size. So, you begin to see the problem. However, as asserted throughout these chapters, it is the artistic performance technique, and not the size of the venue, that truly defines cabaret. Therefore, for the purposes of this book, we will deal exclusively with the intimate performance techniques used in cabaret, regardless of the size of venues.

The cabaret venue, out of financial necessity, hosts every genre and style of singing, character impersonation, and even spoken word. Performances seen at a cabaret venue can consist of one singer onstage or a large cast of performers in a musical revue or showcase format. Even music theater pieces—such as *Nunsense* (1985), *Forever Plaid* (1989), and performances by the all-male operatic parody troupe the La Gran Scena Opera Company (1981–2009), which all went on to great success—started their journey in cabaret venues. But for our purposes, the scope of this work will be limited to the great singers—and great singing—and the requisite training for that singing, in professional cabaret venues, as well as the intimate, performance technique of cabaret.

Cabaret is also often misunderstood to be a close cousin of music theater. This misunderstanding is exacerbated by the fact that a substantial portion of the repertoire performed in cabaret venues comes from music theater and the Great American Songbook. However, upon close examination, one finds concrete stylistic and performance differences between music theater and cabaret, even when singing the same song. This will be discussed further in future chapters.

So, what is cabaret? Cabaret is first and foremost a lyric-driven experience. While one could arguably say that of all vocal music, in no other genre is the lyric of a song so valued. The voice is expected to be in complete service to the lyric, even sacrificing range, pitch duration, and moments of technical vocal brilliance, if necessary. Although technical brilliance is certainly appreciated within this genre, it is not necessarily the hallmark of an advanced elite professional. And above all, the vocal process must never step in front of ("oversing") the lyric or call attention to itself. Additionally, not a single quarter note should be held by the cabaret artist unless the duration of that note is emotionally "earned." By that I mean that the personal—and emotional—connection to the lyric must be present until there is complete offset of tone. This is a goal all singers aspire to regardless of genre, but it is far more challenging than it may initially seem. All too often we see singers—of every genre—begin a phrase with full lyric connection only to have it severed by the thought of pitch preparation, change in dynamic, loss of breath control, or a host of other non-lyric-driven concerns. These disconnections are immediately evident in the intimate performance setting of cabaret, where singer and audience are in extraordinary proximity. However, it is precisely this personal, emotional connection that the discerning cabaret audience has come to not only expect but also insist upon. To lose the connection between lyric and emotion in a performance using a true cabaret technique would be tantamount to coitus interruptus. Authentic connection to the lyric is the fundamental element that separates the novice from the artist in cabaret.

CATEGORIES OF SINGERS

For the purpose of this chapter, we will divide some "previously mistaken-for cabaret" performance styles into a few distinct categories. These are not subcategories within the genre of cabaret. Rather, these are categories of singers who may find themselves performing in a cabaret venue and may (or may not) know what to do once there. Again, to be clear, while one may find these types of singers in cabaret venues across the country, these categories do not represent what will be established as the true performance art of cabaret.

The Theater Singer

The "theater singer" has a strong sense of the fourth wall. He or she is singing not to us but rather at us and always as the character of the show from which the song originates. We are voyeurs watching an intimate moment happening to the character on stage instead of being a participant with the singer. The theater singer's voice generally comes forward as a "remarkable" instrument (but not always). This type of singer may be a strong actor, but only insofar as the portrayal of the character within the show.

The Classical Singer

With the "classical singer," the voice is always front and center. Tone is always maintained, even to the detriment of both emotional connection to (and distinguishability of) the lyric. Notes are held to their fullest duration—and sometimes even longer. There is nothing "spoken" or personal about a classical singer's performance. In addition, although the singer may possess a great emotional connection to the lyric (in any language), that connection is often "leapfrogged" by a vocal tone that "oversings" the lyric. There is also a strong fourth wall present.

The Jazz Singer

The "jazz singer" has a keen sense of rhythmic cadence and harmonic structure. He or she may also strive to "fit into the band" as one of the instruments and not necessarily be the "front sound." The use of voice can be gentle and is often quite musical. The lyric may or may not come forward as the primary element of the performance. Emotional connection is often tied to the musical arrangement and its use of suspended chords and blue notes, as well as other stylistic characteristics. Sometimes there is use of vocal "pyrotechnics" (e.g., scat singing, melismata) that are not necessarily lyric driven. The jazz singer's performance is often mistaken for cabaret because of its intimate nature. Some "jazzys" use a cabaret performance technique—at least on some songs. For the most part, however, the musical arrangements in jazz lend themselves to improvisation of both melody and harmony and complete stylistic retreatment of the song itself, which may also "overplay" the lyric.

The Pop Singer

The "pop singer" is a relatively new species of singer in the world of cabaret, an outgrowth of not only the popularity of modern music but also Broadway's recent acceptance of and reliance on this vocal style. Pop singers tend to think that higher, louder, and longer is always better. Range and decibel are often stretched to their limit, and notes are held longer and straighter with minimal or no perceived use of vibrato. Lyric connection is almost always oversung and often (quite literally) "beat" to death with a constant rhythm that does not allow for variance of thought or emotion. Rather than observing a fourth wall, the pop singer conversely runs to the other extreme and performs as if he or she were singing in a giant stadium, with little regard for the size of the audience, thereby obliterating any sense of intimacy.

The Nightclub Singer

The nightclub singer is a confusingly close cousin to the cabaret singer in that they share repertoire and, very often, venues. In addition, the nightclub singer may employ a cabaret performance technique in one or more of their songs. However, the nightclub singer's main objective is far different from that of the true cabaret artist. In the words of esteemed cabaret critic Roy Sander, "The objective of a nightclub [singer] is to entertain the audience. Not necessarily to move them, to enlighten them, or to make them think."[3] The nightclub singer may take qualities from all the previous categories and blend them in an effort to please everyone who may wander into (and out of) the club. There is generally less attention paid to lyric connection in favor of a presentational approach. Arrangements, even for ballads, may be larger and "slicker," requiring multiple instruments. While this kind of singing and performance style can produce a wonderful show, it doesn't necessarily require the attention or sophistication of the listener.

FINAL THOUGHTS

All of these types of singers may provide a performance that is a completely appropriate and satisfying experience. And these performances may take place on intimate stages or in cabaret venues with patrons sitting at tables instead of in rows of seats. It must also be noted that many performers who work in cabaret venues do morph in and out of these different categories with ease—sometimes within the same performance—thereby further blurring the lines between a performance seen in a cabaret venue and a true cabaret performance. And as previously mentioned, the cabaret venue itself must play host to all types of entertainment out of financial necessity.

In the following chapters you will hear from several elite professionals in the field who will assert that, in the truest sense of the word, these types of performances, even when performed in a cabaret venue, do not truly represent a cabaret performance style. Nor do they use what will be established as the cabaret performance technique. Again, in the words of Roy Sander, "Great cabaret singers uncover layers of meaning that remain hidden in other genres and make the audience feel that they're hearing the song for the first time."[4]

In sum, what does a theater, classical, jazz, pop, or nightclub singer need to do to successfully cross over to the world of cabaret? The answer is simple. The key lies within the lyric of each song and the artist's complete commitment to it. The true cabaret artist performs with a very specific technique that is completely in service to the lyric, striving to create a singular experience. With absolutely no fourth wall and a deeply personal connection to both the song text and the audience, the cabaret artist exemplifies the experience of "singing in the moment"—a moment that will be unlike any other moment before or after it. Musical arrangements will be unique and specific to the artist's personalization of the lyric, but the delivery of that lyric will be first and foremost the priority.

How is this possible, and what are the techniques used by elite cabaret professionals? In the following pages we will examine this question with the help of some award-winning cabaret artists. They will disclose the true nature of cabaret and its unique performance technique and style.

NOTES

1. Nancy LaMott on Dutch television, November 25, 1990.
2. *Cabaret* was written by John Kander (b. 1927) and Fred Ebb (1928–2004). The original Broadway production was directed by Hal Prince (1928–2019) and choreographed by Ron Field (1934–1989). The film version was directed and choreographed by Bob Fosse (1927–1987). There have been three Broadway revivals in 1987, 1998, and 2014.
3. Roy Sander, personal correspondence with author, June 24, 2019.
4. Ibid.

4

CRITICALLY SPEAKING

An Interview with Roy Sander

Roy Sander is the cabaret industry's most ardent fan and esteemed critic. A fixture on the New York cabaret scene—and known as the "Chairman of the Board"—he is one of the industry's most prolific writers, having penned reviews, articles, and columns on the craft of cabaret for more than forty years, including an eleven-year stint at *Backstage* covering cabarets/clubs as well as Broadway and off-Broadway theater through reviews, commentary, and articles. Sander has reviewed cabaret and theater on the *New York Theatre Review* on PBS, WLIM radio, and Citysearch.com and was a voting member of the Drama Desk. He has written columns of advice and commentary for the Manhattan Association of Cabarets (MAC) and has participated in numerous panel discussions on various aspects of cabaret performance and the cabaret scene. Sander was chairman of the judges for the MetroStar Talent Challenge at the Metropolitan Room during the ten years of the contest's existence. He has coached several cabaret performers privately and has twice been a guest instructor at the London School of Musical Theatre. He has received two Bistro Awards in recognition of his contributions to cabaret. Sander is currently chairman of the advisory board of MAC and review editor of BistroAwards.com, where he writes reviews and commentary, serves as a member of the awards committee, and is associate

Figure 4.1. Roy Sander. Photo by Marc Meyerbroker.

producer of the annual awards ceremony. Additionally, he has guided me, David Sabella, as a trusted writing mentor, as both a cabaret reviewer and in the publication of this book.

Roy, thank you so much for sharing your expertise with us today. Some people we've interviewed have suggested not calling the book So You Want to Sing Cabaret *because the word "cabaret" may have some strange and negative connotation. Do you feel there are misunderstandings about the word "cabaret"?*

The term is interpreted differently in different countries and even in different parts of this country. In some places, people think of a floor show with dancing girls. In Germany, there's Kabarett, which frequently refers to an evening of satire but can cover other types of entertainment, and then there's "chanson," which is a program of songs. So, looking at the cabaret scene in New York, I would define cabaret first as a venue, perhaps as "a performance space in which people—the audience—sit at tables and chairs instead of in rows of seats." A term that I think is more descriptive is the term "supper club," which we used to use to suggest intimacy. "Supper club" suggests a certain degree of focus and sophistication—sophistication that comes not from having money but from having taste. However, so many cabarets don't serve dinner, or maybe they serve only peanuts, so it would be tough to use that term.

As far as the art form goes, not the venue, do you feel that cabaret has a specific definition?

Cabaret singing? Yes. While you can do anything in a cabaret, cabaret singing focuses on words and the communication of the meaning of the song. That doesn't mean it has to be a song written long ago—for example, songs from the "Great American Songbook"—it just means that one's interpretation clarifies and illuminates the meaning of the song based on one's own artistic vision and personal interpretation. A cabaret performer isn't merely doing a "cover"—it is much more than that. If a singer has a good voice, maybe she or he can get away with a so-so interpretation that isn't necessarily illuminating the lyric. It'll sound good, but in cabaret, being good enough isn't good enough. The essence of cabaret is deciding on the meaning of the song, and then—unlike performing in music theater where the director is in charge—it is the singer's personal vision that must be realized. In cabaret, the *singer* makes the decisions. *You* are the star. *You* are presenting *your* point of view. So, that's a significant difference. Cabaret is all about point of view and illumination of the lyric.

I think that having a good voice is about 5 percent of what singing is about, except for opera perhaps. But that statement is certainly true in cabaret. Of course, one doesn't want the voice to be painfully bad or the singer to be off pitch, but beyond that it's not about the quality of the voice. My favorite cabaret singer in the world, ever, was Julie Wilson, and for the last twenty or thirty years of her career, it wasn't the voice that we went to hear—it was what she did with the song.

Can we discuss the intimate nature of cabaret performance?

When I saw Lena Horne on Broadway, it was in a theater that seated at least one thousand people, and her performance was intimate. Therefore, intimacy in cabaret is not related to the size of the venue. I think intimacy has to do with what is in the artist's mind, the realization that the performance is not a recital and therefore not presentational. Rather, you're *talking* to the audience. It doesn't matter if the audience is one thousand people or only forty people—you're *talking* to them.

In cabaret singing there is an essential question that every performer must consider for each song he or she sings: "Who am I talking to?" There are so many possibilities! Am I talking to someone? Am I being introspective? Am I talking to the universe? Is the song addressed to some imaginary person or to some specific character, for instance, one's spouse? The answer to this question shapes the entire presentation. First, it will inform the physical performance—for example, where you look. It will also inform your interpretation in very subtle ways. These choices are unique to cabaret. In theater, you always know to whom you're singing the song, because it's dictated to you by the script. For example, I've heard, "It Might as Well Be Spring" sung in different ways with different answers to the question "Who am I singing to?" There is never only one way to perform a cabaret song.

To prepare for a music theater performance, the actor goes through that same kind of process, deciding what their own subtext might be. But in cabaret it almost seems like the subtext becomes the primary text.

In cabaret you quite literally have to invent the subtext from scratch. In music theater, the setup allows for options, but only certain options would be appropriate. For example, you must consider whether your choice is appropriate for the character at this point in the drama, in this setting, and with these other specific characters on stage. In cabaret, on the other hand, you only have the song that you're going to sing—that's it! You start from a blank page. There is no guidance. Now, if it's a selection in a show, part of the guidance might come from its position within the flow of the show, and there might be a reason to choose one answer to the question over another. But there are so many more options in cabaret.

In addition to songs from the music theater canon, I have also heard cabaret renditions of very recent Top 40 songs where performers were incredibly attentive to the lyrics, in addition to singing the songs in a non-pop way.

Right. Very often just taking the beat out of the song . . .

It almost sounds to me like the cabaret approach—or cabaret technique   may require a very different use of voice. In cabaret, the voice is not upfront but rather in service to the lyric. Therefore, it sounds to me like big voices may actually get in the way when singing cabaret.

A bigger voice can be used judiciously and selectively. For example, when the interpretation calls for a swelling of emotion, there are a lot of different ways to swell. One of them is volume, but another is to use a "fuller" sound with more color. So . . . no, a big voice doesn't necessarily get in the way. But I often say, "Just because you can, doesn't mean you should." There's a singer on the scene now who has a glorious voice. Unfortunately, that's what her performances amount to now. You hear glorious music and a glorious voice, but there is nothing else going on. There's no coloration, no nuance, no contours, nor any contrasts.

Some people may have a misunderstanding of cabaret repertoire—historically coming from music theater and the Great American Songbook—and think that it is little more than a recital-style music theater performance in which the singer is standing in the crook of the piano. But cabaret is something uniquely different from music theater. Can you talk about that?

Alright. First up, you just used a term that I don't like to use. I have been known to use it, but I don't like it: Great American Songbook. First, it's not all American. It's largely American, but I prefer "classic popular song." For example, Noël Coward is not American at all, and his songs are great—among the greatest ever written. And there are people today writing songs that are as good as the great ones that we all remember from the twenties, thirties, forties, fifties, or whenever. They're literally writing classic American popular songs in that idiom.

Also, I should say for the record that it is possible to do a successful cabaret show that doesn't even employ cabaret singing—rather, it honors other aspects of cabaret performance. A few years ago, someone did a wonderful show about Motown. What made it great is that she *didn't* rethink the songs in a higher-class idiom—she just did them in the Motown style, and very, *very* well. The show was fun and spirited, had great rhythms, and was very successful. Perhaps most important, she respected the intimacy of the room and "talked" to the audience in a personal way while she sang. *Everything about the show was addressed to the audience.* That is the main difference between cabaret and music theater.

There is no "fourth wall" in cabaret. You truly connect with the audience. In the performance of a song—the same song—in Motown versus in a cabaret setting, or in music theater versus a cabaret setting, do you think there are specific stylistic choices that need to be made so that one "honors the room," as you said? And specifically, how does music theater differ from cabaret in this regard?

I think there are a few key differences. Like I said before, in cabaret you are free from the constraints imposed by the book of the musical and the character that you're playing. Instead, you *invent* the character that you're playing that night and *you* get to choose the style. It could still be sung in a Motown style if you wish, but you could also rethink it, especially if the lyric is good enough. And if the lyric isn't good enough, then it may not be a good choice for a cabaret, unless it fits in with some other agenda such as, "Here's some Motown and we're going to have fun with it and it will be really well done."

In other words, cabaret sets you free because you get to make all the choices. I think that's the main difference. In music theater you have some room for creative interpretation, but you aren't free. And then of course there are also eleven o'clock or "big" numbers in musicals that are accompanied by a full orchestra, so you have less of an opportunity to "bring it in" like you can when you only have a pianist. And then there are the "let's have fun" rhythm pieces that can be great palate cleansers in a big musical. But if that's your whole show in cabaret, it can get a little boring, even if you're really good. A whole show of just lines of rhythmic music with no substance or content is certainly not for me, and it's certainly not cabaret.

What do you think is the most important aspect of a cabaret performance technique that every young performer should try to embody?

The first thing is to be sure the lyric says something that you want to say, even if you might not agree with it. You must find something that you can sink your teeth into. So, make sure it's something you can connect with and understand.

And when talking about a cabaret technique, learn the words of the song before you sing it. Recite it. Get them down cold so you know what you want to say, which lines are important, which words are worth emphasizing. That foundation will inform your performance when you later add the music. You may not be able to emphasize it as much as you might want to because the music might fight that reading, but there's still a wide range of what you can do. There are other ways of expressing the text other than what the music might call for. Remember, you're telling a story; you need to start from that perspective.

Music is notated with dynamics, tempo, and other indications of the composer's intent. If, during the process of rehearsing a song, the singer feels led to do something different, the interpretation is different, for example, he/she sings pianissimo where it says to sing forte; is that acceptable in cabaret?

Oh, absolutely. In fact, it's preferred. Changes should not be arbitrary, but to sing a song the way everyone else sings it is likely not going to be terribly interesting. No matter how good the song is or how good your voice is, you need to make it your own. We've all heard the recording. Have a point of view that might surprise us. Take, for example, Barbra Streisand's famous recording of "Happy Days Are Here Again" where she sings it slowly even though it's an up-tempo song. That works, not because it's different—though that certainly gets our attention—but because she gives you another perspective. It's the perspective of somebody who is so weary that she's wary of the good news; her optimism is really guarded. Therefore, it becomes a valid perspective on the song even though it is nontraditional.

It is very important, however, that you're not arbitrary in your decisions. I have seen situations in which the changes are nothing more than the musical director choosing to be different for the sake of being different. I observed a very, very good singer say to his musical director, "Oh, do something different with this," and I thought, *No, no, no! You! It has to come from you.* The singer needs to decide what he or she wants to say and then communicate that to the musical director. They can then work on it together, but it should never be simply, "Do something different, because I don't want to sing it the way everyone knows it." No, that is unacceptable.

In your experience as a reviewer and a cognoscente of cabaret, what do you believe are the hallmarks of a great cabaret performance? And spe-

cifically, without naming names—unless you want to—give an example of an amazing experience you have had in a cabaret show and why it was so great. And conversely, perhaps you can give us an example of an experience you had that could have been better and why.

I'll start with ones that could have been better, and there have been many. For a show to be terrific, it must hold my attention and interest. If it's just nicely sung but vapid, then I am not interested. As both an audience member and a critic, it's not enough. I want to feel entertained, or wooed, or informed, or just simply involved for my interest to be held. If you are singing to me, I want to hear more of what you have to *say*. Some singers wear out their welcome with me after three songs. However, if you're talking to me through your singing and I am intrigued by what you have to say, then I remain interested. You must present an intelligent, informed, and sometimes very emotional point of view. Cabaret singing is about connecting with the human experience in addition to offering an enriching performance and interpretation. That's the kind of performance that will engage my mind, and of course my emotions. It's about digging deep into a lyric.

I'll give you an example of someone who did that. There is a song that begins "I've got the world on a string, sitting on a rainbow." Now, that's a song we've all heard hundreds of times, if not more. When Julie Wilson did it at the Algonquin, I cried, which I may end up doing now. She found so many layers of meaning. It was an extraordinary experience to hear her sing that song. There was such emotional depth and perception in her interpretation. With Julie there were many experiences like that. And Mabel Mercer, her interpretations were wonderful as well, and it certainly wasn't the voice in her case, especially toward the end of her career. I saw Mabel several times, and it was her interpretations that mattered. She just sat in a chair—which seemed to become a throne because there was a majesty to her—and talked to us. Her interpretations were brilliant because they *said* something. There are other examples of people I think are great exponents of illuminating a lyric. This is my favorite kind of cabaret work. Andrea Marcovicci and Steve Ross come to mind. Steve plays the piano at the same time too! His song interpretations are extraordinary, and he digs down many layers. He takes songs that I have previously not liked, and he finds the meaning. Julie did that too, and more recently Amy Beth Williams—whom I consider to be one of the greats—Barbara Brussell, and Lauren Fox. I am leaving out a lot of others who also do it very, very well. And then there are people who straddle two worlds, like KT Sullivan and Karen Mason. They can get deep into a lyric, but they can also be "performers," never overstated of course. Sharon McNight is an interesting example also. She can be outrageous and do a club act, but she can also do a ballad and really get into the lyric. That's not what she tends to specialize in, but she certainly has a foot in whatever camp she wants to put a foot into.

We've talked a little bit about how cabaret is not limited to the Great American Songbook. But rather, a performer can choose any song, even a contemporary song, if it is interpreted putting the lyric first.

Right. The lyrics must have something to say. If they (and you) have something to say, only then will you do it right.

If there is a great lyric in a contemporary song, it's fair game?

Contemporary can mean two things, either written recently or that the style of the music is contemporary. There are people today writing classic American popular songs in the classic idiom. Examples include songs by John Bucchino, Steven Lutvak, and Francesca Blumenthal—she wrote a lot of wonderful songs, I mean, *really* fine. "Lies of Handsome Men" is a classic. In answer to your question, any contemporary song with a great lyric can become a classic. ♪

Those recently written songs are acceptable in the world of cabaret. But can they be considered new additions to the Great American Songbook or classic popular song?

Of course, if the lyric is meaningful, and the song is well crafted. Classic popular song tends to be well crafted, but not all the lyrics were great. Some were just fun or had a catchy tune or whatever.

It seems to me that the criteria for whether a song becomes a classic song, in the Great American Songbook, depends more on the lyric, than the music.

I think that's right. However, I do think it is possible for a song without the greatest lyric to become a classic. Take "Hey Jude" by the Beatles, for instance. I consider that song to be the contemporary equivalent of Ravel's *Bolero*. I mean, the arrangement is a masterstroke. The first time I heard it I thought, *This is crap . . . it just goes on and on and on*, and then I listened to the whole recorded version of the song and said, "God, that arrangement!" So, yes, I think it's possible for a song to become a classic if other (nonlyrical) factors are strong enough. Sometimes you hear a song in a foreign language and the music has such an impact on you that you want to hear it again and again, even though you don't know what the lyric means. Then later you find out what the lyrics mean and you say, "Ugh, really?" However, the song is a hit in that foreign language simply because the music is so stunning. I wouldn't rule out the music altogether. Music is very important. A song that has a really good lyric but really dull music ain't gonna make it. It's very important not to trivialize the music.

Traditionally, voice teachers spend their whole day sitting on a piano bench dealing with voice production, beauty of tone, breathing, resonance, articulation, phrasing, and so on. What would you ask a voice teacher to spend more time on? And what would you ask them to spend less time on?

I would say let aspiring cabaret singers spend no more than 25 percent of their time receiving that kind of instruction and refer them to other teachers for the rest of the skills they need. If the teacher doesn't know what to focus on to achieve your career goals, then he or she is the wrong teacher for you. There's one singer, one of my favorites of the current scene, who is classically trained and has done a significant amount of opera work. When I first heard her—and I've told her this—I said, "You've got a wonderful voice, but you bored me silly." She continued doing more cabaret work, and now she's one of my favorites. She had to change the way she sings, but it is possible. Her voice teacher may have been fine for what her career was at one time (opera), but that teacher was probably not the right one for her now. I don't know what kind of flexibility teachers have and how much they know about what it takes to sing cabaret in terms of interpretation. Tone is a part of it, absolutely, but it is relatively unimportant compared to other factors.

Other than singing, what are some nonvocal requirements or skills that a cabaret performer needs, even in the business aspect. What does a young singer need to know?

True cabaret shows all have "patter," so that's something with which they need to become comfortable.

The talking?

Yes, and there are so many decisions there. How much talking to have and what to say. Are you going to do just fifteen songs, or are you going to have a theme? To what extent is the theme significant in the show? Is it simply a way of selecting songs—which is fine—and do you really have something to say? Perhaps the theme says something that you want to say in addition to the individual songs? Those are things you must consider. There are singers who are wonderful singers but are awkward when they talk. When that happens, I want to say, "Shut up and sing, because you're so good at it and your interpretations are so rich." But it's never a concert, even though some concerts can have the intimacy and the communication with the audience that a cabaret show should have.

And it's also not a recital.

It's definitely not a recital.

Are there other elements that are important?

I think you need to know what your strengths are—what you're good at and less good at. It's not enough to sing a funny song . . . you must really *be* funny. Take Sidney Myer, for example; he can take a song that was never intended to be funny, he opens his mouth, and he's funny, right off the bat. And then there are other people who sing a funny song, and it just lies there because they just don't get it. They just don't have the spark to pull it off.

The funny bone?

Yes, the funny bone, an antic spirit, or whatever, and if you don't have it, then the solution is that you shouldn't do a funny song. Also, there are performers whose voices and bodies are not fluid enough to do up-tempo numbers, which means they shouldn't do an up-tempo number until they get good enough at it. I have also seen people who don't seem to know what's in their comfort zone and what isn't. I saw a performer recently who was fine when she was leaning against the piano, but when she was standing away from the piano she was nervously fidgeting, which detracted from her interpretation. So, stay by the crook of the piano if you must. On a recording, you may not know that the person is not centered physically, but in a live performance it becomes an important issue. Singers also need to learn how to use the stage. Some performers simply move about too much, confusing motion with action. Motion is just motion, whereas action is purposeful. And in addition to knowing about how to use the stage, there's also mic technique.

Mic technique?

Yes, they need keep several things in mind. For instance, don't cover your mouth with the mic because the audience needs to see your face, not only because it will help us decipher what certain words are (if they are not quite clear aurally), but also because your mouth is part of your communication toolbox. We need to see it. Holding a microphone too close can also screw up the sound.

These are little things that matter other than singing. Another thing you need to know: almost *never* sing directly to one person in the audience. And unless there's a damned good reason, don't leave the stage to go into the audience either. That fails miserably much more often than it succeeds. You should be wary of doing that. Certainly, if it's an introspective ballad, the audience will come to you. Don't worry about turning your head to sing to all parts of the audience—they will come to you. Don't turn your head unless it's called for.

The contrast between "we come to you" versus "you come to us" is interesting. How do you know when to do what? Or is it just a matter of personal style?

When I saw Marlene Dietrich toward the end of her career she spoke to the audience from time to time, but when she performed, we came to her—she didn't come to us. She communicated with the audience, but that wasn't obvious. It wasn't her style then; at that point, she was "empress." However, it was her style when she was younger.

In general, I would say don't move unless it's called for in your interpretation. The other thing you do want to avoid, as we talked about beforehand, is looking stiff, because even when you're talking to one person, if that's your interpretation, you don't look with a determined gaze at that person for two and a half minutes. That's creepy and it's not natural. If it's an "up" number and you really want to perform for the whole audience, do not feel the need to keep turning like an oscillating fan to cover the whole audience. That's another thing that less experienced performers must learn.

Now, about directors: There are some directors who are very knowledgeable, very smart, very good at helping someone structure a show, helping someone with patter and writing clever patter, doing research, and maybe even writing custom lyrics. However, that kind of director only works well when paired with a performer who really knows how to interpret songs. That person is not so good with people who are newer to cabaret and need help with song interpretation.

I also think there are directors who are the opposite—really good at coaching song interpretation.

Oh yes, absolutely, and they may also be good at structuring a show. There are a few directors out there who seem to be good at just about everything. The advice I would give to a young singer is this: If you're going to be doing a show and you want a director to guide you, look around at different shows. You won't necessarily be able to tell what contribution the director has made, but if you see other shows that same director did, you might discern a pattern. Also, you should audition directors by talking to them before you hire them. No matter how good a director may seem, you need to determine whether that person's ideas are going to mesh with yours. The artistic vision should be yours—a director shouldn't give it to you. If you don't have one, then you're not ready to do a show. You must have a vision for each song and know what you want to say with each and every lyric. The director or musical director might guide you away from your interpretation and encourage you to do something else, and if you agree, then fine. But definitely audition the director, maybe via a half-hour interview/conversation. He or she will probably charge you for it, but you need to know that it's the right director for you and your show. Sometimes once you start working with the director, it just feels wrong. If that's the case, fire the director and get someone else. Finally, don't be too impressed by famous people that the director has directed. Those famous people might not need what you need, especially when you are at the beginning of your career.

Another thing I would advise on the business end of things: Don't be too keen on inviting reviewers to your first show. Further, don't invite them to the first performance of your thirtieth show. In the world of theater, plays and musicals have previews. Give yourself a chance to have at least one, two, or maybe even three initial performances totally closed and not open to the press. At that point, if you think everything is working, have another run and invite the press then. *You* manage the press. Make the booking manager and the staff aware of whether you are accepting press coverage or not. If a press person happens to just wander in, as some of them do, make sure that the staff and the booking manager or the room manager notifies the press person and says, "We appreciate your interest, but this is not for review." In my experience, a major mistake that inexperienced performers make is to oversell themselves by inviting critics to view their work prematurely; they oversell themselves out of sheer enthusiasm.

Well, what if someone is only doing one show?

Well then that's a decision to make. Sometimes I go just to see what that person is up to, but then I choose not to write about it. I use my judgment. I have often thought, *Well, you know, this is still so raw. . . . It's not right to write about it.*

As we enter the third decade of the twenty-first century, we find ourselves in a YouTube culture of "post it quick and let's see how many 'likes' I get." The development of craft and artistry via the insular nature of rehearsal is being lost. Nowadays, as soon as a young singer has memorized something, they want to put it "out there" for consumption instead of living with it a while and fleshing it out. Just because you know all the words doesn't mean that it's ready for prime time yet.

That's certainly true of many beginners, and I've also seen other extremely experienced people who have won major awards be reluctant to put themselves out there.

Regarding "the voice": the voice itself does not seem to be something that critics generally even discuss in their reviews of cabaret performances.

It depends on the critic. There are some critics who know a lot about voice and therefore feel equipped to talk about it. Or perhaps, if they were to rank their criteria, they simply give more weight to voice than I do. I give more weight to interpretation because that is my personal preference. I also know of other situations where the voice was gorgeous, but if you look at the person while they are singing, the contortions they go through to produce the sound are counterinterpretative. That is not acceptable in cabaret and is something they need to work on.

Counterinterpretative? That's a great word. I've never heard it before.

Really? I use that word a lot actually. I don't know that it is a word, but I use it. Moving about the stage is counterinterpretative, meaning it undermines interpretation. Moving your mouth a lot, or singing to one person in the audience, is also counterinterpretative because it takes the audience out of what you're doing and makes everyone aware of the person you're singing to, who should be irrelevant. Singing to a particular audience member also makes people think, *God, does that audience member feel uncomfortable with this attention? I would certainly feel uncomfortable.* Also, don't acknowledge people in the audience during the show; it makes the rest of the audience, the other people, feel like outsiders.

What about at end of the show, during "thank yous"?

Well, you could thank the whole audience for coming. If you want to then acknowledge certain, particular people, and if they are people the audience would know—or should know—then yes. But if they're your friend or someone like that, then no, don't do it.

How about luminaries in the audience?

Yes, that is a choice. It's a choice, and it may work, but don't. . . . And here are a few more pet peeves of mine. Never, ever, under any circumstances point to the pianist and ask the audience to applaud. Don't do that. If the audience bursts into applause spontaneously, that's their choice. But when you instigate it, it comes off as "I have to show you that he really is wonderful." Remember, it's *your* show and *your* moment. At the end of a number, you might point to the pianist and say, "Thank you" or "Don did that arrangement," or something. But never do it in the middle of the song, unless it's a real up-tempo selection and you're using the number to introduce the members of the band. That's a different situation.

I notice that custom very often in jazz.

Yes, but that's a different aesthetic.

It is indeed a different aesthetic than cabaret. There are some cabaret artists who also do a lot of jazz. I believe the primary difference between cabaret and jazz is that in cabaret the lyric comes first and foremost, whereas in jazz it's about the musical information, the harmonies, the riffs, the way the song is arranged, and the solos.

Actually, there are a few jazz singers out there who put the lyric first. One of my favorites is Carol Fredette. Her interpretation is as good as Julie Wilson's, and that's saying something. Once I saw a jazz singer named Sally Stark, who was doing a Maxine Sullivan show. At the top of the show she said, "I would appreciate it if you didn't applaud in the middle of the songs," and I thought, *I love you, whoever you are!* I just think the jazz convention is really annoying—it treats the singer like one of the instruments.

I think that's the goal . . . what jazz musicians strive for.

That's how it goes, yes, but it also depends on the singer and what the singer is trying to do. My favorite jazz singers are not necessarily "jazz" singers. They have a jazz singer's *feel* for the music. Barbara Lea is an example of this. I once wrote that I didn't consider her to be a jazz singer but rather that she has a jazz singer's appreciation for music—and she thanked me. Carol Fredette is also considered to be a jazz singer, and that's fair enough. But it's her lyric interpretations that determine her musical choices.

Another exceptional singer associated with the jazz world is the great artist Dee Dee Bridgewater. When her accompanists take solo breaks, they always continue the mood she's set up—it's all one piece. It is never, "Okay, now I'll show off for sixteen bars"; no, it's all one piece. At a concert she gave—I think it was at Town Hall—the drum solo was a very quiet one. I was in tears from the drum solo! I actually wrote, "We've all seen spectacular drum solos, but this is the first one that ever made me cry." But in general, jazz solos too often come off like they are little more than a chance for musicians to show off and show how good they are at improvising. That's a different animal—it's not cabaret at all.

Also, to change the subject, don't tell the audience to tip. It's not appropriate for a cabaret artist to teach the audience good manners. Also, don't thank your husband or your lover. Do that at home.

I think the thank-yous have grown recently, out of an "award" mentality.

Yes, and if it's an awards ceremony, that's okay. Or as I have also written, if it's the final performance of a long run—*then* you can thank the booking manager and the staff. But if it's part of a run, why does the audience care to whom you're grateful? I don't even think the director should be thanked. None of these people should be thanked—they should be *acknowledged*. The musical director . . . the pianist . . . the band . . . *they* should be acknowledged. They worked for the past hour, and the audience should applaud them separately as you acknowledge them, but that's not the same as thanks. People call it thanks, but it's really an acknowledgment. But thanking anyone personally, like someone who flew in from Chicago to see you? No. Keep it professional and thank that person later.

Right. It's not a "friends and family" show.

Exactly. That's the other mantra. As you are conceiving the show and planning it, say to yourself, *No one knows me . . . no one cares about me*, and repeat it often. Do not have any autobiographical patter in your show, unless (a) it sets the song up particularly well; (b) it's very funny, and you're aiming for humor; or (c) it has broader resonance beyond just your personal life. Maybe it illuminates something about *life* or it's simply interesting. Other than that, don't do it. You don't matter—your *artistry* does. When I go to see a show, I don't walk in thinking, *I want to know about this person*. However, I may leave thinking, *I want to know* more *about that person*, and typically, it's not because of anything the person said about himself or herself—it's because of what the person revealed about themselves through song interpretations.

Unless it is in fact interesting—not just to you, but *in fact* interesting. Don't tell us what a song means to you or why you wanted to sing it. After you sing it, let me be the one who is grateful that you chose to sing it. I really don't care *why* you chose to sing it. Make me glad that you chose to sing it because you said so much through the song. This is important because there is a lot of crap being written—and believed today—about needing to "reveal yourself" as a singer. *It's not about you.*

That is advice I would definitely give to an aspiring cabaret singer.

5

THE MAYOR OF
NEW YORK CABARET

An Interview with Sidney Myer

Sidney Myer is a New York cabaret icon and an award-winning
performer, entertaining audiences
from San Francisco to London.
The *New York Times* calls him
"a beloved latter-day vaudevillian
. . . an engaging, mischievous
dispenser of musical repartee."
In addition to cabaret, Myer has
appeared in the Emmy Award–
winning television series *After
Forever*, the film *Headin' for
Broadway*, the off-Broadway hits
Grandma Sylvia's Funeral and
Times Square Angel, and commer-
cials for RCA Victor and the New
York lottery. A cabaret booking

Figure 5.1. Sidney Myer. *Photo by Eric Stephen Jacobs.*

manager for nearly four decades for venues such as Don't Tell Mama,
Rose's Turn, and Panache, he was featured "above the fold" in the Sunday *New York Times* Arts and Leisure section front-page cover story
with the headline "Saviors of the American Songbook." Throughout his

career as a booking manager, Myer's keen eye for talent and gracious spirit has led him to present artists that have gone on to Broadway, television, and motion picture careers and have received numerous awards, including Emmys, Grammys, Tonys, Oscars, and a Pulitzer Prize. We are so grateful that Myer could take time out of his busy schedule to be interviewed for *So You Want to Sing Cabaret*. The following pages offer a snapshot of the "Mayor" talking about the art form to which he has devoted his life. ♪

Thank you for sitting down with us, Sidney. How would you define the "art" of cabaret, separate and distinct from other vocal performance genres, such as music theater and jazz.

My stars! I would say that while cabaret is different than other live musical platforms, each of those categories can be presented in cabaret. In a word, it's a "connection" to yourself, the music, and the audience that does not exist in the same way in other genres.

Define "connection" for us.

In cabaret, it's as if every word is part of a one-on-one conversation you are directly having with another person. If we made a list of all the things that define connection, it would include the following: lyrics, instrumentalists, audience, story, and emotions. You must have a connection to all of them! It's not just a sound of a voice or not having a fourth wall. This kind of connection is completely unlike many other genres from opera to Broadway, and that is ultimately what makes cabaret unique.

When I began booking cabaret, back in 1847 [*laughing*], I only worked with people on the cabaret circuit. As time went on, I started to book people who were already fortunate enough to be employed full time in show business, either in a small role or in the chorus of a Broadway show or on a television soap opera. While they may not have been stars, they were getting to perform for thousands of people a week and making thousands of dollars. So, it mystified me that they were so eager to run over to a fifty-seat cabaret room with a five-dollar cover charge. It slowly became clear to me—and I feel this remains true for the most part today—that people are cast on stage and screen based on their externals;

namely, their appearance and the sound of their voice. Those externals, however, may have nothing to do with their internals: heart, mind, and soul. For example, the gal who is always cast as the innocent ingenue because she is blonde, blue-eyed, and lovely. When she does her cabaret act, she's performing sexy, get-down "I'm a Woman" songs that reflect her true identity, what she wants to express, and why she got into the business in the first place. Or the fellow who may have a very dramatic, dark look and is always cast on *Law and Order* as a sinister villain; his cabaret can be completely comprised of sweet, romantic love songs because that is who he really is. Even the people closest to these performers, from their agent to their manager to their spouses, look at them with different eyes after seeing them in cabaret because they've never seen this aspect of them—this authentic, true self—on any stage previously.

So, there's no "type." It's about presenting one's authentic self.

Yes! You get to cast yourself. Why not make it a dream part, that includes all the facets of you? In every other area—motion pictures, television, theater—there is always someone—a director, a producer, a writer—telling you what to do and how to do it. In cabaret, the only voice you need to listen to is the voice of your own muse or the voice of someone, a director or music director, that *you* have selected to specifically guide you. It's like that burger place: "Have it your way!" That is a rare luxury in the arts that even the biggest stars in other media do not experience.

Cabaret has also taught me there is truly no such thing as competition. A casting director in theater may bring in one hundred people who are your height, size, hair color, and vocal range, which is again all about the externals. On the outside, everyone may indeed be the same "type," but you are the only one with *your* brain, *your* point of view, *your* happiness, and *your* heartbreaks. Ultimately, there's only one of you!

Given the personal nature of connection to the lyric in cabaret, do you think there is such a thing as "cabaret performance technique"? And if so, can you elaborate on what this entails?

Cabaret technique is the ability to reveal yourself and express your true, honest self. You are one of a kind. No one else has your point of view, and hence your phrasing. The goal is for you to bring forth—in whatever song you are singing—who you are as an individual. Any technique that a teacher or director may use to instruct a student must be used as a vehicle to bring out all those aspects of that individual person.

As a performer, booking manager, or even as an audience member, what is more important to you: vocal quality/technique or connection to the lyric?

There is no question that possessing a fabulous voice like Julie Andrews, Barbra Streisand, Frank Sinatra, or Ray Charles is indeed a blessing. But there are many roads to Rome. A great instrument is not always a given in being a singing show-business great. Carol Channing, Jimmy Durante, Randy Newman, Eartha Kitt, Marlene Dietrich, and Bob Dylan, to name only a few, are not known for conventional beauty of voice—but boy, could they put a song over with connection to the lyric, thought, and emotion.

At Don't Tell Mama, we have had countless student classes perform, from the New School and Juilliard to the Ninety-Second Street Y and NYU. While there are always some members of the class with impressive instruments, that does not necessarily guarantee a successful performance. If the words coming out of the singer's mouth have not also passed through their brain first, what comes out is just a disembodied sound and the audience loses interest—and patience—very quickly. The great saloon singer Sylvia Syms once said to me, "If it's just about notes, a trumpet could do it!" Anything one has in the positive column—showmanship, style, vocal acumen, ease of movement, or beauty—is a definite asset when stepping onstage. However, it does not guarantee that you will sell a song or move an audience.

In my case, I never had a conventional voice and regard myself as an "entertainer" as opposed to a singer. In fact, I never wanted to do a CD because I didn't think I would succeed in the one-dimensional world of sound. It was therefore quite a surprise when the Mabel Mercer Foundation (chapter 19) approached me several years ago offering to video my show as a fundraiser and create a DVD that they would then sell. They considered me a vaudevillian who needs to be seen as well as heard.

So, it all comes back to connection again . . .

Absolutely! I have seen singers, making their stage debut, with limited experience and ability—during an evening with many seasoned performers—that were so connected and invested in what they were singing that they received the biggest applause of the night. Often in the local amateur-night contests a person may be the least trained actor or singer, but there is something that is so compelling when putting over the song that the audience goes wild. And in contrast, another person may have a more impressive instrument but does not have that connection, and what we hear is that disembodied sound again.

Like listening to a CD?

Having only a great voice may be preferable on a CD. However, when listening to a CD, the listener provides what isn't there by using their imagination. Before television, radio was called the "theater of the mind." Cabaret, however, is different. If someone is singing right in front of you, and they do not visually or emotionally capture you, the voice becomes incidental very quickly. The ability of an artist to affect an audience—to find a way to connect with them—ultimately takes the day!

On the topic of "you are the only you," what about the value of using a director and how that can help to bring out the you in you? What is the value to having a director?

In my case, I have worked with the same director for over forty-five years. It's true! When I was just beginning, director Peter Schlosser simply "got me." He understood that I was attempting to do things in a way that no one else had done them. Happily, with Peter's counsel, people have now come to "get me" many years later. But back in those days, and in that moment of time, he was a rare individual who was open to what I was trying to accomplish, and he always supported my vision. Peter became my "jeweler's eye."

Just as in life, there are many exceptions. There are some greats—such as Marilyn Maye and the late Julie Wilson—who do not/did not use a director. They created shows themselves or with their accompanist. I think it is fair to say, however, that the lion's share of performers in cabaret do employ the services of a director because it can be very difficult for a pianist on stage with you (or often times behind you) to see what the audience is seeing. When a singer believes a facial expression or gesture may have a certain effect, it may not be landing that way at all. Most everyone has someone to whom they entrust their performance, and with good reason.

Who are some of the famous people that started their careers in cabaret? And is it just singers, or are there other areas of the arts that used cabaret as a starting point?

Oh yes! We would be here for days if I would speak about all those who used Don't Tell Mama as a launching pad to emerge onto the world stage. A few years ago, when James Corden first hosted the Tony Awards, there was a cover story in the arts section of the *New York Times* about him, and they photographed him here! The first line in the interview was, "When I get on stage at the piano bar at Don't Tell Mama . . ." because he regularly comes in and gets up and sings.

And another Broadway and television star—Billy Porter.

I was booking Billy Porter when he was still in high school! It's an unwritten tradition that when you get off of the bus from Peoria or Paris—or Pittsburgh in Billy's case—with your little valise, you put yourself in a show before anyone else puts you in a show. Cabaret is the only door open to you when you arrive, and this is often our first stage experience and exposure. The vast majority are indeed singers/singing actors such as Faith Prince, Alice Ripley, Jennifer Lewis, Karen Mason, Nancy LaMott, Tonya Pinkins, Marin Mazzie, Mira Sorvino, and KT Sullivan, and some are singing pianists such as Billy Stritch, Nellie McKay, Mark Nadler, and Daryl Sherman. What often doesn't come to mind are other talents, as you originally asked: world-famous comedians such as Jim Gaffigan, Aziz Ansari, Seth Rudetsky, Lea Delaria, Kathy Najimy, and Mo Gaffney—the last two of the "Kathy and Mo Show"—all began their careers in cabaret.

And there are the songwriters. What would we do without them? I booked composer Jonathan Larson first at Panache and then at Don't Tell Mama, and he went on to make Broadway history by winning the Tony and Pulitzer Prize for *Rent*. The acclaimed Tony winning–composer Jason Robert Brown presented his first revue of original songs called *The New World* here at Don't Tell Mama. Stephen Sondheim came in to see it, and before long it moved to an off-Broadway theater and was renamed *Songs for a New World*. That show included "Stars and the Moon" and several other songs that have become cabaret classics. Andrew Lippa—composer, lyricist, and playwright for *The Wild Party*—Craig Carnelia, Marcy Heisler and Zina Goldrich, Rick Jensen, Dick Gallagher, and John Wallowitch are a few other important songwriters who have stood out in recent decades.

The Broadway composer and star Steven Lutvak was onstage here for years doing his solo act. Later, with Robert L. Freedman, he won the Tony Award for Best Musical with *A Gentleman's Guide to Love and Murder*. Alexander Dinelaris put his first small play up here and—fast-forward—won an Oscar for the screenplay (with his partners) for the movie *Birdman*, and *then* he wrote *On Your Feet* for Gloria Estefan! Christopher Curtis used to sit at the piano and recount the life of Charlie Chaplin through his original songs. It too wound up on Broadway after germinating in cabaret for year. In the 1980s, the sister of an unknown songwriter brought an actress friend to see the songwriter's show. The sister was Liz Callaway, the songwriter was Ann Hampton Callaway, and the actress was Fran Drescher. When it came time to create a theme song for her new series, *The Nanny*, Fran remembered Ann and asked her to write that theme song, which is now sung all over the globe!

In the last three years, a brilliant two-character original musical began running in the back room at Don't Tell Mama. It then moved to the New York Music Festival (where it won a Bistro Award) before moving up to Provincetown, where it was a huge hit for six weeks. Its final run was at the York Theater in New York, where it got a rave review in the *New York Times*, won the MAC Award for Show of the Year, and won an ASCAP Award. The show was Mark Sonnenblick and Sam Bolen's *Midnight at the Never Get*.

One can mount a project in cabaret at a fraction of the cost of renting even the smallest theater. In theater, you must hire the box office personnel, technical director, and stage manager; bring in the piano and lighting; and obtain insurance, to name only a few things. All these expenses do not exist in cabaret. That's why it is a great "first stop" for so many. You mentioned Billy Porter, who went on to be the one hundred thousand–dollar winner of *Star Search*, and then a Broadway, and now television, star. But in addition, we've had many people debut at Don't Tell Mama who have gone on to win the top awards in the profession, including the Grammy, Emmy, Tony, Outer Critics Circle, Drama Desk, Oscar, and even a Pulitzer Prize. The cabaret stage in New York City was the first experience and exposure for all these artists, and now they are on the world stage.

Cabaret is known as a lyric-driven performance, where the singer's vocal ability should never "oversing" the lyric. In the pedagogical world of "beautiful tone and breath support," what would you ask voice teachers to spend more *time on in studio with their singers?*

Many students work with singing teachers to develop their voice because they want their technique to be as solid as possible. For some vocal teachers, this is their specialty and that's why you go to them. But obviously, that's only half of it. There is so much more that goes into creating a great artist. Once you have control of your instrument, it's wondrously easier to do everything you want with your voice, from belting to singing softly or with rubato. A voice teacher who has given the student the ability to use their instrument in the best way possible should not think that the student's work is done. If it is not the teacher's specialty to go beyond vocal technique, then they should make sure that the student devotes an equal amount of time with a coach or an acting teacher so that they can become a better storyteller and fulfill what each song requires. A song has two halves—the melody and the lyric—and they are equal. You can't have one without the other, and sometimes more than one teacher or coach may be necessary.

What does singing to *someone versus singing* at *someone mean to you?*

Singing *at* someone can often conjure up a fourth wall, such as playing a character or singing with some invisible obstruction to the audience.

Singing *to* someone is much more direct and speaks to that idea of being one's true self onstage. When you sing *to* someone, every idea, every thought, and every feeling is delivered through your mind, heart, and experience. This makes it very personal. It should feel like one person speaking to another.

What nonverbal skills are needed? What else do we need to bring to the stage?

Stage presence is an incalculable gift that comes into play even before the performer speaks. Classes in acting, movement, and dance can work wonders in establishing good stage presence, if one is lacking it. Any training that someone has is a positive thing, but what a specific performer might need to strengthen varies with each individual. For example, someone may have a beautiful voice, but he or she may be timid or awkward. In that case, they need to develop their body skills. One teacher may not be able to help with all those things.

As a booking agent, what makes you sit up and say, "This person has something special." Is this even something that can be taught?

Sometimes I am watching the Tony or Academy or Grammy Awards when I suddenly see someone that I know win. When that happens, my mind instantly enters the "wayback machine." I remember booking them for the first time decades ago and watching their show with maybe ten other people in the room. With some performers, there is an instantaneous verdict that states that this is someone special. However, not being psychic, I stop short of speculating whether they will go on to greatness. But when you see it, you know it—just like love! If the stars align for the person and they continue this path, and if they do not self-sabotage (as many do), they will indeed wind up on the world stage. It must be added, though, that for every person I have booked that has gone on to world-stage fame and fortune, I can point to dozens of others who for whatever reasons—luck, timing, whatever—did not get there. Among all the reasons for not "making it," it has nothing to do with lack of talent. That is never the reason.

Nobody ever sat me down as a child in front of a television and said I should watch Judy Garland, but there she was one night on a television special, and there I sat there mesmerized, feeling that she was looking directly at me. While I could not verbally articulate the feeling at the time, that moment has stayed with me forever. I had the life-changing opportunity to meet her and see her perform live on several occasions. Her presence and her effect on everyone was radioactive. Talk about connection! She was not just singing songs . . . she was living them! It was positively electrifying. As powerful and as emotional as she was on television or in a film or on a recording, it still never fully captured the in-person presence of seeing her live with no degree of separation.

The "Sidney talk" that you do with newcomers is legendary. Why do you do this? How did that start, and is it a "pep talk," a "welcome to the community," or a "chat about the business"?

This is how it began: When I started out as a young aspirant—and in those years prior to audio and video and cassette tapes and computers—you would always audition live at a club's open call. They had a pianist there or you brought one. If you passed the audition, you might have the chance to do your own show on a Sunday or Monday, and the rest of the week was reserved for acknowledged stars like Barbara Cook or Julie Wilson. So after you sang, you would hold your breath waiting for them to say something like "OK, two Tuesdays in May." They would usually have me sign a one-paragraph little letter of agreement and that was that. They did not tell you anything about how or what to do. This predated MAC, which now has seminars, retreats, and symposiums that offer all this information. A book like you're writing now did not exist. There wasn't anything.

When I fell into cabaret management—by chance after being a singing waiter—I thought I would like to provide performers something I did not receive: a one-on-one official welcome, an explanation of how the club did things, basic policies and protocols, and an opportunity to answer the myriad questions that performers starting out inevitably have. Everything I knew about cabaret I learned the hard way, and I wanted to offer a different experience to these newcomers. Some of the facts and figures were indeed in the contract, but not everyone reads those thoroughly. And even if they do, the legalese might not be understood. I think of my talks as a public service. Believe me, when I was starting out a hundred years ago, I wish someone could have sat me down and told me anything about how to proceed.

Over the years, some colleagues have cajoled me, saying things like, "I can't believe you sit down with everyone for an hour and a half!" What wound up happening was that, for many performers, it wasn't just a speech that I gave for one or two nights; with some people, it was a conversation that continued for twenty or thirty years! It never dawned on me then—and at the time I was not thinking of the long term—but it established a relationship and allowed the performer to feel that they would have a person involved with the club who was available to answer any question at any time. People suggested I should do a group talk with several acts, but I said, "No, I don't want anyone to feel inhibited . . . I want them to be able to ask anything." I wanted to do things one-on-one, just like a great cabaret singer. It is the essence of cabaret to make everyone feel like you're singing to them and only them, and I wanted people to feel that I was there just for them. Sometimes I'll see someone from years ago on the street, and they've now "made it" on Broadway or television. They're always so welcoming and they'll say, "Sidney, I remember when you sat down with me." I don't believe the myth that many people forget where they started. I have found that people very vividly remember who was nice to them before it was fashionable.

When cabaret performers work at Don't Tell Mama, they get a lot more than just the "Sidney talk." They get you! You are there at the club for each performer, at the preshow, and very often are standing with them right before they go on. People in the business call you the "Mayor of Cabaret," and you truly are one of the most venerated and celebrated people in cabaret today.

Thank you. That is lovely to hear. It reminds me of a story. Early on in the career of a major singer working today, I arrived at the club immediately before her show and she was crying. I asked what happened. She said that she had just come from the prestigious MetroStar contest, where she had been a contestant, and that she had been eliminated. She was so discouraged and disheartened, and she did not know how she was going to be able to go onstage and sing for an hour. As I spoke to her, I reassured her that she did a great thing by taking a risk and putting herself out there, and that should be the takeaway. In other words, every time we are at bat, we learn something and that falls under the heading of "experience." Well, she went on to do a fabulous show, and PS, the following year she reentered the same contest and won!

. . . and it launched her career . . .

Correct. Whenever we run into one another, she always brings up that night and what a turning point it was for her. It is a business filled with disappointments and rejections. To persevere is our assignment!

What are you most proud of in your career as a singer and performer?

On any stage at any time—be it a small New York club, Town Hall, Lincoln Center, or any concert hall around the county—when an audience member whom I have never met tells me that one minute they were roaring with laughter and the next minute they were wiping away tears, I feel that I have succeeded. This is my goal. It is like I am awake in a dream and it never gets old.

What are you most proud of in your career as a booking manager?

Being an open door in a world that is otherwise filled with "No!"

How do you think cabaret has changed over the course of your career?

Change in life is constant, and cabaret is a part of life, so too is it always changing. One of the most unfortunate changes is that the major newspapers and magazines—which are not even the primary source of news these days—have virtually abandoned all forms of cabaret coverage. Back in the day, the *New York Times*, the *Daily News*, the *New York Post*, *Newsday*, and Bob Harrington's column in the *Backstage* "Bistro Bits" all had reviewers, calendars of cabaret events, picks-of-the week, and full features. While we are now lucky to have websites—such as NiteLife Exchange, Cabaret Scenes, BistroAwards.com, and Cabaret

Hotspot!—which do terrific articles and reviews, the big difference is that these resources are for the initiated: people who already know about cabaret. When cabaret was featured in the daily newspapers as prominently as theater, film, and dance, it reached everyone and thus exposed the uninitiated to the genre. Back then, a lot of people discovered cabaret by seeing a picture or reading a headline, which was a wonderful thing. All of that is gone now.

What is the future of cabaret?

It is said that history repeats itself, and in cabaret that is indeed the case. Whenever a great room closes, a new one suddenly emerges. Cabaret may be a niche art form, but happily there are always people who wish to have the intimate, live experience that this genre offers. Years ago, the Great American Songbook was regularly presented on television programs on the handful of channels that there were back then. No matter where you lived in this country, there were radio stations that came to you with that music. Of course, this has all vanished. Yet even so, every night in a piano bar somewhere, a young person comes through the door eagerly waiting to share their story through this art form. Who knows how they discovered cabaret, but they keep on coming. Thankfully, for them and for us, the music never ends.

SINGING IN CABARET

6

THE GREAT AMERICAN SONGBOOK

An Interview with Michael Feinstein

In addition to his career as a leading musical entertainer, Michael Feinstein's work as an educator, archivist, and interpreter of popular song has established him as the "Ambassador of the Great American Songbook." In 2007, Feinstein founded the Great American Songbook Foundation, which works to preserve and elevate America's rich musical legacy by curating the physical artifacts of its creators and performers; offering programs for the public and research opportunities for scholars, historians, and performers; and providing educational opportunities for student musicians, including the annual Songbook Academy for high school students. Feinstein also serves on the Library of Congress's National Recording Preservation Board, an organization dedicated to ensuring the survival, conservation, and increased public availability of America's sound recording heritage. He earned his fifth Grammy Award nomination in 2009 for *The Sinatra Project*, his album celebrating the music of "Ol' Blue Eyes." *The Sinatra Project, Volume II: The Good Life* was released in 2011. He has released several additional albums, including *The Power of Two* (collaborating with television/Broadway performer Cheyenne Jackson), *Cheek to Cheek* (recorded with Broadway legend Barbara Cook), and *We Dreamed These Days*, for which he cowrote the title song with Maya Angelou. Feinstein's

Emmy Award–nominated television
special *Michael Feinstein: The Sinatra
Legacy* was recorded live at the Palladium in Carmel, Indiana, and aired
across the country. In addition, his
PBS series *Michael Feinstein's American Songbook* was broadcast for three
seasons and is available on DVD; this
critically acclaimed series received the
2010 ASCAP Deems-Taylor Television Broadcast Award. His most recent primetime PBS special was *New
Year's Eve at the Rainbow Room*,
which aired in 2014. ♪

Figure 6.1. Michael Feinstein.
Photo by Kevin Alvey.

Although in recent years newer
popular songs have emerged on the
cabaret scene, the Great American
Songbook is, by all accounts, a staple of cabaret performance repertoire.
This catalogue of songs by some of history's most beloved composers
and lyricists has been performed by legendary singers of all generations,
from Ella Fitzgerald to Lady Gaga, and from Frank Sinatra to Rod
Stewart. This music, with its captivating lyrics and meticulously crafted
melodies, crosses generational preconceptions and hits at the core of the
human condition.

Recently, while riding in a shared-car service, my smartphone automatically synced with the car, and my playlist of great American songs
began to play. The young driver was gracious enough to let the music
keep playing, and to my surprise, by the end of the ride asked me, "What
music is that? It's really nice . . . comforting." This is the power of the
Great American Songbook. But what exactly is the GAS? How do we
define it and preserve it for future generations? For those answers we
turn to the preeminent ambassador of the Great American Songbook,
Michael Feinstein.

*Michael, thank you so much for sharing your time and expertise with us.
Your love of and care for the Great American Songbook has been widely
documented. You have championed the Great American Songbook and*

have brought it to a contemporary audience, possibly more so than any other modern artist. And you've developed a comprehensive and systematic curriculum for teaching the Great American Songbook, doing so through your educational foundation and the American Songbook Academy. So, I'd like to get right to it and talk about all of this, hearing directly "from the source." First, how would you define the Great American Songbook?

The Great American Songbook, for me, is ever evolving. It does not have a "cutoff" date. The largest body of work, and the most significant, dates from the 1910s through the 1950s, and there is so much enduring work from that period that continues on to the present day. The general definition of the Great American Songbook is "music that transcends the time in which it was written, that still touches hearts and minds of people, and has pertinence, continuing to resonate with listeners from generation to generation." If a song is widely known by many people and is part of a cultural shared experience, then it becomes part of the Great American Songbook. So, the songs from the 1960s and 1970s, the songs of Billy Joel, Carole King, Paul Simon, Jimmy Webb, Paul Williams . . . I mean you can go down the list of all the great writers of that period: Harry Nilsson, James Taylor. . . . They all wrote material that is as essential to the Great American Songbook. I also believe that there are songs being composed today that will become part of the Great American Songbook. If they are known and heard widely over the next thirty years, then perhaps they will become a part of it. I suppose the greatest chance of songs to join that category are ones that are written for films or Broadway, such as "Let It Go" from Disney's *Frozen* (2013). That's a song that will probably endure, even though it makes me want to blow my brains out when I hear it. [*laughs*]

Do you make any distinction between a "Classic American Songbook" (1920–1950) and a "New American Songbook" (1950–1970)?

I have never made a distinction between a "classic" and a "new" American Songbook. In addition, I think that assigning a date range is dangerous because Jerome Kern had his first published song in 1902 or 1904, and his first enduring "hit" was in 1914. So, some of his repertoire predates the songbook. Richard Rodgers started writing songs in the mid-1920s but wrote up until 1979, the year of his passing. Therefore, I find it difficult to subcategorize the Great American Songbook by hard dates, especially with the 1950s and the 1960s because there are still so many writers of classics that were working in that period.

In general, what makes a song "Songbook" worthy? What are the defining characteristics of a "Great American Song"?

First of all, it's the craft. A song is a combination of music and lyrics, and they have to be seamlessly combined. If one element is stronger or weaker than the other, then it is not a good song. The words and music have to sound as if they were, or are, inevitable for each other. And that's the magic of these songs! They seem so inevitable. They are songs that were, in most cases, very carefully crafted. But they also have a naturalness and ease . . . at least the best ones do. If a lyric is out of proportion to the melody, then it won't necessarily become an enduring song. However, there are exceptions to that. For example, the song "My Way" has a terrible lyric. But Frank Sinatra—through the force of his personality—turned it into a standard, even though he came to loath the lyric, and that is *not* too strong of a word to use. He regretted having sung it, in the sense that he hated having to repeat it all the time, because he knew it wasn't a well-crafted song. He did *not* regret the success of the thing, mind you. But the song itself he did not admire. And it is not an admirable lyric. It's a very clumsy song. "I ate it up and spit it out"—it's just unfortunately clumsy lyric writing. So, as in the case of "My Way," there can be other elements or circumstances that may catapult a song into the enduring songbook category.

The malleability of a song is also important, when you can take a song like "Body and Soul" and sing it as a torch song, or do it as a piano instrumental as Art Tatum did, or turn it into a big jazz number, or bee bop, and so forth. When a song can be done in so many different ways it is more likely to be performed and recorded hundreds of times. "Over the Rainbow" is probably the best example of a malleable song because it has been done in every conceivable (and inconceivable) way. The songwriter Hugh Martin who wrote "Have Yourself a Merry Little Christmas" said that he was delighted to discover that a group called

"Twisted Sister" had recorded that song. Mel Tormé wrote a great classic called "The Christmas Song," which most people know as "Chestnuts Roasting on an Open Fire." He tells the story that one day he received a recording of "The Christmas Song Cha Cha Cha" played by Hugo Winterhalter, and he said that he loved it because he knew that it was those kinds of interpretations that would add to the longevity of the song.

As a follow-up question, is it possible to identify more modern songs that might qualify for a "Contemporary American Songbook (1970+)"? And if so, what would be the criteria for their acceptance into Songbook status? What elements would make them "Songbook" worthy?

Again, it's the enduring nature of a song and the brilliance of a lyric, its pertinence, and the way a lyric touches the heart and soul of someone. It must be an eloquent expression of the human condition, an eloquent expression of love. That's the thing that made the classic songs so great, and even the songs of the 1960s and 1970s. They found different ways to express often-expressed emotions. It is this kind of cleverness that piques the imagination and "pricks the ear." So to reiterate, it is the *craft* of these songs that helped them to endure, even though most people wouldn't think of it in that way.

Please tell us about your education program, the Great American Songbook Foundation. How did you come to develop the curriculum for this?

The foundation was originally created for the purpose of preserving all of the artifacts that I had collected through the years, including important manuscripts, sheet music, orchestrations, recordings, and other ephemera relating to the Great American Song. I wanted to find a proper place to create a museum—a repository for this material—because I had so much of it helter-skelter, lying around in various and disparate places. I've gotten a lot of things from families of songwriters and heirs and such that are significant in telling the story of the Great American Songbook.

My next priority was finding a way to preserve the Great American Songbook for succeeding generations, and so we created the Songbook Academy. That endeavor is quite fulfilling for me and all the judges that participate in this program, which is a weeklong intensive that happens every summer at the Great American Songbook Foundation headquarters in Carmel, Indiana. The curriculum was developed by Chris Lewis, who is a tremendous educator, and also by many of the other music teachers, professors, and performers whom we engaged for the purpose of creating a well-rounded program that would appeal to high school students.

I remember years ago Liza Minnelli did a recording with the Pet Shop Boys, and one of the tracks was "Losing My Mind," a complete deconstruction of the Sondheim song. The song became a hit in England—a hit single! Liza sang it on the *Top of the Pops* television program, and suddenly at her concerts a lot of young people were coming to hear her do this song, not knowing Liza in any other context. And I asked her, "What are you going to do when these young people come to your shows and expect to hear more pop material?" She looked at me and said, "Honey, all I have to do is get them in the seats."

And the music will do the rest?

And that's how I feel about this body of work, and what we do at the foundation, particularly with the Songbook Academy.

The Songbook Academy . . . tell us a little more about that.

When young people are exposed to this music it resonates with them. It is another choice, in addition to whatever pop or contemporary music they listen to. And it is also a unique expression. The Great American Songbook is as unique as Shakespeare or Beethoven or Michelangelo. These are all examples of timeless art, and that is what I consider this body of work to be. Just like the Italian Renaissance that led to an extraordinary period of artistic expression, it is the same way with American popular music of the twentieth century. The breadth of the work that comes from that time period during which the Great American Songbook was written is unique and is formed as a result of the cultural experience of the time, but the result is art that is timeless.

One of the most fulfilling things about the academy is my continued connection with its participants. They are all like extended family to me. We track and follow their careers and do what we can to help them. I perform with some of the alumni of the academy wherever I can. Our graduates have performed at Carnegie Hall, at the Kennedy Center, and on television shows. Maddie Baillio starred in *Hairspray Live*. And I could go on and on. It is like planting seeds who will go out in the world and propagate this body of work that will be forever timeless. I don't know that the Great American Songbook will ever be mainstream, but it will always hold an important and enduring place in American popular music.

Great American Songbook performances have always flourished in the cabaret setting. They are in fact a staple of this vocal performance genre. In your many years of working in this field, how would you define the art of cabaret? Is it something that is separate and distinct from other vocal performance styles like music theater or jazz?

The word "cabaret" can sometimes have a negative connotation to it in that people may evoke an image of a certain kind of music, and that is unfair and absurd. One of the things that makes me laugh about Simon Cowell is that when he criticizes a performance on *American Idol* he says, "Oh, that's too cabaret," as if that were the ultimate insult. A cabaret is a physical space in which any type of art can be featured, and certainly, in all of the years I have been involved with it, I have seen practically everything you can imagine and heard every imaginable type of music. I have seen comedy performances, and I have seen performance art. I have seen lots of gender-bending performers create lots of new and exciting experiences in that space. The cabaret venue is simply a setting that is smaller in size, and because of that it creates a different and unique connection to the audience. That is the most distinctive aspect of a cabaret. It is very different from music theater, and it is very different from a jazz club. It is different for a number of fundamental reasons.

Another major aspect of cabaret is that usually when a performer is in a cabaret he or she is not assuming the role of a character, and because of this, they must sing "as themselves" to the audience. There is no artifice of a persona. Angela Lansbury, whom I accompanied once for a benefit show, told me that she was most comfortable singing as a character, and she was not at all comfortable singing without the cloak or protection of a character. She said she would get very nervous and did not feel secure. Yet, all those things vanished when she was in character. There are many performers whom I have asked over the years to perform at Feinstein's at the Regency, Feinstein's/54 Below, and

Feinstein's at the Nikko who have said no because they are afraid of being so close to the audience. They don't want to be able to look into the eyes of the people who are seated in such proximity, and simply, they don't know how to do it. That to me is quite surprising.

I've spent my entire life performing in cabarets. I started playing in piano bars when I was in my teens. The funny thing is that now 90 percent of the time I perform in concert halls and have done so for the last twenty-five years. In spite of that, people still think of me as a cabaret performer, which I find fascinating. The only clubs I generally play are my own, but people still think of me as a club performer. I have played at the Hollywood Bowl, the White House, Carnegie Hall, and the Royal Albert Hall. I usually play in large venues, but for whatever reason, my persona is that of a cabaret/nightclub performer.

By the way, in jazz clubs there is a very different experience. People are not necessarily dialed into what is happening with the music. In some clubs being quiet is required, but in other jazz or nightclubs there can be a lot of commotion going on. In the places that I run audiences are quiet, but that is not always the case in a nightclub.

Given the personal nature of connection to the lyric in cabaret, do you think there is a "cabaret performance technique"? And if so, can you elaborate?

Any singer that's great has to have a personal connection to the lyric, so I don't think that is unique to cabaret. You can just be more easily caught in a cabaret if you are not connected to the lyric because of the closeness of the audience. For me, cabaret performance technique is simply a song performance technique in that it does not change when I am onstage in a large situation. And that is, one must *live* the song. You must know the character. You must have some sort of context in mind. You must have a sense of *something* beyond what is on the paper, so that people can see a light in your eyes. However, in a cabaret setting, a small gesture becomes a much larger one, and perhaps in that sense one can do more subtle things. I suppose it's like comparing acting onstage to acting on film. Gestures would inevitably have to change because of the medium. But having said that, the body language and the facial expressions and such generally are the same. It all comes from the lyrics. Everything must come from the lyric. The lyric completely informs the way that I sing a song musically and how I phrase it. Everything comes from the words . . . even key changes. One always has to make sure that they know the meaning of every word of every line that they're singing. Often when I coach people, I'll ask them the meaning of a certain line, or what the song means, and they don't *really* know. That to me is the fatal flaw—the most dangerous flaw—if you're going to be a performer.

We talked earlier about what makes cabaret distinct as a genre, but how does cabaret performance technique *differ from music theater and jazz?*

In music theater you don't look into the eyes of the people. You look at an indeterminate point or you look at another character onstage. With cabaret, you have to play to the people. Even if you don't look them directly in the eye, you at least have to gesture to them. You have to acknowledge them. When I perform in a small setting, I guarantee that every single person feels like I was looking at them at one point or another. I sing and play directly to them. It's about a certain energy—the way we fill up the room with our intention. The other big part of cabaret technique involves where we focus our attention when we are singing. There are many different ways to sing a song. Sometimes one sings a song in a personal reverie—where you are not looking at the audience—but there is still a way to *include* the audience when you are doing that with the appropriate body language and intention.

Remembering back to the time when you were first coming to this repertoire, what attracted you to these songs?

These songs attracted me from my earliest memories. I don't know why that is. I was born in 1956. When I was quite young, I heard the songs on the radio (the pop songs), and they did not appeal to me in the same way that the classic songs appealed to me, the songs that had been written twenty or thirty years earlier. Why that is I cannot tell you, except that when I sat down and started playing the piano at the age of five, I started picking out *those* tunes on the piano, not the popular ones of the day. Musically and harmonically, they always had a tremendous power over me—I felt connection with them. The pop music that was more simplistic did not appeal to me, and even though I could not verbalize why, I knew the difference.

How might we as educators inspire the younger generation to embrace this music again?

I think the first thing is exposure. We have a situation now in which so many young people who listen to pop music don't pay attention to the lyrics because today's pop music is about rhythm. It is not about a character or connection with the words; words are merely sung *with* the music. It's a real problem, but it's a fundamental problem with the world, because nobody has an attention span anymore. Everything around us conspires against it. However, that is the purpose of art. The purpose of art is to bring us back to our hearts and to give us the connection that we need to help make people's lives better. When I have the opportunity to work with young people, I verbalize all of that and talk about how music is one of the great healing gifts of the world and how it is essential for our survival at this time. And I really mean that; I'm not trying to be melodramatic. Music is one of the things that can save us as a society at this time for so many reasons that we don't need to go into right now. So, I think the best way to attract young people to this music is to perform it honestly and to highlight and bring out the elements of these songs that can still resonate with people today.

This book is called So You Want to Sing Cabaret, *and it is sponsored by the National Association of Teachers of Singing. However, cabaret is known as a lyric-driven performance experience, where the singer's vocal ability should never "oversing" the lyric. So, in the pedagogical world of "beautiful tone and breath support," what would you ask voice teachers to spend* more *time on in studio with their singers?*

When I coach young people, I think one of the biggest issues is their body language. They may have fantastic voices, but they can be stiff. They don't know how to use their bodies, which is just as essential an instrument as the voice is. Learning the connection between body and vocal expression is very important. So often young folks, classical kids that I work with, will have robotic hand movements at one point or another, as opposed to looking and being natural. So, body language is something I always have to work with. Another big thing is working with the phrasing of songs. If you look at a lyric, it tells you where to breathe. Quite often people will breathe in the middle of a phrase or sentence, which is like saying, "Hello, how are [breathes] you today?" It isn't at all natural to breathe there. It's all about finding places to breathe that are natural. I also think that learning to relax is one of the essential elements of singing. If we can learn to relax, many other problems go away.

If a young singer came to you asking for advice, what are the three things you would tell them?

One, find a place to perform. I was lucky enough to work in piano bars for years and years, and I would play five hours a night, often without taking a break. Two, find a place to hone your craft. That may mean going to a retirement home or finding a restaurant where they will let you set up in the corner. Even in the subway works. It has to be someplace where you can perform in front of people, and sometimes finding that place requires creative thinking. But believe me, with retirement homes alone, there are millions of people out there who still crave musical performance. Set up a program of going to schools to sing for those students. As I said, it takes creativity, but finding a place to sing is essential. When we are in front of people, we learn. We learn about nerves. We learn about extraneous distractions that can happen. We can see the faces of people and how they react. We learn how to put a set list together—what song should follow another and what to say in between—which is just as important as all the other elements. We learn who we are onstage and who are we as artists.

The third thing is this: learn to play the piano or another accompanying instrument. That can be incredibly valuable. Oh, and a fourth thing: learn about the history of the songs you are singing, and research the time in which they were written (and where). Always try to find the primary elements of a song, such as the original sheet music that isn't adulterated or a vintage recording. You then get a sense of what the song originally sounded like. Unless you know how the original sounded you can't do intelligent or reasoned variations. You can't make it your own without having a fundamental starting point.

As a master class teacher yourself, what do find is lacking in young students and singers today when approaching Great American Songbook repertoire?

The thing that is most lacking is the ability to perform and inhabit a song. Many young people can sing the songs well, but they are awkward—very, very awkward—physically when they perform the songs. In other words, they're great singers, but they're not well-rounded performers. Sometimes I hear or see students who are steeped in music theater, but that is a separate kind of training and technique as we have discussed. There are, obviously, elements that cross over. However, performing as yourself as a solo artist onstage requires a very different persona. Being comfortable with that persona is important.

What is the most important thing a singer must consider or do when learning a Great American Song?

As I've said before, it's about the words. But it's also about learning the melody properly . . . learning the *song* properly. I stress that because so often people don't really *know* the song. They don't know the original song. They'll learn a song from a Frank Sinatra record or an Ella Fitzgerald record or a Barbra Streisand record, and those are all *interpretations* of the song. Often they will copy that artist's vocal phrasing—they'll copy Ella Fitzgerald's scatting, or they'll sing the wrong lyrics that Frank Sinatra sang—and that's death, because then you're just doing a carbon copy. And you can never be as good as the original.

Is there anything that you would like to tell our readers that I have not asked you?

I think that music is a gift. I think it is a privilege. And it is also something that, as I said before, is essential to humanity. I believe that music can change the world. I believe that having music in our lives is so important because it heals us, it gives us a different perspective, and it also builds bridges. It allows us to connect to people with whom we might not otherwise have a connection, such as someone with different political beliefs. We have such polarization now, but it is art that sees and expresses the commonality of all souls, therefore giving us the opportunity to find resolution.

7

THE SINGER-SONGWRITER IN CABARET

An Interview with Ann Hampton Callaway

Ann Hampton Callaway is one of America's most gifted and prolific artists. A leading champion of the Great American Songbook, she has made her mark as a singer, pianist, composer, lyricist, arranger, actress, educator, television host, and producer. Voted by BroadwayWorld.com as Performer of the Year and two years in a row as Best Jazz Vocalist, her unique singing style blends jazz and traditional pop, making her a mainstay in concert halls, theaters, and jazz clubs, as well as on television and in film. She is best known for her Tony Award–nominated performance in the hit Broadway musical *Swing!* and for writing and singing the theme song of the hit television series *The Nanny*. Callaway is also a prolific songwriter whose songs have been featured on seven of Barbra Streisand's albums. The only composer to have collaborated with Cole Porter, she has also written songs with Carole King, Rolf Løvland, Amanda McBroom, and Shelby Lynn. Callaway has shared the stage with great artists across many genres, including George Shearing, Dizzy Gillespie, Stevie Wonder, Dr. John, Liza Minnelli, Betty Buckley, Dianne Reeves, Dee Dee Bridgewater, Audra McDonald, Harvey Fierstein, Ramsey Lewis, Kurt Elling, and Michael Feinstein. Callaway has been a special guest performer with Wynton Marsalis and the Lincoln Center Jazz Orchestra and with Keith Lockhart and the Boston

Figure 7.1. Ann Hampton Callaway.
Photo by Bill Westmoreland.

Pops at Symphony Hall and at Tanglewood. She performed for President Bill Clinton in Washington, D.C., and at Russian president Mikhail Gorbachev's Youth Peace Summit in Moscow. Callaway performed alongside her sister, Broadway star Liz Callaway, in their award-winning show *Sibling Revelry* at London's Donmar Warehouse. Their show *Boom!*, a critically acclaimed celebration of the baby boomer hits of the 1960s and 1970s, was recorded by PS Classics, which debuted in the top twenty-five on the *Billboard* magazine jazz chart. Callaway's performances and recordings have garnered her the Theater World Award, fifteen MAC Awards, several Bistro Awards, the Mabel Mercer Award, the Johnny Mercer Award, and the Norman Vincent Peale Award for Positive Thinking. Stephen Holden of the *New York Times* wrote, "For sheer vocal beauty, no contemporary singer matches Ms. Callaway." Ann's father was Chicago's legendary television and radio journalist, John Callaway. Her mother, Shirley Callaway, was a singer, pianist, and a highly regarded voice teacher, who was also a member of the National Association of Teachers of Singing. We are pleased that this wonderful performer and singer-songwriter agreed to be interviewed and share her knowledge with us. ♪

When and how did you specifically decide to become a cabaret/nightclub singer, or did that unfold in a different way?

I think music chose me from the day I was born. From the time we were babies our mom would sing to us from the piano. As a child, I loved listening to all kinds of music that our parents would play on our turntable—by the age of three I was scat singing to Ella Fitzgerald records. Watching movie musicals also infused our childhood with magic. I remember being four years old and singing along with Judy Garland in

The Wizard of Oz. At six I was enraptured by Barbra Streisand's recording of "People," and at ten I was given a guitar and a rhyming dictionary
for Christmas because I wanted to be the fifth Beatle. At twelve, I had a
music teacher, Miss Morris, who thought I could become a great opera
singer. At thirteen, I started getting serious about writing songs, and I
wanted to be the next Joni Mitchell or Carole King. At sixteen, I fell
totally in love with theater when I played the title role in *Mame* at New
Trier East High School in Winnetka, Illinois. I knew that I needed to do
everything I possibly could to develop my talent.

I enrolled as an acting major at the University of Illinois but quit the
program after "serving two years," choosing instead to move to New
York and create my own education. Three days later, I landed a job singing and playing piano six hours a night at a little joint on Thirtieth and
Third called Sharma's. I quickly expanded my repertoire from twenty
songs to a few hundred. It was an ideal place to learn "on the job," and
I loved the experience of entertaining people from all walks of life who
came through those doors. I remember people saying to me, "What are
you doing in a place like this—you should be on Broadway," and thinking, *Well, if I work hard, maybe in a few years I will be*. However, when
I put myself out there, casting directors thought I was "too tall" (i.e.,
not an ingenue) and told me to come back in ten years "when I am the
age I look like." Then ten years later they said, "You don't have enough
credits."

What I learned during that time is that I loved creating my own shows
and making my own arrangements, blending jazz and traditional pop,
and using my acting training to tell stories through the great songs I was
singing. Working in clubs, I eventually became the singer who "stilled
the room," as the *New York Times* once said. It was such a thrill to finally
perform in "listening rooms" like the Algonquin and Ballroom where
people came just to hear me. The first time I did a one-woman show at
the Guthrie Theater in Minneapolis, I nearly cried because there were
no drinks and there was no noise—just magnificent silence and attentive
people. At that moment I realized that "I am enough." What I found
so compelling about cabaret-style performing is that I could use all my
passions and talents to create something fresh and immediate each and
every night. I loved the intimacy. I loved how music was creating a family of friends for me. I loved going to hear my fellow artists, who were

also creating their own musical experience. Today, no matter how big the venue—whether it is a stadium, theater, or symphony hall—I always try to give my audiences the most intimate, personal, honest, and heart-felt musical experience that I can give.

You are also a prolific songwriter. Did your songwriting career emerge in tandem to your singing career or did it develop later?

Writing songs is an essential part of how I express my heart and soul. I have been writing songs since I was a child and wrote some good songs when I was still in my teens. I wrote my first platinum-selling song, "At the Same Time," in 1987, but it took ten years (to the date) for Barbra Streisand to introduce it to the world on her album *Higher Ground*. I sang original songs in my shows but never quite knew what I needed to do with them to get them "out there." However, I got a big break when Fran Drescher came to my show at Don't Tell Mama, in which I was singing all my own songs. After the show she approached me, and in that inimitable voice said, "You're talented. I want you to write songs for my projects." And so, I did. Then, a few years later, *The Nanny* came along, and my theme was chosen over other top Hollywood songwriters. I never dreamed that the show would become an international syndicated hit for such a long time—my accountant still calls it "my finest work to date." I continue to write all kinds of songs for all kinds of situations. My dream is to record an album of all original songs, and I hope to make that a reality soon.

Please tell us about your early days of study. Your mother was the es-teemed voice teacher and NATS member Shirley Callaway. Did you study formally with her or with another voice teacher? And if so, with whom and for how long?

Growing up with our mom, Shirley, my sister Liz and I learned a great deal from hearing her sing, hearing her talk about singing, and hear-ing her teach. She didn't want to be our official voice teacher at first because she thought it might create competition or tension. When I was fifteen years old I began studying with a great voice teacher named Dora Lindgren. She had been an acclaimed soprano in Sweden, and she was excited about my talent. I learned most of my technique from her, and she inspired me to consider a career in classical music because she thought my voice had the potential to sing opera. At University of Illinois, I met New York City Opera star Nick DiVirgilio and adored him. He was loving and patient and taught me a lot about craft and artistry. (He also liked my original songs and thought I should write for his friend, who happened to be Judy Collins!) Much of what I learned about singing was listening to great singers from all walks of life. Years later, my mom would coach me if I had an issue and would get me where I needed to be. By that time, it was all about the music and being the best that I could possibly be.

What vocal techniques or warm-ups, if any, have you found most useful throughout your performance career?

I sing almost every day, just like a bird. I think singing is part of living, not just my profession. So naturally, singing helps me keep my voice in good shape. I follow Leontyne Price's advice that she shared with my dad, John, who did a television interview with her: "Always sing on your interest, never on your principal." I have various vocal warm-ups I learned over the years, but if I am pressed for time, I do vocal octave leaps on a lip trill. You can never push your voice that way. If I get phlegm on my cords, I do staccato exercises, which I find to be the gentlest way to clear everything. Diction exercises are helpful too. For example, take consonants and do them as quarter notes, then eighth notes, then triplets, and finally sixteenth notes. Deep breathing is important as well, and panting exercises can increase diaphragm awareness. I also believe that studying your lyrics separately and doing acting exercises with them improves your vocal production. The more you are emotionally connected with each part of a song, the better, and more naturally your voice will cooperate. If you want it to be art, it must come from the heart.

Are you usually able to warm up your voice before a performance? And/ or do you program your shows so that the first few songs serve as a vocal warm-up?

I can often do some light warming up at the club, but I try to do some warm-ups in the shower or during the car ride to the venue. Singing lightly to piano tracks or rehearsal tracks before a show not only warms up my voice but also solidifies my muscle memory when I am memorizing songs. I don't program a show to warm up my voice. I like to bring a little thrill factor at the start to build momentum. But I am sensitive to where I am vocally that night or day, and if I am compromised in any way, I sing more simply and let the acting of the song lead the way.

How important is vocal technique to the cabaret performer? And what skills are essential to the cabaret performer that they might not be receiving while studying for a degree in classical or traditional vocal performance?

If a cabaret performer wants full access to the vocabulary of vocal expression—and wants to have a healthy voice ready for all possible performance demands—then mastering vocal technique is imperative. Some singers seem to have a good vocal technique naturally, but even these lucky people would benefit by acquiring more knowledge about the voice. Knowledge is power. I'm fascinated by how many cabaret performers do not work to improve their pitch. Having accurate pitch is a necessity if one wants to be a professional singer. Learning how to place your voice for various sounds is also a great tool. Learning how to manage your breath effectively is foundational as well, but many professional singers don't seem to do this. In addition, many people do not utilize dynamics or employ vibrato judiciously. Also paramount is the expressive power of diction—using vowels and consonants in creative ways.

But the most glaring thing I do not see enough training in, or at least enough awareness of, is the importance of acting and believing in the singing of songs. When I work with singers in master classes, so often they have not done any work on how to read a lyric and find all its meanings, layers, and emotional arcs. They often sing "emotionally," but not with the actual nuances of *true* emotion that the song is creating. Given a few key focus points, their transformation within a moment can be astounding. The process of finding out what you as an artist have to say, how you want to say it, where you want to say it, and with whom you would like to say it is key in cabaret.

I find that too many teachers have not learned how to tell the truth—with love. In other words, they have not learned how to create a safe environment for a singer to learn to be an expressive messenger. Teaching in this way requires great sensitivity. You must get to know each student's personality and learn what makes each individual thrive in order to teach them how to "get it." Teachers should joyfully impart knowledge *and* have a little patience for the time it can take to assimilate technique. No one wants to feel stupid. But it can take a while for technique to feel natural. Encouragement is needed for the many of us who get easily frustrated if we are not "brilliant" immediately. To be the best singer you can be you have to learn who you are and work to heal your inner wounds. So often the traumas of life can close a part of our hearts and affect how "open" we are, both emotionally and vocally. Great teachers can facilitate this healing by listening and empathizing. One last thought: To be the best singer you can be, you must learn how to let go of your ego and be utterly in the moment. Tools that can help you find this include meditation, mindfulness exercises, and improvisation.

Who were your biggest musical influences?

My favorite jazz singers are Ella Fitzgerald, Sarah Vaughan, Billie Holiday, Mel Tormé, Peggy Lee, Nat King Cole, Anita O'Day, Betty Carter, and the trio Lambert, Hendricks & Ross. Traditional pop singers that I love include Judy Garland, Barbra Streisand, Frank Sinatra, Tony Bennett, and Bette Midler. I adore many singer-songwriters; Joni Mitchell, Carole King, James Taylor, and Stevie Wonder are four of my favorites. I listen to soul and love both Ray Charles and Aretha Franklin. My favorite classical singers are Leontyne Price and Luciano Pavarotti.

Some readers may think that cabaret is little more than music theater in the crook of a piano and/or theatrical songs that are sung in a nightclub rather than a theater. Is this impression accurate and/or inaccurate?

For me, the main ingredient of cabaret is intimacy, which can be experienced in venues of any size, large or small. Cabaret is the art of storytelling through music while making an intimate and personal connection with the audience. Cabaret is often about entertaining as well, and it can be thematic and theatrical. It can also feature a variety of musical styles, but there is a strong sense of emotional bonding by the end of the show, regardless of how you get there.

In other interviews there was some discussion about the title, and that the word "cabaret" may have negative connotations. Some have even said it should be called So You Want to Sing Nightclub. *Do you think the word "cabaret" is problematic?*

Over the years I have tried to help market cabaret and its many attributes, but despite its evolution—which has seen many gifted performers enter the field—it somehow remains an ambiguous entity. If cabaret had its own category at the Grammy Awards, then maybe it would be taken more seriously as a genre, but the truth is that if you get branded as a cabaret singer, record labels often don't know what that means. Therefore, if you are striving to have a successful cabaret career and plan on doing many concerts and recording, it helps to clarify what style or styles of music you specialize in.

How would you describe cabaret?

Cabaret is a style of performing that often breaks the fourth wall and invites the experience of interpersonal connection and intimacy between the performer and the audience. Cabaret artists are able to create shows that are like mini-musicals, taking listeners on an emotional journey and sharing the many sides of who they are within their concept or theme, if they have one.

Do you consider yourself to be a cabaret singer, a nightclub singer, or something else entirely?

I am a musical bridge builder. I would call myself a pop/jazz singer-songwriter. I identify cabaret as an important part of my performance style, and I am proud to be in the cabaret community. However, I am also a recording artist, and my musical style takes the lead when I am asked to label myself. I love singing in nightclubs, but I wouldn't want to be branded as a nightclub singer only, because I also sing in concert halls with symphony orchestras. But it is true that I am a cabaret singer because the essence of cabaret—intimacy—is in all my performances.

Let's talk about the ever-expanding Great American Songbook? Can you give an example of a newer song that is now considered to be a part of the Great American Songbook? Or are there stylistic criteria that determine which songs might qualify? What makes a new song eligible to become a great American song?

My friends John Bucchino, Amanda McBroom, Michele Brourman, Susan Werner, and many others are writing songs that imbibe storytelling, theatrical integrity, wit, and seamless craft, all of which are hallmarks of the Great American Songbook. Sting, Paul Simon, and Sara Bareilles are several well-known contemporary songwriters who create songs that feel like moments in time that you can live inside. When I sing Carole King's "Will You Love Me Tomorrow?" or Stevie Nick's "Landslide," I feel like I am being given the same level of honest, in-the-moment music and lyrics as I am when I sing a classic song by Rodgers and Hart. For a song to be in that category, it has to be able to transport my listeners to the very depths of the human experience.

Who are some other iconic performers of cabaret that you admire?

In no particular order: Marilyn Maye, Édith Piaf, Eartha Kitt, Bobby Short, Peggy Lee, Hildegard, Steve Ross, Nancy LaMott, Karen Mason, Mary Cleere Haran, Mabel Mercer, Barbara Cook, Margaret Whiting, Julie Wilson, Amanda McBroom, Liz Callaway, Lucie Arnaz, Clint Holmes, Michael Feinstein, Betty Buckley, Christine Ebersole, Christine Andreas, Rosemary Clooney, Marlene Dietrich, Ute Lemper, Charles Busch, Barb Jungr, Karen Akers, Jason Graae, Faith Prince, Jeff Harnar, KT Sullivan, Andrea Marcovicci, Paula West, Billy Stritch, Eric Comstock, Barbara Fasano, Tovah Feldshuh, Jessica Molaskey, Klea Blackhurst, Catherine Russell, Stacy Sullivan, Lorna Luft, Karen Oberlin, Baby Jane Dexter, Brent Barrett, Carole J. Bufford, Celia Berk, Paolo Szot, Marissa Mulder, and many, many more.

I am sure I am missing some important ones, so I apologize if I forgot to mention them. In addition to these names, there are also many

Broadway artists who "step out of character" for occasional cabaret performances, and that list is long too.

Where do you hope to see cabaret singing in twenty years? In fifty years?

I have faith that cabaret will grow stronger though the years as its many interpreters grow in number and attract more and more lovers of the art form. I would love to see the genre expand in the same way as the Adelaide Cabaret Festival has evolved. That festival has become an international forum for the many faces of cabaret and the many styles of music that can be performed with riveting intimacy. It would be satisfying to see people become even more true to themselves and create even more daring cabaret experiences that honor their individuality and creativity. Finally, I would like to see more collaboration between people of different backgrounds. Wouldn't it be fun to listen to musical dialogues between classical and jazz singers or between rock and Broadway artists?

8

ON "LEGIT" SINGING

An Interview with Dawn Derow

Dawn Derow represents a younger generation of cabaret singer, one that exemplifies both a lyric-driven performance technique and vocal tone and facility born out of a bel canto tradition. A native of Cape Cod, Derow grew up in Eastham, Massachusetts. She attended the Boston Conservatory as a vocal performance major with an opera emphasis. After graduation, she moved to New York to pursue her love of music and has since performed in various clubs such as Birdland, Don't Tell Mama, the Laurie Beechman Theatre, the Metropolitan Room, the Cutting Room, and the Friar's Club. In June 2016, she was part of the Mabel Mercer Foundation Carnegie Hall performance of *It's De-Lovely: A 125th Birthday Celebration of Cole Porter*. Derow won a 2015 MAC award for her work in the duo show *Revolution* with Kathleen France. Her album *Music4Two*, with guitarist Sean Harkness, earned her a 2014 MAC nomination for album of the year. Her show *Legit: A Classical Cabaret* showcased her classical vocal technique, resulting in a Bistro Award as outstanding vocalist of 2016. Most recently, she has found considerable success through her long-running show *My Ship: Songs from 1941*. Known for her versatility, she is the type of songstress that can instantly switch from a jazz number to a Puccini aria, seamlessly moving from one style to the next. ♪

Figure 8.1. Dawn Derow. *Photo by Takako Harkness.*

Dawn, thank you so much for taking the time to speak with us. As a classically trained singer, you received a BFA in vocal performance (opera) from the Boston Conservatory. Tell us about that time in your life, your training, the teachers you had, and how those experiences influence what you do now.

At the Boston Conservatory, I originally studied voice with Irida Pilla, a ninety-five-year-old opera singer who was in her final year of teaching. I was strictly learning bel canto style then, singing Neapolitan songs and various art songs in French, German, and Italian. The summer after my freshman year, I was lucky to be accepted into SSMA Sessione Senese per la Musica e l'Arte, a music program that ran for four weeks in Siena, Italy. I was the soprano soloist.

When I returned, I transferred to Mary Saunders's studio. Mary was the head of the voice faculty at the time. Additionally, I auditioned for *Jesus Christ Superstar*—one of the student-directed, black box theater shows—and was cast as an apostle. I was the only (soon-to-be-opera-emphasis) voice major who was running over to the music theater department to take dance and acting classes, and the only classically trained singer auditioning for the musicals. I received some criticism for that. But I wanted classical training so that when I'm eighty years old I can still sing. That training hasn't let me down. My classical foundation is something that has stuck with me for sure.

I didn't feel that an education in music theater would serve me best. I had been dancing since the age of three and doing local community theater shows since the age of eight. I wanted to be a musician . . . a *singer*. That's why I made the decision to learn the classics first, knowing that all the other styles would soon follow. I still have a *lot* to learn, and I make it a point to always continue learning, growing, and evolving.

At the end of my sophomore year, I was accepted into the opera program. Cecelia Schieve and Trish Weinman, who ran the opera program, were huge influences on me, along with Michael Strauss. Cecelia was a tough professor—she really pushed me. And Trish was one of the first directors I met who really inspired me to become an actress and "make the music happen" through my acting. I didn't want to just "park and bark," as we called it. But it wasn't until later—post 9/11, when I decided to take a break from New York and go to acting school in London at the Method Studio—that I *really* understood what she meant.

I made the most of my time at the Boston Conservatory. I appeared in the opera program's productions as Baby Doe in *The Ballad of Baby Doe*, Lucy in *The Telephone*, and as Adele in *Die Fledermaus*. And with the music theater department I was in *Hair* and *Jesus Christ Superstar* and a few other smaller productions. I also played guitar and wrote songs on my own time. In the evenings, I sometimes sang with some of my friends from Berklee who had a band called Uncle Sammy. We would gig at House of Blues, Middle East, and other grunge bars in Boston. I would sing backup on songs by Bob Marley, Pink Floyd, Steely Dan, Doobie Brothers, and others, even though I was singing the jewel aria from *Faust* during the daytime hours.

You've studied with some well-known pedagogues, including Marilyn Horne and Mary Saunders, for classical and contemporary styles, respectively. Tell us a bit about working with different kinds of teachers and how that has informed your cabaret performance.

I worked with Mary Saunders for four years. I was honored to be in her studio. Mary always made sure that I didn't stray too far from what was asked of me as a lyric soprano in the opera department, but she also allowed me to work on American music theater repertoire. So once again, I got the best of both worlds.

When I moved to New York in 2000, I started auditioning for more music theater. When I was honest with myself, I just couldn't eat, breathe, and sleep opera (and nothing but opera). I had so many interests in different styles of music. I needed a teacher who could break me out of my "opera box" training. It was then that I found Neal Tracy. Neal was my first male voice teacher of real substance and my first teacher in Manhattan. His expansive vocal knowledge made it possible for me to stretch my instrument. I worked with Neal for four years, from about 2003 to 2007, and I learned how to belt!

I only sang for Marilyn Horne a few times. She has seen performances of my show, *My Ship: Songs from 1941*, and heard all my "Legit" material (songs and arias in *Legit: A Classical Cabaret*). Her biggest comment to me was to support more: "It's all about the breath," she'd say. Marilyn continues to be a mentor to me, and I'm delighted to call this opera legend a dear friend.

Can you identify any commonalities between your classical and contemporary vocal study, such as common themes or exercises?

All I can say is, you must warm up your whole voice—it's one instrument. If I'm doing a rock show, I will still warm up my head voice, usually up to a high C, and sometimes higher. I also work on connecting to my breath, so I always start with breath management exercises as well.

Do you feel that your training in classical voice helps you when you sing cabaret, and if so, how?

I don't think "helps me" is the right way of putting it exactly. The voice is like a color wheel, and opera is one of my colors. I still let those colors exist, and I still "exercise those muscles"—again, the trick is to be able to move quickly from one color to the next and do so as truthfully as you can. With the right motivation, material, and musical direction, you can usually accomplish that.

Tell us about your warm-up before a show, what types of exercises you do, when, where, and for how long.

I usually spend about twenty to twenty-five minutes vocalizing. Sometimes I will do it with physical movement, and other times I will do my vocal and movement warm-ups separately. Physically, it's important for me to loosen up my back (thoracic spine) so that my posture isn't slumped over and I'm able to stand in a strong upright position. For years, even after I graduated, I studied the Alexander Technique. If I have time on a show day, I will take a lesson with my Alexander teacher. If not, I will do some of my own yoga poses and mobility stretches. I use a foam roller to roll my back and hips. I will lie on the floor with my arms over my head (knees bent) and do some pelvic tilts as I start my vocalizing. Once I get to the high-range exercises (where I am working on agility and speed), I will add a few hops or maybe even some jumping jacks.

Mark Janas, my musical director for *Legit: A Classical Cabaret*, would always warm me up before we rehearsed and added some wonderful exercises to my repertoire. I currently work with Bill Zeffiro on vocal technique. He too has shared some great techniques for connecting the breath to the sound. Some of them are especially good for the opera singer in me who still wants to "blow the roof off" sometimes—Bill helps to keep me grounded. He always catches me when I am pushing or overly opening my mouth when less could really be more . . . especially in cabaret. As for specific exercises, I think my favorites are the same as everyone else's: lip trills, scales, staccato, inhaling to a count, holding, and exhaling to a count. Then there are some of the fun warm-up tunes: "I love to run in the sun," "I love to sing," "plump jam," and so forth.

What other training did you need (or have gotten) after your formal education in order to have the artistically successful cabaret career that you now have?

One of my favorite introductions to cabaret was by the "King and Queen of Cabaret," Lennie Watts and Lina Koutrakos. In 2008, they did a weeklong course called "Summer in the City" where I met a lot of the friends that I now have in this community. In that class, we had the chance to work with the late great Julie Wilson. Karen Mason was also there, as well as Kristine Zbornik. I learned a lot from all of them. I have worked with both Lina and Lennie as directors—they are so gifted! It was very special getting to have them both in the same room for that workshop because—being as experienced and different from each other as they are—they offered unique and diverse opinions all in one space. I am proud to say that *Revolution*, which was directed by Lennie, won my first MAC award, and *Legit*, which was directed by Lina, won a Bistro Award. I guess my advice would be "listen to your teachers."

Since we're discussing directors, I have to say, it is absolutely *vital* to work with many different directors on different projects. Mix it up. I've had many mentors, teachers, coaches, and directors. I love taking direction and knowing that someone is sitting there observing with a discerning eye so that I will ultimately improve. Also, when learning another style of singing, study and learn from the pros. I didn't know anything about jazz or the Great American Songbook, so I went to work with Barry Levitt in late 2014. I said, "Barry, I will never claim to be a jazz singer, but I'd like to learn some jazz technique anyway." So, for three years we worked together, did a few gigs, and I wound up producing *My Ship: Songs from 1941*.

What first attracted you to cabaret?

Cabaret gives me the chance to do my own shows, with the songs I want to sing, at any given moment in my life. In cabaret, *you* pick the story, content, the arc, and you even learn how to produce it, to boot! With cabaret, there are so many possible avenues to explore, and with the right team of professionals around you, you just might end up with an award-winning show and have a nice long run with it.

Did you always know you'd have a career in cabaret performance, or did it come as a surprise?

I totally fell into cabaret. I got my first and last Manhattan waitressing job at Birdland. For about eight months, I worked "Jim Caruso's Cast Party" and almost always was given the chance to get up and sing at the very end of the night. During that time there were a handful of other servers who were also great singers. So, I took the lead and asked the owner, Gianni Valenti, and Jim Caruso, if we could put on a show—*The Birdland Songbirds*—and he let us do it! You can still catch my "Miss Byrd" from that show on YouTube. Also during that time, I opened my first cabaret show at the Duplex called *Shooting My Arrow*. I wasn't a MAC member yet and didn't know about awards and such, but I did get a review from *Cabaret Scenes* magazine. And I remember being introduced to Lennie Watts. I had a full band (very expensive) and even a backup singer. I loved the material I chose for that show. It was truly about me, and about how astrology plays into who we meet and when, but my patter was *way too long*! I learned from that, and now my shows are much more succinct—the patter is tighter, and I stay closer to the narrative. If you go off course, it can easily become self-indulgent. ♪

You are known for being able to sing in many different styles, including classical, music theater, pop/rock, blues, and others. Was this something you could always do? Also, do you feel that your classical training helped you achieve those styles?

Yes and yes. I mean I could always do it to an extent, but it's definitely gotten better. As a young girl, back on Cape Cod, I was always dancing and singing to a mix of music theater, Madonna, and Janet Jackson songs

. . . even Joni Mitchell, Patsy Cline, and Judy Collins. Later, in my high school years, I got more into singer-songwriters like the Indigo Girls, Sarah McLachlan, Bonnie Raitt, and Jewel. Opera was an accident—a great one—but it wasn't something that I was hearing during my childhood and teenage years. I didn't start listening to opera until I started to sing the repertoire during my conservatory years.

When I sing along to a recording—whether it's an Alanis Morissette or a Kelli O'Hara album—and I *feel* something and I think it will fit in my *color* wheelhouse, I then add it to my collection of songs to sing. That's what's great as you get older as a singer—you are always adding to your knowledge. You have layers upon layers of material and experience in your memory bank that you can pull from, or learn from, when it feels authentic.

Can you identify any necessary skills for a concert/cabaret performance career (artistic or business-wise) that you feel are not being taught in university/conservatory settings?

I think everyone who wants to enter this business should know that "cabaret singer" is synonymous with "producer." It's rather unfortunate but true. I've gotten good at asking for help when I want to produce something, but it continues to be the same struggle, every show. With all the money out there to keep the Great American Songbook alive, who's keeping the *artists alive* who keep the Great American Songbook alive? I always used to joke that if I could trade in the hours I spent at the conservatory, learning the "importance of gesticulation" for a few classes on Manhattan business savvy, I would probably be out there headlining in concert work. What the conservatory did *not* teach me is this: as fabulous as your right-hand gesture is while singing a Mimì's "dying" aria, it will not get you work.

In a short amount of time since your debut, you've won several awards, you've been a featured singer at the Cabaret Convention, and you perform to packed audiences. That takes both great artistry and an understanding of this art form. What have you learned about singing in cabaret, as opposed to other genres?

Be authentic and connect with the audience in front of you. I think that's one thing Broadway performers—some of them, at least—are lacking in concerts or when they do cabaret. Every time you perform cabaret, it must feel like you are singing and telling a story *intimately* to only a few people. Even if you are on a huge stage and in front of a huge audience, you must draw them in, open your eyes, and speak from your heart.

⑨

FINDING YOUR AUTHENTIC VOICE

This chapter will set forth concepts and guidelines for the study of voice within the contemporary commercial music (CCM) genre, which includes many of the styles of singing used in cabaret. It will address pedagogical differences in training for CCM styles versus more traditional and classical styles. For the purposes of this work, the comparisons will be limited within the parameters of CCM versus classical voice study, although I fully acknowledge that many other styles of voice have been written about, with great authority, within the So You Want to Sing series.

This chapter will not offer specific vocal exercises. It is my belief that the study of voice is an experience that must remain live, whether in person or through various online technologies. The feedback given by an experienced professional voice teacher, with knowledge of both the anatomy and acoustics of voice, and the artistic and professional working knowledge within the chosen genre are vital for any measure of success.

WHAT IS THE AUTHENTIC VOICE?

Throughout music history great vocal artists, regardless of genre, have had immediately recognizable voices. Within a few notes one can identify the voice of Frank Sinatra (1915–1998), Ella Fitzgerald (1917–1996), Barbara Cook (1927–2017), Brian Stokes Mitchell (b. 1957), Luciano Pavarotti (1936–2007), or Maria Callas (1923–1977). Each within their own genre is unmistakable. Even in pop music, one can certainly distinguish Lady Gaga (b. 1986) from Ariana Grande (b. 1993) or Ed Sheeran (b. 1991) from Justin Timberlake (b. 1981). Today's cabaret artists—including those mentioned and interviewed in this book—possess this same quality of individuality. And so too should you. ♪

Your authentic voice is the voice with which you speak. It is the sound by which you are immediately recognized. It is not a manufactured sound. By that I mean it is not a sound that is solely used within the genre of music you sing (e.g., most opera singers don't speak the way they sing). Your singing voice in cabaret must be recognizable as, and grow out of, your speaking voice. It can have a substantial range, into and above the passaggio. However, the authentic voice remains unmistakably recognizable as *your voice*.

The development of an unmistakable and immediately recognizable voice (within the bounds of health and safety) should be, in my opinion, the focus of any serious professional vocal study. In recent years, however, the institutionalization of voice pedagogy in universities and conservatories has favored a more homogeneous "beautiful" and "correct" sound, especially in the world of classical voice technique, which rightfully holds all its singers to an Italian bel canto tradition. The sounds that are produced in many voice studios may indeed be beautiful, but there is little individuality of sound, which one might also refer to as the timbre, or color, of the voice.

Individuality of voice is not to be confused with pathological damage or misuse. There are, in fact, many examples of famous singers who are immediately recognizable due to damage or misuse of the voice. A singer whose voice is recognizable due to vocal pathology, illness, or injury is not using their authentic voice. They are using a damaged voice. However unique the sound may be, however famous the singer may become for it, it is still damaged. All forms of damage, whether through illness or injury, must be properly diagnosed and treated by a physician in care of the professional voice, rehabilitated with a speech-language pathologist (SLP), and if indicated, rehabituated (retrained) with a singing voice specialist (SVS).

The authentic voice is free from pathological damage. It is immediately recognizable as the singer's natural, healthy speaking voice throughout the range. It is also effective and appropriate to task, without ever "oversinging" the lyric.

OVERSINGING THE LYRIC

Oversinging the lyric is a common error that one hears in many CCM styles, and especially within the genre of cabaret. It appears to the listener as any type of sound that calls attention to itself, where one may find oneself listening to the tone quality of the voice rather than to the lyric and storytelling. It can also reveal itself as a "wall of sound" mistakenly thought of as "projecting" or "legato" by inexperienced singers. This overbearing use of voice, to the detriment of the lyric or story, is not helpful or artistic in an intimate room.

In a small cabaret venue, especially where amplification is employed, the audience must have some space within the musical phrase to receive the lyric's information, process the story, and breathe with the singer (even unconsciously). A continuous wall of projected singing can have the adverse effect of pushing the audience away. This practice uses the voice as "armor," keeping the audience at a distance as if to say, "Don't look at me, just listen to the sound of my beautiful voice. I paid a lot of money for voice lessons and I'm going to prove it to you." Regrettably, when this is the case, no storytelling can take place, as your audience is presented with more vocal tone than lyric, which is not an authentic way to communicate. A compelling vocal tone, however beautiful, will not in and of itself sustain an entire cabaret performance. That tone must be carried on a *thought* that sustains the lyric throughout the entire *sentence*. In essence, the voice does not *hold a note*. The singer's emotional vehicle must *carry the note* through to its destination: the end of the *thought*.

Oversinging the lyric is a technical problem found in many vocal genres. However, due to the proximity of the audience in a cabaret room, it is perceived as being more aggressive and less inviting. Additionally, oversinging the lyric has the deleterious effect of keeping the singer solely focused on the sound of their own voice, and therefore *not* the lyric. If the use of voice seems to "leapfrog" or step in front of the lyric, then the singer is no longer using a cabaret performance technique.

Does this mean that no one in cabaret sings well or loudly? Of course not. Cabaret singers use a full range of color and dynamics within their singing ability. However, the true cabaret artist never sings higher or louder *just because they can*. Singing higher or louder is reserved only for moments when the storytelling requires it, and even then, only when it can be done without oversinging the lyric. This practice may, in fact, be the one distinction that sets the cabaret artist apart from other types of singers. In cabaret the use of voice must remain in service to the word. The human voice is the *only* instrument on the planet that plays *words*, not notes. Let your pianist, or your band, play the notes. *You sing the words!*

USE OF VOICE

The singer's "use of voice" refers to all the stylistic choices they make, including their resonance strategy (lofted versus pharyngeal [spoken] resonance), vowel structure, the articulation (or disarticulation) of consonants, or even the use of a dialect or accent, which may help to tell the story of the song. Understanding how the use of voice can enhance or betray the storytelling is extremely important. Without the visual or external aids of music theater or opera—that is, the sets, costumes, and context of the plot—the cabaret singer stands alone with only their voice to impart the meaning of both the lyric and the melodic line of music. This is a nuanced endeavor that requires substantial training in both voice technique and performance. However, once onstage, the assimilation of these techniques must be so complete as to appear nonexistent to the audience and effortless to the singer.

In cabaret it is widely considered that the best use of voice is one that does not call attention to itself but rather remains in service to the lyric and storytelling. From a technical point of view this service includes a wide range of options, plus vocal gestures and colors that help to illustrate the story being told. Technical facility is therefore measured by the vocal options available to the singer in terms of color, range, dynamic stylistic flexibility, and resonance and not by the mastery or even presence of a certain type of vocal tone.

These options, once technically mastered and assimilated, are used organically to help the singer create the circumstance of time and place within their storytelling. For example (using the same song in two different scenarios), the song "On the Street Where You Live" from Lerner and Loewe's *My Fair Lady* could be interpreted as an intimate romantic story, pillow talk at 3:00 a.m., or as an exuberant celebration on a crowded street at 2:00 p.m. Each of these scenarios will require a very different use of voice. The 3:00 a.m. interpretation will most assuredly necessitate a gentler use of voice (a more aspirate phonation or a vocal fry, perhaps) to indicate the late hour and intimate context. And even though it may be well within the singer's range, the interpretation of the song may also affect the choice of key. The 3:00 a.m. interpretation may also require both a lower key and softer dynamic in service to a gentler delivery of lyric, again illustrating the hour and circumstance of the story being told.

The use of voice is necessarily dictated by the singer's range of vocal options, which is in turn born out of their own technical ability. Herein lies a main objective for technical voice study in the genre of cabaret: to enhance the singer's vocal ability and options safely and effectively, giving them a greater facility with which to complete the storytelling while at the same time never calling attention to that technical ability while performing. An analogy can be drawn here to weight training and physical fitness. At the gym, one pushes the limits of physical endurance, lifting weight in a specific exercise until near "failure," when another lift in that repetition would not be possible. In life, however, it is never the goal to exhaust one's muscles to failure. Nor does one need the full strength of muscular ability for everyday tasks. You don't lift weights in order to pick up a teacup like a bodybuilder. But as a result of your physical fitness, you do feel stronger and more able to complete everyday tasks. As a singer, *singing* is your everyday task. The goal of voice training should be that the everyday task of singing becomes effortless, with a greater facility and "full range of motion" for the voice, so that one does not have to think about the production of tone, and the communication of the lyric can remain front and center.

Even in the vocally demanding world of grand opera, a singer should never step beyond their vocal comfort zone (their Fach).[1] Leontyne Price (b. 1927) has been famously quoted as saying, "Always sing on your interest, never on your principal." This is perhaps the greatest citation on the importance of investing in proper vocal training, so that the use of voice does not in and of itself pull the listener's attention away from the lyric.

The use of voice must always inform the listener more about the story than it does about the singer. If the song is set as an intimate 3:00 a.m. conversation and the singer uses a fully resonant voice, we are taken out of the story and confronted with a use of voice that tells us more about the singer's vocal training than the story being told. The use of voice *at all times* must be appropriate to the task at hand: to the storytelling.

At the level of professional performance, it is a given that the singer onstage can sing. Therefore, the act of singing, the skill of it, does not need to be proven. Very often it is the singer's own need to *prove* that they can sing that unfortunately backfires and results in highlighting a technical deficit, which might otherwise have gone unnoticed or not even exist. In this case, more attention to the lyric and storytelling would not only aid the singer's interpretation but also help complete the desired vocal gesture without calling attention to the vocal technique (or lack thereof). Concurrently, the singer must continue to work on the mastery of vocal technique to complete the vocal gesture without the anxiety of needing to prove their own merit.

Another analogy: Studying vocal technique can be compared to cooking homemade pasta. You cook the pasta at a certain temperature, for a certain amount of time. In traditional Italian households, when you want to see if the pasta is done, you take a strand out and throw it against the wall. If it sticks, it's done. Similarly, if your vocal technique "sticks" without you having to think about it, it's done. If not, it's not done. Keep cooking.

APPROPRIATENESS TO TASK

Certainly, classical music and other types of unamplified vocal performance will present a completely different series of tasks that contrast sharply with the act of singing in an intimate club with amplification. With real ramifications, the development of personal amplification (handheld microphones and lavaliers) has changed the nature of communication while singing onstage. No longer is it a requirement to "hit the back wall," at least not in music theater, pop, jazz, or cabaret (it never was in cabaret). It is only in classical music where such a requirement still exists. And yet, many voice teachers continue to teach as if self-amplification were a requirement for all students, as if somehow a louder voice were intrinsically more valuable or desirable. This is a vestige of Western classical voice pedagogy and is not an appropriate concern when studying contemporary commercial music.

A solid singing technique gives the singer greater awareness of a safe and effective vocal production without overtraining the singer beyond the needs of the chosen genre. The technical paradigm of "classical voice study works for everything" is simply inefficient. Voice science has advanced considerably in recent years, giving singers (and teachers) a much clearer understanding of many different resonance strategies and techniques to be used in contemporary commercial music. For much more on this subject, see another book within this series, *So You Want to Sing CCM*, as well as Scott McCoy's chapter on singing and voice science within this book (chapter 10). ♪

Appropriateness to task, along with vocal health and safety, must be held up as the gold standard of voice pedagogy within the genre of cabaret, and indeed within all genres of vocal study. It is important to teach singers how to sing safely and effectively *and* make sure that they sound appropriate to the style of music they are singing. Cabaret singers should not sound like opera singers unless, of course, the use of voice for a particular song or effect specifically requires that resonance strategy or sound.

A great example of an elite singer manipulating the use of voice for the appropriateness to task is Eileen Farrell (1920–2002), who enjoyed an international (and vocally healthy) sixty-year, multigenre career. Upon hearing Farrell sing an aria by Richard Wagner (1813–1883) followed by a jazz tune, one would never imagine it was the same singer. This is a goal to which all singers should aspire. ♪

THE TASK AT HAND

For an appropriateness of task to be understood, we must first establish (a) the task at hand, and (b) the vocal requirements specific to that task. Echoing the disclaimer in chapter 3, for the purposes of this work we will limit the scope of this treatise to the specific requirements of a cabaret performance technique and not the many varied performance styles one could experience in a cabaret venue.

Within cabaret performance technique, the first and foremost task at hand is the statement and believability of the lyric. Everything the singer must communicate, the entire scope of the job of singing in cabaret, lies within the lyric. Apart from artists like Stephen Sondheim (b. 1930), who write both the words and music, and among songwriting teams throughout history, the lyric is usually the first information to be written. That lyric is then presented to the composer who sets the lyric to melody and harmony. Herein lies the journey that the cabaret artist must also take, discovering how the lyric inspired the composer and shaped the music's melodic, rhythmic, and even harmonic structure.

Almost universally, the composer's set rhythm will follow the lyricist's natural cadence of language. Rhythmic and dynamic phrasing will also be indicated by the lyricist's specific choice of words. For example, no singer in the history of vocal music has ever shouted the word "moonlight." Analyzing the grammar, punctuation, and keywords of the sentence will give the singer, whether or not they read music, a clear understanding of the musical, rhythmic, and dynamic phrasing of the song. For more information on this, see chapter 13 ("Lyric Connection").

The statement and believability of the lyric is the singer's primary task in cabaret. One must communicate as truthfully as possible, even within the given untrue circumstance of performing onstage in front of a crowd of people. There is no character to lean upon and no point of view to pretend. Cabaret is first and foremost an art form of authentic communication, which also requires an authentic use of voice.

Finding your authentic voice is not as easy as it may seem. Humans are intrinsic imitators. Most, if not all, young singers start their vocal journey by imitating those individual voices who inspired them, singing along with the car radio, or "rocking out" in front of a mirror using a hairbrush as a microphone. Then, when serious vocal study is initiated, the process is often dictated by understanding the "right" sounds to make, often imitating sounds, even unconsciously, that are modeled by the voice teacher. Finding your authentic use of voice in a technically sound way without losing your own vocal identity is essential.

DO YOU REALLY NEED A VOICE TEACHER?

Phrases like "authentic use of voice" and "sing like you speak" may make it sound as if one does not need to study voice in order to sing in cabaret. While there have been many great singers in this genre with little or no vocal training, the truth is that society's vocal performance tastes, after decades of pop and rock music, are now attuned to a "higher, louder, longer" mentality. Even in classical music, holding a note higher, louder, and longer—as if it were a test of endurance—is applauded. As a society, we are now many decades removed from the understanding of how a gentler use of voice can be equally satisfying . . . and even thrilling! This progression of vocal and musical tastes can be traced just as easily in classical music, from baroque opera to bel canto to the verismo. George Frideric Handel (1685–1759) and Giacomo Puccini (1858–1924) require very different uses of the voice, and singing these composers on a professional level requires studying voice. So too must the professional singer of music theater, pop, rock, and jazz understand and study the proper use of voice to sing these styles within the genre of cabaret performance. This cannot be understated. The technical use of the voice in cabaret is significantly different than other vocal genres. Study with a professional voice teacher, in this regard, is absolutely necessary.

The study of voice cannot be done alone. It is not a "do-it-yourself" (DIY) endeavor. Hearing the subtlety of vocal timbre, the amplification and attenuation of harmonic overtones, and understanding how those overtones contribute to the overall sound is a skill honed by professional voice teachers. Further, understanding the acoustic complexity of those overtones—and how to adjust the singer's resonance strategy to acquire the desired sound safely—is a skill that requires diligent study of both voice acoustics and anatomy.

There are many skilled vocal technicians and singing voice specialists to choose from. However, be sure to find the right teacher for your genre of music. Most voice teachers have been trained in the Western classical tradition, and these teachers tend to teach the optimum resonance strategy for the music they themselves sing: art song, oratorio, and opera. But when presented with an alternative resonance strategy—for example, contemporary commercial music—the teacher's own acoustic training and artistic preferences may hinder them from helping the student realize their artistic goals. Therefore, it is vitally important to select a voice teacher that has experience in both performing and teaching the resonance strategies required to sing your selected genre.

In simple terms, if you're not singing opera, you shouldn't sound like an opera singer. You shouldn't be warming up with classical vocalizes. There should be no discussion of Italian vowels. If your vocal genre is contemporary commercial music, you must find a teacher who specializes in that study. There are professional voice teachers with advanced knowledge of voice acoustics and anatomy that specialize in contemporary commercial music. The process of finding the right teacher for your genre of singing must be diligently undertaken. *Interview* each prospective teacher. Ask how many hours a week they spend teaching *your* genre of singing. A teacher may have a roster of thirty to forty students per week, but if they only spend five hours a week teaching your genre, they may not be right for you. As a singer, you must find a teacher that not only hears your voice objectively (and acoustically) but also understands the target resonance strategy of your genre, respects it, and can help you get there safely. The importance of this cannot be understated.

The student must rely upon the teacher's expertise in this regard simply because the singer cannot truly hear their own voice in the same way as an objective listener. This is anecdotally proven by referring to the sound of your voice as revealed on your outgoing voicemail message. How many times did you rerecord the message because you were not happy with the sound of your voice? How many different inflections did you use to try to acquire a sound that you recognized as your own? If you are like most people, after ten or twelve attempts, you simply settled for the best you could get. Meanwhile, everyone who hears your voicemail immediately recognizes your voice and has no problem accepting or understanding it. It is not due to a "flaw" in the technology that your voice records so differently. Rather, the sound you hear *is your voice as others hear it*. It is foreign to you because you experience your voice through the "filter" of the bone conductivity of your own skull. You hear your voice as it sounds inside your head—not acoustically out in the room.

For this reason alone, proper study with a qualified, professional voice teacher—whom you have interviewed, who teaches primarily in your selected genre, and who can help you develop your authentic voice for contemporary commercial music and American popular song—is essential for progress in the genre of cabaret.

THE VOICE TEACHER IN CABARET

Cabaret singing is *beautiful* singing. It is masterfully technical singing. The techniques used are very specific to this genre and fall squarely within a CCM voice pedagogy. Because of this, there are concrete differences in aesthetic and technical preferences that the student must be aware of when working with or interviewing a voice teacher. I posit that there are basically two types of voice teachers: aesthetic teachers and functional teachers.

The aesthetic teacher maintains the aesthetic of the desired sound firmly in their own mind. These are generally Western classical voice teachers, using a paradigm of Italian bel canto vowels and self-amplification. In this paradigm, there is a "target" sound to be acquired. If this specific sound quality is not achieved, the vocal technique is not realized. Students can spend many years with little improvement if the measure of improvement is solely attaining this specific vocal aesthetic.

Conversely, a functional teacher is not focused on a certain aesthetic of sound. The functional teacher strives to impart safe and effective techniques that allow the singer to employ a use of voice that is appropriate to the task at hand, be it music theater, jazz, classical, or any other style of vocal performance. An appropriateness to task must always be maintained within functional training, which means that the specific stylistic idiosyncrasies of each genre should be fully respected and realized. The singer must sound as if they are organically singing within the musical style and that the style itself presents no technical difficulty for them.

The need for functional training has become especially prevalent in music theater and American popular song, both staples of cabaret repertoire. In these genres, there is no established tonal target, no particular sound that we define as the "right" sound. Singers must be able to morph their resonance strategies to fit into many different vocal sounds and styles, according to the song. A music theater singer may audition for Rodgers and Hammerstein's *Oklahoma!* on Monday, Cyndi Lauper's *Kinky Boots* on Tuesdays, and Stephen Sondheim's *Into the Woods* on Wednesday.[2] All three of these shows (and composers) require a different vocal resonance strategy to be sung in a stylistically correct way.

In classical music, one might compare this to the varying vocal requirements within the operatic repertoire; for instance, the vocal differences between baroque and verismo—that is, between composers as different as the aforementioned Handel and Puccini. These eras and composers require substantially different uses of voice. One would never consider singing an opera by Claudio Monteverdi (1567–1643) with the same use of voice as an opera by Pietro Mascagni (1863–1945), or sing Handel as one would sing Wagner. So too must the stylistic differences between composers within the American popular song canon be taken into consideration. Singers in cabaret must use all the stylistic and vocal options available to them, and they must do so as authentically and seamlessly as possible.

In a cabaret concert, the use of voice may vary from "standard" to "legit" to "pop" to "blues." Any number of vocal styles will be used in the course of one evening, and each must sound completely authentic to the singer. Therefore, the voice teacher's role when working with a singer in this genre is not to train the singer to always make the very best sound possible but rather to make the appropriate sound for the song and the singer's unique interpretation of it.

AUTHENTIC TRAINING

In most universities and many private voice studios, the primary focus of vocal training is developing the voice as its own entity or instrument, using guidelines first set forth in the seventeenth and eighteenth centuries. Taking all things into consideration, including the invention of electricity and external amplification, this focus is diametrically opposed to most modern professional uses of voice, where the communication of the lyric—no matter the range or dynamic—must advance the story forward.

Authentic training requires exercises and repertoire that place the singer's voice into the musical environment of chosen genre. Eighteenth-century flexibility exercises are not going to help a young singer develop the ability for jazz improvisation. Italian vowels and lofted resonance are not going to help the singer acquire a spoken sound throughout the vocal range. These studies may be of great value initially, as exercises in the full range of motion within vocal production, but they must soon give way to a more practical and authentic use of voice within the alternative genre. Training must be directed to the task at hand for the professional development of the singer. This means that exercises may be more word or consonant based, that scales using many different resonance strategies will be practiced on both "open" and "closed" vowels, and articulation, communication, and expression may be addressed as "whole body" endeavors, integrating the use of voice with both movement and storytelling. There will be no "park and bark" (stand still and sing). ♪

The statements made above are of practical concern for the voice teacher as well. Within the contemporary commercial music field, and specifically within the genre of cabaret, the voice teaching community has acquired a bit of a bad rap for overtraining singers out of the desired sound. Holding a singer to a Western classical model when that is not the intended repertoire serves neither student nor teacher. The teacher is responsible for helping each singer acquire the desired tonal target of the genre—safely and effectively—to help them reach their desired professional goals.

Popular repertoire, including early music theater and Great American Songbook, can certainly be used in training and developing the voice just as assuredly as the twenty-four Italian songs and arias. The melodic lines of Richard Rodgers (1902–1979), Cole Porter (1891–1964), Irving Berlin (1888–1989), and George Gershwin (1898–1937)—just to name a few—are as "voice building" as any vocal line within the bel canto repertoire. Furthermore, this repertoire can be freely transposed as necessary to best fit the student's needs and progress, and the idea of vocal color can be fully explored, in English, thereby giving the student a greater connection to the text.

Above all, vocal training in this genre should not be in the abstract. The best possible display of technique and technical understanding does not alone prove a singer's merit. This archetype is the result of institutionalized training whereby young singers must fulfill certain benchmarks of technical understanding semester by semester. I assert that this model is designed to fit a performance curriculum into an academic grading structure and is therefore arbitrary and not at all artistic.

Training the voice must always be within the context of the song or story being told. To that end, there is a plethora of repertoire within the popular American songbook from which to choose and work on the various technical aspects of voice, such as breath management, registration balance (mix), resonance, vowel structure, dynamic phrasing, and articulation. All of these vocal tasks can be worked on and mastered without ever singing one word in Italian.

FINAL THOUGHTS

Is the strategic use of an aspirate voice or vocal fry blasphemous to you as a singer . . . or a teacher? Does lowering the key for storytelling purposes strike a blow to your singing ego? These are vocal options that, as a storyteller in cabaret, you must be comfortable with. The voice must remain in service to the lyric at all costs. *At all costs!* In the intimate setting of a cabaret venue, any note that is sung—or oversung—without being connected to story or circumstance will immediately stick out as inappropriate to the task at hand.

In cabaret, one must let go of the need to sing *correctly*. Professional use of voice dictates that there is no *correct* sound. The *right* sound is simply the *best* sound for the story you are telling, which is not necessarily the *prettiest* sound you can make. This concept bears repeating: The *best* sound is not always the *prettiest* sound one can make! It is not a dangerous or unsafe sound, to be sure. It is simply the sound that best communicates the lyric and aids in storytelling.

Are you willing to sacrifice that which, through ardent vocal training, you have previously perceived as "correct," such as beauty of tone or range, in favor of lyric delivery and believability should the storytelling warrant it? Are you willing to trust that the vocal training you have had resides within you and does not need to be *proven* to your audience? If the answer to these questions is yes, then you may very well be on your way to becoming an artistic cabaret singer.

NOTES

1. The German (or Kloiber) Fach system is a method of classifying opera singers by range, weight, and color of voice.

2. The dates of these composers and lyricists are as follows: Richard Rodgers (1902–1979), Oscar Hammerstein II (1895–1960), Cyndi Lauper (b. 1957), and Stephen Sondheim (b. 1930).

10

SINGING AND VOICE SCIENCE

Scott McCoy

This chapter presents a concise overview of how the voice functions as a biomechanical, acoustic instrument. We will be dealing with elements of anatomy, physiology, acoustics, and resonance. But don't panic; the things you need to know are easily accessible, even if it has been many years since you last set foot in a science or math class!

All musical instruments, including the human voice, have at least four things in common, consisting of a power source, a sound source (vibrator), a resonator, and a system for articulation. In most cases, the person who plays the instrument provides power by pressing a key, plucking a string, or blowing into a horn. This power is used to set the sound source in motion, which creates vibrations in the air that we perceive as sound. Musical vibrators come in many forms, including strings, reeds, and human lips. The sound produced by the vibrator, however, needs a lot of help before it becomes beautiful music—we might think of it as raw material, like a lump of clay that a potter turns into a vase. Musical instruments use resonance to enhance and strengthen the sound of the vibrator, transforming it into sounds we identify as a piano, a trumpet, or a guitar. Finally, instruments must have a means of articulation to create the nuanced sounds of music. Let's see how these four elements are used to create the sounds of singing.

PULMONARY SYSTEM:
THE POWER SOURCE OF YOUR VOICE

The human voice has a lot in common with a trumpet: both use flaps of tissue as a sound source, both use hollow tubes as resonators, and both rely on the respiratory (pulmonary) system for power. If you stop to think about it, you quickly realize why breathing is so important for singing. First and foremost, it keeps us alive through the exchange of blood gases—oxygen in, carbon dioxide out. But it also serves as the storage depot for the air we use to produce sound. Most singers rarely encounter situations in which these two functions are in conflict, but if you are required to sustain an extremely long phrase, you could find yourself in need of fresh oxygen before your lungs are totally empty.

Misconceptions about breathing for singing are rampant. Fortunately, most are easily dispelled. We must start with a brief foray into the world of physics in the guise of Boyle's law. Some of you no doubt remember this principle: The pressure of a gas within a container changes inversely with changes of volume. If the quantity of a gas is constant and its container is made smaller, pressure rises. But if we make the container bigger, pressure goes down. Boyle's law explains everything that happens when we breathe, especially when we combine it with another physical law: nature abhors a vacuum. If one location has reduced pressure, air flows from an area of higher pressure to equalize the two, and vice versa. So if we can create a zone of reduced air pressure by expanding our lungs, air automatically flows in to restore balance. When air pressure in the lungs is increased, it has no choice but to flow outward.

As we all know, the air we breathe goes in and out of our lungs. Each lung contains millions and millions of tiny air sacs called alveoli, where gases are exchanged. The alveoli also function like ultra-miniature versions of the bladder for a bagpipe, storing the air that will be used to set the vocal folds into vibration. To get the air in and out of them, all we need to do is make the lungs larger for inhalation and smaller for exhalation. Always remember this relationship between cause and effect during breathing: We inhale because we make ourselves large; we exhale because we make ourselves smaller. Unfortunately, the lungs are organs, not muscles, and have no ability on their own to accomplish this feat. For this reason, your bodies came from the factory with special muscles designed to enlarge and compress your entire thorax (rib cage), while simultaneously moving your lungs. We can classify these muscles in two main categories: any muscle that has the ability to increase the volume capacity of the thorax serves an inspiratory function; any muscle that has the ability to decrease the volume capacity of the thorax serves an expiratory function.

Your largest muscle of inspiration is called the diaphragm (figure 10.1). This dome-shaped muscle originates from the bottom of your sternum (breastbone) and completely fills the area from that point around your ribs to your spine. It's the second-largest muscle in your body, but you probably have no conscious awareness of it or ability to directly control it. When we take a deep breath, the diaphragm con-

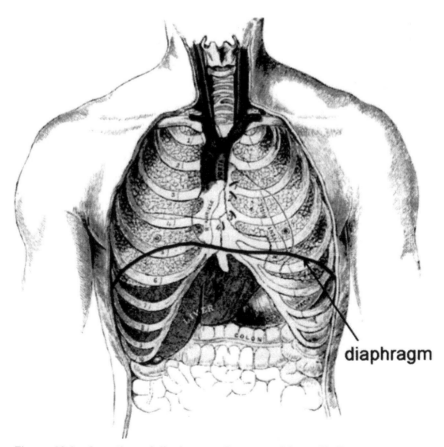

diaphragm

Figure 10.1.   Location of diaphragm. *Courtesy of Scott McCoy.*

tracts and the central portion flattens out and drops downward a couple inches into your abdomen, pressing against all of your internal organs. If you release tension from your abdominal muscles as you inhale, you will feel a gentle bulge in your upper or lower belly, or perhaps in your back, resulting from the displacement of your innards by the diaphragm. This is a good thing and can be used to let you know you have taken a good inhalation.

The diaphragm is important, but we must remember that it cannot function in isolation. After you inhale, it relaxes and gently returns to its resting position through an action called elastic recoil. This movement, however, is entirely passive and makes no significant contribution to generating the pressure required to sustain phonation. Therefore, it makes no sense at all to try to "sing from your diaphragm"—unless you intend to sing while you inhale, not exhale!

Eleven pairs of muscles assist the diaphragm in its inhalatory efforts, which are called the external intercostal muscles (figure 10.2). These muscles start from ribs one through eleven and connect at a slight angle downward to ribs two through twelve. When they contract, the entire thorax moves up and out, somewhat like moving a bucket handle. With the diaphragm and intercostals working together, you are able to increase the capacity of your lungs by about three to six liters, depending on your gender and overall physical stature; thus, we have quite a lot of air available to power our voices.

Eleven additional pairs of muscles are located directly under the external intercostals, which, not surprisingly, are called the internal intercostals (figure 10.2). These muscles start from ribs two through twelve and connect upward to ribs one through eleven. When they contract, they induce the opposite action of their external partners: the thorax is made smaller, inducing exhalation. Four additional pairs of expiratory muscles are located in the abdomen, beginning with the rectus (figure 10.2). The two rectus abdominis muscles run from your pubic bone to your sternum and are divided into four separate portions called bellies of the muscle (lots of muscles have multiple bellies; it is coincidental that the bellies of the rectus are found in the location we colloquially refer to as our belly). Definition of these bellies results in the so-called ripped abdomen or six-pack of body builders and others who are especially fit.

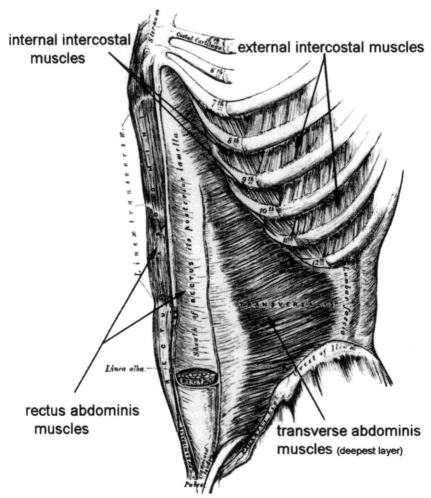

Figure 10.2. **Intercostal and abdominal muscles.** *Courtesy of Scott McCoy.*

The largest muscles of the abdomen are called the external obliques (figure 10.3), which run at a downward angle from the sides of the rectus, covering the lower portion of the thorax, and extend all the way to the spine. The internal obliques lie immediately below, oriented at an angle that crisscrosses the external muscles. They are slightly smaller, beginning at the bottom of the thorax, rather than extending over it. The deepest muscle layer is the transverse abdominis (figure 10.2), which is oriented with fibers that run horizontally. These four muscle pairs com-

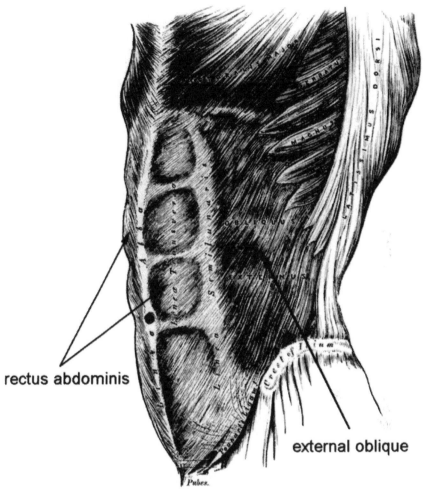

rectus abdominis

external oblique

Figure 10.3. External oblique and rectus abdominis muscles. *Courtesy of Scott McCoy.*

pletely encase the abdominal region, holding your organs and digestive system in place while simultaneously helping you breathe.

Your expiratory muscles are quite large and can produce a great deal of pulmonary or air pressure. In fact, they can easily overpower the larynx. Healthy adults can generally generate more than twice the pressure that is required to produce even the loudest sounds; therefore, singers must develop a system for moderating and controlling airflow and breath pressure. This practice goes by many names, including breath support, breath control, and breath management, all of which rely on the principle of muscular antagonism. Muscles are said to have an antagonistic relationship when they work in opposing directions, usually pulling on a common point of attachment, for the sake of increasing stability or motor control. You can see a clear example of muscular antagonism in the relationship between your biceps (flexors) and triceps (extensors) when you hold out your arm. In breathing for singing, we activate inspiratory muscles (e.g., diaphragm and external intercostals) during exhalation to help control respiratory pressure and the rate at which air is expelled from the lungs.

One of the things you will notice when watching a variety of singers is that they tend to breathe in many different ways. You might think that voice teachers and scientists, who have been teaching and studying singing for hundreds, if not thousands of years, would have come to agreement on the best possible breathing technique. But for many reasons, this is not the case. For one, different musical and vocal styles place varying demands on breathing. For another, humans have a huge variety of body types, sizes, and morphologies. A breathing strategy that is successful for a tall, slender woman might be completely ineffective in a short, robust man. Our bodies actually contain a large number of muscles beyond those we've already discussed that are capable of assisting with respiration. For an example, consider your latissimi dorsi muscles. These large muscles of the arm enable us to do pull-ups (or pull-downs, depending on which exercise you perform) at the fitness center. But because they wrap around a large portion of the thorax, they also exert an expiratory force. We have at least two dozen such muscles that have secondary respiratory functions, some for exhalation and some for inhalation. When we consider all these possibilities, it is no surprise at all that there are many ways to breathe that can produce beautiful singing. Just remember to practice some muscular antagonism—maintaining a degree of inhalation posture during exhalation—and you should do well.

LARYNX: THE VIBRATOR OF YOUR VOICE

The larynx, sometimes known as the voice box or Adam's apple, is a complex physiologic structure made of cartilage, muscle, and tissue.

Biologically, it serves as a sphincter valve, closing off the airway to prevent foreign objects from entering the lungs. When firmly closed, it is also used to increase abdominal pressure to assist with lifting heavy objects, childbirth, and defecation. But if we gently close this valve while we exhale, tissue in the larynx begins to vibrate and produce the sounds that become speech and singing.

The human larynx is a remarkably small instrument, typically ranging from the size of a pecan to a walnut for women and men, respectively. Sound is produced at a location called the glottis, which is formed by two flaps of tissue called the vocal folds (a.k.a. vocal cords). In women, the glottis is about the size of a dime; in men, it can approach the diameter of a quarter. The two folds are always attached together at their front point but open in the shape of the letter V during normal breathing, an action called abduction. To phonate, we must close the V while we exhale, an action called adduction (just like the machines you use at the fitness center to exercise your thigh and chest muscles).

Phonation is only possible because of the unique multilayer structure of the vocal folds (figure 10.4). The core of each fold is formed by muscle, which is surrounded by a layer of gelatinous material called

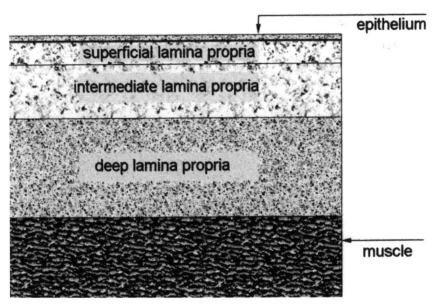

Figure 10.4. Layered structure of the vocal fold. *Courtesy of Scott McCoy.*

the lamina propria. The vocal ligament also runs through the lamina propria, which helps to prevent injury by limiting how far the folds can be stretched for high pitches. A thin, hairless epithelial layer that is constantly kept moist with mucus secreted by the throat, larynx, and trachea surrounds all of this. During phonation, the outer layer of the fold glides independently over the inner layer in a wavelike motion, without which phonation is impossible.

We can use a simple demonstration to better understand the independence of the inner and outer portions of the folds. Explore the palm of your hand with your other index finger. Note that the skin is attached quite firmly to the flesh beneath it. If you poke at your palm, that flesh acts as padding, protecting the underlying bone. Now explore the back of your hand. You will observe that the skin is attached quite loosely— you can easily move it around with your finger. And if you poke at the back of your hand, it is likely to hurt; there is very little padding between the skin and your bones. Your vocal folds combine the best attributes of both sides of your hand. They provide sufficient padding to help reduce impact stress, while permitting the outer layer to slip like the skin on the back of your hand, enabling phonation to occur. When you are sick with laryngitis and lose your voice (a condition called aphonia), inflammation in the vocal folds couples the layers of the folds tightly together. The outer layer can no longer move independently over the inner, and phonation becomes difficult or impossible.

The vocal folds are located within the five cartilaginous structures of the larynx (figure 10.5). The largest is called the thyroid cartilage, which is shaped like a small shield. The thyroid connects to the cricoid cartilage below it, which is shaped like a signet ring—broad in the back and narrow in the front. Two cartilages that are shaped like squashed pyramids sit atop the cricoid, called the arytenoids. Each vocal fold runs from the thyroid cartilage in front to one of the arytenoids at the back. Finally, the epiglottis is located at the top of the larynx, flipping backward each time we swallow to prevent food and liquid from entering our lungs. Muscles connect between the various cartilages to open and close the glottis and to lengthen and shorten the vocal folds for ascending and descending pitch, respectively. Because they are sometimes used to identify vocal function, it is a good idea to know the names of the muscles that control the length of the folds. We've already mentioned that

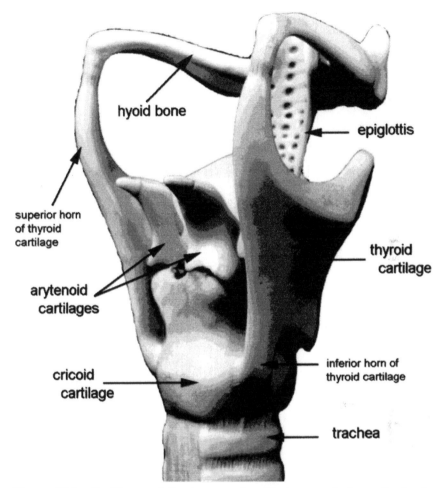

Figure 10.5. Cartilages of the larynx, viewed at an angle from the back. *Courtesy of Scott McCoy.*

a muscle forms the core of each fold. Because it runs between the thyroid cartilage and an arytenoid, it is named the thyroarytenoid muscle (formerly known as the vocalis muscle). When the thyroarytenoid, or TA muscle, contracts, the fold is shortened and pitch goes down. The folds are elongated through the action of the cricothyroid, or CT muscles, which run from the thyroid to cricoid cartilage.

Vocal color (timbre) is created by the combined effects of the sound produced by the vocal folds and the resonance provided by the vocal tract. While these elements can never be completely separated, it is useful to consider the two primary modes of vocal fold vibration and their resulting sound qualities. The main differences are related to the relative thickness of the folds and their cross-sectional shape (figure 10.6). The first option depends on short, thick folds that come together with nearly square-shaped edges. Vibration in this configuration is given a variety of names, including mode 1, thyroarytenoid (TA) dominant, chest mode, or modal voice. The alternate configuration uses longer, thinner folds that only make contact at their upper margins. Common names include mode 2, cricothyroid (CT) dominant, falsetto mode, or loft voice. Singers vary the vibrational mode of the folds according to the quality of sound they wish to produce.

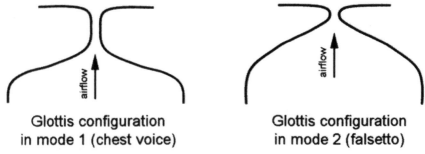

Glottis configuration
in mode 1 (chest voice)

Glottis configuration
in mode 2 (falsetto)

Figure 10.6. Primary modes of vocal fold vibration. *Courtesy of Scott Mc-Coy.*

Before we move on to a discussion of resonance, we must consider the quality of the sound that is produced by the larynx. At the level of the glottis, we create a sound not unlike the annoying buzz of a duck call. That buzz, however, contains all the raw material we need to create speech and singing. Vocal or glottal sound is considered to be complex, meaning it consists of many simultaneously sounding frequencies (pitches). The lowest frequency within any tone is called the fundamental, which corresponds to its named pitch in the musical scale. Orchestras tune to a pitch called A-440, which means it has a frequency of 440 vibrations per second, or 440 hertz (abbreviated Hz). Additional frequencies are included above the fundamental, which are called overtones. Overtones in the glottal sound are quieter than the fundamental.

In voices, the overtones usually are whole number multiples of the fundamental, creating a pattern called the harmonic series (e.g., 100 Hz, 200 Hz, 300 Hz, 400 Hz, 500 Hz, etc., or G2, G3, D4, G4, B4—note that pitches are named by the international system in which the lowest C of the piano keyboard is C1; middle-C therefore becomes C4, the fourth C of the keyboard) (figure 10.7).

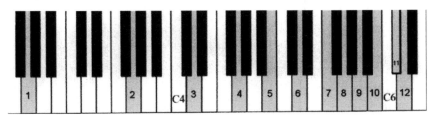

Figure 10.7. Natural harmonic series, beginning at G2. *Courtesy of Scott McCoy.*

Singers who choose to make coarse or rough sounds as might be appropriate for rock or blues often add overtones that are inharmonic or not part of the standard numerical sequence. Inharmonic overtones also are common in singers with damaged or pathological voices.

Under most circumstances, we are completely unaware of the presence of overtones—they simply contribute to the overall timbre of a voice. In some vocal styles, however, harmonics become a dominant feature. This is especially true in throat singing or overtone singing, as is found in places like Tuva. Throat singers tune their vocal tracts so precisely that single harmonics are highlighted within the harmonic spectrum as a separate, whistle-like tone. These singers sustain a low-pitched drone and then create a melody by moving from tone to tone within the natural harmonic series. You can learn to do this too. Sustain a comfortable pitch in your range and slowly morph between the vowels /i/ and /u/. If you listen carefully, you will hear individual harmonics pop out of your sound.

The mode of vocal fold vibration has a strong impact on the overtones that are produced. In mode 1, high-frequency harmonics are relatively strong; in mode 2, they are much weaker. As a result, mode 1 tends to yield a much brighter, brassier sound.

VOCAL TRACT: YOUR SOURCE OF RESONANCE

Resonance is typically defined as the amplification and enhancement (or enrichment) of musical sound through supplemental vibration. What does this really mean? In layman's terms, we could say that resonance makes instruments louder and more beautiful by reinforcing the original vibrations of the sound source. This enhancement occurs in two primary ways, which are known as forced and free resonance (there is nothing pejorative in these terms: free resonance is not superior to forced resonance). Any object that is physically connected to a vibrator can serve as a forced resonator. For a piano, the resonator is the soundboard (on the underside of a grand or on the back of an upright); the vibrations of the strings are transmitted directly to the soundboard through a structure known as the bridge, which also is found on violins and guitars. Forced resonance also plays a role in voice production. Place your hand on your chest and say /a/ at a low pitch. You almost certainly felt the vibrations of forced resonance. In singing, this might best be considered your private resonance; you can feel it and it might affect your self-perception of sound, but nobody else can hear it. To understand why this is true, imagine what a violin would sound like if it were encased in a thick layer of foam rubber. The vibrations of the string would be damped out, muting the instrument. Your skin, muscles, and other tissues do the same thing to the vibrations of your vocal folds.

By contrast, free resonance occurs when sound travels through a hollow space, such as the inside of a trumpet, an organ pipe, or your vocal tract, which consists of the pharynx (throat), oral cavity (mouth), and nasal cavity (nose). As sound travels through these regions, a complex pattern of echoes is created; every time sound encounters a change in the shape of the vocal tract, some of its energy is reflected backward, much like an echo in a canyon. If these echoes arrive back at the glottis at the precise moment a new pulse of sound is created, the two elements synchronize, resulting in a significant increase in intensity. All of this happens very quickly—remember that sound is traveling through your vocal tract at more than seven hundred miles per hour.

Whenever this synchronization of the vocal tract and sound source occurs, we say that the system is in resonance. The phenomenon occurs at specific frequencies (pitches), which can be varied by changing the position of the tongue, lips, jaw, palate, and larynx. These resonant frequencies, or areas in which strong amplification occurs, are called formants. Formants provide the specific amplification that changes the raw, buzzing sound produced by your vocal folds into speech and singing. The vocal tract is capable of producing many formants, which are labeled sequentially by ascending pitch. The first two, F1 and F2, are used to create vowels; higher formants contribute to the overall timbre and individual characteristics of a voice. In some singers, especially those who train to sing in opera, formants three through five are clustered together to form a super formant, eponymously called the singer's formant, which creates a ringing sound and enables a voice to be heard in a large theater without electronic amplification.

Formants are vitally important in singing, but they can be a bit intimidating to understand. An analogy that works really well for me is to think of formants like the wind. You cannot see the wind, but you know it is present when you see leaves rustling in a tree or feel a breeze on your face. Formants work in the same manner. They are completely invisible and directly inaudible. But just as we see the rustling leaf, we can hear, and perhaps even feel, the action of formants through how they change our sound. Try a little experiment. Sing an ascending scale beginning at B♭3, sustaining the vowel /i/. As you approach the D♯ or E♭ of the scale, you will likely feel (and hear) that your sound becomes a bit stronger and easier to produce. This occurs because the scale tone and formant are on the same pitch, providing additional amplification. If you change to an /u/ vowel, you will feel the same thing at about the same place in the scale. If you sing to an /o/ or /e/ and continue up the scale, you'll feel a bloom in the sound somewhere around C5 (an octave above middle C); /a/ is likely to come into its best focus at about G5.

To remember the approximate pitches of the first formants for the main vowels, /i–e–a–o–u/, just think of a C-major triad in first inversion, open position, starting at E4: /i/ = E4, /e/ = C5, /a/ = G5, /o/ = C5, and /u/ = E4 (figure 10.8). If your music theory isn't strong, you could use the mnemonic "every child gets candy eagerly." These pitches might vary by as much as a minor third higher and lower but no farther; once a formant changes by more than that interval, the vowel that is produced must change.

Formants have absolutely no preference for what they amplify—they are indiscriminate lovers, just as happy to bond with the first harmonic

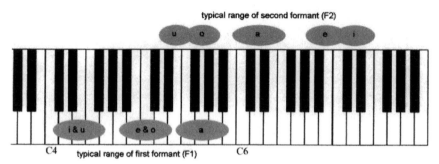

Figure 10.8. Typical range of first and second formants for primary vowels. *Courtesy of Scott McCoy.*

as the fifth. When men or women sing low pitches, there will almost always be at least one harmonic that comes close enough to a formant to produce a clear vowel sound. The same is not true for women with high voices, especially sopranos, who must routinely sing pitches that have a fundamental frequency higher than the first formant of many vowels. Imagine what happens if she must sing the phrase "and I'll leave you forever," with the word "leave" set on a very high, climactic note. The audience won't be able to tell if she is singing "leave" or "love"; the two will sound identical. This happens because the formant that is required to identify the vowel /i/ is too far below the pitch being sung. Even if she tries to sing "leave," the sound that comes out of her mouth will be heard as some variation of /a/.

Fortunately, this kind of mismatch between formants and musical pitches rarely causes problems for anyone but opera singers, choir sopranos, and perhaps ingenues in classic music theater shows. Almost everyone else generally sings low enough in their respective voice ranges to produce easily identifiable vowels.

Second formants can also be important, but more so for opera singers than everyone else. They are much higher in pitch, tracking the pattern /u/ = E5, /o/ = G5, /a/ = D6, /e/ = B6, /i/ = D7 (you can use the mnemonic "every good dad buys diapers" to remember these pitches) (figure 10.8). Because they can extend so high, into the top octave of the piano keyboard for /i/, they interact primarily with higher tones in the natural harmonic series. Unless you are striving to produce the loudest unamplified sound possible, you probably never need to worry about the second formant; it will steadfastly do its job of helping to produce vowel sounds without any conscious thought or manipulation on your part.

If you are interested in discovering more about resonance and how it affects your voice, you might want to install a spectrum analyzer on your computer. Free (or inexpensive) programs are readily available for download over the internet that will work with either a PC or a Mac computer. You don't need any specialized hardware—if you can use Skype or FaceTime, you already have everything you need. Once you've installed something, simply start playing with it. Experiment with your voice to see exactly how the analysis signal changes when you change the way your voice sounds. You'll be able to see how harmonics change in intensity as they interact with your formants. If you sing with vibrato, you'll see how consistently you produce your variations in pitch and amplitude. You'll even be able to see if your tone is excessively nasal for the kind of singing you want to do. Other programs are available that will help you improve your intonation (how well you sing in tune) or enhance your basic musicianship skills. Technology has truly advanced sufficiently to help us sing more beautifully.

MOUTH, LIPS, AND TONGUE: YOUR ARTICULATORS

The articulatory life of a singer is not easy, especially when compared to the demands placed on other musicians. Like a pianist or brass player, we must be able to produce the entire spectrum of musical articulation, including dynamic levels from hushed pianissimos to thunderous fortes, short notes, long notes, accents, crescendos, diminuendos, and so on. We produce most of these articulations the same way instrumentalists do, which is by varying our power supply. But singers have another layer of articulation that makes everything much more complicated: We must produce these musical gestures while simultaneously singing words.

As we learned in our brief examination of formants, altering the resonance characteristics of the vocal tract creates the vowel sounds of language. We do this by changing the position of our tongue, jaw, lips, and sometimes palate. Slowly say the vowel pattern /i–e–a–o–u/. Can you feel how your tongue moves in your mouth? For /i/, it is high in the front and low in the back, but it takes the opposite position for /u/. Now slowly say the word "Tuesday," noting all the places your tongue comes into contact with your teeth and palate and how it changes shape as you produce the vowels and diphthongs. There is a lot going on in there—no wonder it takes so long for babies to learn to speak!

Our articulatory anatomy is extraordinarily complex, in large part because our bodies use the same passageway for food, water, air, and sound. As a result, our tongue, larynx, throat, jaw, and palate are all interconnected with common physical and neurologic points of attachment. Our anatomical Union Station in this regard is a small structure called the hyoid bone. The hyoid is one of only three bones in your entire body that do not connect to other bones via a joint (the other two are your patellae, or kneecaps). This little bone is suspended below your jaw, freely floating up and down every time your swallow. It is a busy place, serving as the upper suspension point for the larynx, the connection for the root of the tongue, and the primary location of the muscles that open your mouth by dropping your jaw.

Good singing—in any genre—requires a high degree of independence in all these articulatory structures. Unfortunately, nature conspires against us to make this difficult to accomplish. From the time we were born, our bodies have relied on a reflex reaction to elevate the palate and raise the larynx each time we swallow. This action becomes habitual: palate goes up, larynx also lifts. But depending on the style of music we are singing, we might need to keep the larynx down while the palate goes up (opera and classical) or palate down with the larynx up (country and bluegrass). As we all know, habits can be very hard to change, which is one of the reasons it can take a lot of study and practice to become an excellent singer. Understanding your body's natural reflexive habits can make some of this work a bit easier.

There is one more significant pitfall to the proximity of all these articulators: tension in one area is easily passed along to another. If your jaw muscles are too tight while you sing, that hyperactivity will likely be transferred to the larynx and tongue—remember, they all are interconnected through the hyoid bone. It can be tricky to determine the primary offender in this kind of chain reaction of tension. A tight tongue could just as easily be making your jaw stiff, or an elevated, rigid larynx could make both tongue and jaw suffer.

Neurology complicates matters even further. You have sixteen muscles in your tongue, fourteen in your larynx, twenty-two in your throat and palate, and another sixteen that control your jaw. Many of these are very small and lie directly adjacent to each other, and you are often required to contract one quite strongly while its next-door neighbor must remain totally relaxed. Our brains need to develop laser-like control, sending signals at the right moment with the right intensity to the precise spot where they are needed. When we first start singing, these brain signals come more like a blast from a shotgun, spreading the neurologic impulse over a broad area to multiple muscles, not all of which are the intended target. Again, with practice and training, we learn to refine our control, enabling us to use only those muscles that will help, while disengaging those that would get in the way of our best singing.

FINAL THOUGHTS

This brief chapter has only scratched the surface of the huge field of voice science. To learn more, you might visit the websites of the National Association of Teachers of Singing (NATS), the Voice Foundation (TVF), or the National Center for Voice and Speech (NCVS). You can easily locate the appropriate addresses through any internet search engine. Remember: knowledge is power. Occasionally, people are afraid that if they know more about the science of how they sing, they will become so analytical that all spontaneity will be lost or they will become paralyzed by too much information and thought. In my forty-plus years as a singer and teacher, I've never encountered somebody who actually suffered this fate. To the contrary, the more we know, the easier—and more joyful—singing becomes. ♪

⓫

VOCAL HEALTH FOR SINGERS

Wendy LeBorgne

GENERAL PHYSICAL WELL-BEING

All singers, regardless of genre, should consider themselves as "vocal athletes." The physical, emotional, and performance demands necessary for optimal output require that the artist consider training and maintaining their instrument as an athlete trains for an event. With increased vocal and performance demands, it is unlikely that a vocal athlete will have an entire performing career completely injury free. This may not be the fault of the singer, as many injuries occur due to circumstances beyond the singer's control such as singing through an illness or being on a new medication seemingly unrelated to the voice. ♪

Vocal injury has often been considered taboo to talk about in the performing world as it has been considered to be the result of faulty technique or poor vocal habits. In actuality, the majority of vocal injuries presenting in the elite performing population tend to be overuse or acute injury. From a clinical perspective over the past seventeen years, younger, less experienced singers with fewer years of training (who tend to be quite talented) are generally the ones who present with issues related to technique or phonotrauma (nodules, edema, contact ulcers), while more mature singers with professional performing careers tend to present with acute injuries (hemorrhage) or overuse and misuse injuries (muscle tension dysphonia, edema, GERD) or injuries following an illness. There are no current studies documenting use and training in correlation to laryngeal pathologies. However, there are studies that document that somewhere between 35 and 100 percent of professional vocal athletes have abnormal vocal fold findings on stroboscopic evaluation. Many times these "abnormalities" are in singers who have no vocal complaints or symptoms of vocal problems. From a performance perspective, uniqueness in vocal quality often gets hired, and perhaps a slight aberration in the way a given larynx functions may become quite marketable. Regardless of what the vocal folds may look like, the most integral part of performance is that the singer must maintain agility, flexibility, stamina, power, and inherent beauty (genre appropriate) for their current level of performance taking into account physical, vocal, and emotional demands.

Unlike sports medicine and the exercise physiology literature where much is known about the types and nature of given sports injuries, there is no common parallel for the vocal athlete model. However, because the vocal athlete uses the body systems of alignment, respiration, phonation, and resonance with some similarities to physical athletes, a parallel protocol for vocal wellness may be implemented/considered for vocal athletes to maximize injury prevention knowledge for both the singer and teacher. This chapter provides information on vocal wellness and injury prevention for the vocal athlete.

CONSIDERATIONS FOR WHOLE-BODY WELLNESS

Nutrition

You have no doubt heard the saying "You are what you eat." Eating is a social and psychological event. For many people, food associations and eating have an emotional basis resulting in either overeating or being malnourished. Eating disorders in performers and body image issues may have major implications and consequences for the performer on both ends of the spectrum (obesity and anorexia). Singers should be encouraged to reprogram the brain and body to consider food as fuel. You want to use high-octane gas in your engine, as pouring water in your car's gas tank won't get you very far. Eating a poor diet or a diet that lacks appropriate nutritional value will have negative physical and vocal effects on the singer. Effects of poor dietary choices for the vocal athlete may result in physical and vocal effects ranging from fatigue to life-threatening disease over the course of a lifetime. Encouraging and engaging in healthy eating habits from a young age will potentially prevent long-term negative effects from poor nutritional choices. It is beyond the scope of this chapter to provide a complete overview of all the dietary guidelines for young children, adolescents, adults, and the mature adult; however, a listing of additional references to help guide your food and beverage choices for making good nutritional decisions can be found online at websites such as Dietary Guidelines for Americans, Nutrition.gov Guidelines for Tweens and Teens, and Fruits and Veggies Matter. See the online companion web page on the National Association of Teachers of Singing (NATS) website for links to these and other resources. ♪

Hydration

"Sing wet, pee pale." This phrase was echoed in the studio of Van Lawrence regarding how his students would know if they were well hydrated. Generally, this rule of pale urine during your waking hours is a good indicator that you are well hydrated. Medications, vitamins, and certain foods may alter urine color despite adequate hydration. Due to the varying levels of physical and vocal activity of many performers, in order to maintain adequate oral hydration, the use of a hydration calculator based on activity level may be a better choice. These hydration calculators are easily accessible online and take into account the amount and level of activity the performer engages in on a daily basis. In a recent study of the vocal habits of musical theater performers, one of the findings indicated a significantly underhydrated group of performers.[1]

Laryngeal and pharyngeal dryness as well as "thick, sticky mucus" are often complaints of singers. Combating these concerns and maintaining an adequate viscosity of mucus for performance has resulted in some research. As a reminder of laryngeal and swallowing anatomy, nothing that is swallowed (or gargled) goes over or touches the vocal folds directly (or one would choke). Therefore, nothing that a singer eats or drinks ever touches the vocal folds, and in order to adequately hydrate the mucous membranes of the vocal folds, one must consume enough fluids for the body to produce a thin mucus. Therefore, any "vocal" effects from swallowed products are limited to potential pharyngeal and oral changes, not the vocal folds themselves.

The effects of systemic hydration are well documented in the literature. There is evidence to suggest that adequate hydration will provide some protection of the laryngeal mucosal membranes when they are placed under increased collision forces as well as reducing the amount of effort (phonation threshold pressure) to produce voice. This is important for the singer because it means that with adequate hydration and consistency of mucus, the effort to produce voice is less and your vocal folds are better protected from injury. Imagine the friction and heat produced when two dry hands rub together and then what happens if you put lotion on your hands. The mechanisms in the larynx to provide appropriate mucus production are not fully understood, but there is enough evidence at this time to support oral hydration as a vital component of every singer's vocal health regime to maintain appropriate mucosal viscosity.

Although very rare, overhydration (hyperhidrosis) can result in dehydration and even illness or death. An overindulgence of fluids essentially makes the kidneys work "overtime" and flushes too much water out of the body. This excessive fluid loss in a rapid manner can be detrimental to the body.

In addition to drinking water to systemically monitor hydration, there are many nonregulated products on the market for performers that lay claim to improving the laryngeal environment (e.g., Entertainer's Secret, Throat Coat, Grether's Pastilles, slippery elm). Although there may be little detriment in using these products, quantitative research documenting change in laryngeal mucosa is sparse. One study suggests that the use of Throat Coat when compared to a placebo treatment for pharyngitis did show a significant difference in decreasing the perception of sore throat.[2] Another study compared the use of Entertainer's Secret to two other nebulized agents and its effect on phonation threshold pressure (PTP).[3] There was no positive benefit in decreasing PTP with Entertainer's Secret.

Many singers use personal steam inhalers or room humidification to supplement oral hydration and aid in combating laryngeal dryness.

There are several considerations for singers who choose to use external means of adding moisture to the air they breathe. Personal steam inhalers are portable and can often be used backstage or in the hotel room for the traveling performer. Typically, water is placed in the steamer and the face is placed over the steam for inhalation. Because the mucus membranes of the larynx are composed of a saltwater solution, one study looked at the use of nebulized saline in comparison to plain water and its potential effects on effort or ease to sound production in classically trained sopranos.[4] Data suggested that perceived effort to produce voice was less in the saline group than the plain water group. This indicated that the singers who used the saltwater solution reported less effort to sing after breathing in the saltwater than singers who used plain water. The researchers hypothesized that because the body's mucus is not plain water (rather it is a saltwater—think about your tears), when you use plain water for steam inhalation, it may actually draw the salt from your own saliva, resulting in a dehydrating effect.

In addition to personal steamers, other options for air humidification come in varying sizes of humidifiers from room size to whole house humidifiers. When choosing between a warm air or cool mist humidifier, considerations include both personal preference and needs. One of the primary reasons warm mist humidifiers are not recommended for young children is due to the risk of burns from the heating element. Both the warm mist and cool air humidifiers act similarly in adding moisture to the environmental air. External air humidification may be beneficial and provide a level of comfort for many singers. Regular cleaning of the humidifier is vital to prevent bacteria and mold buildup. Also, depending on the hardness of the water, it is important to avoid mineral buildup on the device and distilled water may be recommended for some humidifiers.

For traveling performers who often stay in hotels, fly on airplanes, or are generally exposed to other dry-air environments, there are products on the market designed to help minimize drying effects. One such device is called a Humidflyer, which is a face mask designed with a filter to recycle the moisture of a person's own breath and replenish moisture on each breath cycle.

For dry nasal passages or to clear sinuses, many singers use Neti pots. Many singers use this homeopathic flushing of the nasal passages regularly. Research supports the use of a Neti pot as a part of allergy relief and chronic rhinosinusitis control when used properly, sometimes in combination with medical management.[5] Conversely, long-term use of nasal irrigation (without taking intermittent breaks from daily use) may result in washing out the "good" mucus of the nasal passages, which naturally helps to rid the nose of infections. A study presented at the 2009 American College of Allergy, Asthma, and Immunology (ACAAI) annual scientific meeting reported that when a group of individuals who were using twice-daily nasal irrigation for one year discontinued using it, they had an increase in acute rhinosinusitis.[6]

Tea, Honey, and Gargle to Keep the Throat Healthy

Regarding the use of general teas (which many singers combine with honey or lemon), there is likely no harm in the use of decaffeinated tea (caffeine may cause systemic dryness). The warmth of the tea may provide a soothing sensation to the pharynx, and the act of swallowing can be relaxing for the muscles of the throat. Honey has shown promising results as an effective cough suppressant in the pediatric population.[7] The dose of honey given to the children in the study was two teaspoons. Gargling with salt or apple cider vinegar and water are also popular home remedies for many singers with the uses being from soothing the throat to curing reflux. Gargling plain water has been shown to be efficacious in reducing the risk of contracting upper respiratory infections. I suggest that when gargling, the singer only "bubble" the water with air and avoid engaging the vocal folds in sound production. Saltwater as a gargle has long been touted as a sore throat remedy and can be traced back to 2700 BCE in China for treating gum disease. The science behind a saltwater rinse for everything from oral hygiene to sore throat is that salt (sodium chloride) may act as a natural analgesic (painkiller) and may also kill bacteria. Similar to the effects that not enough salt in the water may have on drawing the salt out of the tissue in the steam inhalation, if you oversaturate the water solution with excess salt and gargle it, it may act to draw water out of the oral mucosa, thus reducing inflammation.

Another popular home remedy reported by singers is the use of apple cider vinegar to help with everything from acid reflux to sore throats. Dating back to 3300 BCE, apple cider vinegar was reported as a medicinal remedy, and it became popular in the 1970s as a weight-loss diet cocktail. Popular media reports apple cider vinegar can improve conditions from acne and arthritis to nosebleeds and varicose veins. Specific efficacy data regarding the beneficial nature of apple cider vinegar for the purpose of sore throat, pharyngeal inflammation, and reflux has not been reported in the literature at this time. Of the peer-reviewed studies found in the literature, one discussed possible esophageal erosion and inconsistency of actual product in tablet form.[8] Therefore, at this time, strong evidence supporting the use of apple cider vinegar is not published.

Medications and the Voice

Medications (over the counter, prescription, and herbal) may have resultant drying effects on the body and often the laryngeal mucosa. General classes of drugs with potential drying effects include antidepressants, antihypertensives, diuretics, ADD/ADHD medications, some oral acne medications, hormones, allergy drugs, and vitamin C in high doses. The National Center for Voice and Speech (NCVS) provides a listing of some common medications with potential voice side effects including laryngeal dryness. This listing does not take into account all medications, so singers should always ask their pharmacist of the potential side effects of a given medication. Due to the significant number of drugs on the market, it is safe to say that most pharmacists will not be acutely aware of "vocal side effects," but if dryness is listed as a potential side effect of the drug, you may assume that all body systems could be affected. Under no circumstances should you stop taking a prescribed medication without consulting your physician first. As every person has a different body chemistry and reaction to medication, just because a medication lists dryness as a potential side effect, it does not necessarily mean you will experience that side effect. Conversely, if you begin a new medication and notice physical or vocal changes that are unexpected, you should consult with your physician. Ultimately, the goal of medical management for any condition is to achieve the most benefits with the least side effects. Please see the companion page on the NATS website for a list of possible resources for the singer regarding prescription drugs and herbs. ♪

In contrast to medications that tend to dry, there are medications formulated to increase saliva production or alter the viscosity of mucus. Medically, these drugs are often used to treat patients who have had a loss of saliva production due to surgery or radiation. Mucolytic agents are used to thin secretions as needed. As a singer, if you feel you need to use a mucolytic agent on a consistent basis, it may be worth considering getting to the root of the laryngeal dryness symptom and seeking a professional opinion from an otolaryngologist.

Reflux and the Voice

Gastroesophageal reflux disease (GERD) and laryngopharyngeal reflux (LPR) can have a devastating impact on the singer if not recognized and treated appropriately. Although GERD and LPR are related, they are considered slightly different diseases. GERD (Latin root meaning "flowing back") is the reflux of digestive enzymes, acids, and other stomach contents into the esophagus (food pipe). If this backflow is propelled through the upper esophagus and into the throat (larynx and pharynx), it is referred to as LPR. It is not uncommon to have both GERD and LPR, but they can occur independently.

More frequently, people with GERD have decreased esophageal clearing. Esophagitis, or inflammation of the esophagus, is also associated with GERD. People with GERD often feel heartburn. LPR symptoms are often "silent" and do not include heartburn. Specific symptoms of LPR may include some or all of the following: lump in the throat sensation, feeling of constant need to clear the throat/postnasal drip, longer vocal warm-up time, quicker vocal fatigue, loss of high-frequency range, worse voice in the morning, sore throat, and bitter/raw/brackish taste in the mouth. If you experience these symptoms on a regular basis, it is advised that you consider a medical consultation for your symptoms. Prolonged, untreated GERD or LPR can lead to permanent changes in both the esophagus and the larynx. Untreated LPR also provides a laryngeal environment that is conducive for vocal fold lesions to occur as it inhibits normal healing mechanisms.

Treatments of LPR and GERD generally include both dietary and lifestyle modifications in addition to medical management. Some of the dietary recommendations include elimination of caffeinated and carbonated beverages, smoking cessation, no alcohol use, and limiting tomatoes, acidic foods and drinks, and raw onions or peppers, to name a few. Also, avoidance of high-fat foods is recommended. From a lifestyle perspective, suggested changes include not eating within three hours of lying down, eating small meals frequently (instead of large meals), elevating the head of your bed, avoiding tight clothing around the belly, and not bending over or exercising too soon after you eat.

Reflux medications fall in three general categories: antacids, H2 blockers, and proton pump inhibitors (PPI). There are now combination drugs that include both an H2 blocker and a proton pump inhibitor. Every medication has both associated risks and benefits, and singers should be aware of the possible benefits and side effects of the medications they take. In general terms, antacids (e.g., Tums, Mylanta, Gaviscon) neutralize stomach acid. H2 (histamine) blockers, such as Axid (nizatidine), Tagamet (cimetidine), Pepcid (famotidine), and Zantac (ranitidine), work to decrease acid production in the stomach by preventing histamine from triggering the H2 receptors to produce more acid. Then there are the PPIs: Nexium (esomeprazole), Prevacid (lansoprazole), Protonix (pantoprazole), AcipHex (rabeprazole), Prilosec (omeprazole), and Dexilant (dexlansoprazole). PPIs act as a last line of defense to decrease acid production by blocking the last step in gastric juice secretion. Some of the most recent drugs to combat GERD/LPR are combination drugs (e.g., Zegrid [sodium bicarbonate plus omeprazole]), which provide a short-acting response (sodium bicarbonate) and a long release (omeprazole). Because some singers prefer a holistic approach to reflux management, strict dietary and lifestyle compliance is recommended and consultation with both your primary care physician and naturopath are warranted in that situation. Efficacy data on nonregulated herbs, vitamins, and supplements is limited, but some data does exist.

Physical Exercise

Vocal athletes, like other physical athletes, should consider how and what they do to maintain both cardiovascular fitness and muscular strength. In today's performance culture, it is rare that a performer stands still and sings, unless in a recital or choral setting. The range of physical activity can vary from light movement to high-intensity chore-ography with acrobatics. As performers are being required to increase their onstage physical activity level from the operatic stage to the pop-star arena, overall physical fitness is imperative to avoid compromise in the vocal system. Breathlessness will result in compensation by the larynx, which is now attempting to regulate the air. Compensatory vocal behaviors over time may result in a change in vocal performance. The health benefits of both cardiovascular training and strength training are well documented for physical athletes but relatively rare in the literature for vocal performers.

Mental Wellness

Vocal performers must maintain a mental focus during performance and a mental toughness during auditioning and training. Rarely during vocal performance training programs is this important aspect of per-formance addressed, and it is often left to the individual performer to develop their own strategy or coping mechanism. Yet, many performers are on antianxiety or antidepressant drugs (which may be the direct re-sult of performance-related issues). If the sports world is again used as a parallel for mental toughness, there are no elite-level athletes (and few junior-level athletes) who don't use the services of a performance/sports psychologist to maximize focus and performance. I recommend that performers consider the potential benefits of a performance psycholo-gist to help maximize vocal performance. Several references that may be of interest to the singer include the audio recording *Visualizations for Singers* (1992) and the classic voice pedagogy book *Power Performance for Singers: Transcending the Barriers* (1998).[9] ♪

Unlike instrumentalists, whose performance is dependent on accu-rate playing of an external musical instrument, the singer's instrument is uniquely intact and subject to the emotional confines of the brain and body in which it is housed. Music performance anxiety (MPA) can be career threatening for all musicians, but perhaps the vocal athlete is more severely affected. The majority of literature on MPA is dedicated to instrumentalists, but the basis of definition, performance effects, and treatment options can be considered for vocal athletes. Fear is a natural reaction to a stressful situation, and there is a fine line between emotional excitation and perceived threat (real or imagined). The job of a performer is to convey to an audience through vocal production, physical gestures, and facial expression a most heightened state of emotion. Otherwise, why would audience members pay top dollar to sit for two or three hours for a mundane experience? Not only is there the emotional conveyance of the performance, but also the internal turmoil often experienced by the singers themselves in preparation for elite performance. It is well documented in the literature that even the most elite performers have experienced debilitating performance anxiety. MPA is defined on a continuum with anxiety levels ranging from low to high and has been reported to comprise four distinct components: affect, cognition, behavior, and physiology. Affect comprises feelings (e.g., doom, panic, anxiety). Affected cognition will result in altered levels of concentration, while the behavior component results in postural shifts, quivering, and trembling. Finally, physiologically the body's autonomic nervous system (ANS) will activate, resulting in the "fight or flight" response.

In recent years, researchers have been able to define two distinct neurological pathways for MPA. The first pathway happens quickly and without conscious input (ANS), resulting in the same fear stimulus as if a person were put into an emergent, life-threatening situation. In those situations, the brain releases adrenaline, resulting in physical changes of increased heart rate, increased respiration, shaking, pale skin, dilated pupils, slowed digestion, bladder relaxation, dry mouth, and dry eyes, all of which severely affect vocal performance. The second pathway that has been identified results in a conscious identification of the fear/threat and a much slower physiologic response. With the second neuromotor response, the performer has a chance to recognize the fear, process how to deal with the fear, and respond accordingly.

Treatment modalities to address MPA include psycho-behavioral therapy (including biofeedback) and drug therapies. Elite physical performance athletes have been shown to benefit from visualization techniques and psychological readiness training, yet within the performing arts community, stage fright may be considered a weakness or character flaw precluding readiness for professional performance. On the contrary, vocal athletes, like physical athletes, should mentally prepare themselves for optimal competition (auditions) and performance. Learning to convey emotion without eliciting an internal emotional response by the vocal athlete may take the skill of an experienced psychologist to help change ingrained neural pathways. Ultimately, control and understanding of MPA will enhance performance and prepare the vocal athlete for the most intense performance demands without vocal compromise.

VOCAL WELLNESS: INJURY PREVENTION

In order to prevent vocal injury and understand vocal wellness in the singer, general knowledge of common causes of voice disorders is imperative. One common cause of voice disorders is vocally abusive behaviors or misuse of the voice to include phonotraumatic behaviors such as yelling, screaming, loud talking, talking over noise, throat clearing, coughing, harsh sneezing, and boisterous laughing. Chronic or less-than-optimal vocal properties such as poor breathing techniques, inappropriate phonatory habits during conversational speech (glottal fry, hard glottal attacks), inapt pitch, loudness, rate of speech, and hyperfunctional laryngeal-area muscle tone may also negatively affect vocal function. Medically related etiologies, which also have the potential to affect vocal function, range from untreated chronic allergies and sinusitis to endocrine dysfunction and hormonal imbalance. Direct trauma, such as a blow to the neck or the risk of vocal fold damage during intubation, can affect optimal performance in vocal athletes depending on the nature and extent of the trauma. Finally, external irritants ranging from cigarette smoke to reflux directly affect the laryngeal mucosa and can ultimately lead to laryngeal pathology.

Vocal hygiene education and compliance may be one of the primary essential components for maintaining the voice throughout a career. This section provides the singer with information on prevention of vocal injury. However, just like a professional sports athlete, it is unlikely that a professional vocal athlete will go through an entire career without some compromise in vocal function. This may be a common upper-respiratory infection that creates vocal fold swelling for a short time, or it may be a "vocal accident" that is career threatening. Regardless, the knowledge of how to take care of your voice is essential for any vocal athlete.

Train Like an Athlete for Vocal Longevity

Performers seek instant gratification in performance sometimes at the cost of gradual vocal building for a lifetime of healthy singing. Historically, voice pedagogues required their students to perform vocalises exclusively for up to two years before beginning any song literature. Singers gradually built their voices by ingraining appropriate muscle memory and neuromotor patterns through development of aesthetically pleasing tones, onsets, breath management, and support. There was an intensive master-apprentice relationship and rigorous vocal guidelines to maintain a place within a given studio. Time off was taken if a vocal injury ensued or careers potentially were ended, and students were asked to leave a given singing studio if their voices were unable to withstand the rigors of training. Training vocal athletes today has evolved and appears driven to create a "product" quickly, perhaps at the expense of the longevity of the singer. Pop stars emerging well before puberty are doing international concert tours, yet many young artist programs in the classical arena do not consider singers for their programs until they are in their mid- to late twenties.

Each vocal genre presents with different standards and vocal demands. Therefore, the amount and degree of vocal training are varied. Some would argue that performing extensively without adequate vocal training and development is ill advised, yet singers today are thrust onto the stage at very young ages. Dancers, instrumentalists, and physical athletes all spend many hours per day developing muscle strength, memory, and proper technique for their craft. The more advanced the artist or athlete, generally the more specific the training protocol becomes. Consideration of training vocal athletes in this same fashion is recommended. One would generally not begin a young, inexperienced singer on a Richard Wagner (1813–1883) aria without previous vocal training. Similarly, in nonclassical vocal music, there are easy, moderate, and difficult pieces to consider pending level of vocal development and training.

Basic pedagogical training of alignment, breathing, voice production, and resonance are essential building blocks for development of good voice production. Muscle memory and development of appropriate muscle patterns happen slowly over time with appropriate repetitive practice. Doing too much, too soon for any athlete (physical or vocal) will result in an increased risk for injury. When the singer is being asked to do "vocal gymnastics," they must be sure to have a solid basis of strength and stamina in the appropriate muscle groups to perform consistently with minimal risk of injury.

Vocal Fitness Program

One generally does not get out of bed first thing in the morning and try to do a split. Yet many singers go directly into a practice session or audition without proper warm-up. Think of your larynx like your knee, made up of cartilages, ligaments, and muscles. Vocal health is dependent upon appropriate warm-ups (to get things moving), drills for technique, and then cooldowns (at the end of your day). Consider vocal warm-ups a "gentle stretch." Depending on the needs of the singer, warm-ups should include physical stretching; postural alignment self-checks; breathing exercises to promote rib cage, abdominal, and back expansion; vocal stretches (glides up to stretch the vocal folds and glides down to contract the vocal folds); articulatory stretches (yawning, facial stretches); and mental warm-ups (to provide focus for the task at hand). Vocalises, in my opinion, are designed as exercises to go beyond warm-ups and prepare the body and voice for the technical and vocal challenges of the music they sing. They are varied and address the technical level and genre of the singer to maximize performance and vocal growth. Cooldowns are a part of most athletes' workouts. However, singers often do not use cooldowns (physical, mental, and vocal) at the end of a performance. A recent study looked specifically at the benefits of vocal cooldowns in singers and found that singers who used a vocal cooldown had decreased effort to produce voice the next day.[10]

Systemic hydration as a means to keep the vocal folds adequately lubricated for the amount of impact and friction that they will undergo has been previously discussed in this chapter. Compliance with adequate oral hydration recommendations is important and subsequently so is the minimization of agents that could potentially dry the membranes (e.g., caffeine, medications, dry air). The body produces approximately two quarts of mucus per day. If not adequately hydrated, the mucus tends to be thick and sticky. Poor hydration is similar to not putting enough oil in the car engine. Frankly, if the gears do not work as well, there is increased friction and heat, and the engine is not efficient.

Speak Well, Sing Well

Optimize the speaking voice using ideal frequency range, breath, intensity, rate, and resonance. Singers are generally vocally enthusiastic individuals who talk a lot and often talk loudly. During typical conversation, the average fundamental speaking frequency (times per second the vocal folds are impacting) for a male varies from 100 to 150 hertz and 180 to 230 hertz for women. Because of the delicate structure of the vocal folds and the importance of the layered microstructure vibrating efficiently and effectively to produce voice, vocal behaviors or outside factors that compromise the integrity of the vibration patterns of the vocal folds may be considered phonotrauma.

Phonotraumatic behaviors can include yelling, screaming, loud talking, harsh sneezing, and harsh laughing. Elimination of phonotraumatic behaviors is essential for good vocal health. The louder one speaks, the farther apart the vocal folds move from midline, the harder they impact, and the longer they stay closed. A tangible example would be to take your hands, move them only six inches apart, and clap as hard and as loudly as you can for ten seconds. Now, move your hands two feet apart and clap as hard, loudly, and quickly as possible for ten seconds. The farther apart your hands are, the more air you move and the louder the clap, and the skin on the hands becomes red and ultimately swollen (if you do it long enough and hard enough). This is what happens to the vocal folds with repeated impact at increased vocal intensities. The vocal folds are approximately 17 millimeters in length and vibrate at 220 times per second on A3, 440 on A4, 880 on A5, and more than 1,000 per second when singing a high C. That is a lot of impact for little muscles. Consider this fact when singing loudly or in a high tessitura for prolonged periods of time. It becomes easy to see why women are more prone than men to laryngeal impact injuries due to the frequency range of the voice alone.

In addition to the amount of cycles per second (cps) the vocal folds are impacting, singers need to be aware of their vocal intensity (volume). One should be aware of the volume of the speaking and singing voice and consider using a distance of three to five feet (about an arms-length distance) as a gauge for how loud to be in general conversation. Using cell phones and speaking on a Bluetooth device in a car generally result in greater vocal intensity than normal, and singers are advised to minimize unnecessary use of these devices.

Singers should be encouraged to take "vocal naps" during their day. A vocal nap would be a short period of time (five minutes to an hour) of complete silence. Although the vocal folds are rarely completely still (because they move when you swallow and breathe), a vocal nap minimizes impact and vibration for a short window of time. A physical nap can also be refreshing for the singer mentally and physically.

Avoid Environmental Irritants: Alcohol, Smoking, and Drugs

Arming singers with information on the actual effects of environmental irritants so they can make informed choices on engaging in exposure to these potential toxins is essential. The glamour that continues to be associated with smoking, drinking, and drugs can be tempered with the deaths of popular stars such as Amy Winehouse (1983–2011) and Cory Monteith (1982–2013) who engaged in life-ending choices. There is extensive documentation about the long-term effects of toxic and carcinogenic substances, but here are a few key facts to consider when choosing whether to partake.

Alcohol, although it does not go over the vocal folds directly, does have a systemic drying effect. Due to the acidity in alcohol, it may increase the likelihood of reflux, resulting in hoarseness and other laryngeal pathologies. Consuming alcohol generally decreases one's inhibitions, and therefore you are more likely to sing and do things that you would not typically do under the influence of alcohol.

Beyond the carcinogens in nicotine and tobacco, the heat at which a cigarette burns is well above the boiling temperature of water (water boils at 212°F; cigarettes burn at over 1400°F). No one would consider pouring a pot of boiling water on their hand, and yet the burning temperature for a cigarette results in significant heat over the oral mucosa and vocal folds. The heat alone can create a deterioration in the lining, resulting in polypoid degeneration. Obviously, cigarette smoking has been well documented as a cause for laryngeal cancer.

Marijuana and other street drugs not only are addictive but also can cause permanent mucosal lining changes depending on the drug used and the method of delivery. If you or one of your singer colleagues is experiencing a drug or alcohol problem, research or provide information and support on getting appropriate counseling and help.

SMART PRACTICE STRATEGIES FOR SKILL DEVELOPMENT AND VOICE CONSERVATION

Daily practice and drills for skill acquisition are an important part of any singer's training. However, overpracticing or inefficient practicing may be detrimental to the voice. Consider practice sessions of athletes; they may practice four to eight hours per day broken into one- to two-hour training sessions with a period of rest and recovery in between sessions. Although we cannot parallel the sports model without adequate evidence in the vocal athlete, the premise of short, intense, focused practice sessions is logical for the singer. Similar to physical exercise, it is suggested that practice sessions do not have to be all "singing." Rather, structuring sessions so that one-third of the session is spent on warm-up; one-third on vocalises, text work, rhythms, character development, and so on; and one-third on repertoire will allow the singer to function in a more efficient vocal manner. Building the amount of time per practice session—increasing duration by five minutes per week, building to sixty to ninety minutes—may be effective (e.g., week 1: twenty minutes three times per day; week 2: twenty-five minutes three times per day).

Vary the "vocal workout" during your week. For example, if you do the same physical exercise in the same way day after day with the same intensity and pattern, you will likely experience repetitive strain–type injuries. However, cross-training or varying the type and level of exercise aids in injury prevention. So when planning your practice sessions for a given week (or rehearsal process for a given role), consider varying your vocal intensity, tessitura, and exercises to maximize your training sessions, building stamina, muscle memory, and skill acquisition. For example, one day you may spend more time on learning rhythms and translation and the next day you spend thirty minutes performing coloratura exercises to prepare for a specific role. Take one day a week off from vocal training, and give your voice a break. This means not complete vocal rest (although some singers find this beneficial) but rather a day without singing and limited talking.

PRACTICE YOUR MENTAL FOCUS

Mental wellness and stress management are equally as important as vocal training for vocal athletes. Addressing any mental health issues is paramount to developing the vocal artist. This may include anything from daily mental exercises/meditation/focus to overcoming performance anxiety to more serious mental health issues/illness. Every person can benefit from improved focus and mental acuity.

ADDITIONAL VOCAL WELLNESS TIPS

When working with singers across all genres, the most common presentation in my voice clinic relates to vocal fatigue, acute vocal injury, and loss of high-frequency range. Vocal fatigue complaints are generally related to the duration of their rehearsals, recording sessions, "meet and greets," performances, vocal gymnastics, general lack of sleep, and the vocal requirements to traverse their entire range (and occasionally outside of physiological comfort range). Depending on the genre performed, singing includes a high vocal load with the associated risk of repetitive strain and increased collision force injuries. Acute vocal injuries within this population include phonotraumatic lesions (hemorrhages, vocal fold polyps, vocal fold nodules, reflux, and general vocal fold edema/erythema). Often these are not injuries related to problematic vocal technique but rather due to "vocal accidents" or overuse (due to required performance/contract demands). Virtually all singers are required to connect with the audience from a vocal and emotional standpoint. Physical performance demands may be extreme and at times highly cardiovascular and acrobatic. Both physical and vocal fitness should be foremost in the minds of any vocal performer, and these singers should be physically and vocally in shape to meet the necessary performance demands.

Advanced and professional singers must possess flexible, agile, and dynamic instruments and have appropriate stamina. Singers must have a good command of their instrument as well as exceptional underlying intention to what they are singing as it is about relaying a message, characteristic sound, and connecting with the audience. Singers must reflect the mood and intent of the composer requiring dynamic control, vocal control/power, and an emotional connection to the text.

Commercial music singers use microphones and personal amplification to their maximal capacity. If used correctly, amplification can be used to maximize vocal health by allowing the singer to produce voice in an efficient manner while the sound engineer is effectively able to mix, amplify, and add effects to the voice. Understanding both the utility and the limits of a given microphone and sound system is essential for the singer for both live and studio performances. Using an appropriate microphone can not only enhance the singer's performance but also reduce vocal load. Emotional extremes (intimacy and exultation) can be enhanced by appropriate microphone choice, placement, and acoustical mixing, thus saving the singer's voice.

Not everything a singer does is "vocally healthy," sometimes because the emotional expression may be so intense it results in vocal collision forces that are extreme. Even if the singer does not have formal vocal training, the concept of "vocal cross-training"—which can mean singing in both high and low registers with varying intensities and resonance options—before and after practice sessions and services is likely a vital component to minimizing vocal injury.

FINAL THOUGHTS

Ultimately, the singer must learn to provide the most output with the least "cost" to the system. Taking care of the physical instrument through daily physical exercise, adequate nutrition and hydration, and focused attention on performance will provide a necessary basis for vocal health during performance. Small doses of high-intensity singing (or speaking) will limit impact stress on the vocal folds. Finally, attention to the mind, body, and voice will provide the singer with an awareness when something is wrong. This awareness and knowledge of when to rest or seek help will promote vocal well-being for the singer throughout his or her career.

NOTES

1. Wendy LeBorgne et al., "Prevalence of Vocal Pathology in Incoming Freshman Musical Theatre Majors: A 10-Year Retrospective Study," Fall Voice Conference, New York, 2012.

2. Josef Brinckmann et al., "Safety and Efficacy of a Traditional Herbal Medicine (Throat Coat) in Symptomatic Temporary Relief of Pain in Patients with Acute Pharyngitis: A Multicenter, Prospective, Randomized, Double-Blinded, Placebo-Controlled Study," *Journal of Alternative and Complementary Medicine* 9, no. 2 (2003): 285–98.

3. Nelson Roy et al., "An Evaluation of the Effects of Three Laryngeal Lubricants on Phonation Threshold Pressure (PTP)," *Journal of Voice* 17, no. 3 (2003): 331–42.

4. Kristine Tanner et al., "Nebulized Isotonic Saline versus Water Following a Laryngeal Desiccation Challenge in Classically Trained Sopranos," *Journal of Speech Language and Hearing Research* 53, no. 6 (2010): 1555–66.

5. Christopher L. Brown and Scott M. Graham, "Nasal Irrigations: Good or Bad?" *Current Opinion in Otolaryngology, Head and Neck Surgery* 12, no. 1 (2004): 9–13.

6. Talal N. Nsouli, "Long-Term Use of Nasal Saline Irrigation: Harmful or Helpful?" American College of Allergy, Asthma and Immunology Annual Scientific Meeting, Abstract 32, 2009.

7. Mahmoud Norri Shadkam et al., "A Comparison of the Effect of Honey, Dextromethorphan, and Diphenhydramine on Nightly Cough and Sleep Quality in Children and Their Parents," *Journal of Alternative and Complementary Medicine* 16, no. 7 (2010): 787–93.

8. Laura L. Hill et al., "Esophageal Injury by Apple Cider Vinegar Tablets and Subsequent Evaluation of Products," *Journal of the American Dietetic Association* 105, no. 7 (2005): 1141–44.

9. Joanna Cazden, *Visualizations for Singers* (Burbank, CA: Voice of Your Life, 1992); Shirlee Emmons and Alma Thomas, *Power Performance for Singers: Transcending the Barriers* (New York: Oxford University Press, 1998).

10. Renee Gottliebson, "The Efficacy of Cool-Down Exercises in the Practice Regimen of Elite Singers" (PhD diss., University of Cincinnati, 2011).

THE CRAFT OF CABARET

12

CRAFTING YOUR SHOW

The art of cabaret is much more than simply picking a few tunes and "doing a show." There is a step-by-step process, as well as many other factors that need to be considered when creating an authentic cabaret show. This chapter walks you through the process of crafting your cabaret show, covering essential topics such as concept/theme, team building, song selection and placement, and connective patter writing, the entire process of "putting it together" in a cohesive way. The chapter concludes with the basics of microphone technique.

FIRST STEPS: CONCEPT, SONGS, AND PATTER

Before you can begin to think about producing a show, you must first carefully consider what kind of show you would like to create. What is the concept of your show? What is it that you want to say, and how do you want to say it? Once this is established, then you are ready to choose songs. Your song list will evolve as the process unfolds, and songs on the list will come and go. You will also need to have several extra songs in mind that could be included, or substituted, as you advance your concept. Then you are ready to begin writing a connective script, called "patter." Your connective script should read like a book, meaning that every song lyric and line of patter must move your story/concept ahead, regardless of the musical content within the songs. The lyrics must remain your primary focus. If every lyric of every song and all connective patter unite to tell a cohesive story, then you are on the right track.

DIFFERENT TYPES OF SHOWS

Once you have developed a concept, selected a few songs, and written some connective patter, it is then time to decide what kind of show you will do. In cabaret, there are really no rules. You are free to create any type of show your artistic impulse envisions. Over time, however, certain types of shows have emerged as "tried and true." If you go to see a show, chances are it will fall into one of these major categories. In addition to considering one of these types of shows, you may also create a hybrid. You can also create something completely new. But your choice must always represent your true, authentic self.

Theme Shows

The theme show is centered on a specific topic that is not only personal to you but also universally relatable to a larger audience. This can include topics such as follows:

- Your job (past jobs): What crazy jobs did you have while you were in school? A singer who had previously been a dog walker did a show called *The Dog Walking Diva* about the lessons she learned from the dogs.
- Dating/love life: A wealth of material, both heartfelt and comic, is available on this subject.
- Married life or family life: The good, the bad, the ugly, and the funny.
- Politics: Political shows can be tricky. You run the risk of alienating a certain percentage of your audience. Nevertheless, they are frequently done.

- Second chances: This can be about re-creating yourself, returning to the stage after raising children, or leaving your day job to pursue your dream.

These are just a few of dozens of possible themes. A good place to start is by asking yourself what kind of theme show you would be interested in seeing, and then let your imagination wander. When creating a theme show, also think about where it could be booked. For example, if your show is animal related, perhaps you could contact a dog shelter or adoption agency and offer to do a benefit for them. Is it about cooking or food? Perhaps there is a restaurant in your area that would be willing to sponsor a dinner-show evening. As will be covered in another chapter, you are your own producer (chapter 17). Think about your marketing options from the beginning.

Personal Story Shows

A personal story show will place the focus on you and your life. You might choose to talk about how (or why) you became a singer, delve into a specific portion of your life, or reveal a personal struggle that you overcame. An autobiographical show, however, needs to be presented in such a way that it is also universally relatable to your audience. For example, we can all relate to the trials and tribulations of newfound (or lost) love, experiencing a health scare, or facing age-related issues in your peer group. Many personal story shows are tales of overcoming challenges and persevering in the face of adversity. Just remember that your show should enlighten your audience and make *them* feel better. Ultimately, it's not about you. It's about how you relate your story to the *audience*. There must, however, be a "generic" aspect to how you write and present it. It's not a therapy session—it cannot be solely about you. Instead, your show must have the common denominator of a human experience to which your audience can relate.

Composer/Lyricist Shows

This type of show is self-explanatory—Cole Porter, the Gershwins, Irving Berlin, Harold Arlen, the Beatles, Johnny Mercer, Fats Waller,

Alan and Marilyn Bergman, Noël Coward, Carole King, Tom Waits, Rodgers and Hart, Rodgers and Hammerstein . . . the list goes on. When you do a composer/lyricist show, there are literally thousands of options. However, these shows need a personal point of view as well. Was he or she your grandparents' favorite lyricist? Did you see *Kiss Me Kate* and fall in love with Cole Porter? Was Carole King's *Tapestry* the music of your teens? What did those songs mean to you at that age? When doing a composer/lyricist show, you must thoroughly research your subject. Audiences enjoy hearing anecdotal tidbits or things about a composer or lyricist that are less well known. Educate your audience with information that intrigued or meant something to you when you discovered it for the first time. In cabaret, all your choices should mean something to you.

Artist Tribute Shows

Again, for artist tribute shows—such as the Carpenters, Peggy Lee, Sophie Tucker, Liberace, Frank Sinatra, Bette Midler, Bobbie Gentry, Johnny Mathis, Ella Fitzgerald, Sammy Davis Jr., the Rat Pack, Cher, and Reba McEntire—the list goes on and on. Again, do your research to see what's been done—or is currently being done—in your area. Also, as mentioned earlier, let your audience know the reasons this artist is important to you or speaks to you. This is a crucial. It's not just about their music or their body of work—it's about *how* and *why* you chose to interpret this music.

Both composer/lyricist and artist tribute shows can be profitable ventures. Whenever there is an educational aspect to your work, these shows have the potential to be booked in libraries, senior facilities, and schools. For example, you can pitch an Irving Berlin show on his birthday, a Dorothy Fields show during Women's History Month, or a Celtic show on St. Patrick's Day. One of the most popular shows in New York (at time of publication) is an ongoing monthly tribute series at Birdland, produced and presented by multi-MAC (Manhattan Association of Cabarets) award winner Natalie Douglas.[1] Her shows are personal and informative. They pay tribute to the artist being honored, but she never tries to impersonate them. Again, it must be authentic to *you*.

Broadway or Legit Singing Shows

Are you a theater or legit-voiced singer? Play to your strengths and think outside of the box. You could do a show about

- *Songs I'll Never Get to Sing*: Why? Are they against your type? Are you an ingenue who longs to do the funny second-banana songs? Are you a character man who wants to sing leading roles? This is the beauty of cabaret. There is no "type." You can sing whatever you want to sing!
- *Broadway Backwards*: This is a show performed in New York every year by Broadway stars in which the girls sing the boy's songs and the boys sing the girl's songs.
- "Sweet Little Follies on a Seesaw in the City of Angels": Create your own mini-musical using songs from different Broadway shows.
- *Puccini to Porter*: Do you have opera chops? Show them off! Do a mixed bag of songs from the opera world alongside your favorite American Songbook composers. Remember to show a relationship between the two worlds and what both worlds mean to you.

It is very important to remember that your interpretation of these songs must remain personal. You must not perform them within the context of the show from which they originate. Broadway and legit cabaret shows can be captivating, but only if *your* interpretations take the audience to new and unexpected places. Your audience wants to hear these songs as if for the first time.

These are only a few of the many kinds of shows one can perform in a cabaret venue. For the purposes of this book, only the more solo singer-oriented shows have been listed. However, cabaret clubs have played host to other types of shows including

- musical comedy and comedic shows;
- recurring series/interview shows;
- drag/impersonation shows (including live singing);
- group or benefit shows; and
- jazz, nightclub, and saloon sets.

Now you have developed a concept, chosen a few songs, written some connective patter, and know what type of show you want to do. Now it's time to . . .

BUILD YOUR TEAM

Your next order of business will be building your team. In cabaret we define the word "team" as your musical director, director, band members, and, depending upon how involved they are in the total production of your show, the technical director. These are the people you've hired, presumably because you have done your research and believe they can bring what you need to the table. These are people you should trust. These are also the only people you should listen to before and after your show—not your friends, not your voice teacher, and not your adoring spouse or your Aunt Mary. Your team will be the best barometer of your work, the process, and your progress. When you get a review, it will be your team with whom you'll discuss what you agree or disagree with in order to grow. And if you hire them—and yes, you are hiring them—with the expectation and understanding that they will be honest with you, then certainly you will grow in this art form.

Do you have a music director or a director already picked out? If not, start by seeing as many shows as you can or by taking a class in cabaret performance. Many directors are also teachers in this field. Sitting in on a class or two can be an important part of your research. If you can, go to see other cabaret shows in your area. Analyze which shows you've really enjoyed, and ask yourself why you enjoyed them. What did you notice about the musical director and their musical arrangements, musicality, and demeanor onstage? Does their style fit your concept? Are they having fun with the singer onstage, collaborating in the process, or does it appear as if they are simply "paid to play"? Use the same process for your director. If you liked the flow of a show, its patter, and the staging of the songs, make a note of who directed the show. Once you have compiled a list, you should narrow it down to three musical directors and three directors to interview as possible members of your team. If you're still not sure where to find a musical director or director, the website CabaretHotspot.com offers a list of professionals who work in this industry, including teachers, music directors, directors, photographers, and other types of consultants. ♪

PUTTING IT TOGETHER

Once you have decided the kind of show you would like to do and you have picked your team, you will begin building your show. Most shows have thirteen to sixteen songs, and there are many possibilities for the order of songs. Your musical director and director can also help you and should be encouraged to offer suggestions. The following are a few guidelines for "putting it together."

- Open with two or three up-tempo songs to excite your audience.
- Consider making your first couple of tunes a "welcome" to the audience. Or do a song relevant to the show's theme. For example, if your theme is animals, then you might open with "If I Could Talk to the Animals."
- A 9:5 ratio of up- or medium-tempo songs to ballads is also recommended. This allows the ballads to stand out. This is not a rule, just a personal preference of the authors based on professional experience.
- If you are singing an original song, one that you've written or is unknown to the audience, this can be a harder sell. Be sure to place these originals between more familiar songs. This order allows your audience to relax into a tune they are more familiar with and be better prepared to hear another unknown lyric.
- Try to cluster tunes that go together to make mini "arcs" so you won't need to talk as much.
- An "eleven o'clock number" is usually a big tune or a tune that brings the theme of the show full circle. This song should be positioned toward the end of the show.
- The last one or two tunes should be delivered with an "attitude of gratitude" toward the audience. Perform these *after* your "thank you" to the club, the band, your musical director, and the audience.
- If you do an encore, do it without apologies or excuses. You can walk offstage after your last song and return to sing an encore. Or

as you are taking your final bow, the VOG ("voice of God"—your technical director) will announce your name and as you continue to bow you can acknowledge the musical director, thank the audience for coming, and then sing your encore. This is acceptable, especially in smaller cabaret rooms where trying to navigate a graceful exit and return for an encore might be awkward. In that case, it would be better to make that journey only once, after the encore.

Song Order

As you are finalizing your song list, you'll also need to decide where you will insert patter. Place a mark between the songs that need a verbal setup. This process may very well happen organically as you are selecting your songs. You should absolutely chat after your first, second, or third number (depending on how many songs you decide to open with). Always welcome your audience no later than your third song. After your welcome, briefly talk about yourself, make a joke or two, and communicate the theme of your show. Or if there is no theme, then move directly into setting up the next song or first cluster of songs. When choosing the order of songs, analyze the lyrics and make note of which songs, when placed one after the other, seem to lyrically read in a way that tells a complete story (beginning, middle, and end). If the set is already cohesive, there may be no need to speak between these songs.

Script (Patter)

You should always write more than you need. You and your team will make edits during the rehearsal process. And if you only want to add an occasional one-liner, that's fine. You certainly don't need a paragraph of patter between each song. Be succinct and carefully choose when you will speak. Trust the lyrics of the songs to do their job. Cabaret audiences are sophisticated; they'll get it. When researching your show, look for anecdotes that jump out at you. Figure out why you want to sing these tunes or pay tribute to this composer or artist. What might your audience find interesting or amusing? If you are doing a theme show, make sure to advance your theme throughout the show so the audience knows how each song relates to the overall concept.

Other Considerations

Now that you have a song list mapped out, you need to consider the "feel" of each number as well as how the show will flow and be heard by the audience. How many ballads are in your show? How many power ballads? How many up-tempo songs? How do your songs end—with a tag, a triple tag, or no tag at all?[2] You don't want to program three songs in a row that all end with a triple tag. Be aware of these things and mix it up. This doesn't mean you should upset the order of songs or disrupt the story that your lyrics tell. Instead, change the arrangements of the songs (and their endings) if need be. The lyrics must tell a coherent story throughout the evening. That always comes first.

Some more questions you should ask yourself:

- How many funny songs (novelty pieces) or show tunes are in your show?
- How many "medium-feel" tunes are there?
- Are there any duets?
- Will you have a guest singer?
- If you are using a trio (piano, bass, and drums), are there any songs with just piano and voice. Or maybe only bass and voice?
- In which songs are the musicians given solos?
- Is there a stylistic mix within the show? Are there any Latin, jazz, waltz, or blues songs in your show?

Look at your song list and note the musical "feel" of each song. Also note any solos and how each song begins and ends. If you have a few songs that start *colla voce* (voice ad lib) and build in tempo, and, like the ballads, spread these songs over the course of the evening. Add an element of surprise when you can. For example, try a comic setup followed by a sad song, or vice versa: set up a number as dark or sad and then do an up-tempo or comic song!

Ask yourself why you need, or want, to sing these songs. Are there personal stories attached to them? The audience wants to hear those stories. But again, tie them into a universal message, relatable to everyone in the room.

Do you have an idea and script but no music? Write the script first and then look for songs that tell your story. Or conversely, look at your

SONG ORDER WORKSHEET

NOTE: The following order and patter placement are suggestions, not rules. You may chat <u>wherever</u> you wish, and should when it is needed to keep the story of the show moving. But be careful not to chat too much. As mentioned, try to cluster a few tunes to create a mini arc and then bring the show full circle by bringing the overall concept to a natural conclusion.

Title of Show_____	Intro/Outro	Feel/Type	Solos
1. _____ (up-tempo, welcome, or theme)	_____	_____	_____
2. _____ (2nd up-tempo or medium-tempo)	_____	_____	_____

"Welcome" patter, followed by a brief introduction of the show's premise, followed by set-up patter for a cluster of tunes.

3. _____ (ballad?)	_____	_____	_____
4. _____	_____	_____	_____
5. _____	_____	_____	_____

Possible insert of patter.

6. _____	_____	_____	_____
7. _____	_____	_____	_____
8. _____	_____	_____	_____

Possible insert of patter.

9. _____	_____	_____	_____
10. _____	_____	_____	_____

Possible insert of patter.

11. _____	_____	_____	_____
12. _____ (eleven o'clock #?)	_____	_____	_____

Acknowledgments and/or last patter.

13. _____ (closer and/or gratitude)	_____	_____	_____

Possible encore.

14. _____	_____	_____	_____

Figure 12.1. Song order worksheet. *Courtesy of the authors.*

pile of tunes and see if there is a theme or story that emerges from them and then start writing. There are no rules to art!

In sum, the structure of the show that you design (with or without a director) can take many different shapes. In order to help you make decisions as you plan your show, the following serves as a song order template. A PDF version of this template can also be downloaded in the online resource page on the NATS website. ♪

MICROPHONE TECHNIQUE

A very practical aspect of the craft of cabaret is microphone technique.[3] This is the "what to do and when to do it" of working with a microphone. Proper mic technique translates to your audience as confidence in your ability, preparedness, and respect for the art form. Conversely, a lack of proper mic technique can make the performer appear less confident or unprepared and leave your audience feeling nervous.

When using a mic, the top of the mic should be just under your chin and should not cover your face or your mouth. Your audience needs to see your mouth and lips as part of the communicative expression of your face. Whether handheld or in the stand, the mic should be about five inches away from the mouth. Without a ruler you can gauge the proper distance between your lips and the mic by placing the thumb of your hand on your chin with your hand outstretched. The mic should be placed at the distance of your pinky. Allowing for type and quality of microphone being used, this is generally the farthest distance the mic should be from the mouth to achieve a good balance between the direct source signal and room-reflected sound. And most important, *do not hold on to the microphone while it is in the mic stand, and do not hold the mic stand itself*. You want to take your audience into the world of your imagination. The minute you hold the mic stand, you lock the audience into the world of the club. In their minds, the mic and the stand will disappear if you don't call attention to them.

If you cannot hear yourself on the monitor, it is vital to ask your technical director to correct this, preferably at your tech rehearsal by simply (while singing) pointing to the monitor, then to your mouth, and raising your flat hand up. This will indicate "more voice in the monitor please."

You should also establish a private "in performance" signal beforehand such as lifting two or three fingers off the microphone or lightly touching your ear. This will signal to your technical director that you cannot hear yourself in the monitor. This direction may seem counterintuitive to performers who may never want to "break character" while singing. Remember, however, that in cabaret *you* are the character, and there is no fourth wall. If the technical issue cannot wait until the end of the song to be addressed (obviously the better option), you can certainly privately signal the tech director. He or she will be looking closely at you and will understand.

If you are holding the mic for your song, *always* lower the stick, and move the mic stand away from where you are singing (behind you). There are few things more distracting than a singer holding a mic and singing with the empty mic stand directly in front of them. Why hold the mic at all if you're going to keep the stand in front of you? The great cabaret artist Marilyn Maye uses and teaches a specific technique for this: gripping the mic stand with an underhand grip (thumb down), which allows the singer to move the mic without "cracking" their elbow, thereby creating an elegant line of the arm as you move the mic out of the way.

Most of the newer mic stands have a squeeze mechanism. You squeeze the handle to lower or rise—very simple. Another type is the "righty tighty/lefty loosey" mechanism to raise and lower the stand. In this case, be sure to adjust the height before you remove the mic.

Do *not* hold the mic cord while holding the mic. It's ultimately distracting, and more important, it translates to the audience as nerves. Rehearse holding the mic while singing and be sure to move about with it. As you move you may have to adjust the cord to your location. Touching the cord in this instance is perfectly acceptable. But once you are stationary, let it go. This kind of "chord-ography" may be daunting at first, but with practice it will become second nature and something you don't have to think about while performing.

FINAL THOUGHTS

Crafting a cabaret show is a multilayered endeavor. It's not just a matter of picking a few songs to sing. It is also vastly different than a classical recital, a jazz set, or another type of concert. Hopefully this chapter has given you some practical guidelines for how to proceed. It may seem intimidating and rather overwhelming, but with the right team the process can be personally revealing, artistically fulfilling, and, most important, lots of fun!

NOTES

1. See Natalie Douglas's interview in chapter 23.

2. "Tag" and "triple tag" refer to the practice of repeating the ultimate or penultimate phrase (or part of the phrase) of music, sometimes with a key change, for emphasis of the lyric and or musical ending. A tag repeats the phrase once, whereas a triple tag repeats the phrase three times.

3. In chapter 14, Matt Edwards discusses the technical aspects of how a microphone works and how the voice works best when being amplified. As a precursor to his chapter, we offer some basic instruction on microphone technique.

13

LYRIC CONNECTION

Lyric connection—the ability to interpret and personalize the lyric of a song, devoid of other character needs or artifice—is perhaps, more than any other aspect of performance, the hallmark of a great cabaret artist. This chapter will offer several examples of how one might connect to a lyric. Each of these techniques can be used to help you discover what the song means to *you* personally. Your director may also guide you to different techniques for lyric connection. You can never have too many. Remember, cabaret is primarily a personal and lyric-driven experience. This is the work that separates the novice from the professional.

OWN THE LYRIC

When you speak in real life, you "own" everything you say. Within each breath you take and for each thought that you have, you decide how to communicate, what inflections of voice to use, where to pause for emphasis, and what volume to use to best make your point and get what you want. This is a naturally occurring phenomenon that happens instantaneously and goes unnoticed. It is simply the way we communicate. As people who are out in the world and talking with others, we are always striving to make our point and achieve our goals. Similarly, when you communicate through song, you must remember that these same principles exist. You are still communicating with people, just as you are in speech, striving to make your point and achieve your goals. To do that you must "own" the lyric as much as you "own" everything else you say. The difference is that you did not create the lyric. You have not thought it up out of a circumstance of need. Rather, you have read it on a page. Therefore, you have come to the lyric much differently than if you had created it yourself.

As a singer, you must strive to be a creative artist, not a re-creative artist. Therefore, it is important to own each lyric. One way to do this is by deconstructing the text. Analyze the grammar and punctuation of the lyric. Write the text, margin to margin, as a monologue (not as poetry). Notice where the music editor has placed capitalizations and punctuations, and what type of punctuation has been used. In some cases, capitalization and punctuation will be placed to honor the form of poetry and not necessarily the spoken sentence. It is important to notate where and how *you* interpret the structure of the sentence. If, in your interpretation, you feel the sentence needs a comma and there is none, put one in. If there is an errant capital letter confusing your interpretation, take it out. Write out the text as you would a letter to a friend, placing punctuation and emphasis where *you* speak in the natural cadence of language.

During this process you should also note the grammatical structure of the lyric. (Oh no, it's English class all over again!) Where are the nouns, pronouns, adjectives, verbs, adverbs, and so forth? What or who is the subject of the sentence? These are often the important "keywords." There may be a high note on the word "of," but is that really the critical word in the sentence? (Hint: The preposition is *never* the critical word in a sentence.) So, no matter how high that note may be, it's probably not going to be very loud. And it's certainly not going to be louder than any of the other words around it.

There are also context clues to consider within the lyric. Even if you don't read music, the *lyric* will inform your phrasing. Certain words have inherent color and dynamic. Be mindful of the imagery created by the text and its implicit dynamic phrasing. No one in the history of vocal music has ever shouted the word "moonlight."

Last, note where there are musical rests in the phrasing of the lyric. These rests may in fact be important clues as to the composer's intent.

Or they could just as easily be place-markers, which allow the math of each measure to add up correctly. Musical notation is a mathematical attempt to convey an artistic concept. Music does not happen on the page. It happens in imagination. It happens in the air. The point being, it *happens* first, and *then* it gets written down. And in that writing process a lot can be left out, especially in music that is many decades old and has inherent within it a common performance practice.

Common performance practices are musical gestures or technical elements that are expected within the genre but not necessarily written down. Classical music has common performance practices that include the use of ornamentation and embellishments. Jazz has many common performance practices, including harmonic and rhythmic variance. In this same way, American popular song has very specific common performance practices, including the lack (or delay) of vibrato, the requirement of a "speechlike" mix within the singing voice, and above all, the absolute necessity for the cadence of language to guide the rhythmic delivery. In other words, not all notes are created equal. A string of notes of equal value will be stressed (held or shortened) as appropriate to the emphasis of the syllable within the cadence of language. If this common performance practice were not observed—and the composer had to accurately notate the cadence of language—the vocal line would be filled with double- or triple-dotted rhythms. It would, in fact, be so intricately rhythmed that it would intimidate even the most accomplished musician. The answer then is to write out even notes (usually quarter notes or eighth notes) and rely upon the common performance practice of a cadence of language lyric delivery.

Ownership of the lyric through analysis of grammar, punctuation, inherent imagery within the text, and the observance of the cadence of language will greatly inform your interpretation and personalization of the song.

SUBTEXT (LYRIC PERSONALIZATION)

Subtext (subconscious text) refers to the thoughts you are thinking while you are speaking. For example, a simple phrase like "thank you" can be said in an almost infinite number of ways depending on how you feel about the circumstance and to whom you are talking. It can be said with tears in your eyes or as a genuine expression of love and gratitude. Or it could just as easily be muttered under your breath, sarcastically, to dismiss the person or change the subject. Subtext, therefore, colors the spoken text with emotion and relevance. We do it "subconsciously" and constantly. There is always a thought behind what we are saying— a motivation, if you will. And often the spoken text and subtext do not match. The subtext supports the spoken text in the given circumstance, but they do not exactly match.

This technique of analyzing the thought behind the word or action is a common practice among all vocal performing arts disciplines. And if you are reading this book, chances are you may already understand this technique and its importance. While there may be a deeper understanding and explanation of subtext found in many books on the subject of acting, this technique is so important to the cabaret artist that it bears addressing.

The cabaret artist uses subtext to personalize the lyric of a song. And while the lyrics themselves are not changed, the personalization of the lyric (the use of subtext) can completely change the singer's interpretation. In music theater, the subtext would be considered from the point of view of the character. But in cabaret, the point of view *must be yours*, personalized and in no way informed by an external character's needs. The "golden moment" in acting, singing, or any performing arts discipline is when your personalization of the text and your character's needs seem to so closely match that they become indistinguishable.

THE FIVE Ws

Within the lyric personalization, the "five Ws"—who, what, why, where, and when—must be defined. These are as follows:

1. *Who* are you talking to? Who in your *real life* can you say these words to (past or present) and they would make sense? Be very specific, with the name of an actual person in your life. In the case of a soliloquy, where you are talking to yourself, you are in fact seeking counsel from a "part" of yourself, an "archetype" (e.g., inner

warrior, god/goddess, sage, child). How you speak to your inner warrior will be very different from how you speak to your inner child. Always make a clear choice.

2. *What* do you want from them? Defining your objective is essential to your communication of the lyric. Your *what* will be specific to your *who* and can therefore change your interpretation of the song dramatically. Sometimes you may not achieve your objective within the song. That happens often. However, whenever you do achieve your objective, the song must end. Be sure to pick one that can sustain the entire song.

3. *Why* don't they give it to you right away? This is your obstacle, the conflict within the song. Storytelling requires conflict, the overcoming of an obstacle or at least the attempt. The definition of your *why* will also inform your "actions" within the song. In many cases you will not achieve your objective within the song, but you must never stop trying.

4. *Where* are you? On a beach, in a restaurant, or in your home? Be very specific. The circumstance of your setting will have ramifications for your use of voice.

5. *When* is this conversation taking place? At 2:00 p.m. or 3:00 a.m.? Again, this will make a difference in both your lyric delivery and your vocal production.

These "five Ws" must be considered from *your* perspective, devoid of any other character's needs, and will help to establish your personal point of view within each song.

THE ACTIONS

Once the five Ws have been established, you then need to place "actions" on each sentence. The "action" is stated as a one-word verb. It is what you are "doing" while you are talking. The action is not a state of being (happy, sad, etc.)—it is what you are doing *to the other person* in order to overcome the *why* and get the *what*. Are you flirting with them? Are you chastising them? Placing an action verb on each sentence (not musical phrase) within the song will keep you in a constant state of doing, rather than being, or feeling, which will help you stay grounded to the lyric in a very personal and captivating way.

Below is an example of lyric personalization using three techniques: owning the lyric, creating subtext, and using the five Ws. A more familiar theater song is intentionally used to show how you can interpret the lyric using your own story and subtext in order to personalize the song. ♪

Title: "I Dreamed a Dream"
Lyric: Herbert Kretzmer (original text by Alain Boubil and Jean-Marc Natel)
Music: Claude-Michel Schönberg
From: *Les Miserables*
Year: 1980
Who: (Who are you talking to?) My father.
What: (What do you want from them?) To get his approval to go to a performing arts school.
Why: (Why don't they give it to you right away?) He wants me to have a "real" career/security.
When: (When is it?) Early morning, before work, and your acceptance is due today (give a sense of urgency).
Where: (Where are you?) In the kitchen.
Actions: What are you *doing* to this person to overcome the *why*?

In the personalization and subtext chart in table 13.1, boldface and italics are used for ease in publication. You can choose to mark these any way you like, with color pencil, underline, circle, highlighter, and so on. Here, punctuation and subjects (nouns) are in boldface, verbs and descriptives (adjectives and adverbs) are in italics, and important words or phrases are underlined. Actions are in the left column.

The lyric has been purposefully set in a very "desperate" example of subtext with which a young student might identify. The point being that in this song—in all songs—the stakes must be high. This exercise is usually done privately and shared only with your team (as described in chapters 15 and 16), if at all. So, be as honest as possible when doing it. And when you sing, it is this subtext that will inform your performance, making it a personal experience for both you and the audience. The audience will not know exactly what you are thinking, but your specificity

Table 13.1.

Action:	Text:	Personalization/subtext:
Ease (into the conversation)	I dreamed a **dream** in **time** gone by; when **hope** was high and **life** worth living. I dreamed that **love** would never die. I dreamed that **life** would be forgiving.	Hey dad, you know, I've always wanted to be an actor/singer. That's what got me through middle/high school. I knew a better life was coming.
Remind	Then **I** was young and unafraid, and **dreams** were made and used and wasted. There was no **ransom** to be paid; no **song** unsung, no **wine** untasted.	On stage I was confident and bold. I dreamed about winning a Tony! I never wanted to do anything else. My life was filled with joy.
Challenge	But the **tigers** come at **night** with their **voices** soft as **thunder**, as they tear your **hope** apart, as they turn your **dream** to shame.	And now you want me to turn away from my dream. You threaten not to pay for college unless I choose a different career. You invalidate my life choice.
Guilt	**He** slept a **summer** by my side. **He** filled my days with endless **wonder**. **He** took my childhood in his stride, but he was gone when autumn came.	I've had a glimpse of my future, filled with doing what I love. But now you tell me, "No! That was just a childish dream."
Insist	And still I dreamed **he'd** come to me, that **we** would live the years together.	I will have this career. I am talented. I will keep singing and live the life I choose.
Demand	But there are **dreams** that cannot be, and there are **storms we** cannot weather.	I will not fulfill your dream for my life. I cannot live that way.
Invoke	**I** had a **dream** my life would be, so different from this hell **I'm living.**	I remember when I was a kid. I had a different plan, a better plan.
Plead	So different now from what **it** seemed. Now **life** has killed the **dream** I dreamed.	Please, Dad, I can't give up my dream. And I can't do this without you.

of thought will allow them to personally identify with the song in their own way. Always remember the following rule in cabaret: *tear down that fourth wall*. Speak directly to your audience with truth in your heart. The audience is your scene partner. It's the hardest thing in the world to do, but it's what defines you as a cabaret artist.

THE MOMENT BEFORE

In addition to the techniques listed above, another quick way to connect with a lyric is to create a "moment before." Ask yourself, in the scenario you are creating for the song, "What was the last thing said to me before my first words?" Although the subtext, personalization, and grammatical work referenced above are absolutely necessary for every song you sing, this type of "instant" lyric connection can help you immediately remember the scene or mood and your emotional context. Several examples are listed below. ♪

Song: "Since I Fell for You" (Lyric and Music by Buddy Johnson, 1945)

The refrain of this song begins with "You made me leave my happy home." And now, by using a "moment before"—BOOM—you're right there emotionally, be it sad, angry, or hurt.

Table 13.2.

Lyric	Moment before (right before the lyric)
"When you just give love, and never get love, you better let love depart."	"I can't believe I fell for your lies! I don't want to see you anymore!"

Song: "You Must Believe in Spring" (Lyric by Alan and Marilyn Bergman; Music by Michel Legrand, 1977)

Admittedly this is a very sad scenario, but this extremely dramatic setup is great for a song about hope. Think about it. What would motivate you to be the voice of reassurance better than something as horrific as this circumstance? The energy you bring to the song would be

Table 13.3.

Lyric	Moment before (right before the lyric)
"When lonely feelings chill the meadows of your mind, just think if winter comes, can spring be far behind?"	You just found out a friend or relative has cancer.

devastatingly honest and strong. By imagining something that is opposite and contrasting, you can get there with one line.

SINGING IN THE MOMENT

This is by far the hardest, and at the same time truest, lyric connection to make. It is a wonderful technique to use in rehearsal. It is not recommended as a first choice or for a novice. And very rarely, due to its unpredictability, can this technique be used in performance. However, as a rehearsal device, it can reveal different colors in your interpretation that enable you to "dig deep" into the lyric.

You've already done the subtext and lyric personalization work and you have decided what you believe the song means to you. Let's say, in this instance, it is a love song, but on the day that you are going to sing it you have a huge fight with your romantic partner. How does this reality affect the way you've chosen to approach the song, based on your subtext and personalization? And if that approach suddenly becomes irrelevant, what can you do? Remembering that cabaret performance requires a very personal connection to the lyric, there are several ways to channel an honest and expressive energy, allowing for a new (and maybe surprising) interpretation to emerge.

1. You can allow yourself to feel upset, but use the lyrics to convince yourself, as you are singing, why you fell in love with this person in the first place.
2. You can direct the song at the person who upset you (even if they are not there) with an attitude of, "You hurt me, and this is how I feel about you," which may translate to the audience as vulnerable, heartfelt, or passionate.
3. You can interpret the lyric as if you feel your relationship *is* breaking up, and the emotional, fearful passion you feel may translate as

the exact emotion you wanted the song to have, but from another perspective. Once again, the audience will not know exactly what you are thinking, but they *will* sense the truthful connection you have to the lyric.

Of course, if the circumstance is too overwhelming, you may simply decide to perform another song. But if you decide to get onstage and deliver that song, trusting your real emotions will be available without overwhelming you, then you are practicing the technique of "singing in the moment." This is a heightened level of singing because you do not predetermine the outcome as you would in a more traditional performance experience. You sing the song with the mood you are in and trust that new colors will be revealed.

Singing in the moment keeps you honest and real, provided that the reality of your circumstances won't impede your ability to sing the song. There is a fine line between "singing in the moment" and "needing to take a moment." But history shows us that legendary performances happen when singers allow themselves to unabashedly express what they are feeling in front of an audience. Ultimately, that's what any performance technique should do; it should allow you to be truthful within the context of a given circumstance. Most of the time the circumstance is a "given *untruthful* circumstance." But sometimes the circumstance can become unexpectedly truthful. When that happens—if your singing and acting techniques are strong and you have the courage to create—you are singing in the moment.

As mentioned earlier, the audience will not know exactly what you are thinking or feeling, nor should they. Performing is not about how *you* feel. It's about how you make the *audience* feel. This is your job as a performer. In any of these circumstances, you must reveal the truth of who you are in that exact moment, present and ready to communicate. The words will do the rest.

When singing a song that you love *as yourself*, with all that you bring to it, it feels less like *acting* and more like *sharing*. And more important, it is both real and authentic to you—and therefore to an audience. With this comes the beauty of finding new feelings while singing a song you may have sung hundreds of times before. This can only happen when you are totally in tune with how you feel and are singing in the moment.

FINAL THOUGHTS

Perhaps you've never considered diving into a lyric in this way, creating such a personal backstory and taking full ownership of the text by analyzing the grammar, punctuation, and imagery. Perhaps you were unfamiliar with the common performance practice of cadence of language lyric delivery. Maybe using "the moment before" or a "singing in the moment" technique has never occurred to you. Ultimately, the choice is up to you about how you would like to work. However, be sure to take risks during your preperformance process when it is safe to explore. Be open to all processes. Try them and then decide which ones you prefer.

If all of this seems daunting or even frightening, never fear. You are not alone. So many people believe that singing a song consists solely of learning the notes and words. As a true cabaret artist, however, you have the ability to effect real change in the hearts and minds of your audience. For that to happen, the change must happen in *you* first. Remember, all these interpretive techniques and lyric analyses evolve one song at a time over the many weeks/months of your preparation. Once you have mastered these techniques and have done the written work for ten to fifteen different songs, you will begin to see the page differently. You will make these choices more immediately, your lyric connection will grow more personal and more immediate, and your performance will therefore be more professional. Just start with one song . . . you can do it!

14

USING AUDIO ENHANCEMENT TECHNOLOGY

Matthew Edwards

In the early days of popular music, musicians performed without electronic amplification. Singers learned to project their voices in the tradition of vaudeville performers with a technique similar to operatic and operetta performers who had been singing unamplified for centuries. When microphones began appearing onstage in the 1930s, vocal performance changed forever since the loudness of a voice was no longer a factor in the success of a performer. In order to be successful, all a singer needed was an interesting vocal quality and an emotional connection to what he or she was singing. The microphone would take care of projection.[1]

Vocal qualities that sound weak without a microphone can sound strong and projected when sung with one. At the same time, a singer with a voice that is acoustically beautiful and powerful can sound harsh and pushed if he or she lacks microphone technique. Understanding how to use audio equipment to get the sounds a singer desires without harming the voice is crucial. The information in this chapter will help the reader gain a basic knowledge of terminology and equipment commonly used when amplifying or recording a vocalist as well as providing tips for singing with a microphone.

THE FUNDAMENTALS OF SOUND

In order to understand how to manipulate an audio signal, you must first understand a few basics of sound including frequency, amplitude, harmonics, and resonance.

Frequency

Sound travels in waves of compression and rarefaction within a medium, which for our purposes is air (see figure 14.1). These waves travel through the air and into our inner ears via the ear canal. There they are converted via the eardrums into nerve impulses that are transmitted to the brain and interpreted as sound. The number of waves per second is measured in hertz (Hz), which gives us the frequency of the sound that we have learned to perceive as pitch. For example, we hear 440 Hz (440 cycles of compression and rarefaction per second) as A4, the pitch A above middle C.

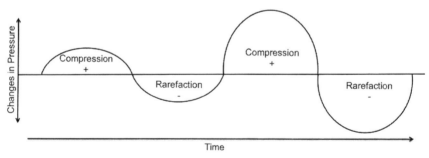

Figure 14.1. Compression and rarefaction. *Creative Commons (CC BY-SA 4.0).*

Amplitude

The magnitude of the waves of compression and rarefaction determines the amplitude of the sound, which we call its "volume." The larger the waves of compression and rarefaction, the louder we perceive the sound to be. Measured in decibels (dB), amplitude represents changes in air pressure from the baseline. Decibel measurements range from zero decibels (0 dB), the threshold of human hearing, to 130 dB, the upper edge of the threshold of pain.

Harmonics

The vibrating mechanism of an instrument produces the vibrations necessary to establish pitch (the fundamental frequency). The vibrating mechanism for a singer is the vocal folds. If an acoustic instrument, such as the voice, were to produce a note with the fundamental frequency alone, the sound would be strident and mechanical like the emergency alert signal used on television. Pitches played on acoustic instruments consist of multiple frequencies, called overtones, which are emitted from the vibrator along with the fundamental frequency. For the purposes of this chapter, the overtones we are interested in are called harmonics. Harmonics are whole number multiples of the fundamental frequency. For example, if the fundamental is 220 Hz (A3), the harmonic overtone series would be 220 Hz, 440 Hz (fundamental frequency times two), 660 Hz (fundamental frequency times three), 880 Hz (fundamental frequency times four), and so on. Every musical note contains both the fundamental frequency and a predictable series of harmonics, each of which can be measured and identified as a specific frequency. This series of frequencies then travels through a hollow cavity (the vocal tract) where they are attenuated or amplified by the resonating frequencies of the cavity, which is how resonance occurs.

Resonance

The complex waveform created by the vocal folds travels through the vocal tract where it is enhanced by the tract's unique resonance characteristics. Depending on the resonator's shape, some harmonics are amplified and some are attenuated. Each singer has a unique vocal tract shape with unique resonance characteristics. This is why two singers of the same voice type can sing the same pitch and yet sound very different. We can analyze these changes with a tool called a spectral analyzer as seen in figure 14.2. The slope from left to right is called the spectral slope. The peaks and valleys along the slope indicate amplitude variations of the corresponding overtones. The difference in spectral slope

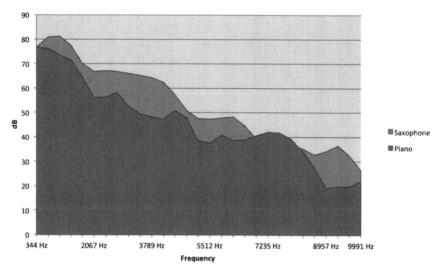

Figure 14.2. The figure shows two instruments playing the same pitch. The peak at the far left is the fundamental frequency, and the peaks to the right are harmonics that have been amplified and attenuated by the instrument's resonator, resulting in a specific timbre. *Courtesy of Matthew Edwards.*

between instruments (or voices) is what enables a listener to aurally distinguish the difference between two instruments playing or singing the same note.

Because the throat and mouth act as the resonating tube in acoustic singing, changing their size and shape is the only option for making adjustments to timbre for those who perform without microphones. In electronically amplified singing, the sound engineer can make adjustments to boost or attenuate specific frequency ranges, thus changing the singer's timbre. For this and many other reasons discussed in this chapter, it is vitally important for singers to know how audio technology can affect the quality of their voice.

SIGNAL CHAIN

The signal chain is the path an audio signal travels from the input to the output of a sound system. A voice enters the signal chain through a microphone, which transforms acoustic energy into electrical impulses. The electrical pulses generated by the microphone are transmitted through a series of components that modify the signal before the speakers transform it back into acoustic energy. Audio engineers and producers understand the intricacies of these systems and are able to make an infinite variety of alterations to the vocal signal. While some engineers strive to replicate the original sound source as accurately as possible, others use the capabilities of the system to alter the sound for artistic effect. Since more components and variations exist than can be discussed in just a few pages, this chapter discusses only basic components and variations found in most systems.

Microphones

Microphones transform the acoustic sound waves of the voice into electrical impulses. The component of the microphone that is responsible for receiving the acoustic information is the diaphragm. The two most common diaphragm types that singers will encounter are dynamic and condenser. Each offers advantages and disadvantages depending on how the microphone is to be used.

Dynamic   Dynamic microphones consist of a dome-shaped Mylar diaphragm attached to a free-moving copper wire coil that is positioned between the two poles of a magnet (figure 14.3). The Mylar diaphragm moves in response to air pressure changes caused by sound waves.

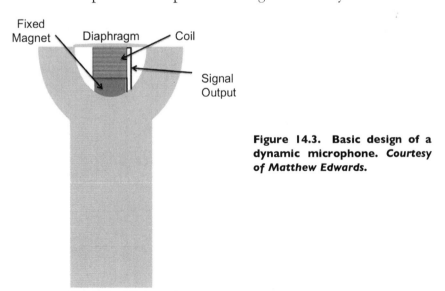

Figure 14.3. Basic design of a dynamic microphone. *Courtesy of Matthew Edwards.*

When the diaphragm moves, the magnetic coil that is attached to it also moves. As the magnetic coil moves up and down between the magnetic poles, it produces an electrical current that corresponds to the sound waves produced by the singer's voice. That signal is then sent to the soundboard via the microphone cable.

The Shure SM58 dynamic microphone is the industry standard for live performance because it is affordable, nearly indestructible, and easy to use. Dynamic microphones such as the Shure SM58 have a lower sensitivity than condenser microphones, which makes them more successful at avoiding feedback. Because of their reduced tendency to feedback, dynamic microphones are the best choice for artists who use handheld microphones when performing. ♪

Condenser Condenser microphones are constructed with two parallel plates: a rigid posterior plate and a thin, flexible anterior plate (figure 14.4). The anterior plate is constructed of either a thin sheet of metal or a piece of Mylar that is coated with a conductive metal. The plates are separated by air, which acts as a layer of insulation. In order to use a condenser microphone, it must be connected to a soundboard that supplies "phantom power." A component of the soundboard, phantom power sends a 48-volt power supply through the microphone cable to the microphone's plates. When the plates are charged by phantom power, they form a capacitor. As acoustic vibrations send the anterior

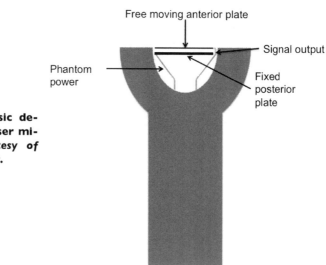

Figure 14.4. Basic design of a condenser microphone. *Courtesy of Matthew Edwards.*

plate into motion, the distance between the two plates varies, which causes the capacitor to release a small electric current. This current, which corresponds with the acoustic signal of the voice, travels through the microphone cable to the soundboard where it can be enhanced and amplified.

Electret condenser microphones are similar to condenser microphones, but they are designed to work without phantom power. The anterior plate of an electret microphone is made of a plastic film coated with a conductive metal that is electrically charged before being set into place opposite the posterior plate. The charge applied to the anterior plate will last for ten or more years and therefore eliminates the need for an exterior power source. Electret condenser microphones are often used in head-mounted and lapel microphones, laptop computers, and smartphones.

Recording engineers prefer condenser microphones for recording applications due to their high level of sensitivity. Using a condenser microphone, performers can sing at nearly inaudible acoustic levels and obtain a final recording that is intimate and earthy. While the same vocal effects can be recorded with a dynamic microphone, they will not have the same clarity as those produced with a condenser microphone.

Frequency Response   Frequency response is a term used to define how accurately a microphone captures the tone quality of the signal. A "flat response" microphone captures the original signal with little to no signal alteration. Microphones that are not designated as "flat" have some type of amplification or attenuation of specific frequencies, also known as cut or boost, within the audio spectrum. For instance, the Shure SM58 microphone drastically attenuates the signal below 300 Hz and amplifies the signal in the 3 kHz range by 6 dB, the 5 kHz range by nearly 8 dB, and the 10 kHz range by approximately 6 dB. The Oktava 319 microphone cuts the frequencies below 200 Hz while boosting everything above 300 Hz with nearly 5 dB between 7 kHz and 10k Hz (see figure 14.5). In practical terms, recording a bass singer with the Shure SM58 would drastically reduce the amplitude of the fundamental frequency while the Oktava 319 would produce a slightly more consistent boost in the range of the singer's formant. Either of these options could be acceptable depending on the situation, but the frequency response must be considered before making a recording or performing live.

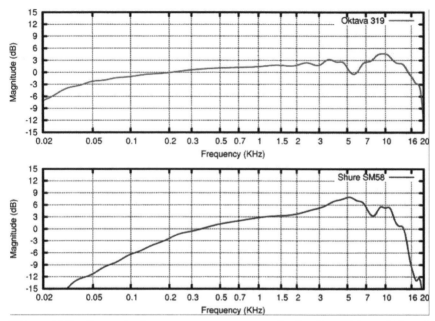

Figure 14.5. Example frequency response graphs for the Oktava 319 and the Shure SM58. *Creative Commons (CC BY-SA 4.0).*

Amplitude Response   The amplitude response of a microphone varies depending on the angle at which the singer is positioned in relation to the axis of the microphone. In order to visualize the amplitude response of a microphone at various angles, microphone manufacturers publish polar pattern diagrams (also sometimes called a directional pattern or a pickup pattern). Polar pattern diagrams usually consist of six concentric circles divided into twelve equal sections. The center point of the microphone's diaphragm is labeled 0° and is referred to as "on-axis" while the opposite side of the diagram is labeled 180° and is described as "off-axis."

Although polar pattern diagrams appear in two dimensions, they actually represent a three-dimensional response to acoustic energy. You can use a round balloon as a physical example to help you visualize a three-dimensional polar pattern diagram. Position the tied end of the balloon away from your mouth and the inflated end directly in front of your lips. In this position, you are singing on-axis at 0° with the tied end of the balloon being 180°, or off-axis. If you were to split the balloon in half vertically and horizontally (in relationship to your lips), the point at which those lines intersect would be the center point of the balloon. That imaginary center represents the diaphragm of the microphone. If you were to extend a 45° angle in any direction from the imaginary center and then draw a circle around the inside of the balloon following that angle, you would have a visualization of the three-dimensional application of the two-dimensional polar pattern drawing.

The outermost circle of the diagram indicates that the sound pressure level (SPL) of the signal is transferred without any amplitude reduction, indicated in decibels (dB). Each of the inner circles represents a –5 dB reduction in the amplitude of the signal up to –25 dB. Figures 14.6 and 14.7 are examples. Figures 14.8, 14.9, and 14.10 show the most commonly encountered polar patterns.

When you are using a microphone with a polar pattern other than omnidirectional (a pattern that responds to sound equally from all directions), you may encounter frequency response fluctuations in addition to amplitude fluctuations. Cardioid microphones in particular are

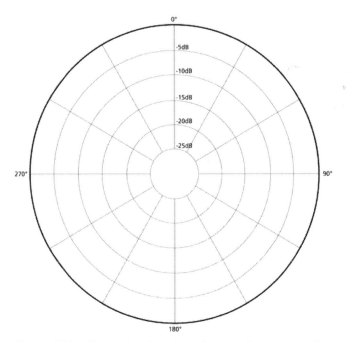

Figure 14.6. Example of a microphone polar pattern diagram. *Creative Commons (CC BY-SA 4.0).*

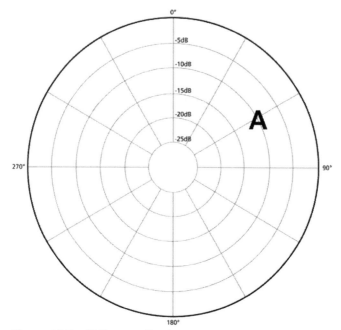

Figure 14.7. If the amplitude response curve intersected with point A, there would be a 10-dB reduction in the amplitude of frequencies received by the microphone's diagram at that angle. *Creative Commons (CC BY-SA 4.0)*.

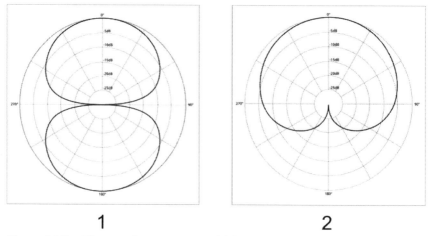

1   2

Figure 14.8. Diagram 1 represents a bidirectional pattern; diagram 2 represents a cardioid pattern. *Creative Commons (CC BY-SA 4.0)*.

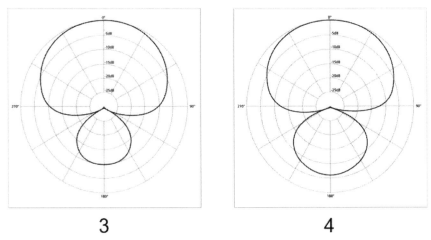

Figure 14.9. Diagram 3 represents a supercardiod pattern; diagram 4 represents a hypercardioid pattern. *Creative Commons (CC BY-SA 4.0).*

known for their tendency to boost lower frequencies at close proximity to the sound source while attenuating those same frequencies as the distance between the sound source and the microphone increases. This is known as the "proximity effect." Some manufacturers will notate these frequency response changes on their polar pattern diagrams by using a combination of various lines and dashes alongside the amplitude response curve.

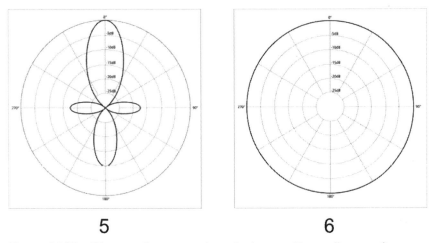

Figure 14.10. Diagram 5 represents a shotgun pattern; diagram 6 represents an omnidirectional pattern. *Creative Commons (CC BY-SA 4.0).*

Sensitivity   While sensitivity can be difficult to explain in technical terms without going into an in-depth discussion of electricity and electrical terminology, a simplified explanation should suffice for most readers. Manufacturers test microphones with a standardized 1 kHz tone at 94 dB in order to determine how sensitive the microphone's diaphragm will be to acoustic energy. Microphones with greater sensitivity can be placed farther from the sound source without adding excessive noise to the signal. Microphones with lower sensitivity will need to be placed closer to the sound source in order to keep excess noise at a minimum. When shopping for a microphone, the performer should audition several next to each other, plugged into the same soundboard, with the same volume level for each. When singing on each microphone, at the same distance, the performer will notice that some models replicate the voice louder than others. This change in output level is due to differences in each microphone's sensitivity. If a performer has a loud voice, he or she may prefer a microphone with lower sensitivity (one that requires more acoustic energy to respond). If a performer has a lighter voice, he or she may prefer a microphone with higher sensitivity (one that responds well to softer signals).

Equalization (EQ)

Equalizers enable the audio engineer to alter the audio spectrum of the sound source and make tone adjustments with a simple electronic interface. Equalizers come in three main types: shelf, parametric, and graphic.

Shelf   Shelf equalizers cut or boost the uppermost and lowermost frequencies of an audio signal in a straight line (see figure 14.11). While this style of equalization is not very useful for fine-tuning a singer's tone quality, it can be very effective in removing room noise. For example, if an air conditioner creates a 60 Hz hum in the recording studio, the shelf can be set at 65 Hz, with a steep slope. This setting eliminates frequencies below 65 Hz and effectively removes the hum from the microphone signal.

Parametric   Parametric units simultaneously adjust multiple frequencies of the audio spectrum that fall within a defined parameter. The engineer selects a center frequency and adjusts the width of the bell curve surrounding that frequency by adjusting the "Q" (see figure 14.12). He or she then boosts or cuts the frequencies within the bell

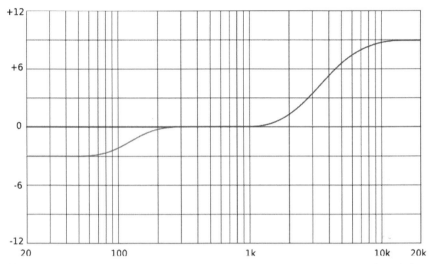

Figure 14.11. The frequency amplitude curves show the effect of applying a shelf equalizer to an audio signal. *Creative Commons (CC BY-SA 4.0).*

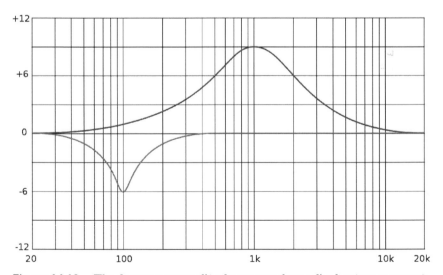

Figure 14.12. The frequency amplitude curves above display two parametric equalizer settings. The top curve represents a boost of +8 dB set at 1 kHz with a relative large bell curve—a low Q. The lower curve represents a high Q set at 100 Hz with a cut of 6 dB. *Creative Commons (CC BY-SA 4.0).*

curve to alter the audio spectrum. Parametric controls take up minimal space on a soundboard and offer sufficient control for most situations. Therefore, most live performance soundboards have parametric EQs on each individual channel. With the advent of digital workstations, engineers can now use computer software to fine-tune the audio quality of each individual channel using a more complex graphic equalizer in both live and recording studio settings without taking up any additional physical space on the board. However, many engineers still prefer to use parametric controls during a live performance since they are usually sufficient and are easier to adjust midperformance.

Parametric adjustments on a soundboard are made with rotary knobs similar to those in figure 14.13. In some cases, you will find a button labeled "low cut" or "high pass" that will automatically apply a shelf filter to the bottom of the audio spectrum at a specified frequency. On higher-end boards, you may also find a knob that enables you to select the high pass frequency.

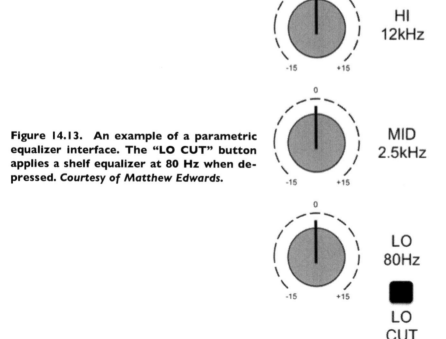

Figure 14.13. An example of a parametric equalizer interface. The "LO CUT" button applies a shelf equalizer at 80 Hz when depressed. *Courtesy of Matthew Edwards.*

Graphic   Graphic equalizers enable engineers to identify a specific frequency for boost or cut with a fixed frequency bandwidth. For example, a ten-band equalizer enables the audio engineer to adjust ten specific frequencies (in Hz): 31, 63, 125, 250, 500, 1K, 2K, 4K, 8K, and 16K. Graphic equalizers are often one of the final elements of the signal chain, preceding only the amplifier and speakers. In this position, they can be used to adjust the overall tonal quality of the entire mix.

Utilizing Equalization   Opinions on the usage of equalization vary among engineers. Some prefer to only use equalization to remove or reduce frequencies that were not a part of the original sound signal. Others will use EQ if adjusting microphone placement fails to yield acceptable results. Some engineers prefer a more processed sound and may use equalization liberally to intentionally change the vocal quality of the singer. For instance, if the singer's voice sounds dull, the engineer could add "ring" or "presence" to the voice by boosting the equalizer in the 2–10 kHz range. See figure 14.14 for an example of a graphic equalizer interface.

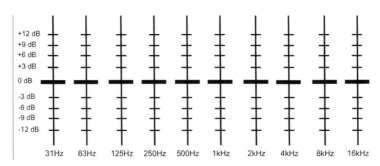

Figure 14.14.   Example of a graphic equalizer interface. *Courtesy of Matthew Edwards.*

Compression

Many singers are capable of producing vocal extremes in both frequency and amplitude levels that can prove problematic for the sound team. To help solve this problem, engineers often use compression.

Compressors limit the output of a sound source by a specified ratio. The user sets the maximum acceptable amplitude level for the output, called the "threshold," and then sets a ratio to reduce the output once

it surpasses the threshold. The typical ratio for a singer is usually between 3:1 and 5:1. A 4:1 ratio indicates that for every 4 dB beyond the
threshold level, the output will only increase by 1 dB. For example, if
the singer went 24 dB beyond the threshold with a 4:1 ratio, the output
would only be 6 dB beyond the threshold level (see figure 14.15).

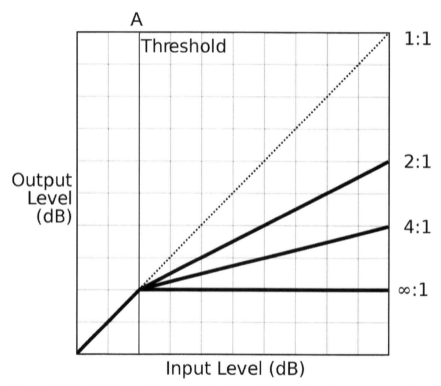

**Figure 14.15. This graph represents the effects of various compression
ratios applied to a signal. The 1:1 angle represents no compression. The
other ratios represent the effect of compression on an input signal with the
threshold set at line A.** *Creative Commons (CC BY-SA 4.0).*

Adjusting the sound via microphone technique can provide some of
the same results as compression and is preferable for the experienced
artist. However, compression tends to be more consistent and also gives
the singer freedom to focus on performing and telling a story. The additional artistic freedom provided by compression is especially beneficial

to singers who use head-mounted microphones, performers who switch between vocal extremes such as falsetto and chest voice, and those who are new to performing with a microphone. Compression can also be helpful for classical singers whose dynamic abilities, while impressive live, are often difficult to record in a manner that allows for consistent listening levels through a stereo system.

If a standard compressor causes unacceptable alterations to the tone quality, engineers can turn to a multiband compressor. Rather than affecting the entire spectrum of sound, multiband compressors allow the engineer to isolate a specific frequency range within the audio signal and then set an individual compression setting for that frequency range. For example, if a singer creates a dramatic boost in the 4 kHz range every time they sing above an A4, a multiband compressor can be used to limit the amplitude of the signal in only that part of the voice. By setting a 3:1 ratio in the 4 kHz range at a threshold that corresponds to the amplitude peaks that appear when the performer sings above A4, the engineer can eliminate vocal "ring" from the sound on only the offending notes while leaving the rest of the signal untouched. These units are available for both live and studio use and can be a great alternative to compressing the entire signal.

Reverb

Reverb is one of the easier effects for singers to identify; it is the effect you experience when singing in a cathedral. Audience members experience natural reverberation when they hear the direct signal from the singer and then, milliseconds later, they hear multiple reflections as the acoustical waves of the voice bounce off the side walls, floor, and ceiling of the performance hall (see figure 14.16).

Many performance venues and recording studios are designed to inhibit natural reverb. Without at least a little reverb added to the sound, even the best singer can sound harsh and even amateurish. Early reverb units transmitted the audio signal through a metal spring, which added supplementary vibrations to the signal. While some engineers still use spring reverb to obtain a specific effect, most now use digital units. Common settings on digital reverb units include wet/dry, bright/dark, and options for delay time. The wet/dry control adjusts the amount of direct signal (dry) and the amount of reverberated signal (wet). The bright/dark control helps simulate the effects of various surfaces within a natural space. For instance, harder surfaces such as stone reflect high frequencies and create a brighter tone quality while softer surfaces such as wood reflect lower frequencies and create a darker tone quality. The delay time, which is usually adjustable from milliseconds to seconds, adjusts the amount of time between when the dry signal and wet signals reach the ear. Engineers can transform almost any room into a chamber music hall or concert stadium simply by adjusting these settings.

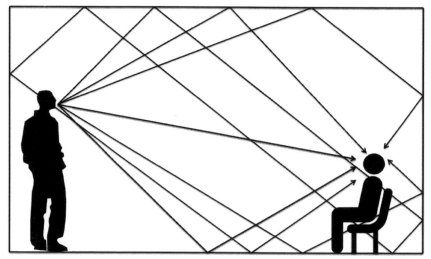

Figure 14.16. This diagram illustrates the multiple lines of reflection that create reverb. *Courtesy of Matthew Edwards.*

Delay

Whereas reverb blends multiple wet signals with the dry signal to replicate a natural space, delay purposefully separates a single wet signal from the dry signal to create repetitions of the voice (figure 14.17). With delay, you will hear the original note first and then a digitally produced repeat of the note several milliseconds to seconds later. The delayed note may be heard one time or multiple times, and the timing of those repeats can be adjusted to match the tempo of the song.

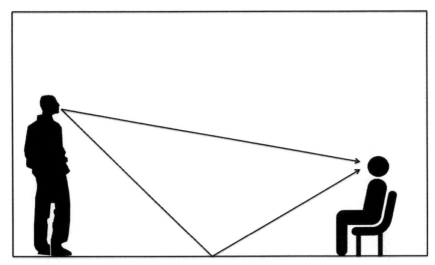

Figure 14.17. This diagram illustrates how a direct line of sound followed by a reflected line of sound creates delay. *Courtesy of Matthew Edwards.*

Auto-Tune

Auto-Tune was first used in studios as a useful way to clean up minor imperfections in otherwise perfect performances. Auto-Tune is now an industry standard that many artists use, even if they are not willing to admit it. Auto-Tune has gained a bad reputation in the past few years, and whether you agree with its use, it is a reality in today's market. If you do not understand how to use it properly, you could end up sounding like T-Pain (b. 1985).[2]

Both Antares and Melodyne have developed Auto-Tune technology in both "auto" and "graphical" formats. "Auto" Auto-Tune allows the engineer to set specific parameters for pitch correction that are then computer controlled. "Graphical" Auto-Tune tracks the pitch in the selected area of a recording and plots the fundamental frequency on a linear graph. The engineer can then select specific notes for pitch correction. They can also drag selected pitches to a different frequency, add or reduce vibrato, and change formant frequencies above the fundamental. To simplify, the "auto" function makes general corrections while the "graphic" function makes specific corrections. The "auto" setting is usually used to achieve a specific effect (for instance, "I Believe"

[1998] by Cher [b. 1946]), while the "graphic" setting is used to correct small imperfections in a recorded performance.

Digital Voice Processors

Digital voice processors are still relatively new to the market and have yet to gain widespread usage among singers. While there are several brands of vocal effects processors available, the industry leader as of this printing is a company called TC-Helicon. TC-Helicon manufactures several different units that span from consumer to professional grade. TC-Helicon's premier performer-controlled unit is called the VoiceLive 3. The VoiceLive 3 incorporates more than twelve vocal effects, eleven guitar effects, and a multitrack looper with 250 factory presets and 250 memory slots for user presets. The VoiceLive 3 puts the effects at the singer's feet in a programmable stomp box that also includes phantom power, MIDI in/out, a USB connection, guitar input, and monitor out. Onboard vocal effects include equalization, compression, reverb, and "auto" Auto-Tune. The unit also offers μMod (an adjustable voice modulator), a doubler (for thickening the lead vocal), echo, delay, reverb, and several other specialized effects.[3] ♪

One of the most impressive features of digital voice processors is the ability to add computer-generated harmonies to the lead vocal. After the user sets the musical key, the processor identifies the fundamental frequency of each sung note. The computer then adds digitized voices at designated intervals above and below the lead singer. The unit also offers the option to program each individual song with multiple settings for every verse, chorus, and bridge.

THE BASICS OF LIVE SOUND SYSTEMS

Live sound systems come in a variety of sizes from small practice units to state-of-the-art stadium rigs. Most singers only need a basic knowledge of the components commonly found in systems that have one to eight inputs. Units beyond that size usually require an independent sound engineer and are beyond the scope of this chapter.

Following the microphone, the first element in the live signal chain is usually the mixer. Basic portable mixers provide controls for equalization, volume level, auxiliary (usually used for effects such as reverb and compression), and on some units, controls for built-in digital effects processors. Powered mixers combine an amplifier with a basic mixer, providing a compact solution for those who do not need a complex system. Since unpowered mixers do not provide amplification, you will need to add a separate amplifier to power this system.

The powered mixer or amplifier connects to speaker cabinets, which contain a "woofer" and a "tweeter." The woofer is a large round speaker that handles the bass frequencies while the tweeter is a horn-shaped speaker that handles the treble frequencies. The crossover, a component built into the speaker cabinet, separates high and low frequencies and sends them to the appropriate speaker (woofer or tweeter). Speaker cabinets can be either active or passive. Passive cabinets require a powered mixer or an amplifier in order to operate. Active cabinets have an amplifier built in and do not require an external amplifier.

If you do not already own a microphone and amplification system, you can purchase a simple setup at relatively low cost through online vendors such as Sweetwater.com and MusiciansFriend.com. A dynamic microphone and a powered monitor are enough to get started. If you would like to add a digital voice processor, Digitech and TC-Helicon both sell entry-level models that will significantly improve the tonal quality of a sound system.

Monitors are arguably the most important element in a live sound system. The monitor is a speaker that faces the performers and allows them to hear themselves and the other instruments onstage. Onstage volume levels can vary considerably, with drummers often producing sound levels as high as 120 dB. Those volume levels make it nearly impossible for singers to receive natural acoustic feedback while performing. Monitors can improve aural feedback and help reduce the temptation to oversing. Powered monitors offer the same advantages as powered speaker cabinets and can be a great option for amplification when practicing. They are also good to have around as a backup plan in case you arrive at a venue and discover they do not supply monitors. In-ear monitors offer another option for performers and are especially useful for those who frequently move around the stage.

MICROPHONE TECHNIQUE

The microphone is an inseparable part of the contemporary commercial music singer's instrument. Just as there are techniques that improve singing, there are also techniques that will improve microphone use. Understanding what a microphone does is only the first step to using it successfully. Once you understand how a microphone works, you need hands-on experience.

The best way to learn microphone technique is to experiment. Try the following exercises to gain a better understanding of how to use a microphone when singing:

1. Hold a dynamic microphone with a cardioid pattern directly in front of your mouth, no farther than one centimeter away. Sustain a comfortable pitch and slowly move the microphone away from your lips. Listen to how the vocal quality changes. When the microphone is close to the lips, you should notice that the sound is louder and has more bass response. As you move the microphone away from your mouth, there will be a noticeable loss in volume and the tone will become brighter.
2. Next, sustain a pitch while rotating the handle down. The sound quality will change in a similar fashion as when you moved the microphone away from your lips.
3. Now try singing breathy with the microphone close to your lips. How little effort can you get away with while producing a marketable sound?
4. Try singing bright vowels and dark vowels and notice how the microphone affects the tone quality.
5. Also experiment with adapting your diction to the microphone. Because the microphone amplifies everything, you may need to under-pronounce certain consonants when singing. You will especially want to reduce the power of the consonant sounds /t/, /s/, /p/, and /b/.

FINAL THOUGHTS

Since this is primarily an overview, you can greatly improve your comprehension of the material by seeking other resources to deepen your knowledge. There are many great resources available that may help clarify some of these difficult concepts. Most important, you must experiment. The more you play around with sound equipment on your own, the better you will understand it and the more comfortable you will feel when performing or recording with audio technology.

NOTES

1. Paula Lockheart, "A History of Early Microphone Singing, 1925–1939: American Mainstream Popular Singing at the Advent of Electronic Amplification," *Popular Music and Society* 26, no. 3 (2003): 367–85.

2. For example, listen to T-Pain's track "Buy You a Drank (Shawty Snappin')."

3. "VoiceLive 3," TC-Helicon, accessed May 2, 2016, www.tc-helicon.com.

(15)

BUILDING YOUR TEAM

The Music Director

*A Conversation with Alex Rybeck, Tracy Stark,
and Gregory Toroian*

In cabaret, the music director is one of the most important people on your team and perhaps the first person you should hire. Once you have compiled your list of possible music directors (chapter 12), contact each of them and book a session. Bring several different songs/charts with you—for example, a jazz chart, pop music, a show tune, and a comedy—to make sure that they have the skill set that your show requires. Not all music directors are comfortable with all styles of music, or music notation for that matter. Ask if they are comfortable reading a "lead sheet." Note their energy and whether they are coaching you, collaborating with you, or just playing for you. Ask if they write arrangements (and what each chart will cost). Ask them how they deliver the charts. You should always have a hard copy and an electronic copy of any chart you have paid for.

It is important to treat this session like a job interview—theirs, not yours. *You* are interviewing *them*. Get all the answers you need in order to make your final decision. If your show requires a trio or additional instruments, ask them if they know and can hire the additional players. It's always better for the music director to have an established relationship with the other musicians. Ask your prospective music director things like: (a) Do they bring all the charts to the gig or is that your responsibility? (b) Do they teach a class? If so, ask if you can audit or take the class. (c) How do they prefer to have their music organized? Do they want it in a book, in plastic sheets, or taped together "accordion" style? Be as concise and polite (but direct) as professionalism dictates. Ask which directors they have worked with and who they would recommend. This could augment—or confirm—the list of prospective directors you have compiled.

The music director and the singer must collaborate, and in cabaret it is the singer that ultimately leads the team. However, the singer must also trust the music director, allowing them time to lead the session, using the expertise that they possess to coach the music, and, most important, create the musical arrangements needed for the authentic interpretation of the songs. The collaboration between music director and singer must be built on mutual respect for each other's time, talent, and taste.

Depending on your region of the country and your level of expertise, your voice teacher/vocal coach may offer to be your music director. This is not always the best idea for three specific reasons. First, you want to be able to get different (and more objective) feedback from someone who does not know your voice, its pitfalls, progress, or potential. Second, an objective ear may also be beneficial in picking song keys and creating arrangements. And third, and perhaps most important, the teacher-student dynamic need not be present during rehearsals for *your* show. You do not want to find yourself onstage concerned about how you sound because your voice teacher is at the piano. Cabaret is a lyric-driven performance art. You cannot spend a single second in "tech head" (worrying about how you sound).

We spoke with the following professionals, each of whom is an accomplished music director. There are, of course, many highly qualified music directors currently working to great acclaim in the cabaret industry today. As a means of narrowing the criteria for interview, we selected three recent awards winners, each with their own unique style and perspective.

* * *

Alex Rybeck is a pianist, arranger, and composer recognized for his work in theater, cabaret, concert, and recording. His Broadway credits include the original productions of *Merrily We Roll Along* and *Grand Hotel*. He conducted the world premiere of *What the World Needs Now* with Burt Bacharach. His work in cabaret has earned him numerous MAC, Bistro, Nightlife, and Broadway-World awards for musical direction and songwriting. His many albums include *Sibling Revelry* and *Boom!* (Liz and Ann Hampton Callaway); *Leap of Faith* and

Figure 15.1. Alex Rybeck.

Total Faith (Faith Prince); *The 1959 Broadway Songbook* (Jeff Harnar); *Better Days* (Karen Mason); and every solo album by Liz Callaway, including *The Story Goes On* and *The Beat Goes On*. In addition to these artists, he has also accompanied or arranged for Tommy Tune, Michael Feinstein, Kitty Carlisle Hart, Marni Nixon, Donna McKechnie, Amanda McBroom, Tovah Feldshuh, Avery Sommers, Sally Mayes, Roslyn Kind, Jason Graae, Lee Roy Reams, and Karen Akers. ♪

Tracy Stark is a pianist/arranger/conductor/singer/songwriter and an eleven-time MAC Award winner for Music Director, Piano Bar Enter-

Figure 15.2. Tracy Stark.

tainer, and Song of the Year. She is a Bistro Award winner for Musical Direction and a recipient of Stu Hamstra's Cabaret Hotline Songwriter of the Year award. Stark has worked with Sarah Dash (Labelle), Randy Jones (Village People), Lesley Gore, Phoebe Snow, Karen Black, Barb Jungr, Brenda Braxton, Eric Millegan (television's *Bones*), Tonya Pinkins, Nathan Lee Graham, and hundreds of other rock, jazz, and Broadway vocalists. She creates and music directs seventy-five to one hundred different shows per year and has three albums of original music. ♪

Figure 15.3. Gregory Toroian.

Gregory Toroian is an award-winning music director, arranger, songwriter, and accompanist. He plays across all genres and chiefly concentrates on jazz. He has worked with Jon Hendricks, Cab Calloway, Donna Summer, and Tony Bennett, among others, and has appeared in almost every jazz and cabaret club in New York City. Toroian produced and served as music director for a revue of Michel Legrand's music called *How Do You Keep the Music Playing?*, which has been performed in New York City, Toronto, Chicago, and Lake Placid. He has worked as music director for famed recording artist Jane Olivor. When not performing, Toroian coaches singers both privately and in master class format. He has been a faculty member at the New School and the Lee Strasberg Institute, and currently offers an array of performance workshops, with topics including how to work with piano, bass, and drums; phrasing and styling jazz vocals; group harmony; and scatting. ♪

It was a pleasure to have a wide-ranging conversation with each of these individuals.

Thank you all so much for sharing your time and expertise. Let's start with Tracy. How did you discover the genre of cabaret?

[Stark] When I moved to NYC in 1997, I started getting into the cabaret scene by playing in the piano bars and meeting singers. There was a thriving cabaret community here, and I gravitated to it very naturally, especially since the piano bars I was playing in also housed some of the more popular cabaret rooms. Fast-forward two decades: I have now literally musically directed and played thousands of cabaret shows.

The thing that brings me the most bliss in this art form is to play with great singers. I have been playing for and collaborating with singers my entire life in all musical genres. When I was (much) younger, I didn't know what the term "cabaret" meant, even though a large percentage of my income came from doing cabaret shows. I just thought I was doing "shows" with singers. I simply didn't know that there was a name for the specific type of show I was doing. I also thought that there was a specific genre of music I had to do for it to be considered "cabaret"— you know, old-timey music, show tunes, torch songs, and so forth—but that is simply not true. Cabaret is about communication. It is inclusive of all genres.

And a question for all of you: What are the three most important things you strive to get out of a singer?

[Rybeck] Making music with someone is collaborative, or at least it should be. What I strive for is to establish a creative partnership and provide the desired musical support that best serves the singer. I strive for seamlessness in the result. In other words, the singer and the accompanist should be on the same page as far as communicating the meaning and feeling of the song.

Four things that go a long way toward establishing rapport between singer and music director are humor, honesty, respect, and enthusiasm. It's always easier to create in an environment that's fun. That's where humor and enthusiasm come in. Respect is evident in how someone approaches every aspect of the collaboration, such as respect for someone's time. There should also be respect for the song itself, both the music and the lyric. In planning a show, there should also be respect for the intended audience. Honesty is essential, meaning that it's okay for a singer to say, "I am not comfortable with that accompaniment, what else can we try?" or for me to say, "I would love to hear this in a lower key," or even, "I don't think this song serves you well." The most important words in a musical partnership are, "Can we try it?"

[Stark] This question could have different answers depending on the person. Each artist has different strengths and weaknesses, and my goals with each individual artist may vary. For me, the most important thing in cabaret above all others is communicating a story or, at the very least, an emotion or situation. I try to work with and support the vocalist in any way I can to facilitate getting their story across. And then there's phrasing: finding the best way to communicate the story in the most effective and musically interesting way. Any one phrase can be communicated in an infinite number of ways. Your unique and specific personality/outlook/viewpoint is what will make you interesting as a per-former. I encourage a unique expression, one that isn't just a re-creation of somebody else's version of the same song. It is also important to find/collaborate on an arrangement that enhances the story being told. And finally, there has to be some *joy* involved!

[Toroian] The number one thing I like to draw out of people is for them to be themselves. They need to be the best "them" they can be, to have passion for what they're doing, and be very clear about why they're do-ing it and what they're trying to accomplish. They must also understand the work ethic and the discipline required to do this unique artistic endeavor.

Describe the job of the music director in cabaret.

[Toroian] It's evaluating the singer's strengths and weaknesses and then playing to their strengths while working on their weaknesses. Helping them really find who they are as a singer and, of course, putting every-thing together musically, figuring out how we want to do the arrange-ments, and refining from that point forward.

[Stark] I agree that it depends on the strengths and weaknesses of the artist. There are artists who don't need much other than a musical col-laboration. I have done gigs where I will be asked to show up an hour before a show, at which point I am handed a book of charts and told,

"Just follow me!" On the other end of the spectrum, many of the artists who call me like for me to help create a show from scratch. I may need to suggest songs, help create a set list, write arrangements and orchestrations, put together a band, lead the band, write charts, help to shape the show, and help with the script (patter).

[Rybeck] If one thinks of the singer as a filmmaker whose job it is to "project" their mental movie (the song's subtext) upon the audience, then my job as accompanist and/or arranger is to underscore that movie. Just as a successful film score enhances the mood and drama, but subtly so as not to steal focus, a good arrangement helps to communicate the story, providing atmosphere, texture, and drama. A good arrangement frames the lyric. A good arrangement can make a funny song funnier, a sad song sadder, and a sexy song sexier. A bad arrangement is one that fights the words and/or forces the singer into vocal discomfort.

And what does the job become when a singer decides not to use a director?

[Toroian] If there isn't a director involved, the job tends to expand into doing a partial director's job, including microphone technique, patter writing, song order, and things like that. In these situations, I try to be more of a "third eye" (outside of the musical aspects of the show), but this can be difficult to do at times because I am physically behind the piano and cannot see the whole picture.

[Stark] When I watch videos of cabaret shows I have done in the past where I am playing the piano, I realize how much of the artist's performance I missed because my focus was on the music. This is just because when I play the piano, I have a side view of the performer, which makes it easy to miss a good amount of the artist's communication. For that reason, if there isn't a director, I will always encourage the artist to have a knowledgeable person watch a rehearsal or two, so there's at least one "third eye" that isn't mine. I really do prefer (and encourage) having a proper director, especially if there is complexity of any sort in the show, which is all of them.

[Rybeck] I believe that if there is no director, the music director may fill that role, but only if the music director has the proper background and experience. I have written light plots and have suggested staging. I am very often the cowriter of a singer's patter. I usually have input into the act's structure. These are all "directorial" duties. Some music directors are comfortable and adept at making such suggestions, whereas others are not. If a singer is looking for a music director who can also serve as a director, this should ideally be established at the beginning of the collaboration.

How do you find new singers to work with? Or do they find you? And do you have a "bar" or talent level that you prefer to work with?

[Rybeck] In my cabaret work, I haven't ever sought singers directly; they find me. When it comes to choosing to work with someone, the artist's level of experience is only a partial consideration. I will always take a talented up-and-comer over an untalented veteran. I am just as proud of the work I have done with newcomers as I am of working with Tony Award winners. My goal with up-and-comers is to help make their work shine as brightly as that of famous stars.

[Toroian] I'm not sure I find singers. They seem to find me by word of mouth, seeing me at an open mic, or playing a show—things like that. I do not have a bar. I will gladly work with anybody who loves to sing, is enthusiastic about their work, and who is hopefully open-minded about exploring their talent.

[Stark] Most of the singers who contact me do so because they have seen my work with other artists. My advice to pianists who are new to any musical scene: *Get out there and play!* Show up. Say yes to everything, especially playing in piano bars if you have that skill. That is where singers gather. The more you play with singers, the more singers will seek you out. Also, playing in piano bars forces you to work on skills that will enhance your musical direction skills. Transposing, playing with all sorts of singers, dealing with crowds that aren't easy, coming up with "arrangements while you wait," and so forth, are all valuable skills. I enjoy working with both experienced talent and up-and-comers. I even enjoy working with complete beginners if they have musical intuition, a strong work ethic, and enthusiastic curiosity. If I have a good rapport (musical and otherwise) with someone and I feel I have something to offer them—and I have time in my schedule—then I will add them to my roster. If there is someone I'm on the fence about working with, I ask myself if the project will fulfill me creatively, spiritually, and of course . . . financially. I am also a realist, so sometimes work is work, and bills need to be paid.

When someone books an initial session, what should they bring?

[Stark] First, I would ask them about themselves and their experience. Then I ask them where they are in the process of putting the project together. If they are just starting a project, I then ask them to bring whatever they like to sing and anything they feel might be included in the show. That way, I can get a solid glimpse into who they are musically, what they might need from me, and where to go from there. I like to perform together at the very first meeting. I believe that people either have immediate musical connections or do not. So, first things first. Do we have a connection? That is the most important thing. After that is established, we can then talk about what the singer's goals are and how I can assist in achieving them.

[Rybeck] When first meeting someone whose work I don't know, I usually ask them to bring a lot of music. I want to get to know their voice and their repertoire, even if it's material that will largely be irrelevant to the upcoming project. I want to infuse my ear with their voice, including their range and their "sweet spots." I usually don't give a lot of feedback in a first session. I am more interested in absorbing what the singer has brought to the table. You can learn a lot just by hearing someone sing through a batch of material: their sense of rhythm, sense of phrasing, connection to lyrics (or lack thereof), and predilection for certain kinds of material. You can also learn what their repertoire "gaps" are. For instance, are there no "up-tempos," nothing written after 1970, or before 2000, and so forth?

[Toroian] I tell them to bring whatever songs that they want to try (hopefully in a variety of styles and tempos), a recording device to record the entire session, or just portions of it, or the accompaniments I might play for them. The first meeting is about beginning to know each other both musically and otherwise. I am also interested in learning about their past experience, what they want their future experience to be, why they are here, and what is it that they would like me to do for them.

If something intrigues you at this first session, what makes you say to yourself, "This person has it"?

[Rybeck] For me, it's usually the combination of an extraordinary voice with an active, interesting brain. I respond to artists who bring a strong point of view to their material.

[Toroian] To begin with, their philosophy about why they sing, if they sing for the joy of it and for the communication of it—like perhaps all art should be!

[Stark] Of course, I love playing with someone who can really *sing*! But there are also many other factors. I want to be emotionally touched. I want to be able to follow the artist so deeply into their story that I'm afraid to inhale at the end, for fear of breaking the spell. That is the most beautiful extreme.

Besides the voice, what else intrigues or attracts you when it comes to working with someone?

[Stark] It's always a plus when someone is prepared. It's also a plus when people have great taste, or at least similar taste in music, as I do. However, one of the things I appreciate most is an open mind and a willingness to experiment. I tend to use the phrase "Let's try it and see how it feels!" a lot. Equal respect in collaboration is so important.

[Rybeck] What it simply boils down to is chemistry. Why do any two people click? Chemistry! It's either there or it isn't.

[Toroian] The voice is not the first thing on the list for me—it's a few notches down. Yes, they have to be able to sing in tune and keep time, but again, I'm more interested in their philosophy as to why they do it and how open-minded they are, as well as—to some degree—their ability to listen, absorb, and take direction. Their charts are irrelevant at this point—I usually help with their music choices anyway. My wheelhouse is more jazz, pop, and rhythm and blues as opposed to musical theater.

And conversely, what would send a "red flag" up for you? What might lead you to believe that this may not be a person you would want to work with?

[Toroian] Somebody who comes off as being completely closed-minded and doesn't want to hear anything that I, or perhaps anyone, has to say. To circumvent this, on the phone conversation before we meet, I'll usually ask somebody what it is they want from me. Or what is it that you want to get out of our work? Hopefully we are able ascertain at that time, to some degree at least, whether this collaboration should move forward. "Chemistry" is important, but no one can predict or even control that.

[Rybeck] For me it boils it down to one word again: negativity! Negativity is a "red flag." Fortunately, I haven't encountered blatant negativity very often. It's more subtle. Sometimes you just wind up realizing you don't "click" with one another musically. Sometimes a singer will resist suggestions and not be willing to try different approaches. Other times, the artist may require a certain kind of musical expertise that is not in my wheelhouse. I have talked myself out of gigs after becoming aware the style of music is not something that I can deliver at the level the act deserves. I am happy to recommend other music directors who I think would be better, considering the material.

[Stark] It all depends on the individual person. There are traits in one person that might drive me nuts, but those same traits might be completely acceptable (or even charming) in another person. Basically, I expect people to be honest, upfront, open-minded, and kind—and hopefully, not too high maintenance.

Do you teach voice technique or lyric connection, or are you part of a director/music director team that teaches? If so, describe that process and tell us why it's important to take these classes.

[Stark] I absolutely work with lyric connection. That is probably the main goal of most of my sessions. Granted, I am a music director, so there are other goals as well, but everything stems from the music-lyric connection. There are numerous reasons classes are desirable. First, just the fact that you are surrounded by other people—some of whom are sitting inches away from you—is invaluable. It is much more difficult and nerve-racking to sing in front of a few people who are inches away from you than it is to sing in front of a packed stadium. I know that sounds odd, but people who have been in both situations understand what I am talking about. A class like that gives you the opportunity to work in that type of situation. It also gives you a chance to get immediate feedback on your performance, not just from the teacher, but also from the other students. You can always feel if something is working and/or if you are losing the crowd. Another positive aspect of classes is the fact that you get to learn from and experience the work your classmates are doing. Inevitably, there is going to be something you can relate to with what someone else is working on that's in tune with what you need to learn.

[Toroian] I do not teach voice. I'm a vocal coach. I do not work on mechanical or technical things with a singer. I am totally into the lyric and how the singer connects to it, and what it means to them as opposed to who wrote it or who else sang it. I am definitely a part of teams—different teams with different directors—and I love the collaboration process. I also teach workshops that involve teams. What I like about workshops is that there is an audience. When we go out to do this live, there will be an audience. The good news is that the audience in the workshop is already on your side. There's usually a lot of camaraderie and support, and that's good, especially when you're learning new or unfamiliar things, or delving into strange territory. It can be more freeing and less intimidating when there is that support in the room. In all my workshops—the trio class, the jazz harmony class, or the scat class—you learn from listening to the feedback that another director or I give to everyone in the workshop. These classes seem to be a win-win situation for everyone involved.

[Rybeck] I have coached singers since 1980, my first year in NYC, helping them find repertoire for auditions and club acts and helping them with lyric connection, interpretation, and personalization. Since the early eighties, I have accompanied and cotaught classes with Sara Louise Lazarus. Sara is the finest teacher of performance I know. We still teach workshops together. I have also taught master classes, both by myself and with artists I work with in cabaret, including Jeff Harnar, Faith Prince, Liz and Ann Hampton Callaway, Donna McKechnie, Jason Graae, Todd Murray, and others. I enjoy teaching very much because I am learning as much about the material as the singer being coached. I am a firm believer that all the answers are in the lyrics, and too many singers gloss over the lyrics. They are more concerned with "how they sound" and "how they feel" and tend to be less involved with *what they are saying, to whom they are saying it, why they are saying it*, and *what is at stake*. I find it very helpful to have singers speak the words and meticulously deconstruct the lyric until every word choice is justified with intention. There are many techniques that I use to hopefully guide singers toward connecting more deeply and personally with the lyrics.

Classes (as opposed to one-on-one coaching) are valuable for several reasons. For one thing, it is invaluable to *watch* other people's work, because when you're the one receiving feedback, you can't see the result, the transformation. However, when watching someone else deal with the same issues you are dealing with, the "corrections" are more clearly perceived and remembered. You can more easily trust a teacher or coach when you see positive transformations occurring before your eyes. Another important takeaway is exposure to repertoire. In addition, I also think it's very important to get out and *see* cabaret, especially young people and individuals who are just beginning to explore this genre for the first time. It's necessary to know what's happening in the clubs and at all levels of the industry. And it's especially important to see the headliners perform—the people who are masters of the art form. You need to know what you're aiming for. A bunch of songs is not an "act." In order to understand what differentiates an "act" from a "set" requires *seeing* an act!

Describe the "art of cabaret" and how it differs from musical theater. Are there any similarities, and do you have a different process when it comes to approaching each genre?

[Rybeck] I believe that both cabaret and musical theater involve story-telling. But the essence of cabaret is that each song is a self-contained story, delivered from one person *directly to the people in the audience*, without the conceit of the "fourth wall." There are exceptions, such as theatrical songs that are written to be delivered directly to the audience and cabaret acts that are extremely stylized and theatrical. But in general, cabaret is more a baring of the singer's soul. The singer, after all, is the one who has picked the songs! Theater is more about creating a self-contained world, with the audience eavesdropping on a character. In theater you are being *sung at*. In cabaret, you are being *sung to*.

[Stark] I agree, cabaret and musical theater seem similar at first, and yet the very basic premises of each genre are completely opposite. Cabaret is such an open genre and can easily include repertoire from the musical theater canon. And there have certainly been theater pieces that would fit into the definition of what a cabaret show is. For example, *Springsteen on Broadway* was a perfect example of what a great intimate cabaret show can be, even though it was technically a Broadway show. The basic premise of theater is to tell stories while incorporating a fourth wall, whereas the basic premise of cabaret is to allow the audience to feel as if they are with you in a more intimate setting . . . even in a large venue. After a successful cabaret show, the audience often feels like they just came from somebody's living room having participated in a great conversation, even though they sat and watched.

Greg, is there a difference in answering this question from a jazz pianist's perspective?

[Toroian] The similarities are that it's all music. It's "what you are singing about" and "how you feel about it." However, there will be differences just because of the genres, the idiom, and even the venue. Musical theater—which I don't work in very often—most of the time involves you playing a character. In cabaret and jazz, however, you are not. In cabaret, *you are you*. Cabaret is a very personal thing, but I still think that this concept can apply to jazz as well. Although jazz usually focuses on the music, I still believe it should be all about the lyric. We don't have to compromise the music to make that happen.

How has cabaret changed over the course of your careers?

[Rybeck] The material is more diverse. Beyond the general staples of Great American Songbook standards, jazz, and Broadway, one can hear virtually any category of music in a club act now. Contemporary, pop, rhythm and blues, and other genres have found their way into cabaret venues, and this music can all work beautifully if the lyrics are meaningful enough to resonate in intimate environments and are stripped of glossy "production." But the basics of what works hasn't really changed: the power of a talented performer to reach audience members' hearts by singing personally chosen songs directly into their eyes.

[Stark] Going back to the onset of cabaret . . . according to my knowledge, in Germany—specifically Berlin—in the early 1900s, the artists and creative types would gather for secret parties and perform. Cabaret was their personal expression. It was political, sexy, sexual, gender-bending, and often humorous—things that they could not necessarily express in public venues. In my own cabaret experience, it is an extremely varied genre that expresses whatever an individual artist wants or needs to express. As the decades have passed, cabaret has evolved into people telling their own personal stories . . . or stories they feel need to be told.

[Toroian] Since I began, some time ago, cabaret has changed. Repertoire-wise, it used to be much more theatrically oriented. Now, it can be anything: rock, jazz, bluegrass . . . anything. There are also more musicians involved, much more so than in the past: bass players, saxophonists, horns, backup singers, and so forth.

What is the future of cabaret?

[Rybeck] I believe that cabaret will continue to go through cycles of popularity. As long as people want to gather in small rooms, have a drink, and hear good music, it will continue. It has always been a fragile art form, and it continues to be under the radar for the general public, ignored by television and most other media outlets. And yet . . . it goes on. Young people are still filling classes to study it and filling clubs when they perform. The more technology takes over our lives, perhaps there will be a stronger attraction to hear live music in a small room, where there is a palpable human connection and genuine interaction occurring between the singer and the audience. You don't experience that at a rock concert or any other form of entertainment.

[Stark] I can only hope that the younger generations will understand this incredibly expansive, individualistic, and creative genre and continue to keep it alive.

[Toroian] Cabaret will continue because it is virtually the only outlet where you can completely do your own thing for an hour. Almost everything else in our lives is prescribed. If it's a jazz club, it had better be jazz that's performed. If it's a theater, well then, there better be show tunes. Whether you sing at a piano bar or a wedding . . . all of those things are valid and a way to pay the bills, but cabaret still allows you to do what you want, when you want to do it. I don't think it's going anywhere.

Is there anything you would like to share with our readers that we haven't already covered?

[Rybeck] I would just like to add that I am hugely grateful for every singer and director with whom I have worked in the cabaret world. I have learned something valuable from each collaboration—not just musically but as a human being. As I stated, I see my musical partnerships as personal relationships. Nothing brings people together more closely and more quickly than making music. I am happy to say that most of the people I have worked with have become personal friends. Sharing music is inherently a very personal gesture, so after only a few sessions, people who make music together naturally form a relationship with one another. I think for most of us who choose music as a profession, music is connected to our deepest feelings, memories, yearnings, joys, and sorrows. It is connected to our identity. Therefore, creating a common musical expression (via arrangements and performances) is a precious act and an endeavor to be taken seriously. The singer and the accompanist must rely on each other completely, and it requires enormous courage, faith, trust, and willingness on the part of both parties. When it comes together and the intended result is achieved—making the audience laugh, cry, or even simply pay attention—there is no better reward.

16

BUILDING YOUR TEAM

The Director

Interviews with Jeff Harnar, Lina Kputrakos, and Tanya Moberly

When looking for directors, interview them just as you did with your music director. Do they teach a class? If so, ask to audit one so you can watch them in action. Take notes. How do they work with each singer? Would their process work for you? Then, book a session to discuss your ideas. Bring along your show concept, song list, and draft script, and be open to his or her feedback. Ask them what music directors they have worked with and which ones they would recommend for your show. Again, it's always better for the singer when the members of the team have a connection and relationship with one another.

If after this first meeting, you are in disagreement or feel it's not the right fit, then move on to the next person on your list. It is vitally important that you trust your director unequivocally. They will work with you on lyric connection and will come to know a lot of your "secrets." You must trust them, and they must respect you.

You may have a clear idea of what you want to say and how you want to say it, in which case you may opt to self-direct. And if you're not sure, you can always start the process and then ask a director to "consult" on your show as need be. Another option is to take a class offered by a director or a director/music director team and begin to work on your material in class. A group class can offer unique benefits very different from those acquired when working one-on-one. Toward the end of your process, the teacher/director can be hired privately to help fine-tune your performance.

As with the music directors interviewed in the previous chapter, there are many highly qualified directors we could have spoken to. As a means of narrowing down the criteria for interview, we have chosen two recent award-winning directors: Tanya Moberly, the 2019 Bistro Award winner, and Jeff Harnar, the 2019 MAC Award winner. We have also included a section of our interview with Lina Koutrakos, who—in addition to being an award-winning director—is featured in chapter 24 as one of this industry's most highly regarded teachers.

* * *

DIRECTOR INTERVIEW I: JEFF HARNAR

Jeff Harnar is an award-winning cabaret performer and director. He has appeared in every major New York City venue, including Feinstein's/54 Below, the Laurie Beechman Theatre, Birdland, the Oak Room, Café Carlyle, Iridium, the Russian Tea Room, and Carnegie Hall. Together with KT Sullivan, Harnar created and performed the 2016 award-winning Stephen Sondheim revue *Another Hundred People* that played extended New York engagements; toured Chicago, St. Louis, and London; and was broadcast nationally on PBS. In London, Harnar was artistic director and host for three seasons of *The American Songbook in London* at the Jermyn Street Theatre and Pizza on the Park. And he has headlined engagements at the Crazy Coqs and the Pheasantry. He has won three BroadwayWorld Cabaret Awards for Best Male Vocalist, four MAC Awards (including Major Male Artist), and three Bistro Awards. He is also the winner of the 2015 Donald F. Smith Award and the 2012 Noël Coward Foundation Cabaret Award. Harnar served as artistic director and host for the acclaimed New York *Lyrics and Lyricists* series and, together with Andrea Marcovicci, has cohosted several star-studded evenings for the Mabel Mercer Foundation's annual Cabaret Convention at both Jazz at Lincoln Center's Rose Hall and the New York Town Hall. Marcovicci and Harnar also shared the bill

Figure 16.1. Jeff Harnar. Photo by Heather Sullivan.

at Town Hall for a duet celebration of Cole Porter's 125th birthday. As a director, he won the BroadwayWorld Cabaret Award, the Backstage Bistro Award, and two MAC Awards. His directorial credits include Tovah Feldshuh's critically acclaimed one-woman shows *Tovah Is Leona!* and *Aging Is Optional*, as well as award-winning cabaret acts for Celia Berk, Dawn Derow, Josephine Sanges, and Rita Gardner. ♪

Jeff, thank you for sharing your expertise. As an award-winning director and performer, you have a unique perspective.

Well, as a performer I know what I'm looking for in a director, and *that* helps me as a director. In addition, I've also learned from all the singers that I've worked with, and that helps me as a performer too. All these experiences have helped me solidify my own beliefs.

Tell us about directing in cabaret versus directing in any other medium.

My training was acting, and I have always believed that there should be a third eye. The music director usually has his eyes on the music, so it's hard for him to be that objective third eye. Also, it's nice to have a deciding vote if there is some issue that's fifty-fifty and can go either way. When that happens, it's nice to have someone say, "Well, I'm out front watching and this is what works the best or what reads the best." Directors even chime in on musical issues, song choices, song order, endings of songs, and so forth. Certainly, when Alex (Rybeck, chapter 15) and I work together, we've had a director come in and say things like, "No, that needs a big ending! We need a big note at the end of that. It can't be a fade."

Because of where it was positioned in the show?

Exactly. However, one of the big things the director really helps with in cabaret—and I try to do this for my clients as well—is that, in general, a cabaret act is the "appearance" of a person being *themselves* in front of an audience. Obviously, it's a heightened sense of yourself—certain qualities that you're illuminating onstage—but you still must be authentically *you*. Also, a director helps to not be tone deaf in one's patter and intentions. You need to be accessible and loveable. Commanding attention for an hour is a very special and challenging thing to do. For me as a performer, I really need someone to come in and say, "Yes, you're on the right track" or, "When you say it that way, I don't love you as much" or, "This would be smarter here."

When you talk about not being tone deaf in the patter, do you mean you write the patter with them?

Oh absolutely! I believe everyone is talented. Everybody has some light, some gift, something they're trying to say, and my goal is to help them weed out what is unnecessary. I liken it to an arrow coming out of a quiver—I want the show to be a direct shot. If I can keep the intention in line with the arc of the show and help the evening to have a beginning, middle, and an end, those are the things that I am most mindful of as a director.

What is your opinion about whether or not to use a director? Is a director necessary in cabaret?

No. I know many people who don't use a director. Andrea Marcovicci is a great example of someone who had a twenty-five-season career at the Algonquin Hotel with critically acclaimed shows, and she never once had a director. Andrea is a wonderful actress. She came from a theater and film background. She has a very clear understanding of who she is, what her "it" is, and how she should deliver it. She also works symbiotically with her music director, and they implicitly trust one another.

If a young singer decides that they want to work with a director, how do they go about finding one? For example, how would they find you?

I'm easy to find in this day and age of electronics. Most of us are. I would suggest identifying two or three names of directors that you're aware of and would possibly like to work with. You can find them by going to shows and looking at other artists' work. Seek out someone who is doing what you envision for yourself, and take note of who is directing them. This is important because, for instance, the kind of show I would direct is much different than a show directed by Marilyn Maye. Her approach is more from the nightclub world, which is very different.

What is the difference between a nightclub act and a cabaret act?

For me, "nightclub" is a word that harkens back to an era where shows were often forty-minute sets that went from ten o'clock at night until two in the morning. In a nightclub, you are pretty much background music in a smoke-filled room with people drinking cocktails. There might also be an opening act. However, cabaret has a much more attentive audience. You usually have the audience's rapt, delighted attention. They came there to listen to you. If there's dining, it happens discreetly during the show or beforehand. There's no smoking anymore. Oh, what a wonderful time we live in! I began my career at the tail end of the smoking era. Also, cabaret is a much more inclusive umbrella than nightclub singing.

Would you say cabaret requires more of the audience?

Yes, it does. First of all, it demands their attention. In cabaret, people are predisposed to give you audience. That's why they're there. You're not a surprise that's thrown in the background of a ritzy night at the Persian room. And you have the pleasure of knowing the audience is there to see the show and pay attention.

What if a singer comes to you and says they want to do a show, but they don't know what they want to do yet?

Then they have come to me too soon. [*laughing*]

They need to have a concept first?

Yes, I think so. The singers that I have enjoyed working with have a very clear intention of what it is they want to do, whether it's a song, a book show, or theme show. I like to work with singers who have determined a point of view and already have a list of songs they're gravitating toward.

When they bring their song list to you, do you change or augment it?

Oh, absolutely.

Do you say this *song instead of* that *song?*

Most certainly. When Dawn Derow (chapter 8) came to me with songs for her show *1941*, she initially had twelve songs written down. Now, *1941* has an enormous wealth of material to look at, listen to, and think about. As her director I asked, "Where's the 'novelty song'? (a comical or nonsensical song). We need humor." We looked on Wikipedia, and the first thing that popped up is "The Hut Sut" song, which ended up being the showstopper for her. I love hopping on the bandwagon of a concept that someone has come up with. For instance, Josephine Sanges (chapter 25) and her Harold Arlen show. What could be more exciting than to have a voice like that and focus it on a particular songwriter, knowing that what you want is for somebody to hear the best Josephine we can deliver. It's not going to be Judy Garland's show or Frank Sinatra's—all the song choices will reflect *her* point of view and *her* unique set of talents. I love doing that! That's what really lights me up.

When a singer comes to you with a new show, what are you looking for—in that person or project—that makes you say either, "Yes, I want to work with this person" or "No, it's too soon"?

The only time I say, "It's too soon" is if they just want to do a show and don't know anything more than that. I would rather spend my time working with someone who has a more specific vision. I am looking for people who are willing, open, trusting, and brave. It takes so much tenacity to do this that it must be someone I really think will be able to follow through.

And what should they be looking for in a director?

It's just such an important relationship. Now, I'm going to quote myself, but only because someone just quoted this back to me. When I won the MAC Award two years ago, I said, "The great thing about cabaret is that it's a car you're driving from point A to point B, and you get to choose who's in the car with you." When you're picking a director, make sure it's someone who can put gas in that car, someone who lights you up, affirms you, and makes you feel safe. Those are the things that I try to do. Tovah Feldshuh says I am one of the five best directors she's ever worked with, which is outrageous when you think of the body of work she's done. However, she said, "It's because I always feel safe. I can try anything with you, and I know it's a safe space." Perhaps that empathy comes from also being a performer. I know firsthand how frightening it can be to take a risk.

When someone brings something to you that is new to them or they feel insecure, how do you make them "feel safe"? What is it like when a singer is trying something, and they don't have it fully fleshed out? Perhaps they don't even know whether it's a good idea? How does that moment become crafted? How do you, as a director, look at that moment and say yes or no?

It's so different with everybody. Sometimes I can see something in a singer that they may not see themselves. I know it's there, and I simply ask them to have faith and to continue exploring. What I love about working with Tovah—and I think it's because of her background in theater—is that if I give her a suggestion, she will give it back to me 100 percent . . . even if she doesn't believe in it! She will say, "I'm not sure about that, but I want you to see it." And she'll do it. And afterward I'll say "Thank you. I was wrong." [*laughter*] But she gives it to me 100 percent. She's fearless. So again, it's different with each performer. Ideally, you want to work with someone you really trust has your best interests at heart. I really do believe most everybody already knows what they have inside them. They just need a little encouragement, someone to affirm what's right, to guide them and say, "This is where you're at your best.

This is where I love you. Do more of this." The process of discovery should be a joyful one.

How long is the whole process?

It's different with everybody. I say to every singer, "My wish for you is time. Give yourself time." Everybody seems to want to rush to get something onto the stage. It's of course important to have a performance deadline, because I don't think great creativity happens without some sense of urgency or deadline. You can't create inside a vacuum. But some of my favorite moments are when singers must postpone their shows because some "life" event comes up and they say, "We're pushing the dates back a month." When that happens, I think, "Yippee! We have more time?" I am just now, as a performer, feeling like I am mastering some of the Cole Porter material that I have been doing for twenty-five years. There is so much more that goes into it than memorizing the words and music in time for opening night. You must really get the song into your bones.

And it changes over the course of your performing life?

Of course. That's the great thing about being a cabaret singer. You'll never outgrow the role because if you keep growing and informing your material, you'll make different choices. I am now revisiting shows I first did at the start of my career. In September, we're doing a show I haven't performed for thirty years. I can't wait to try it on again knowing what I know today, which I didn't know then.

Back then, maybe your interpretation had youthful zeal, but now you're a different person and you need to approach the material differently. Doesn't that make the entire show different? And is that good, considering what the show was originally intended to be? Do you try to revive some of that original intent, or does it simply become a "new" show with known material?

When Alex Rybeck and I first did our show *The 1959 Broadway Songbook* in 1991, it was my debut show at the Algonquin. Michael Feinstein suggested the song, "I Wish It So" from *Juno*, a Mark Blitzstein song. It's a wonderful, hopeful song. The same month that we opened that show at the Algonquin, Rosemary Clooney opened at Rainbow & Stars singing "I Wish It So," from *Juno*, which her husband, José Ferrer, directed at that time. One of the reviews compared what it's like to see a thirty-year-old singing that song as opposed to a sixty-five or seventy-year-old. The reviewer remarked that although it is the same song with the same lyric, the readings were completely different—and absolutely valid for each interpretation. That's what I'm hoping to find as we revisit some of these shows. I am interested in seeing what these songs mean to me now. ♪

Do you have a favorite type of show that you like to see or direct?

Yes. My favorite shows to *see* have a theme. I like to know that I'm going to be taken care of as an audience member, and that's what I try to do when I am directing as well. I want the audience to know by the second song that they're going to be taken care of—and whether each song has a point of view and that there is some sense of the journey ahead. Ideally, a show should feel inevitable. It should feel like each song births the next, and whatever song is eighth could not possibly have been second. That's the kind of show I like to see. Those shows take me on a ride, and I can simply sit back and be entertained.

You work on lyric interpretation with your singers, and there are many different techniques for doing this. Can you describe your favorite techniques?

As performers, the lyric is our script. So, it had better be something that you want to say, that needs to be said, that needs to be said right now, and that needs to be said by you. *And* it must be believable when it is coming out of your mouth. If the right lyrics are selected, you can speak your entire show and the text of it will make sense.

It should read like a book. It should flow, as you say, in an inevitable way.

Yes, and the great thing about writing out your lyrics, besides being a good memorization tool, is that it forces you to pay attention to the punctuation, which informs your phrasing.

A lot of sheet music is not very accurate in the use of punctuation or capitalization. Lyrics are written within the conventions of poetry, and the singer must make sense of it, as a monologue, sometimes taking out (or putting in) capitalization and/or punctuation in order to reclaim the thought within the complete sentence.

The biggest gift a singer could get is to find a lyric first and say, "Oh, I love this lyric." Then, challenge yourself as an actor to think, "How would I say it? How would it come out of me? What inflections would I use if this were my speech?" And, "Look what I do with my hands when I *say* these words." I'm going to remember that when I sing it. I want my hands to do what they would normally do. Singing should be as natural as talking. A good deal gets unlocked when I go back to the text, look at the punctuation, and challenge myself to make those sentences come out of me. That's what I love about singing Sondheim, trying to figure out, "How would I *say* that?" as opposed to "How would I *sing* that?"

How hard is it to get someone to backtrack into the lyrics when they already know the song? They've never had the experience of saying the sentence without the rhythm of the musical phrase.

It can be really hard for some people . . . really, really difficult.

How do you get someone to focus only on the lyrics and forget the music that's on the page?

I just keep pushing back by saying, "I don't believe that. I don't believe that's how you would say that." I had a great teacher in Julie Wilson. She was the queen of talking on pitch. Her inflections and innuendos were a master class. She'll always be in my head as an example of what to do. Sometimes you really need to see someone do it to understand, "Oh I don't need to sing it that way."

Many readers of this book will be trained singers and teachers with stellar voices. In cabaret, very often that stellar voice can get in the way and "leapfrog" over the lyric. What do you do in that situation?

Aghhh! That is so challenging. When that happens, I sometimes say to people, "You've got the curse of a beautiful voice and a beautiful sound." We just must check that at the door for a while. Something Sara (Lazarus) says that I borrow is, "The way you're singing right now is so beautiful and will always work, and you know it works. I'm not asking you *not* to sing it that way, but let's just safely put it aside and know that it's there, and for the sake of experiment let's just try it a whole other way." Then I'll say, "You can't sing until a third of the way, or even halfway, into the song." I want the transition to be as seamless as it can be from the patter to when the song starts, so that someone might not even know the moment when it's become a song. Let's try to go that far, and then maybe we can marry the two. Again, I know what it's like as a performer to have someone come at me with a radical idea, so I really try to be gentle with it. Some people take it very well. It can be a big revelation—it certainly was for me. With others, it simply takes longer.

Have you had the experience where a singer with a classically trained voice comes in singing beautifully, but the voice is oversinging the lyric, and then—through working on the story—they are able to change the nature of their sound and they're telling the story more and "singing" less, but now they hate it because they don't think they sound like themselves?

That can happen, but thankfully I have not had that experience *yet.* But I will say—going back to the story I told before about "I Wish It So"— the genesis of Michael Feinstein suggesting that song to me was that he asked me, "Is there any show from 1959 you can't find a song in?" And I said, "Yes, *Juno.*" And he asked, "What about 'I Wish It So'?" I had listened to it a dozen times. It's a gorgeous song, sung by a soprano. But at Michael's urging, I went back and listened to the lyric, and the lyric is extraordinary. So that, to me, is what a cabaret singer can do that a music theater singer sometimes can't. We have a real opportunity to make someone hear a song completely differently. "I've Got You under My Skin" is probably my favorite example of this, because most people think of the Frank Sinatra/Nelson Riddle arrangement. But if you detach that lyric from that arrangement, the lyric is one of the most gorgeous examples of a three-dimensional, profound expression of personal angst ever written. That lyric *by itself* is saying something so different than the Nelson Riddle arrangement. So, we have a real opportunity as cabaret singers to affect that kind of change. How many times have you heard a song in a cabaret and thought, *I've never heard the words like* that *before?* After a good cabaret act, that's what you should be hearing—things like, "I never listened to the lyric before" or "I never understood what that song was about before" or "I never even knew that it was a good lyric." If you're hearing that kind of feedback after your show, you've done the work. . . and that's the fun! ♪

Has cabaret changed over the past twenty-five years?

It has definitely evolved. I understand that the change we see today began before my time, when the audience really started to give focus to the performer and the performer started to do more than just a set of songs. The idea of songbook shows, or theme shows, was born slightly before I started performing. I have certainly seen cabaret flourish through the creativity of what people bring to the cabaret rooms, as well as the kinds of themes they create. It has become an extraordinary and rich art form.

Finally, where do you think cabaret is going as we head into the future?

I certainly am hoping that there will continue to be hunger for live experiences . . . immediate, interpersonal, and communal experiences. Cabaret is not something you can "stream" into your living room. It is about the live, in-the-moment experience of actually being in congregation with a room full of people and having a performer bare their soul. It can feel like a mother singing a lullaby to you. It can feel like a cheerleader giving you the zest to go out and live again. It can feel like an oracle, a healer, soothing your aching heart. That very special thing can only happen in a cabaret room. And most people that experience it are led back to it, and ask themselves, "How long has this been going on?"

* * *

DIRECTOR INTERVIEW 2: LINA KOUTRAKOS

Figure 16.2. Lina Koutrakos.

Award-winning singer and director, Lina Koutrakos is also one of the cabaret industry's most esteemed pedagogues (chapter 24). As part of her interview as a teacher, we spoke with Koutrakos about the directing side of her career. Those comments have been placed here for continuity. Please see chapter 24 for her complete biography. ♪

Lina, we've talked about teaching, but does anything different happen in a directorial process that might not happen during the teaching process?

Yes, I think so, because now you are putting together an entire one-person show. When I direct people's first shows, I realize that a lot of what I am teaching them—along with everything else they learned in the solo performance class—is how to put the show together. A lot of singers don't realize—especially the first time out—that even if they are the singer and they have a piano player and a director, they are also leading the way, *producing* and *writing* the show. You're the writer, the producer, you're *everything* else that you have to be, *before* you become the singer who is center stage. After all of that, you are also the person you "cast" in the part. You pick the songs. You bring your subtext to me and say things like, "'It Had to Be You' is not a happy song for me. This is what it's about for me. I want to sing it about having to marry my first husband. It was not a good relationship, but it had to go that way for me so that I could become who I am today. Can I do that with this song?" Well, let's see! And then *you*, the singer/writer/producer interviews arrangers, and they shape the arrangement and help with the interpretation. *That* is the process I have to guide my singers through and remind them that this process unfolds organically over time.

And you help the singer choose songs?

I always ask, "Why did you pick this song?" If the song is one that is overperformed, I may say something like, "This song has been done to death. Tell my why you picked it, and let me try to find you something a bit more pointed toward the feelings you want to express." In other words, someone might *really* want to sing "New York, New York," but that is probably not a good idea, *especially* in New York.

So then the conversation becomes . . . "What do you love about that song? The big notes or the lyric about this beautiful city?"

Exactly. You must start somewhere. If the person says, "Well, I think it's because I want to pay homage to New York," I would then move the conversation forward by saying things like, "Great! Let's start looking for other songs. And just exactly *how* do you feel about this city?" As a director, there are a lot of things to teach. In addition to all of this, there is the spoken word.

You mean the patter?

Yes, what you say in between each song that walks you into the next mood. The patter sets you up so that the minute the song begins, your audience is on that trip with you at the first note and the first lyric. They shouldn't have to sit there for eight to sixteen bars wondering what you're singing about. I used to do a lot of patter writing for people, but I am presently working with several people who write their own patter really well. With them, I simply edit for the entertainment value and the acting beats. I also advise them *not* to chitchat their butts off between songs. Don't explain what you're going to sing next, and why. If you are going to do that, don't bother singing. You just told the whole story to me! So, those are the things that are being "taught" while directing that are not necessarily being taught in a performance class.

Shows have a journey. I hate that word, but they do. They have an ebb and flow. They are little plays that must remain authentic. All the pieces must come together, and it is my duty and job to teach the singer what we're doing and why we're doing it. It is an intense process, and I take my lead completely from the person that's center stage. I have gotten better at that because I didn't want to impose the same "Lina formula" on everybody's show. I am hellbent on the "Lina formula" being known as helping to make the person as authentic as possible. To make that happen I need to stay completely out of *their* way. It isn't about my vision. Rather, it's my job to help them create their vision and translate it as clearly and with as much entertainment value as possible.

Logistically speaking, how long is the process of putting together a show? How much time should you spend working with a director?

First, it's a financial endeavor as well because you pay for your musicians and your director's time, as well as studio space if you need it. So, you must be smart about that and figure out what you can manage financially. Let's pretend finances are not an issue. The most important thing I tell people is keep the time with your director consistent. If you want to meet once a week for three hours a week, great. If you want to do that two times a week for two or three hours, great. If you can only afford to do that once every few weeks, great. But consistency matters to the process. I don't think it is a good idea to get started and then let the ball drop for a few months. Whatever you decide to do, be consistent.

For most people, I have them meet with me first and tell me the songs they're thinking of. Then we'll begin fleshing those out. I'm interested in listening to people tell me about themselves because that's how I go about finding song ideas for them. After I have heard their voice, I need to hear who *they* are. Being in the industry for over thirty years, I have a lot of song ideas. Once we have come up with a song list, I then send them off to an arranger. And in New York, we're lucky. We have incredible pianists with honed arranging skills for authentic singers. I'm not going to arrange a song for my voice, my story, or my personality the same way you're going to. We're going to do it very differently, and I know both of us are going to be very effective. But you need to find that person, that arranger, who can hear what you are trying to say.

That's unique to cabaret. No one sings the same song in exactly the same way. You are encouraged to make it different and create your own arrangement of the song.

Exactly. And yet, you don't want to go so far out of your way that you're bastardizing the Great American Songbook or are just showing off. It must always come from someplace authentic in you. Your "It Had to Be You" can be about the newborn baby you're holding in your arms. That's a very different song than someone else's "It Had to Be You" about an abusive ex-husband.

And the musical arrangement, what's being played underneath the singer, is going to be different, depending on the singer's interpretation.

Absolutely. Once again, the arrangement is informed by who you are and what the lyric of the song means to *you*. Until you figure that out, the director or arranger can't help you.

Some clients want to rush the process. They just want to get their songs down as quickly as possible and get their show up and running. With these performers, I try to convince them to breathe a bit because there's something to be said for sitting and letting ideas percolate. And then there is the other extreme—people who get so involved in the process that they *only* want the process to happen. With them, you must set some goals so that a show will happen.

Push them onto the stage, in a sense?

Correct. Because if you work on a show for too long, you'll wind up changing it and never settling on anything. At some point you have to say, "This is the piece I'm going to do." So, if I were to outline a typical time line, I would say that if we have everything available to us and we work together once a week and you go home and work on it consistently, you're looking at three to four months.

Three-hour rehearsals once a week?

Two to three hours. Sometimes that would be with just your director and sometimes just your accompanist/musicians or your musical director. And sometimes you go off and work on your own. You don't need to pay for everybody to sit in the room while you work. And you don't need a rehearsal pianist either. If your music director is the person you're paying top dollar (to play the show and arrange it), then ask him or her to put everything down on tracks so you can practice on your own and work on other aspects of the music with your director. You'll know when it's time to bring your entire team together, and your director should tell you when you need to do that as well.

So, that's about twelve hours a month for four months. That's about fifty hours of rehearsal for one hour onstage.

Yeah, that sounds about right. And that's why you need to enjoy the process. If you don't enjoy the process, then don't bother doing it. Some people love to go on cruise ships. They save their money and they do that. Some people want to take ballroom dancing. Some people want to put a pool in their backyard. All of these are great things to spend your money on. If you're a middle-aged person who wants to sing again (even if your show is not going to reap any financial benefits), then you better enjoy the hell out of it, because the process can be just as much fun as your hour onstage!

* * *

DIRECTOR INTERVIEW 3: TANYA MOBERLY

Figure 16.3. Tanya Moberly.
Photo by Takako Harkness.

Tanya Moberly is the recipient of the 2019 Bistro Award for Directing. She is also a six-time MAC Award winner for *The Salon*, one of the industry's longest-running open-mic shows. Moberly has been in many theatrical productions and currently works as one of the booking managers at Don't Tell Mama. She recently directed *A Life behind Bars* starring Dan Ruth, which won the 2018 Bistro Award for Solo Play, a 2018 MAC Award for Spoken Word, the 2018 Hollywood Fringe Festival Encore Producers' Award, and the 2016 United Solo Award for Best Autobiographical

Show. Moberly has been performing in cabaret since 1997 when she co-created *The Blonde Leading the Blonde*, which ran for five years at Don't Tell Mama. Solo cabaret shows include *Songs I Feel Like Singing: Four Different Shows with Four Different Musicians*, which was the 2016 MAC Award winner for Female Vocalist. She also received the 2014 Bistro Award for Theme Show and a MAC nomination for Major Female Artist in 2018. ♪

Tanya, thank you for sharing your expertise with us. Can you describe the cabaret director's job?

I think a director's job is to bring cohesion to an artist's vision, to unearth what an artist's instincts are, and to succeed in conveying his or her ideas. A director will make a performer shine. A director is not a dictator, but merely a guide. The artist should always have veto power over any idea because it is the performer's show. If an artist feels secure in their vision and doesn't need any assistance, then he or she does not need a director. A director is simply there to offer help and another perspective if desired.

Why should a singer use a director?

Sometimes people just need an eye. I have been hired on many occasions to work with someone for an hour or two on their show as a consultant/coach. The role of a consultant/coach is like that of a director—it's just condensed.

Does the singer bring a concept to you, or do you decide that together?

Singers usually come to me with an idea. Often this is something about their life, something they care to express, or just a kind of music that they love, such as particular composers and/or styles. For me it always, always, always starts with a list of songs. Ultimately, the songs fight it out and a show is born.

In a new project interview, what do you look for in a singer? What should they be looking for in a director?

I try to get an idea of what it is they are trying to express. And if we are having a discussion, then they have already seen something in me that made them seek me out. The rest is logistics. I always make sure I am super clear about the way I work, what I charge, and so forth.

What attracts you to a singer/project?

What attracts me is the person, the artist, and their spirit. Quite often, I have no idea what the show will look like when we begin. As I said earlier, every show begins with a list of songs. Sometimes, people come to me with a show that is relatively complete already, maybe even one they have performed before. When that happens, it is my job simply to be an editor or "show doctor," concerning myself only with the craftsmanship and construction of the show. However, most people are starting a show from scratch, so that first step is making a list of songs that the performer feels called to sing. Then, as I said, the songs "fight it out." Which ones are calling the loudest? The songs, and especially their lyrics, are always the meat of the show, and they are what the show is really about. The rest is just sculpting.

What are your views on interpreting and connecting to a lyric?

Lyrics are everything. It always helps if a song is well written, musically speaking, but the most important thing is to convey the lyric to its fullest capacity.

What techniques do you use to help a person connect? Do you consider this part of the director's job?

Helping a singer connect to the lyric is absolutely my job. It's always in the acting, which comes from the lyric/text. Who are you singing/talking to? Why? Why now? What just happened that evoked this? What is your "action" (verb)? What are you actively doing to the person/people you are singing to in this song? After that, it is about deepening the specificity of everything, including any images or memories inherent in the song or words. Those techniques are different for every individual. I work with everyone differently according to what works for them.

How involved are you with the overall look and sound of the show, the technical aspects: lighting cues, musical underscoring, song flow, patter, and so forth?

Very. I usually have strong feelings about most aspects of a show, so I offer them.

Beside the voice, what other nonverbal skills does a singer need?

Performing requires all kinds of physicality—including dealing with microphones, cords, stools—as well as matching your body language to whatever you're singing about.

You work with people of all ages. Do you think age and life experience matter, or is it just about whether a singer emotionally connects to the song?

Sometimes it's an age thing. I was judging a junior talent contest once, and all these eight-to-twelve-year olds were singing "Rose's Turn" and "As Long as He Needs Me." My reaction was, "There is so much great material for young artists, go find it!" And then again, sometimes it's just about how a song fits a particular person or show, or doesn't.

How do you think cabaret has changed over the years?

I started my career in cabaret in 1997, and I have certainly seen a lot of clubs close, and I am so grateful for the ones that are still around. I'm also very grateful for organizations like MAC, the Mabel Mercer Foundation, and the American Songbook Association for their continued dedication to preserving the art form, as well as publications and websites like Cabaret Scenes, NiteLife Exchange, Theater Pizzazz, and Cabaret Hotspot!

What is the future of cabaret?

I think the future is ours to write. I think the future is open to anyone who cares to participate. As Lennie Watts (chapter 19) says, "Cabaret's not going anywhere. If all the clubs were gone, we'd still be singing in the frozen food aisle at Gristedes."

FINAL THOUGHTS

The use of a director in cabaret is a recent development, and whether one decides to use a director is entirely up to each performer. The points made here by each of these award-winning directors, however, remain true. Cabaret performance is a live expression of art, experienced in the singular moment. How one is "translating" to the audience cannot be discerned by the singer nor the music director. A watchful eye, a close friend, a teacher, or a director should always be engaged to ensure the singer's expressive goals are being realized. The difference between a friend/teacher and a director lies within the parameters of their respective tasks and their relationship to the singer. The role of the voice teacher is traditionally very personal, and of course a friendship is built upon years of trust and understanding. These people may already know your voice, your backstory, and personal history within the context of your life. Therefore, they may be able to subconsciously "fill in the blanks" of your storytelling in a way that the objective audience member may not. A director, on the other hand, focuses moment to moment on the task at hand, absorbing your storytelling, connecting the dots, and ensuring the entertainment value of your production. Remember, *you* are the star, and you are also the writer and the producer. It is my opinion that hiring a director is certainly a good investment that will positively affect the quality of your production.

THE BUSINESS OF CABARET

17

DIY ("DO-IT-YOURSELF") PRODUCTION

Cabaret is, for the most part, a self-produced art form. A young Barbra Streisand (b. 1942) booked herself into the Bon Soir in Greenwich Village. And Bette Midler (b. 1945) played the Continental Baths in the Ansonia Hotel, with Barry Manilow (b. 1943) at the piano, no less. These small, and sometimes alternative, venues are where many cabaret artists hone and develop their craft. Yes, there are booking managers and publicity managers, and as your career progresses, *they* will find *you*. Your job is to create art, and until you find a third-party producer, your job is to *produce* art.

Cabaret clubs are the backbone of this small-venue, live-performance industry, and they are eager to showcase your talent. At the same time, these clubs are running a business and must always keep their own bottom line in mind. We can learn a valuable lesson from these clubs by considering our own bottom line and honoring our art with an equal amount of business savvy via the skill of "do-it-yourself" (DIY) production. DIY production is the one necessary skill, or set of skills, that is not currently taught in any university, conservatory, or otherwise artistic curriculum. However, it is a vital set of skills that when mastered can immeasurably help you reach your artistic goals.

BOOKING YOUR SHOW

How do you book a show? The short answer is, carefully. First you must discern in which venue, or venues, you think your show would best fit. Start by asking the professionals on your team, namely, your director and musical director. Each club has its own certain personality, and some might work better than others depending on the concept of your show. For example, some venues can only support shows with piano accompaniment (or piano and bass only) and may not allow or have the stage space for a drum kit. Others, however, may provide a larger stage where a trio or other instruments would fit comfortably. Some venues serve food, whereas others only serve drinks. Which venue would be better for your show and target audience? Finances may be another concern, as some clubs may simply have a higher financial requirement that might not work for your budget.

Most cabaret shows can be performed in any venue. However, if your show consists of "new" music theater and contemporary tunes and you are not doing standards or jazzy tunes, you may not want to approach a club that usually caters to jazz. On the other hand, a jazz or contemporary set can easily fit into a traditional cabaret, nightclub, or supper club venue. And as mentioned previously, if your show has an educational component or celebrates a specific composer, an alternative venue, such as a library or a church, might want to produce your show as part of their arts series. Carefully consider where and why your show concept would be welcome, and then market your show to those venues first.

Marketing your show could be as simple as calling the venue and asking for their protocols when booking a show. Find out to whom to send your materials, and then email, mail, or deliver those materials to that individual with a formal cover letter. Standard promotional materials include the following: your headshot and résumé, the title of your show and concept, and previous performance reviews, if applicable. In most cases, if the club does not know you, they may also ask for a video or YouTube clip of one of your previous performances. However, if a member of your team has a relationship with the venue, he or she may be able to broker a booking for you. If your director or musical director already has a relationship with the club and recommends you, then you may be booked as a courtesy to the referring team member because you are a trusted commodity.

Once you have decided *where* you want to book your show, the question becomes *when* to book your show. This can be tricky, because most clubs and venues book several months ahead. Additionally, in order to promote the show, you need a minimum of two months' lead time to get your press release to the publicity outlets that list shows in your area. Publications that review shows need to be notified as well so that they can list your show on their calendars and possibly assign a reviewer (*if* you decide you want one). That means in most cases you may need to pick a club and set a date before you have finished putting the show together.

There is another angle to consider. You have the show concept ready to go, you've picked your team, you are in rehearsals, and you decide it is time to book it. In this case, the date you wind up with could be anywhere from two months to six months away. Two months can put pressure on you with a real goal to strive toward, and alternatively six months could lengthen or stall out your rehearsal process as you wait for distant performance dates. And yes, "dates" in the plural. If you are going to book one date, you should go ahead and book two or three. This way you can amortize the expense of producing your show over two or more performances and get more "bang for your buck." Also, a single date may not work for all the friends and family who will want to attend, let alone the general audience whose interest you want to pique.

Your dates will probably not be two to four nights in a row; that kind of run is generally reserved for an established professional. Try booking one show per week over two to four weeks, or even once a month for two to four months. This is currently fashionable in the New York cabaret scene and makes sense for several reasons: first, it spreads your show over time and makes room for publicity "buzz" to help secure future performances; second, it amortizes your initial expense to pay for the musical director and band, thereby increasing your profit potential; and third, spreading your dates out over a few months allows the material to artistically ruminate. The show, and your performance, will grow over time with continued rehearsal between shows.

So . . . you've picked a club, you've picked your dates, and you're in negotiation with the club. Here are some things to consider:

- Does the club do any publicity for you?
- Can you place your show's advertising postcards there?
- Do they have a dressing room? If they do, take a look at it so you know what you can and cannot bring.
- Do you or your band have to bring any equipment?
- Is their sound system adequate for the demands of your show?
- Do they have a vocal monitor?
- Do they provide a drum kit?
- Do they take credit cards or just cash (from your audience)?
- What is their minimum? Is it a cash value or "two drinks"?
- If they have food, does the food count in the minimum?
- Do you have to guarantee a certain number of seats?
- Can they cancel the show if you have less than a certain number of reservations by a certain day prior to opening?
- Are you financially responsible for anything if the show does not go up or if they cancel?
- And most important, when will you receive payment from the club?

Finally, have they given you a contract that puts all of this in writing? If so, be sure to read it carefully. The following section details the different types of contracts you may encounter in the cabaret world.

CLUB CONTRACTS

There are various types of club contracts with which you should familiarize yourself. This section will cover four of the most common types of cabaret contracts—standard contracts, "percentage split," "singer guarantee," and the elusive "paid gig" contract—and explain the differences between them.

Standard Contracts

In a standard contract, the artist generally sets and receives the cover charge, and the club receives the minimum food and drink charge. You will also need to pay for your technical support, which usually runs $80 to $150 per show. This may appear on some standard contracts as a "tech fee." Some contracts may also specify that the club has a right to cancel the show if you have less than a certain number of reservations by a certain day before the performance. In this case, you may also be responsible for a minimum balance due so that the club can cover the cost of their staff.

"Percentage Split" Contracts

The "percentage split" contract is a relatively recent development in the world of cabaret. This "split" can range from 20 to 40 percent, which means although you would still set the cover charge, that charge would be shared between you and the club, sometimes including tech fee and sometimes not. To explain further, let's consider the example of a $1,000 night (a $20 cover charge and fifty people in the room) with a 60/40 percentage split. This would mean that 60 percent of the "pot" would go to you ($600) and that the club would keep the other 40 percent.

If your percentage split contract does not include the tech and room fees, then it in reality becomes more of a 50/50 split. Your gross profit is now just $500, which we will discuss briefly in the "creating a budget" section below. Instead of walking away with $500 under a standard contract, this 60/40 split leaves you at a "break even" of $0 for a show with a musical director only! The percentage split sometimes can be negotiated to 70/30 or even to 80/20. However, these more attractive arrangements will usually be contingent on the notoriety of the talent, the capacity of the room, and how many people you will have in your audience. Most clubs doing a percentage split contract take a *minimum* of 20 percent. When negotiating, ask yourself what justifies the percentage split offered. Does the club provide an in-house publicity service that has proven results? Do they guarantee an audience for you? And from the club's perspective, what can you guarantee them? Do you *know* you can fill the room for one night or more? Your power in negotiating stems from your reputation as an artist and the proven track record of your team.

"Singer Guarantee" Contracts

This is an even newer development in the world of cabaret contracts, mostly occurring in the higher-end supper clubs. In this scenario, the singer guarantees the club a certain amount of patronage or a minimum dollar value. The supper club may offer a "prix fixe" dinner for a certain amount (e.g., $60) as well as a cover charge (e.g., $40) for the show, which goes to the artist. Dinner and a show for $100! Sounds like a great deal, especially for the audience. However, be careful . . . the contract may require you to guarantee a certain number of seats. This means that a forty-seat guarantee would require a financial commitment or earning potential of $1,600 just to step onstage, plus the cost of your musical director or band! What if you cannot meet this requirement? What if you brought in twenty people instead of forty? Your earning potential has now been reduced to $800, and those missing twenty people are costing you $800! That means you have net profit of $0 . . . and you still must pay your musical director. Before signing one of these contracts, you will need to work through the math carefully.

"Club Guarantee" Contracts

Some jazz clubs will offer the singer a "guarantee." As with most contracts, the amount of the guarantee will vary depending on the singer's notoriety. Many clubs will initially guarantee $500 per night. Over time, if they see an increase in attendance—that you are a "draw"—they will offer an incentive of an additional $100 to $200. Most musical directors would be in the $250 range for one show, so under this guarantee, you can both be guaranteed that you make some money. However, a trio can cost up to $850—you are now *losing* money. Therefore, you must negotiate the club guarantee based on the number of instruments you are planning to have and what your own minimum income expectation is—never forget to pay yourself. Finally, remember that you can also negotiate with your band. If the club is a well-known venue, musicians may take the gig at a lower fee just to have the opportunity to play there. It's worth asking!

"Paid Gig" Contracts

While these are the rarest of all contracts, there are clubs and venues that will pay a performer outright. For example, the library circuit and senior centers are places that often pay anywhere between $500 and $1,000 per performance. These venues are also usually program-specific types of shows based on their clientele. Therefore, be sure you do a little research before marketing your show to these venues. Of course, larger, more established clubs produce headlining talent at much greater fees. In this scenario, at any level, it is still the responsibility of the headlining artist to pay the music director and band out of the total fee received.

The Bottom Line

Over the course of time, you are likely to encounter many different types of contracts. The most important thing to remember before signing a contract is to read the contract very thoroughly and ask a lot of questions. A cabaret singer, like any other self-employed professional, must do the math carefully to be sure they are always coming out "in the black."

CREATING A BUDGET

This section will guide you through the cost of doing a show with the understanding that these expenses are incurred over a long period of time, usually at least four to six months and in some cases up to an entire year. Knowing how much your show will ultimately cost to produce, inclusive of all the preshow costs, will allow you to create a realistic budget. The budget estimates below show both the cost of doing a show using only a music director/pianist (90 percent of all cabaret shows follow this format) and the cost of this same show with an instrumental trio (piano, bass, and drums).

Show Cost versus Ticket Price

Using only a piano, your primary expenses for each show will include your musical director, room fee/percentage, and technical director (who

runs the lights and sound). The essential question to ask is how many audience members you will need to break even. So, let's create an example
of a simple budget. Again, this scenario is for one show with a musical
director/pianist only.

Let's assume you are charging a $20 cover charge and that the room
seats seventy people. That's a maximum income potential of $1,400 if
you sell out the room. Let's budget for audience attendance of both
fifty people (realistic) and seventy people (full capacity). As stated in
the contracts section above, most rooms now require a "per head" or
percentage charge that comes out of the cover fee. For this example,
we will assume that we are using a standard contract and a $3 per head
charge. (See table 17.1.)

Table 17.1. Producing costs and profits per performance (piano only)

Earnings ($20 Cover)	**$1,400** (70)	**$1,000** (50)
Expenses:		
Musical director/pianist	$250	$250
Tech fee	$100	$100
Room cost ($3 per head)	$210 (70)	$150 (50)
TOTAL	**$560**	**$500**
Profit:	**$840**	**$500**

Now, let's consider the same scenario, but with a trio of instruments
(piano, bass, and drums) instead of a piano only. We will use the same
formula and statistics as above. (See table 17.2.)

Note that adding a bassist and drummer to your roster results in a
significant difference in take-home profit. You could also take a "middle
road": with only a piano and bass player (a common instrumental con-

Table 17.2. Producing costs and profits per performance (trio)

Earnings ($20 Cover)	**$1,400** (70)	**$1,000** (50)
Expenses:		
Musical director/pianist	$250	$250
Bass player	$150	$150
Drummer	$150	$150
Tech fee	$100	$100
Room cost ($3 per head)	$210 (70)	$150 (50)
TOTAL	**$860**	**$800**
Profit:	**$540**	**$200**

figuration) your total show expense with seventy people in attendance would be $710, leaving you a profit of $690. With fifty people in the room, your show expense would be $650, leaving you with a net profit of $350. There are also expenses you will encounter in the weeks leading up to the show. These are outlined in table 17.3.

Table 17.3.   Preshow costs

10 hours of rehearsal with music director/pianist:	$90 × 10	$900
3 hours of tech rehearsal:	$90 × 3	$270
Charts:	$100 × 15	$1,500
Total preshow costs (piano only):		**$2,670**
With a bass player (3-hour rehearsal)	$50 × 3	$150
Revised total (with bass):		**$2,820**
With a drummer (3-hour rehearsal)	$50 × 3	$150
Revised total (with bass and drums):		**$2,970**

One should also note that you will likely do only one band or tech rehearsal, which will occur before your first show. Therefore, if you are performing the same show two or more times, these expenses can be amortized over the run of shows. Lastly, let's examine the total cost to produce one show with various configurations of instruments. (See table 17.4.)

Finally, remember that the more shows that you book, the more you will amortize the preshow expenses. Also, remember the formula that was used here isn't the only one—formulas can change. For example, you could charge a $25 or $30 cover. Also, depending on the room and evening, you could have fewer than fifty or more than seventy people in attendance. Changes like these would obviously affect your net income.

Add-On Costs

Additional items that you might spend money on could be the following: a director (between $70 and $100 per hour), your vocal coach (between $80 and $150 per hour), acting classes, hair products and makeup, studio rentals for rehearsals (usually between $20 and $30 per hour), a publicity person (which can cost you anywhere from $1,000 to $2,500), postcards (which range from $250 to $500), and your outfit or costume. All of these are optional costs, but common ones in cabaret.

Table 17.4.   Total cost to produce one show

	Piano	Piano & Bass	Trio
70 People in Attendance			
Preshow costs	$2,670	$2,820	$2,970
Show costs	$560	$710	$860
Total show cost	**$3,230**	**$3,530**	**$3,830**
Net profit (70 × $20)	–$1,400	–$1,400	–$1,400
Net loss (after first show)	**–$1,830**	**–$2,130**	**–$2,430**
Second show net profit	$840	$690	$540
Third show net profit	$840	$690	$540
Fourth show net profit	$840	$690	$540
Total net profit/loss (4 shows)	**$690**	**–$60**	**–$810**
50 People in Attendance			
Preshow costs	$2,670	$2,820	$2,970
Show costs	$500	$650	$800
Total show cost	**$3,170**	**$3,470**	**$3,770**
Net profit (50 × $20)	–$1,000	–$1,000	–$1,000
Net loss (after first show)	**–$2,170**	**–$2,470**	**–$2,770**
Second show net profit	$500	$350	$200
Third show net profit	$500	$350	$200
Fourth show net profit	$500	$350	$200
Total net loss (4 shows)	**–$670**	**–$1,420**	**–$2,170**

Offsetting the Budget

Although you are the lead producer of your own show, even lead producers don't go it alone. As the lead producer you can find sponsors or a coproducer, sell advertising space in your program if you have one (and this is a good reason to have one), or open a donation or funding page on social media. Also, consider asking family members to help you produce a show in lieu of an upcoming birthday or holiday gift.

Finally, *be prepared.* The more prepared you are in your rehearsals, the less time you will need to spend paying your team to do something you can do for yourself. Remember to read your contracts carefully so you do not get stuck with any mystery costs. And last but not least, treat your show like a business venture—it is one!

FINAL THOUGHTS

There is no denying that crafting a show, finding a team, self-promoting, and self-producing is hard work, time consuming, and expensive. But there are also tangible returns on this investment. How many hours have you spent in voice lessons, vocal coachings, or acting lessons? And how often do you actually get to perform? The learning experience of performing onstage cannot be underestimated. As singers, we learn by spending time "on the boards" honing our craft. Certainly, your singing life cannot be relegated to auditioning. The audition can be a very vapid experience, where you are not receiving the necessary feedback from the audience to answer questions such as "Does this song work for me?" or "Am I connecting to the lyric and to the audience?" Performing artists learn from performing, not from auditioning.

I am reminded of something that was once said to me by the great Broadway actress Chita Rivera (b. 1933): "*Nobody* gets paid what they are worth in this business. We do this because we have to, because we love it, because we breathe it. If you're in this business for the money, then get out now, because you will always be disappointed." The development of your craft—your *individual* craft—comes from your ability to create art, not your ability to "get the job." You will discover that, over time, if this is your chosen path of artistic expression, you will start to "play" under different and more lucrative contracts. Cabaret offers a unique opportunity to develop skills required in every other aspect of performance art *and* to do so with full ownership of your artistic ability. *That's* why we do it.

18

DIY ("DO-IT-YOURSELF") PROMOTION

Cabaret is both an art and a business. There are no longer "auditions" for cabaret. It is an entirely self-produced and self-promoted art form. After you've crafted a compelling show, built your team, started re-hearsals, and have your club dates, it's time to promote your show. To that end, this chapter will guide you through many different options for self-promotion and marketing. Remember, your audience may start out largely as friends and family, but your goal is to reach a much wider audience. To that end, it is imperative that you use every means of pro-motion available within your budget.

There are many current social media platforms that can be of tremen-dous service in promoting your show. Facebook, Instagram, and Twitter are just a few in a sea of "apps" that can be very beneficial, especially when you are on a limited budget. And of course a YouTube channel is a ubiquitous tool for performing artists. To that end, we have devoted a section of this chapter to a "how to" guide for optimizing your social media presence, as well as a portion that discusses how to seek the help of a public relations (PR) professional. These sections were graciously contributed by Rosalyn Coleman Williams and Betsyann Faiella who are experts on these topics. Before that, however, let's go over several traditional and reliable methods of self-promotion that are frequently used in the world of cabaret.

SHOWCARDS

Show postcards are one of the most reliable forms of advertisement in cabaret. They can be distributed at local spots where people who are interested in live entertainment may congregate: coffeehouses, jazz clubs, social clubs, libraries, salons, restaurants, theaters, and of course other cabaret and entertainment venues. And although social media can (and probably will) be a major component in your advertising efforts, postcards are still considered to be an industry standard.

How to design your postcard and where to have it produced is entirely up to you. But do think about what might be visually appealing to *look* at, not just to read. It's not enough that all the information is there—we see a picture of you. Your potential audience needs to be drawn to your postcard on a visual level first before they will read the details. Think about what kind of postcards you are drawn to. What would make your postcard more memorable than someone else's?

To Spend or Not to Spend

High-end cards (glossy card stock, color photos, unique size/shape) send a psychological message of quality. Postcards are entirely about the initial impression, and a quality card indicates an investment. From a marketing point of view, this investment generally gets a higher rate of return. In other words, don't skimp on your postcard!

Creating a "Look"

This *Animal Magnetism* postcard uses a photograph with a playful, almost cartoonlike jungle scene in the background, which indicates the comic nature of this performer and show. Marketing-wise, this image allows the card to stand out in a sea of images.

Figure 18.1. *Lynda Rodolitz: Animal Magnetism.*

Figure 18.2. *Kristine Zbornik at the Metropolitan Room.*

Multi-award-winner Kristine Zbornik (figure 18.2) provides another effective example. The energy and design of the card is unique. You know exactly what to expect from this show just by looking at the card.

Consistent Branding

Establish your "brand" with the use of a consistent format, font, or image within your advertising campaign. This is an important part of any marketing strategy, especially for cabaret singers doing their second, third, and future shows. Creating a brand by keeping certain elements of the design consistent (such as font style, postcard size, and the use of a logo or similar image) will attract an audience member even *before* they read the content. Over time they will come to visually know this is *your* card and *your* show. Each show should have a slightly different look within your established branding. You don't want your audience to think this is the exact same show you did last time. However, consistency when creating your "look" will ultimately create your unique brand.

Figure 18.3. Mark Nadler: Razzle Dazzle. Postcard by Frank Dain | Photo by Heather Sullivan.

Figure 18.4. *Mark Nadler: Does This Room Make My Act Look Big? Postcard by Frank Dain | Photo by Heather Sullivan.*

Mark Nadler establishes his brand by consistently using full-color cards with an energetic and atmospheric image as opposed to a head-shot. The energy of the image jumps off the card and conveys an artistic uniqueness, which itself establishes his brand. These two cards (seen here in black and white) use a similar color, yellow, to highlight the title, thereby establishing a consistency of branding.

Regina Zona's postcards (figures 18.5 and 18.6) exemplify both consistent branding and an eye-catching "look." This woman is a former opera singer, now performing in cabaret. In opera she performed internationally as the Queen of the Night in Mozart's *Die Zauberflöte*. Staying authentic to her brand, these images pay homage to her past and indicate a certain level of artistic gravitas. The pictures are regal and classy, foreshadowing both the music one will hear (probably not rock 'n' roll) and the overall quality of the production. Once again, the quality of your card subliminally communicates the quality of your show to your prospective audience.

Figure 18.5. *Regina Zona: Becoming . . . the Queen—One Woman's Self-Help Journey to Authenticity. Postcard by Regina Zona | Photo by Susan Stripling.*

Figure 18.6. *Regina Zona: Becoming the Queen 2.0. Postcard by Regina Zona | Photo by Susan Stripling.*

Return Engagements

If you know you will do three shows in May and then bring the show back in the fall, it will be cost effective to order more cards than you need. Then you can simply add a "RETURN ENGAGEMENT" or "ENCORE PERFORMANCE" label with the new performance. This label subconsciously adds a sense of excitement or urgency to the return engagement. Consider this possibility when designing your original cards.

You may also opt to print postcards in bulk (one thousand plus) with your branded image and title of the show on the front. You can use the same cards for all your future engagements of this show and simply use larger labels or have the details printed on the back of the card for each run of the show.

Other Considerations

Society today is extremely visually oriented. Too many words and too much detail guarantees your postcard will wind up in the wastebasket immediately. Keep it simple. One or two brief reviews (one-liners)—if you have them—always help, but keep the card clean.

Your photo should be a true representation of who you are now—not ten years or forty pounds ago. It should represent not only your look but also your energy. If you're doing a theme show, your photo should communicate the energy you will bring to the stage. Are you selling a brassy musical comedy show or an elegant evening of the Great American Songbook? The look of each of these postcard should be completely different.

Most clubs will display your cards for distribution. They may even display a poster-sized card in the window. If you're going to invest in a poster, why not make a few? Although it is not recommended to post outside, strategically placed posters inside different venues can be very effective.

Although design and printing fees have fallen substantially in the last few years, the question remains: Will these cards bring in the necessary amount of people you need in order to justify their cost? Think about the size of the club, your cover charge, and the seating capacity versus the cost ratio. In other words, how many seats will you need to fill in order to pay for the cards? If you are doing four to six performances, postcards will most likely pay off.

The Manhattan Association of Cabarets (MAC) offers an email list as well as a mailing label list of its membership as a perk to members. This is an excellent way to reach those who are truly interested in cabaret performance but who may not be on social media. Many people prefer the visual and tactile feel of a postcard to remind them not to miss your show.

THE OPEN MICROPHONE

The "open mic" is also an essential part of promoting your show, especially in metropolitan areas. As someone who is producing and starring in a show, it is essential to sing at any and all open mics in your area for at least two months before your show opens. Your voice and performance will be your best advertisement and should have people approaching you asking when and where you'll be singing. Be prepared to pass out your postcards and accept your colleagues' cards in return.

In New York there is an open mic on almost every night of the week. Many have featured guests who sing more than one tune. Let the host/producer of the open mic know that you have a show coming up and hand them a postcard. You might just book a featured spot in the weeks leading up to your show.

Keep in mind that being seen and remembered favorably is your *best* advertising! Open mics have a certain protocol. Be sure to follow this protocol in order to make the best impression.

1. Rule number 1: *Just sing!* The host/producer has one job, and that is to get as many people up to sing as possible. If you talk for ten minutes before you sing, two other people may not be able to sing. This is professionally unacceptable. Just sing your song and pass out your cards. Rehearse what you are going to say before your song. This should be one or two sentences of the patter at most. Keep it concise and clean.
2. When you arrive, check in with the host. If you have to sign up to sing, be sure to give them your name, even if you think they already have it. ("Hi, I'm _____. I'd love to be on the list tonight.")

3. Silence your cell phone and *do not text* during the show. Give the other performers your complete attention.

4. Have your music prepared in your key with as few page turns as possible. Have your music printed on *card stock* (yes, card stock) and taped edge to edge (accordion style). Do you have a special arrangement of your tune? Does it have a lot of "returns," "D. S. al codas," and so forth? If so, do yourself a favor and arrange the music with no returns. (You will need to do the cutting and pasting yourself.) Have your arrangement written out completely so the person accompanying you never needs to flip to a previous page. With your music arranged in this way, you (a) will spend less time showing the pianist the "road map" of your tune, and (b) will be less likely to become the victim of errant page turns.

5. The one caveat to the previous statement is if you are using a jazz chart and the entire song is printed on one page. Even with the standard "return to A" and "tag ending," a one-page chart of a well-known standard in your key is preferred over multiple pages.

6. Your sheet music must match your performance practice. In other words, sing the music as written or have someone create a chart specifically for you. Keep in mind that the sheet music you just downloaded is not likely to be written in the style of the artist you are emulating. Sometimes digital sheet music providers will indicate that the arrangement is "in the style of" someone. But most often what you download is the "standard" version. The lesson here: *Don't ever bring an untried piece of sheet music to an open mic.*

7. When you are called up to sing, give the music to the pianist and tell them (briefly) what you need. The host may ask you questions about your upcoming show. Give a one-line introduction to your tune (if you must) and sing. *This is the process. Don't drag it out.* Afterward, quickly thank your audience/pianist/host, take your music, and leave.

8. Listen to your fellow singers. They listened to you. And above all, *do not leave* right after you sing. If you *must* leave early, tell the host/producer when you arrive. But be careful; you don't want to become known as a "hit and run" singer. Give your colleagues the courtesy and professional respect that they gave you. Your reputa-

tion is fragile in this regard. In other words, follow the golden rule and treat other singers the way you would like to be treated.

* * *

DIGITAL PROMOTION

Rosalyn Coleman Williams is the creator of Acting in the Digital Age, a platform that helps performers optimize their use of digital marketing, harness the power of social media, and understand the importance of an ethically responsible digital footprint.[1] She also created the first live, online acting class called "Zoom in Acting" where performers learn to use current technology and their own craft to create transformative self-tapes/video.

An esteemed teacher for more than twenty-five years, we asked Coleman Williams to contribute her expertise to this chapter. She has taught students at NYU's Tisch School of the Arts, SUNY Purchase,

Figure 18.7. Rosalyn Coleman Williams. *Photo by Audrey Foto.*

the Actors Center, the American Conservatory Theater, Actors Connection, Howard University, and the Duke Ellington School of the Arts in Washington, D.C. In addition, she has conducted acting workshops at film festivals around the country.

As an actor, Coleman Williams's professional experience includes Broadway, film, and television. She has acted with Meryl Streep, Viola Davis, Samuel L. Jackson, Halle Berry, and Tom Cruise. She stars in the recently released second season of the Emmy-nominated web series *Ctrl Alt Delete* and will soon be seen in the feature film *Miss Virginia*. Although she is best known as an actor, she is also the director of two award-winning short films, *Allergic to Nuts* and *Drawing Angel*. Both have been seen nationally on television as well as in film festivals in the United States and abroad. Coleman Williams is currently preparing to direct the feature film *Hanging by a Thread*, written and produced by her husband and partner Craig T. Williams and executive produced by Academy Award winner Viola Davis and her husband Julius Tennon. ♪

THE CABARET SINGER AND SOCIAL MEDIA

For many singers, social media can be both overwhelming and intimidating. It can be especially scary when it comes to sharing your professional desires, ambitions, and accomplishments. You may worry about whether you've shared too much or appear to be bragging—or even worse, boring people with mundane musings about what you had for breakfast. When it comes right down to it, you just don't have the time.

The purpose of social media for a singer is simple: *it is to help you do your job*. Your job is not only to sing; it is also to become known so people will be drawn to what you are selling, which is your voice and performance. Every performer must create a public persona—the public side of you that is authentic, good at your craft, and ready to share your gifts with the world. You must build a group of loyal followers who will become comfortable enough with you to join your mailing list and ultimately show up to see you perform. You must create an authentic digital version of *you*.

Does it feel unnecessary? Here's what you should know: When you submit your material to a club or meet someone professionally, the first thing they will do (when you leave the room) is look for you online or on social media. Many clubs will ask you to submit an example of your work via YouTube or Vimeo. And a simple Google search should immediately yield beneficial information. In this digital day and age, if you can't be found online, people may become suspicious. They wonder what you are hiding and, more important, *why* you are hiding.

Maybe you aren't online because social media platforms are always changing. It is hard to keep up with the latest thing or the newest app. Maybe you are online and choose to keep your settings "private." Keeping everything private won't work. In fact, it can actually hurt your career, especially one that heavily relies on self-promotion. Make yourself discoverable.

In real life we show up for someone we know, admire, and trust. Social media is where many professional and fan-based relationships are fostered. They are solidified in person, of course, by the authenticity of your performance. That authenticity must be reflected in your social media presence. Social media extends your voice. The images, audio, and the video you share, as well as in your content and the way you write is the digital version of you. Twitter, Instagram, Facebook, and Snapchat simply package it for their market. It is a way to stay current and be in touch with your audience. The ability to effectively communicate with your audience is essential to the art of cabaret.

Safety First

Turn off location services so you can't be followed in real time. Read privacy policies and realize that *nothing* is private. Create an email account and establish a phone number exclusively for the public. Social media requires that you share this information, so set up contact information separate from the phone number and email account you use for intimate friends and family members. Google Voice can be used to generate a separate phone number that rings to your existing device. And be sure to have a separate Google email address for the public and one for work/personal use. Most important, be an honest broker. Consider how would you feel if *everyone* read what you shared and posted online.

Do the Math

Let's say you have three thousand followers on your platform of choice, and you have a cabaret show coming up. How wonderful would it be to fill the house with one hundred of those followers! You would need to add performances, and each night those followers would buy your CD and spend lots of money on drinks. The club is thrilled and offers you a future booking. How amazing would that feel? This is a very achievable goal.

In entertainment casting it has become common practice to consider a performer's social media presence. Performers who do not have social media followers or who have no online presence lose jobs. Why? They have no way of promoting their project. There's no guarantee they'll put bodies in seats. If you have 250,000 followers on any platform, you have power as an influencer and can attract serious collaborators for creative endeavors.

Best Practices

It is important to follow the culture of the platform you are on. For instance,

1. Twitter is a short and fast medium; it's not intended for essays.
2. Facebook is a little bit of everything.
3. Snapchat is temporary but provides a channel for ongoing content.
4. Instagram is all about images and videos, and you don't need permission to be "friends."

With all of these platforms, it's best to go slow. Choose the platform that works best for your immediate needs. As you become more comfortable, try another and expand your reach. Here are some important tips to keep in mind:

1. Remember that *nothing* is private.
2. Platforms rise and fall in popularity.
3. Advertising your profession can be tedious and annoying (unless you're on LinkedIn). However, it's called *social* media for a reason. Make nine out of ten posts fun. You can do this by sharing your interests (e.g., music, movies, art, sewing, travel, animals, food). Make sure you are sharing *real* experiences. You are revealing who you are, and like-minded people will be drawn to you. Promote your show or your career, yes, but balance that out with more fun posts than "come see my show" requests.
4. Self-promotion should be short and simple. It should have one message or request. You should ask your audience to do one thing only, such as push this button, listen to this song, read this message. It should never be more complicated than that.
5. Make it user-friendly. Your content should be easy to understand and useful. It should be delightful.

6. Don't ignore a huge social topic or news item. It makes you seem tone deaf. Chime in! Share what matters to you. It's your public persona. It's *you* on the *Today* show.
7. Back up your social media shares with a link to your website in the information section of the platform.
8. Follow and interact *authentically* with industry professionals.
9. Share a mix of behind-the-scenes and candid photos.
10. Do not hide. You should be the focus—not your pet, your kids, or the shrubbery outside your apartment. You don't want people to think you're uncomfortable with your appearance.
11. Post consistently and post authentically.
12. Always include a link to your website. Don't you want people to see what you were put on this earth to do?

A few of my best jobs started with being "discovered" on social media. The journey from a Facebook post to my website to my contact information resulted in a real-world meeting. Social media is the beginning of a relationship between like-minded people. Whether you are beginning a professional working relationship or trying to attract an audience to your show, you want to reach people who share common interests and temperaments. That discovery can begin on social media.

What you share does not have to be perfect—that's not authentic. Rather, be *real*! It is just as important to share disappointments as it is triumphs. Share as you would with an acquaintance. Create connections by sending people to your website where they can get to know your work.

Social media is also where your audience and fans can see behind the scenes. Give them a glimpse of what you're doing and what's next. You should always be conversing with your audience and regularly contributing to the social fabric of the community. Social media can be the most powerful tool in your arsenal. Share and follow up.

One last thing: Convert followers into an email list. It becomes the list you can directly email friend to friend. I get one from Tyler Perry each time he debuts a film. And guess what? I go every opening weekend because those emails make me feel so close to him. It works!

* * *

WHEN TO HIRE A PRO

At some point in your cabaret/perfor-
mance career you may seek the advice
and help of a professional public relations representative.[2] But what exactly
does that mean? What can and should
you expect from this professional? We
asked Betsyann Faiella, an independent public relations manager and
media producer, to share her expertise
on the working relationship between
artist and PR manager. Faiella has a
deep background in producing advertising for major brands, as well as
creative coaching and performing. She

Figure 18.8. Betsyann Faiella.
Photo courtesy of Frank Dain.

is well respected throughout the cabaret industry. Her company, Savoy
PR, helps clients identify and realize their PR goals. ♪

HIRING A PUBLIC RELATIONS PROFESSIONAL

What does a publicist do? What is public relations? Do I need a publicist? Is a publicist my agent? Does a publicist ensure an audience for
my show? What's the difference between a PR person and a publicist?
These are some of the questions performers ask themselves when they
have a show to promote or a burgeoning career in show business and
think they might be ready for the press.

What is PR? Public relations is a plan meant to build positive relationships between you and the public (your audience/your customers).
Once you've hired a PR professional, they help craft and communicate
your message. They reach out with that message in the form of a press
release and a spoken pitch that's ready at a second's notice. A publicist
is a spokesperson for you—communicating by phone calls and emails
to editors, producers, news programmers, and journalists who might
be interested in what you have to offer. If you need crisis management,
they can be your public face in front of news cameras. But don't worry;
as a rule, there's very little crisis management in cabaret!

Before you hire a PR person, why not interview a few? Talk about your goals and expectations and ask about *their* background. Look at what they've done for others. Make sure they have experience. If you're a beginner and they promise you an appearance on NBC's *Today* show, you should run for the door. Discuss fees and payment terms. They will also ask you questions so they can determine if your goals seem realistic. A publicist knows the marketplace, and as tough as it may be to hear, an ethical person is going to be honest with you about what they think they can do and what is probably not going to happen immediately.

If there's *already* a plan and a pitch in place, you might just hire a *publicist* to get you "published," so to speak, on news or entertainment platforms and social media. Some PR pros specialize in social media as a primary focus.

PR pros also provide media training. If you're anticipating interview opportunities on radio or television, you need to be ready. Almost everyone can use a little media training. Some people are shy and introspective, and others are so enthusiastic that they sound like a runaway train, barely taking a breath and giving the interviewer no opportunity to ask the next question. Interviews are easier for everyone when you've done some preparation. My favorite type of interview is when you actually have a conversation with the interviewer, perhaps asking questions of your own.

Publicists open doors for you that you can't, don't want to, or don't have time to open yourself. I learned this when (in another life) I was a media producer and a singer in Los Angeles cabarets. Between producing media and rehearsing—and everything else that goes into earning a living while pursuing your dreams—I didn't have time to worry about press. And frankly, I hadn't the foggiest idea how to do it! So, I hired a PR person, and boom—I got a review in *Variety*. Other high-profile items followed. I experienced firsthand the value of a good publicist!

When Do You Need a PR Pro?

At what point do you need to hire a PR pro? Here are five common situations:

1. When you have a new project to promote. However, proceed with caution; you and your project should be ready for press. Press

coverage is not always pretty and not always what you think you're going to hear. If you're underprepared, that may upset the press. Conversely, being unprepared *emotionally* for what the press might say may upset you. Because there are fewer journalists, critics, and influential press outlets than there were ten or twelve years ago (even though the number of creatives seeking press coverage continues to grow), a performer may not get another chance with a publication/platform for a year or even more if they're deemed too green.

2. Another time you might choose to work with a publicist is when you've already managed to generate some buzz. A publicist can help you capitalize on the perceived or real demand you've created. An editor likes to know there's interest—and that they'll be publishing something their audience is eager to read.

3. You intuit or know there will be a news peg (story hook) that you believe could tie in to what you're promoting. A news peg is a reason for the editor/journalist/producer to publish the story (or to interview you). Maybe your solo show is about Vincent van Gogh (1853–1890) and the Met has just announced a major retrospective of his work in the next year, or you're planning a show celebrating an important birthday or anniversary of a composer or lyricist. You'll probably want to hire a PR pro immediately to get the word out about your show!

4. You're a little further down the road with your career and receiving more inquires than you can handle on your own. Remember, if you're fielding inquiries, there are even more out there to be had.

5. You're ready to be perceived as a "player." Having a representative gives you some cachet. However, as previously mentioned, your project should be ready for press.

A PR pro does not book you into venues—that is not part of their job description. However, if they have a good relationship with a venue they may be able to facilitate it. It is also not part of their job description to fill a room, but some may be willing to help you put bodies in seats. If you've begun to build a fan base on social media, the fans will hopefully come. You need to work on a fan base, whether you're doing it yourself or you hire a social media maven who "gets" you.

What PR can do is this: When you begin to get significant, positive, or provocative pieces of press, the show-going or music-buying public will eventually respond. But don't forget, there is a rule that people have to see your name repeatedly—it's actually called the "Rule of Seven"—before they consider spending money on you.

Does a PR pro advertise you? Advertising is different than PR. PR is earned. Advertising is purchased. Advertising isn't in a PR budget unless it is specifically placed there. Is advertising suggested? Yes, with several low-cost means available. Budget some money for advertising, but not immediately (particularly if you are a beginner).

What does it cost to hire a PR pro? (Are you sitting down?) Large firms cost from three thousand to more than ten thousand dollars per month. Small firms, however, may consider each potential client on an individual basis. Many firms have a minimum fee, however, for each type of job. PR is extremely time consuming; a client isn't just paying for a PR pro to write a press release and send it out to a pack of journalists in a mass email. A client is paying for time, experience, and access to the PR pro's contacts.

The Client's Responsibilities

A client needs to give publicity lead time. As mentioned earlier, there are far fewer journalists covering music and theater than there were a dozen years ago. You cannot call a PR firm looking for representation just two weeks before your show. Reviewers plan their schedules well over a month in advance. Newspapers often need six weeks to consider the simplest feature. Most magazines need at least three months. Radio needs at least a few weeks to schedule an interview, unless you get lucky or it's an extremely timely "story" (remember the news peg). Simple listings are requested a minimum of two weeks in advance. You need at least two months if you're not going after any long lead (magazine) platforms. Allow five to six months for magazines.

Try to be responsive to the publicist when they contact you since it could be a last-minute thing and you'll miss out if you don't get back to them right away. Be prepared and on time for your interviews and meetings. Budget allocation is also your responsibility. If you've spent a fortune on a CD or crafting a show, hopefully you've set aside money for public relations. I can't tell you how many times someone has come to me with a CD that cost thousands of dollars to produce, yet they completely neglected to budget for promotion of their product.

FINAL THOUGHTS

Understanding the role of self-promotion in the success of any performing arts career, and especially in a cabaret career, is paramount. The use of social media—often thought of as the "holy grail" of publicity—is only one of many components used in promoting your show and building your audience. Postcard design and placement, directed emails, open mics, and publicity management are all additional resources available to you when you are ready. However, the best publicity resource you have—at any time—is *you!* Your reputation, not only as a performer but also as a member of the cabaret performing arts industry, is your best calling card. Throughout this book you will read the words "authentic" and "intimate" many times. Even when considering publicity, these words ring true. Don't forget, your audience is coming to see *you* and to hear what *you* have to say. No matter how you choose to publicize your show, do so *authentically* and with the purpose of *intimately* sharing your storytelling with the audience.

NOTES

1. This portion of the chapter was written by Rosalyn Coleman Williams with introductory paragraphs by David Sabella.

2. This portion of the chapter was written by Betsyann Faiella with an introductory paragraph by David Sabella.

19

ORGANIZATIONS AND ASSOCIATIONS

Interviews with Marilyn Lester,
KT Sullivan, and Lennie Watts

Cabaret, like any other industry, has its own trade associations and support organizations. Three of the most important of these are the American Songbook Association, the Mabel Mercer Foundation, and the Manhattan Association of Cabarets. These organizations, each in their own unique way, work tirelessly to advance the education, appreciation, and performance of cabaret in the United States and abroad. In addition, each of them presents coveted awards every year in recognition of achievements in cabaret performance. This chapter provides an introduction and overview of these important organizations through direct conversations with their leaders: Marilyn Lester (American Songbook Association), KT Sullivan (Mabel Mercer Foundation), and Lennie Watts (Manhattan Association of Cabarets).

THE AMERICAN SONGBOOK ASSOCIATION

The American Songbook Association (ASA) is a nonprofit arts and education organization dedicated to stimulating and promoting public interest in the legacy of the Great American Songbook (both classic and new) as well as the unique art form of cabaret. Under the editorial leadership of Frank Dain, the ASA also publishes *Cabaret Scenes* magazine, the only print magazine in the world with a focus on the art form of cabaret. The magazine is published six times a year with news, photos, and feature articles, while the *Cabaret Scenes* website hosts additional content including performance reviews from all over the world. The ASA also bestows a Lifetime Achievement Award at its annual gala, as well as the Margaret Whiting Award in association with Debbi Whiting and My Ideal Music. This award goes to a cabaret performer who exhibits a potential for growth in his or her performance abilities. ♪

Marilyn Lester is the executive director of the ASA as well as a contributing writer and reviewer for *Cabaret Scenes*. She is also an editor, contributing writer, and reviewer for the web-based Nite-Life Exchange, reviewer for the web-based Theater Pizzazz, and a contributing writer for the *New York City Jazz Record*. Before coming to the ASA, Lester served as the executive director for the Duke Ellington Center for the Arts. Additionally, she serves on the boards of the New York chapter of the Duke Ellington Society and the American Popular Song Society (APSS). Lester is also a member of the League of Professional Theatre Women and the Coalition of Professional Women in the Arts and Media.

Figure 19.1. Marilyn Lester. *Photo by An-Khang Vu-Cong.*

We were fortunate to have the opportunity to speak with Lester about the ASA, the Great American Songbook, and the history of cabaret performance style and technique.

Marilyn, I am thrilled to be able to speak with you about the Great American Songbook, as well as the ASA. Let's start with a definition of the Great American Songbook. What are your thoughts on this?

The ASA actively seeks to define the American Songbook. We have classified it into two distinct realms: "classic/golden age"—essentially pre-World War II—and the "new" songbook, which is everything since. The term "Great American Songbook" refers to the classic/golden age songbook, the songs that became standards and were popular from about the ragtime period to World War II. They encompass a range of styles that includes jazz, ragtime, swing, and anything written by the great composers of the era: Duke Ellington and Fats Waller (these composers come to mind first as the ASA just produced a gala celebrating the "Black American Songbook"), as well as Irving Berlin, Jerome Kern, Hoagy Carmichael, Johnny Mercer, Harry Warren, and many others. They are songs you would hear Frank Sinatra and others sing—classic songs of that era and still cabaret favorites. Post World War II, there was a shift in the stylistic approach to what was being written. The result was a sound that is slightly different. That "post" era leads up to today. There are many modern songwriters who are writing great songs that have already become standard songs. A standard is not only a song that you hear over and over and over again but also one that has lyrical and musical complexity—that is, something that has substance. A true standard has something to say in both the tune and the lyric. I am compelled to quote Duke Ellington, who said, "There are two kinds of music, *good music* and the other kind." So, for us it's the *good music* that makes a song a standard worthy of the Great American Songbook.

You mentioned the criteria for inclusion in the American Songbook includes musical and lyrical complexity. Is part of that criteria the presence of—and/or the lack of—a constant beat? Is that what differentiates a standard from a pop song?

The Smithsonian Institution did a study in which several musicologists determined that one of the progressions of American music was that many songs of the modern/pop era lack the kind of complexity seen in the Great American Songbook. From the musicologist's point of view, it's not just the beat—it's *everything* that constructs a song from a songwriter's point of view. If you look at a Duke Ellington song, it is quite complex: the notes, the harmonies, the chord progressions, and so forth. A tune like "Sophisticated Lady" is a great example of this complexity. It has a beautiful melody and a complexity in the lyric that tells a story. That's another component of what makes a standard a standard and why complexity is important. Ultimately, a song that makes the songbook tells a story. A lyric that goes "I love you baby, yeah, yeah" clearly does not.

Is there any singer's version you particularly recommend for "Sophisticated Lady"?

For interpreting Duke I would go straight to Ella [Fitzgerald]. She recorded the entire Duke Ellington songbook as part of her songbook series for Verve Records. ♪

You made a distinction about jazz. Do you feel that jazz is a separate and distinct genre from cabaret? How does jazz interface with the Great American Songbook?

Going back to Duke Ellington, he was notoriously against categories and labels. He has a catalogue of three thousand tunes, and not all of them are in a style that you would consider jazz. He referred to what he wrote as "American music." I like that term. I think that's a really good way of identifying the Great American Songbook.

So then, what about jazz?

With jazz, the lines blur. A standard song can be interpreted in several ways. While some songs initially seem to be jazz, they may not turn out that way when sung. It depends upon the interpretation of the singer and the way the song is arranged. Many tunes can be interpreted in either a straight or a jazz arrangement. The difference is in the way the singer approaches the lyrics and melody, as well as their unique delivery of the song. Also, of course, jazz involves improvisation.

Jazz is about the singer's interpretation of both the melody and lyric?

Yes, both. If the arrangement allows for improvisation, for slightly adjusting the melody, then I would call it jazz. In jazz you bend the rules as far as the music is concerned—you can extend a note, shorten a note, or introduce creative phrasing. That's what makes it jazz.

You also mentioned that you had an event for the "Black American Songbook." Tell me about how that distinguishes itself from the Great American Songbook.

Well, it shouldn't! Previously, I was executive director of the Duke Ellington Center for the Arts (DECFA). I worked with Mercedes Ellington (Duke's granddaughter), and after years of writing many reviews of cabaret and jazz, I realized that you would often hear people refer to the works of Cole Porter, the Gershwins and Irving Berlin, but never anybody of color. So, when the American Songbook Association launched our first gala, I felt we had to rectify that unfortunate trend. It became my personal mission. I want the names Duke Ellington and Fats Waller to come off a person's tongue as trippingly as do Cole Porter and Irving Berlin. As a result, we dedicated our first gala to the "Black American Songbook," or perhaps I should say "standards written by African Americans."

In this current era of political correctness, do you think that there is any risk of cultural appropriation if someone who is not of color were to sing those songs?

No, not at all. If you didn't know who wrote them you wouldn't think for a moment, "Oh, that was written by a black person" or "that was written by a white person." Early Irving Berlin draws from ragtime, so you might think an African American wrote it. But no! It was Irving Berlin.

Cabaret is not exclusively the Great American Songbook. One hears many different types of music in a cabaret club or show. And yet, I perceive a dividing line between those cabaret singers who specialize in Great American Songbook and everyone else.

I would say that was right.

Does the Great American Songbook in any way define cabaret? Would a definition for cabaret be . . . to sing a majority of Great American Songbook repertoire in any given performance?

That may have been true a decade ago, but it's changing now. The entire business of cabaret is changing. Cabaret at its core will always be an art form that presents material in an intimate space: not a stadium, and not a concert hall. What used to be called a nightclub or supper club is now a smaller space in which people gather to hear a performer. The notion of "what to perform" in that space has historically been the golden age songbook—the standards of the prewar era. But that's largely because we were chronologically closer to the music and singers of that era. Now, we are decades further away from that era, and the repertoire is becoming more contemporary. There is at least as much material written since World War II as there was before World War II. Modern songs are lovely, fabulous, and should be sung. For example, we now have the whole Stephen Sondheim Songbook, just to name one composer.

So, let's compare and contrast a Sondheim song. How would one perform it differently in a cabaret setting compared to the same song on the music theater stage.

If you are performing in a theatrical production, you are playing a role. You're interpreting the song through that character. That necessity disappears once you walk into a cabaret room. In cabaret, you are in control of your own delivery. The performer has the luxury of determining how he or she wants to sing that song, free of a character.

Yet, so many singers put themselves back in the constraints of a character. They put up a strong fourth wall and deliver the song in the same way they would in a musical.

Yes, unfortunately, that often occurs.

So, is that still cabaret?

Well, now you're getting to the point. Cabaret is really about how one personally delivers the lyric and makes sense of the material. Unless one does that, it's not cabaret.

Can we then define cabaret as being a more intimate performance style, devoid of the fourth wall, and with a more personal lyric delivery?

Absolutely, yes! I think that's what makes cabaret great! That wall must be down. Now, I've also seen remarkable cabaret shows where the wall is up, but then you're talking about someone with an "a-list" reputation and a larger-than-life stage presence. And even with that, there is an unavoidable intimacy that comes through.

Thinking about the stadiums in which Barbra Streisand performs, they might as well be a five-hundred-seat room, or even a one-hundred-seat room, because she is that communicative and personal.

Correct, and that's what I am saying—it takes a Barbra Streisand to pull that off. There are those who just totally give themselves to the audience. It's as if you're in their living room and they're singing only to you. That is what *really* makes cabaret "cabaret"—that ability to drop all defenses and give 100 percent of yourself to the person who is there. Great cabaret singers make the audience feel as if they are your best friend, sitting there saying, "Hey, this is a song I love. Want to hear it?" There's no pretense, no artifice—it's just pure "me to you." That is the apex of what makes good cabaret.

"Me to you"—meaning there is a constant communication with the audience?

Yes. You want the people in the audience to come out of the room feeling uplifted and feeling as though something special has happened, perhaps even be moved to tears by a song. There's something really special about that kind of intimate exchange in which the person in the audience, in the cabaret room, feels a connection with the performer. It's not an abstract. It's not watching TV. It's somebody up there. It's somebody with whom you can make an emotional connection. That's what makes cabaret special.

How long has the ASA been in existence, and how long have you been the executive director? Could you tell us a bit about your mission statement, the events, opportunities, and education you offer?

The American Songbook Association was originally called the Cabaret Scenes Foundation and was founded when *Cabaret Scenes* magazine was incorporated. It was originally a not-for-profit foundation primarily focused on publishing the magazine. Along with that there was also a mission statement, which included a statement on the importance of education. I had been writing for *Cabaret Scenes* magazine, so I asked Frank Dain (the editor) and Peter Leavy (the publisher) for a meeting, and I said, "Look, I have the experience. I can do this for you." I proposed my position, and they said "okay." As part of this restructuring, we constructed a new mission statement. In order to make the broader mission statement a reality, that necessitated the organization to have a different name. After a lot of thought, we decided on "American Songbook Association," and we officially launched the organization in January 2018. *Cabaret Scenes* magazine continues to be published under the same title.

Carolyn Montgomery was also a key element in this transformation. Unbeknownst to me, she approached Peter and Frank as well with her desire to bring the Great American Songbook into schools. The educational system is not what it used to be, and a lot of schools unfortunately don't have music at all. We decided to step up and fill that void. By the time I had come knocking on the door, Carolyn had already set up a program into a school that she knew, and the kids loved it.

Do you continue to bring the Great American Songbook into schools?

Yes. Throughout the five boroughs of New York City.

And, if someone reading this were to say, "Hey I'd like to have a program like that come into my school," can they can contact the ASA?

Absolutely. I don't want to ever again hear someone ask me, "Who is Cole Porter?" Or Duke Ellington or Fats Waller, for that matter. We will entertain any request.

OK, a new topic: Can you give a few examples of exemplary interpreters of the Great American Songbook, living or dead?

Well, Ella Fitzgerald has got to be up there. Frank Sinatra also. There's a reason that everybody loves Frank Sinatra. When it comes to interpretation, he is the master, the absolute master. And then also, female wise, you cannot get better than Margaret Whiting and Peggy Lee—especially early Peggy Lee. ♪

What about some of the female singers that come to mind immediately for most people, such as Judy Garland, Barbra Streisand, Liza Minnelli?

Garland is amazing. But I just cannot get into Streisand or Minnelli. For me they are too mannered. I prefer "clean," straightforward singing. ♪

So, their personal and vocal mannerisms invade the song too much for your taste?

Yes, in a way. I think that there's an unnecessary vocal trickery that happens in their singing.

At some point you feel that their vocal pyrotechnics overplay the lyric?

Yes, that is a good way of putting it. Cabaret is storytelling. And when I hear a story told to me, I want it to be told straight and true. I don't want fireworks or anything other than the story itself.

On this point, many great cabaret singers confine themselves to a certain range. Frank Sinatra was a baritone. Most of the Great American Songbook males topped out at F4 or G4. The women of that era, the belters, did not go above a C5, and the sopranos hardly ever above an E5. Do you think that there is a "range component" to be considered in great cabaret singing? As Roy Sander often says, "Just because you can sing that high doesn't mean you should" (paraphrased).

Right, exactly.

A lot of cabaret teachers and music directors lower the keys of songs even though the singer is saying, "That's not high for me. I can sing that." But it's not about what you can do. It's about what you need to do for the lyric, for the story.

Exactly. Let me invoke Sandy Stewart, who is now eighty-two years old. Because of her age, she cannot do vocally what she once did as a young woman. But talk about interpretation! She can possess a stage now as surely as she ever did. She knows that her range is limited. She sings lower than she used to, but she sings with such power. She inhabits the lyric and tells the story in a way that makes up for everything else. Again, it's about storytelling.

* * *

THE MABEL MERCER FOUNDATION

Named after one of the supreme cabaret artists of the twentieth century, the Mabel Mercer Foundation was established in 1985 to preserve and advance both the classic popular song and the performance and education of American cabaret. The foundation provides outreach to students across the country via workshops, seminars, competitions, concert tickets, and scholarships. Since its creation, the foundation has sponsored live performances throughout the year, by both new and established cabaret artists, including the annual New York Cabaret Convention at Jazz at Lincoln Center. Additionally, the Mabel Mercer Foundation continues its efforts outside of New York City, sponsoring cabaret conventions in San Francisco, Long Island, Chicago, Philadelphia, and Palm Springs, as well as international events in London and Sydney. ♪

KT Sullivan was named artistic director of the Mabel Mercer Foundation in 2012. Prior to this appointment, she starred in the 1995 Broadway revival of *Gentlemen Prefer Blondes*, as well as the 1989 revival of *The Threepenny Opera*. In addition to these two significant productions, Sullivan headlined for almost two decades in the Oak Room of the Algonquin Hotel. Her show, *Rhyme, Women, and Song*, was presented on the PBS station WNET 13, and her award-winning *Sondheim Montage*, also starring Jeff Harnar, was filmed for PBS from the New Jersey Performing Arts Center. She appears regularly in such New York venues as the Laurie Beechman Theatre and Birdland. Sullivan stars annually at the Pheasantry in London and has been showcased at Lincoln Center, Carnegie Hall, the Kennedy Center, the Spoleto

Figure 19.2. KT Sullivan. *Photo by Stacy Sullivan.*

Festival USA, the Chichester Festival, Club RaYé in Paris, and the Adelaide Festival in Australia. She has also guest starred on Garrison Keillor's *A Prairie Home Companion* and toured China as the star vocalist with the Manhattan Symphonie. Sullivan has recorded several albums on the DRG label, including *Crazy World* and *Live from Rainbow & Stars: The Songs of Bart Howard*, which won a Bistro Award. We had the opportunity to speak with Sullivan in her office at the Mabel Mercer Foundation. ♪

Thank you so much for sharing your time and expertise with us, KT. Tell me about the Mabel Mercer Foundation, its history, and your involvement with the organization.

Donald Smith started the Mabel Mercer Foundation when Mabel died in 1985, and the reason he started it was because all the obituaries said that Mabel was a "jazz" singer. He wanted her to be remembered correctly; he wanted Mabel to be remembered for what she truly was: a cabaret singer! I came into town in 1985, the year of her death, just in time for her memorial at Town Hall, which Donald produced. I was in the audience, and from the audience I saw Cy Coleman onstage along with Bart Howard, Julie Wilson, Dorothy Loudon, Elaine Stritch, Murray Grand, and the list goes on! They were all there to salute Mabel Mercer, and I didn't even know who she was! Some friends called me to ask if I would go with them because they had an extra ticket, and said, "Oh, sure," but I didn't know who she was. ♪

Frank Sinatra said, "Everything I learnt, I owe to Mabel Mercer." He would sit "ringside" along with Peggy Lee and Lena Horne, and they would try to figure out how she did it. Billie Holiday loved her. In fact, Billie Holiday would say, "Let's go by and see that classy singer." They would go to see her for her last set. They all wanted to figure out how she could bring you in to her realm, sitting on a chair telling a story. She would sing, and it was like she was talking on pitch.

By 1989, Donald had raised enough money to start the Cabaret Convention at Town Hall. There are all the years up here. [*KT gestures to a wall full of posters.*] Donald hoped by seeing these wonderful singers on that stage at Town Hall, the audience would then go see that person in a small room. It was a way to build a following. People would know who you were because you were exposed to 1,200 to 1,500 people in one night.

The year before Donald died, in 2011, he called me into the office and sat me down. Because his health was failing, he asked me, "Do you think this has really run its course, or do you think it should go on after myself?" I replied, "Donald, it should of course go on." He said, "Would you like to do it?" I fell out of my chair. That's how I got involved. ♪

Before coming to the Mabel Mercer Foundation, I was president of the Dutch Treat Club. Meetings were held at the National Arts Club, which is now called the Players Club. I produced a National Arts Club event for Donald, and he saw me officiating at the podium. He saw me as president of that and realized I could take over after he stepped down. And now, working with Rick Meadows and Jason Martin, it just keeps getting better. The foundation is a center in the world of cabaret. Our stationery says "The future of cabaret." That's how we're keeping the art form alive: by showing the world how it's done.

How does the Mabel Mercer Foundation manifest its mission of keeping cabaret alive?

Every week we send out a performance "spotlight" email. I try to only recommend people that I have seen or who have been in the convention. We also have a midyear concert every May. The first was in 2014, celebrating Margaret Whiting's career. In 2015 we celebrated people born in 1915 like Billie Holiday, Frank Sinatra, Alice Faye, and Bart Howard in a concert called "A Very Good Year." The next year we did a Cole Porter concert, and this May, we celebrated Jerome Kern.

You also produce the Cabaret Convention in October—and have educational programs as well.

Yes, we produce the high school American Songbook competition. Our board members, Adela and Larry Elow, endow this competition. We have participants from the Professional Performing Arts School (PPAS), LaGuardia High School, Frank Sinatra High School, and Talent Unlimited. And they are clamoring to participate! One teacher, from just one school, said to me, "I have eighteen students who want to compete this year." I can only have eighteen students in the *entire competition*!

They're all doing Great American Songbook repertoire?

Yes, from 1900 to 1970. I love that period. I think that the craft of songwriting took a real nosedive around 1970. Unfortunately, a lot of newer songs don't seem to have a beginning, middle, or end. Sometimes, a song just repeats one phrase over and over and over again until it just . . . ends. I call them "tapeworm" songs. I would rather have a song with some structure.

Where do you see the Mabel Mercer Foundation in five years? What are your goals, things the foundation hasn't yet done?

We've done conventions in Chicago and San Francisco, but we find them economically very difficult. I wish we could do more of those. We tried to go back to Chicago last year, but it was just too expensive. Our Cayman Islands master classes are underwritten by the Cayman Arts Festival, and if an organization like this can send us the money, it is easy for us to send them the faculty and the singers. We have to keep the

outreach going so we can nurture the next generation of cabaret singers. That is our mission. We have noticed through our work with the
public schools that kids truly do like this music when they're exposed to
it. After they hear the songs and sing them—and hear the approval of
their peers going nuts because these songs really go somewhere—then
they're hooked.

*KT, you have a truly lovely lyric soprano voice (and a solid technique),
but it's clear in your performance that your priority is the lyric and not
showing off the voice.*

No matter how great your voice is, it's never about the voice.

*The minute the voice steps in front of the lyric, we're not in cabaret
anymore.*

Right. You are correct.

*That's a very hard thing for singers to understand. You can have a beau-
tiful voice, but that doesn't mean you have to use all of it all the time. I
really admire that about you. Always, in your show, there is a moment
or two where this glorious voice comes out. And we think, "Oh my God,
she can do that?" But ultimately, it's not about that. You reserve that use
of voice as a lovely "back pocket" gem.*

Thank you.

*Is there such a thing as a specific cabaret performance technique? For
instance, take a song like "Send in the Clowns." If you're singing that
song in* A Little Night Music *on Broadway versus singing that same
song in cabaret, how is it different?*

In cabaret, you're singing *to the people* in the audience. On Broadway,
you're playing a character, and there's always a fourth wall. *It's very different.* I've seen a lot of Broadway people do their first cabaret show,
and the fourth wall is a hard box to break out of. They just can't do it.

I don't think the public at large understands the specificity of cabaret training or the art of cabaret versus music theater. Many singers think of cabaret as "music theater in the crook of the piano."

Well, a lot of the songs we sing are from early music theater. Maybe that's where the confusion starts. Cabaret is so much more personal. That's the very reason why the two art forms are so different.

So, how do you teach that?

It is hard. It can throw you off at first. I remember my first time. My first cabaret was the scariest thing I ever did. I was so used to that fourth wall. When you can see people's faces, you notice immediately if someone doesn't like the song or if someone has had a bad night. But it's also lovely if you're singing a romantic ballad and two people take each other's hands across the table. You get to see that. In the theater, you don't see that.

So, it is about connecting with the audience "in the moment" and reacting to what you see there?

Yes, and sometimes when that happens, we reenvision the song on the spot, because of what is happening at that moment. You react, and it affects what you do next.

Walk me through your process for reenvisioning a song you know from music theater when singing it in a cabaret show.

When you do a Broadway show, because you've done that and you know you're not thinking about how you're going to play this to your audience, you've got to be in character throughout the show. The audience almost doesn't exist, and they certainly don't influence how you prepare your performance. But for cabaret, you have to break down a song through the lyrics first. Never mind a character. What does lyric mean to you? You must find a way to personally paraphrase it.

And that becomes a very different story than it would be if it were still in the show.

Oh yes. It becomes *your* story.

Do cabaret artists only pick songs with lyrics that relate to their own personal story?

That's what's so great about cabaret. You can like every song you sing, or you don't have to sing it! Sometimes, you're stuck in a show, and you must sing a song you don't necessarily want to sing or hear a song you don't particularly like. And you think, *Oh God, I'm in this show.*

We call that "trapped in a hit."

Most important, you must love the lyric. Mabel, by the way, sang contemporary songs. She sang "Both Sides Now," just after it was written. She sang it before Judy Collins did. If she liked the lyrics, she would sing it. Plain and simple.

Cabaret repertoire, and especially the Great American Songbook, has such a depth to the lyric. It seems to me that one must've lived their life a little bit in order to be "truthful in the lyric." How then do we teach young people, who may not yet have had the life experience to fully understand the lyrics they are singing?

That is an interesting question. I recently saw this one little girl sing "The Ladies Who Lunch" from Stephen Sondheim's *Company*. She was so cute. She was all of seventeen. There was so much wrong with her performance. First of all, it was too high. Elaine Stritch's key is so low, and she was doing it an octave higher. So, the first thing we did is find a better key for her. And then, she didn't know who "Mahler" was, and she was saying "captain," instead of "caftan." However, she was funny, and the idea was right. She knew enough to know the song was funny, and good for her having that sensibility. She knew that it was a "good song." That same little girl also sang "Someone to Watch over Me," which was perfect for her. There are songs that are perfect for young girls, especially ones with lyrics that convey longing. But the "wizened" songs, they should stay away from them until . . . ♪

The what?

The "wizened" songs. The "no regrets, no complaints" type of songs. A child hasn't lived enough to sing about those things. But the longing songs . . . [*KT sings*] "I have dreamed that your arms are lovely . . ." Those are great. As you get older, there are a lot more songs that become available for you, but there are some that are perfect for young kids.

Do you think that a cabaret performance technique is not necessarily relegated to an small and intimate venue? Can the same technique be used in a venue of any size, provided the performer can reach across the footlights and communicate in an intimate way?

Barbara Cook played both Carnegie Hall and the Sydney Opera House. She also played the Metropolitan Opera. She could bring the audience in completely. It was different than when she was playing Marian the Librarian in *The Music Man*. In Carnegie Hall, she was not a character. She was Barbara Cook up there saying, "Can you come join me for my song?" ♪

So then, the definition of "cabaret" is not specifically tied to the size of venue but rather a specific and intimate performance technique?

Yes. When Maureen McGovern sang "Somewhere over the Rainbow" without a microphone at Rose Hall, she reached all of them, and it was quite moving. And that was 1,200 people.

Is there anything else you want to impart to our readers about the Mabel Mercer Foundation?

Cabaret is an art form through which I think more people can express themselves, even more so than art songs. Donald Smith always called cabaret the "fragile art." Most of us are not going to be playing Madison

Square Garden. That's just not going to happen. And we don't want that to happen, because cabaret is an intimate genre. It is this core value that we need to sustain. It's not a dying art. It's a fragile art, and we are going to keep it alive. This mission is also not a big movement, because we're not going to outsell Lady Gaga. However, people like that are now singing these songs.

Lady Gaga recently sang with Tony Bennett.

Yes, people will return to these songs again and again. That's what Mabel believed. People wanted to hear her sing these songs because they wanted to be moved, like Rex Reed, who said, "She could break your heart. This little old woman sitting in a chair could break your heart." These songs touch people. These stories touch people. We must keep this fragile art form alive. That's what we are all about.

* * *

THE MANHATTAN ASSOCIATION OF CABARETS

The Manhattan Association of Cabarets (MAC) was founded in 1983 primarily as an organization for cabaret owners, managers, and booking agents. The organization opened its enrollment to performers in 1985. MAC's first president was Curt Davis who, upon his death, was succeeded by founding member Erv Raible, co-owner of several New York piano bars and cabarets. Other past presidents include Jamie deRoy, Michael Estwanick, Barry Levitt, Judy Barnett, Scott Barbarino, and Ricky Ritzel. The current president is Lennie Watts, who began his appointment in 2009. MAC strives to advance the education, art, and business of cabaret entertainment. A trade association first and foremost, its activities are designed to heighten public awareness of cabaret's artistic contributions and vitality, to honor its creativity, to build its current and future audiences, and to speak out as an influential voice on behalf of MAC members and the industry at large. To help educate members in the art and business of cabaret, MAC presents seminars and panel discussions throughout the year on a variety of subjects:

"They Write the Songs" is a songwriting competition in honor of songwriters John Wallowitch and Dottie Burman. Through an endowment bequeathed by the Burman estate, the competition awards a cash prize to songwriters/composers over the age of forty who have not yet received recognition for their writing talents, while the Wallowitch prize honors songwriters under forty. Songwriters' submissions are accepted in the fall, and finalists are chosen by a panel of judges. Award winners are chosen by a celebrity judge. Past judges include Barb Jungr (2014), Lauren Molina (2013), Ann Hampton Callaway (2012), and Karen Mason (2011). Winners then perform at an annual event also called "They Write the Songs," which highlights the songwriter and their contributions to cabaret. ♪

"MAC Roving Mic" is a monthly open mic night for MAC members only. Nonmembers may attend, but do not sing. At these events, members try out new material, network with industry colleagues, and advertise their own upcoming shows. Songwriters are encouraged to perform or have their songs performed for the membership as well. This "roving" open mic moves to a different cabaret venue each month, which allows members to perform and be seen in various clubs. Each evening is hosted by a MAC board member and offers members the opportunity to work with different music directors throughout the season.

"MAC to School," which was launched in 2015, is an annual two-day educational symposium that includes workshops, classes, seminars, and more. This event is open to both MAC members and nonmembers alike. The curriculum changes each year but has included the following: Cabaret 101: Getting Started; Cabaret 201: The Next Level; The Business of Cabaret; Marketing; Vocal Workshops; Vocal Technique and Style; Scat and Jazz Improvisation; Utilizing Social Media; You-Tube Videos/Presence; Image Consulting; Original Music; and Opening Number Showcases. Each day ends with a master class taught by some of the biggest names and most honored teachers in the cabaret industry. ♪

Lennie Watts is a fifteen-time MAC, five-time Bistro, and three-time NiteLife Exchange Award winner, as well as the recipient of a 2014 BroadwayWorld Award. He is the only person to receive awards as an outstanding vocalist, director, producer, and booking manager. Watts has been active in the New York cabaret scene for more than

twenty-five years. In addition to directing in small cabaret venues, he
has directed events in New York at
Symphony Space, the Town Hall,
the B. B. King Blues Club, and Sony
Hall. As a performer, he has toured
nationally and internationally and has
performed at the Town Hall in several concerts, including *Broadway
Unplugged* and *Broadway by the
Year: 1949*. As a theater director,
he has directed productions of *How
to Succeed in Business without Really Trying, Godspell, Dames at Sea,
Joseph and the Amazing Technicolor
Dreamcoat*, and *Phantom*. Watts is
also the creator of Singnasium, Cab
Lab, Summer in the City, the Arrangement Experience, and Cabaret

Figure   19.3. Lennie   Watts.
Photo by Helane Blumfield.

Boot Camp, all critically acclaimed professional cabaret performance
workshops. He is on the faculty of Marymount Manhattan College and
is a master teacher for the Eugene O'Neill Cabaret and Performance
Conference. The *Village Voice* calls him "a one-man cabaret army!" He
is the longest-serving president of MAC in the organization's history. It
was a pleasure to speak with him about his teaching, directing, and the
Manhattan Association of Cabarets. ♪

*Thank you, Lennie, for sharing your time and expertise with us. How
long have you been associated with MAC, and how long have you served
as the president?*

I have been involved with MAC on and off for the last twenty years. I
decided to run for the board and was elected as vice president while
Ricky Ritzel was serving as president. I have now been the president for
over eleven years.

You come from a theater background. How did you find cabaret? Or how did cabaret find you?

Randi Lester introduced me to cabaret. We did a show at the Duplex called *Ain't Missin' Dinner*; that's how I met her. When she started to work at Don't Tell Mama, she said to me, "You should come to see some of these shows." I didn't know what cabaret was. I was at the very first MAC Awards with a friend, and I didn't know what cabaret was. My introduction to cabaret was in a smoked-filled room, with pieces of cheese on paper plates. But I got to see Sylvia Sims, Sidney Myer, and John Adams, and so many wonderful performers. I thought, *What is this?!* I got hooked. I saw some wonderful shows like *The Jenny Burton Experience*, and I remember seeing Terri Lynn Paul singing pop music with a band and backup singers. I thought, *This is kind of cool.* I was tired of being cast in the Stubby Kaye roles in every show, and my voice is not really suited for that. And it's not the way that I like to sing. I thought, *Wow, this is a way I can put together my own show.* I started doing that and really loved it.

Tell us about MAC, the board, your mission, and the programs the organization offers.

The MAC board is comprised of thirteen membership-elected volunteers and nine active advisory board members, all of whom are professionals in the art of cabaret . . . as well as professionals in their own industries (day jobs). We are not paid, and on average—at our busiest times—some of us volunteer from ten to thirty hours a week on MAC-related tasks and functions. Our board members are very approachable. We are all here to serve the membership, and members are encouraged to offer their opinions directly to us at any time via email or telephone or at our annual meeting.

In my tenure as president, I'm proud to say that many things I wanted to do with (and for) MAC have come to fruition. We produce the MAC Awards and several educational programs throughout the year, including the songwriting contest "They Write the Songs," the "MAC Roving Mic," and "MAC to School."

MAC members may also submit selections from their CDs to the MAC channel on AccuRadio. We offer a calendar on our website on which members can list their upcoming performances. We maintain a Google Group and two Facebook pages where members can post show advertisements and network with other members. We participate in the annual Broadway Cares/Equity Fights AIDS (BC/EFA) Flea Market and Grand Auction, and we partner with other organizations for additional outreach programs. And we have an annual holiday party—just for fun!

As the president of MAC, how would you define the art and craft of cabaret, and how does it differ from other vocal performance genres?

Cabaret is a very personal experience. A lot of wonderful theater performers struggle with cabaret just because they can't be themselves and they don't have (or want to have) that intimacy. I think that my cabaret work has helped me in my theater work because it has made me more comfortable with who I am. I can tap into that quicker than some people who have not had cabaret training. So, in that aspect, one kind of feeds the other. But they are different animals.

What are some of the hallmarks of a great cabaret performance?

A great cabaret act makes me laugh, makes me cry, makes me think, and makes me feel something. I am in awe of people who have their own "take" on a song and arrangements. I love to listen to songs that I know in a new way and am not a big fan of people simply singing out of a vocal selection songbook. I love it when I leave (the show) knowing the artist's point of view. I don't necessarily need to know all the intimate details of a performer's life, but I do like to know how they feel about things. I love great arrangements of music and thoughtful patter. I like to go to the show and feel like that person put time, thought, and their heart and soul into this hour of entertainment.

What do you think are the biggest misconceptions about cabaret?

Some people define cabaret as just the Great American Songbook, and I totally disagree with that. Cabaret can be contemporary music or any kind of music for that matter. It could can also include monologues and storytelling. If you are having an intimate connection with a group of people in an small venue, then that's cabaret.

In the twenty-five years that you have been singing, directing, producing, booking, and teaching, how has cabaret changed?

The finances of cabaret have changed over the years. It has become more costly to do cabaret because it's more costly to do *anything* in New York than it was in the 1980s and early 1990s. I also feel there was a time in the early 2000s where people started doing "safe" work. There was not a lot of interesting stuff going on. Not all of it, but the bulk of it for me was not exciting. Now, however, cabaret performers are thinking outside of the box again and coming up with interesting ideas and concepts. I'm excited about cabaret and excited about the young people who are discovering cabaret for the first time.

I teach at Marymount College, which was the first college to offer a cabaret class as part of its music theater curriculum. I have been teaching it from the beginning, and I've seen these kids go on to do their own cabaret shows. So again, I'm really excited about the future of cabaret. I think that people will always crave this kind of entertainment and intimacy. I also believe that—especially as people become more attached to their devices and all of that sound-bite stuff—cabaret will become even more in vogue because people will need the human contact that you can only get in a cabaret setting. I have high hopes for that.

FINAL THOUGHTS

The organizations and associations within the cabaret industry provide a glimpse into the ever-changing nature of this art form. Organizations that were once considered the domain of the "blue-hair set" are now actively reaching younger generations. What these organizations need are the three *T*s: time, treasure, and talent. The American Songbook Association, the Mabel Mercer Foundation, and the Manhattan Association of Cabarets would certainly welcome interest or assistance from any interested party. Do you want to start a Great American Songbook competition in your high school or college? Want to bring established cabaret talent to your city to do a master class? How about a weekend symposium? These organizations are at your fingertips—literally, via Google—and can provide you with both time and talent that you will certainly treasure.

THE ROYAL FAMILY OF CABARET

Interviews

20

THE QUEEN OF CABARET

An Interview with Andrea Marcovicci

In a career spanning more than five decades, Andrea Marcovicci has appeared on Broadway, performed at the White House, sold out Carnegie Hall, and ushered in the millennium with the Chicago Symphony Orchestra. A champion of the Great American Songbook, Marcovicci's recordings reflect not only her deep devotion to classic songwriters of the past but also her encouragement of new voices composing in that same tradition. Her many honors include MAC, Bistro, and Mabel Mercer Foundation awards. She holds the record of performing an unprecedented twenty-five seasons at the legendary Oak Room of the Algonquin Hotel, where she was the final performer to grace that stage. Marcovicci began her cabaret career with appearances on *The Today Show* and *The Merv Griffin Show* before appearing at the legendary New York nightclub Reno Sweeney and mounting a solo concert at Carnegie Hall. Highly regarded as the "Queen of Cabaret," Marcovicci has performed extensively throughout the country in clubs, theaters, and on concert stages, including more than thirty years at the Gardenia in Los Angeles, more than twenty years at the Plush Room in San Francisco, more than fifteen years at the Tilles Center on Long Island, nine years at Davenport's in Chicago, and of course for twenty-five years at the Oak Room. Additionally, she's headlined at the Rrazz Room, the

Colony Theatre, the Vilar Performing Arts Center, the New Jersey Performing Arts Center, Wolf Trap, and
Steppenwolf Theatre. In New York
she's appeared at Lincoln Center,
Town Hall, Symphony Space, the
Café Carlyle, Joe's Pub at the Public
Theatre, and Feinstein's/54 Below.
Abroad she's performed at the Liceu
Opera House in Barcelona, as well
as Pizza on the Park and the Jermyn Street Theatre in London. We
are delighted that Marcovicci could
share her expertise with us in spite of
her very busy schedule. ♪

**Figure 20.1. Andrea Marcovicci.
Photo by Daniel Reichert.**

*Andrea, thank you so much for shar-
ing your expertise. Your career has been so varied. You have been a
television and film star as well as an award-winning cabaret artist. As an
actress and singer, is your process of working on a monologue different
than your process of working on a song?*

Working on a song is very much like working on a monologue. I have
always thought of the processes as being somewhat the same. I tend to
work lyric first and music second, and I devote a lot of time to analyzing the lyric so that with or without the music the lyric would work as a
theater piece. With or without the music . . . that is the key.

*And what do you do in those instances where the character and style of
the music want to take you in one direction, but your interpretation of
the lyric sends you in another?*

I recently had an experience with that. I wanted to sing "Not a Day Goes
By" from Sondheim's *Merrily We Roll Along*, but as a happy song. I saw
in the lyric a great deal of happiness, and I felt it as a bossa nova. By
slightly changing the rhythm and keeping a bright smile on my face—

but always keeping the lyric intact—I was able to interpret it as a happy song. It was a great deal of fun!

Do you feel that is an important aspect of cabaret, being able to reinterpret or reinvent a song?

Yes, I think that's what we do. That is our purpose. We are charged with keeping the extraordinary Great American Songbook alive and interpreting it in new ways for future generations. We keep it alive with our sense of humor and innovation. I once took the song "Bill" (from *Showboat* by Jerome Kern and Oscar Hammerstein II), which is a torch song, and did it as a comedy number. With the right arrangement and the right interpretation, you can do practically anything.

When/how did you first decide to become a singer? And did you specifically decide to become a cabaret singer or did that unfold in a different way?

I started as a singer/songwriter/folk singer is the late sixties. In the midseventies I sang at a wonderful spot called Reno Sweeney where I did as much rock 'n' roll as true cabaret. I would sing David Bowie one moment and "Young at Heart" (by Johnny Richards and Carolyn Leigh) the next, then a Fred Astaire medley, and then "My Ship" (from *Lady in the Dark* by Kurt Weill and Ira Gershwin). It wasn't until 1985 at the Gardenia in Hollywood that I began to develop a cabaret repertoire and following by singing every Saturday at midnight! Did I make a conscious choice to become a cabaret singer? I was mostly acting at the time and I needed an outlet for my self-expression. The success of my shows led me to become a cabaret singer.

How would you define the art of cabaret, separate and distinct from other vocal performance genres (music theater, jazz, etc.)?

Cabaret is, by its very nature, more intimate. It's the most personal art form there is. The artist makes all the decisions: what to sing and *how* to sing it, where to stand, how to move, in what order the songs should be presented, and so forth.

Given the personal nature of lyric connection in cabaret, do you think there is a "cabaret performance technique"? And if so, can you elaborate on this technique?

A successful cabaret artist can make you feel like she or he is singing *only* to you. This is done by lowering your gaze and connecting truly with every member of the audience. In other words, there should be no "fourth wall" as there is in the theater. There are a lot of people who seem to be afraid to engage with the audience. But if you don't engage with the audience you might as well stay home. It's not as if you pick one person and gaze down at them until they're uncomfortable. But you should lower your gaze. People should feel that they were sung *to*, not *at*.

That seems to be a cabaret mantra.

Yes, absolutely.

When you are working with someone or directing them, and they are not used to this approach, how do you get them to do that?

I have them sing to me, in the audience, and then I move around the room. They must keep their eyes on me. They must keep singing *to* me. "I'm here now. Focus on me." And then I move. "Now I'm here, look at me. Watch. I'm moving." And I'll have them continue to focus on me as I move around until they are comfortable with the direction of their gaze and the intensity of focus, person to person. It's not easy.

So, then, is the technique of it, for the actor, that the gaze becomes intimate with each person in room, but the actor's internal monologue is directed toward one person moving around the room?

Yes, I've always said when you have a conversation with someone in the real world, they don't always stay still. They move around. Nobody stays absolutely still. Your gaze, as you are talking, naturally follows them.

How does the cabaret performance technique differ from music theater, jazz, and so forth?

Well, there is absolutely no fourth wall in cabaret. We look directly into the eyes of our patrons and welcome them with open arms! We don't sing to the back of the house either, the way so many theater singers are taught. We sing to the front of the house, engaging the people at ringside and then extending that intimacy to people that cannot be seen in the darkness. You take that energy of *seeing* and push it out toward the back of the room. You imagine that you are extending that same *seeing* energy, that connection, out to the few seats that you *can't* see.

Jazz performers, in my humble opinion, seem more interested in grooving with the music and the rhythms than interacting with the audience. There are exceptions of course.

How do you define the phrase "lyric connection"? What does it mean to you?

It means that you are bringing past experiences of your own into the song you are singing, which enriches and brings it to life. Otherwise it's just words and a melody well sung.

How do you connect to a lyric?

By separating the lyric from the music and treating it only as monologue. By insisting that it makes sense as a monologue. By reciting it without the music being played. It's the simplest technique of all.

The world of cabaret is filled with legendary artists whose gifts were interpretive, and not necessarily vocal.

No, not at all . . . Mabel (Mercer) . . . Julie (Wilson) . . .

Yes, exactly. How do we communicate to young artists that it's not always about the voice?

Well, if you're truly interpreting, you're not worrying about how "fabulous" each note is. You're trying to get the story across. Sometimes that means there's a breathy quality one minute and a nice mix the next. There might be a belted note, but that's not the point. The point is getting the story across—to make the song a conversation. You rarely shout in the middle of a conversation unless it's called for. And if you're concentrating on loving your audience, you're thinking less about yourself.

Love your audience, not your voice.

Exactly! Yes. Yes. Yes!

This book is called So You Want to Sing Cabaret *and sponsored by the National Association of Teachers of Singing. However, cabaret is known as a lyric-driven performance experience, where the singer's vocal ability should never "oversing" the lyric. In a world of beautiful tone and breath support, what would you ask voice teachers to spend more time on with their singers? And, conversely, what should they spend less time on?*

Voice teachers should spend time helping a singer have the supplest voice possible so that all the colors of their voice are available at a moment's notice. It's not about belting or hitting high notes or even beautiful tone. It's about *variety* of tone and making an evening *interesting*.

Besides a good voice and superb lyric connection, what other skills (on- or offstage) do new singers need to learn for a career in cabaret?

They need to learn movement and microphone technique, how to get the best out of the lighting and sound technicians, and how to stage themselves throughout the course of an act so that the evening isn't too static.

Have you ever used a director for your shows? And if so, do you think a director is necessary in cabaret?

Only lately have directors become a fixture in cabaret. I admit to being self-directed my entire career, and yet, and this is important, I have some very savvy friends and have bounced ideas off of them all these years, so I've hardly been flying blind.

And as a follow-up, I recently saw a show that you directed, Ann Kittredge at Feinstein's/54 Below. It was a fantastic show. Will we be seeing more directing in your future?

Absolutely. Ann is my latest client, and I think she's sensational, but I also work with Sandy Bainum, whom I have great respect for as well!

Ann has a beautiful voice with impeccable technique. How important is vocal technique to the cabaret performer?

Vocal technique is very important so as not to abuse your voice or the audience's ears!

Do you have a warm-up ritual before a performance?

Absolutely! I warm up a few times during the day of the performance!

You've championed newer music being sung and included in the Great American Songbook. Are there new songs being written that would work well in a cabaret performance?

Many fabulous songs are entering the canon from music theater and independent songwriters, even someone like the artist Pink.

When you pick new repertoire, even very recent songs, what do you look for?

It has to have a lyric that is as sophisticated and clever as music of the past. The melody has to be a true, beautiful melody. I had no problem singing Pink's "Glitter in the Air." I was very taken with it when I heard it. I put it in my show at the Carlyle, and my audience was quite surprised. ♪

And you rearranged it?

Oh yes, it didn't sound like the way Pink did it. But as long as the lyric is clever and there aren't too many refrains, I will consider it. One of the problems with contemporary songs written in the 1970s and 1980s is that the songs are too refrain heavy. If you have the same repetition in the refrain, you don't have anywhere to go as a cabaret artist. A good song for cabaret is a conversation. Don't give me two refrains that say the same thing. Give me the "meat and potatoes." You have to build. You have to have a beginning, middle, and an end in a cabaret song.

Lyrics that mean something?

Yes, and I have found that in the words of writers like John Bucchino, Craig Carnelia, Tom Toce, and Christine Lavin—the people that I put on my *New Words* album. ♪

It must have been magical playing the Oak Room. Can you describe the room and maybe a wonderful memory of a night (or nights) during your tenure?

Well, I had an enviable position. To be able to come back for twenty-five straight years, to move in—really move in—lock, stock, and barrel for ten weeks at a time was a blessing. Not only was it a joy to see and sing for the same people each year; it was also my muse in a way. I had to create a new show every year. I didn't have a choice. I would be singing for the same audience that saw me the year before, so it had to be new.

The thing about the Algonquin was that it was so warm and inviting before, during, and after the show. I knew my crowd—actually *knew* them intimately. I knew who was marrying whom, who had been ill, and who had breast cancer and conquered it.

And that influenced your programming?

Yes, I would often think about what the right thing would be to sing for my audience the following year. Or people would request things. I once did a whole show called *By Request*. I placed all of the requests in a top hat and literally pulled them out of a hat. And don't forget, I also got to *live* there. It was magical and miraculous.

When you performed there in a long run, ten weeks, was it the same show for all ten weeks?

Once I did a sixteen-week run and six separate shows. And at the same time planned a wedding and got married two days after the run.

Any other special memories of the Oak Room?

Whew! Too many nights to single out one or two memories, but I loved this crazy rectangle of a room that taught me how to constantly give attention to every last face in the place. I used to joke that they should place me on a revolving stage so that I could be seen from all angles. That's how sitting on the piano evolved! It was the best vantage point to see and be seen in that delightful, historical, elegant rosy-colored room.

Can you share with us some of your current favorite cabaret venues?

I love Feinstein's/54 Below and Feinstein's at Vitello's and my home room, the Gardenia in Hollywood. And the Beach Cafe in New York seems to have welcomed many of my friends with open arms.

And who are your favorite singers on the scene now?

My favorite singers include my pal Jeff Harnar, Karen Akers, KT Sullivan, and of course my own Ann Kittredge. ♪

You recently retired from cabaret performance with a "final" show at Feinstein's/54 Below despite an adoring public begging you not to. What went into this decision? And could you ever be talked back onto the cabaret stage?

Well, let's clear this up right now! I did not retire from *singing!* I retired from *touring.* I retired from *packing suitcases.* I sing regularly at the Gardenia in Hollywood, and I will always do the New York Cabaret Convention.

Where do you see, or hope to see, cabaret singing in twenty years?

I hope it will be constantly reinventing itself . . . just like it is now!

And lastly, if a young singer came to you for advice, what are the three things you would tell them?

To thine own self be true, lower your gaze, and love your audience before you ask to be loved.

㉑

THE CROWN PRINCE OF CABARET

An Interview with Steve Ross

Steve Ross is widely regarded as the "Crown Prince of New York Cabaret." He has performed across the United States in cabarets, theaters, and prestigious concert halls including Carnegie Hall and Lincoln Center. As an international ambassador of cabaret, he has performed in London, Paris, Tokyo, São Paulo, Rio de Janeiro, Melbourne, and Sydney. An articulate man with a keen knowledge of the Great American Songbook and its history, Ross has hosted radio series on both the BBC and American Public Media. As a teacher, Ross regularly conducts workshops and master classes and for eight years was on the lecture/performance roster at the Metropolitan Museum of Art. Born "forty-five minutes from Broadway" in New Rochelle, New York, and raised in Washington, D.C., by an opera-loving father and a piano-playing mother, Ross grew up listening to grand operas as well as the songs of George Gershwin, Cole Porter, and Irving Berlin. His first major job in New York was as a singer/pianist at Ted Hook's Backstage. In 1981 he reopened the legendary Oak Room at Manhattan's famed Hotel Algonquin where he performed for more than fifteen years. He has appeared on Broadway in Noël Coward's *Present Laughter* and off-Broadway in *I Won't Dance*, Ross's tribute to Fred Astaire. His last show at the Algonquin, *Puttin' on the Ritz: The Songs of Fred Astaire*, prompted Stephen

Holden of the *New York Times* to
describe Ross as "the personification
of the bygone dreamworld that his
music summons."

I had the opportunity to speak
with Steve Ross about his long career
and the nature of cabaret very soon
after his successful run of shows at
Birdland, New York's legendary jazz
club and cabaret theater. ♪

*Thank you, Steve, for sharing your
time and expertise with us. I thoroughly enjoyed your performance the
other night at Birdland. This book is
geared toward singers and their voice
teachers, so I would love to start our*
conversation talking about your experience with your own voice and
voice teachers.

**Figure 21.1. Steve Ross. Photo
by Stacy Sullivan.**

I came to town in 1968. I think I had sung a couple of songs in public at
a bar once in Washington, D.C., where I'm from. But I never dreamed
that I was a singer—never—until I came to town and I went to work at
this bar. I used to hang out at the bar every Sunday night. And one night,
when the singer/pianist left, the manager came to me and asked, "Do
you want the job?" (I had sat in a couple of times.) And I said, "Yes."
"And you have to sing too," he said to me. Well, I think I sang the only
song that I really knew, which was from an album by a name not known
to you, I'm sure (Beatrice Kay) who sang the songs of the "naughty nineties," a.k.a. the Gay Nineties. And I loved them. Many of them were
English music hall songs. She had this one song called "Don't Go in
the Lion's Cage Tonight." So, I learned that just from listening to it—I
played by ear at the time. Then I said, "Oh my God! I've got to learn
how to sing out!" I asked a couple of friends about singing teachers and
soon got involved with Helen Gallagher, who still teaches, I believe, all
of these years later. Helen was a two-time Tony Award winner (for *Pal
Joey* and *No, No, Nanette*). She was a terrific, down-to-earth, wonder-

ful lady. She taught every Saturday and I played the piano for her class. That went on for a couple of years and I learned so much. And then, I began playing the piano for a classical teacher, Ruby Schaar. So . . . I was listening and learning by playing the piano for both of these people. In exchange for playing for Helen, she let me sing on one of the Saturdays when somebody else played. When I sang in front of the class for the first time there was a very good response. It was absolutely thrilling for me to sing. I'd never sung before.

Next, I got another job in a bar on Fifth Avenue, and it was one where I had to sing. But I realized that when I "sang out" I was always hoarse the next day. I didn't know how to sing. I didn't know anything about anything except that I heard Judy Garland sing and a lot of other people. But when I sang, I always was hoarse afterward. So, I thought *I'd better fix this. I need a much better—and bigger—voice.* So, Helen passed me along to her teacher who lived on Seventy-Third Street, a marvelous old gentleman named Olly Olson. He was much older, the generation before her. I don't know what exactly his technique was, but he at least steered me in the right direction. He was my first real voice teacher. I then went to another teacher after him. Each teacher that I've had seems to have come along right at the very moment when I needed him or her. Joan Kobin was a rather well-known teacher . . . she was Barbara Cook's teacher. Barbara was her star pupil. She did this "suppressing of the tongue" routine. You know that one? Anyway, I went along with it. I didn't know anything. So, I just went in and thought somehow it would be OK. (She taught Barbara Cook, what could be wrong with her?) So, I did that for a while, and it seemed to help me. And then I went to one of her co-teachers, who taught the same method—the "Kobin method," whatever that was. After a bit of study, I could sing higher and last longer. So, I improved my technique enough to get through a night of singing in a smoky bar.

So, the years went by—many, many years went by—and I somehow eventually figured it out. There may have been other teachers . . . oh yes, Mayan Bishop was a gentleman who taught me for a while. He was a student of a teacher named Sarah Lee. And after him I had a wonderful teacher—now we're almost up to the present—named Larry Taylor from Park Avenue who had theories about vowel modification and all that stuff. That was all wonderful. He got me through a couple of years until he passed away. And then, about seven years ago, I started studying with a woman named Maria Zhorella. She was an extraordinary teacher who lived to teach. She passed away at 102, but she taught me for four years, beginning when she was ninety-eight. She was an operetta star and a radio program hostess in the 1940s in Vienna, and she made her way—a couple of marriages later—to America. She never had a big career for whatever reason. . . . I don't think she wanted it. She loved teaching. She lived for that. I went to her twice a week for four years. She never charged me a cent. And it was the greatest thing that has ever happened to me. I mean, we both know I don't have an operatic voice, but it's a functioning voice and it allows me hold to notes and hit certain notes that I wasn't able to hit before I was with her.

That's wonderful to hear. Thank you so much for sharing.

No, no, no, it *is* possible for an old dog like me. I was over seventy when she started teaching me. And I don't think I sound like an eighty-year-old now. And I want to tell you something about this woman, Maria Zhorella. When I met her—at age ninety-eight—whenever she was demonstrating, her singing voice sounded like forty-year-old women. But her voice—her speaking voice—sounded like an old lady. I've never understood how she could go into "sopranoland" and sing *The Merry Widow* (which she sang for years) with all those high notes without any trace of a quiver or a wobble. I was so impressed and grateful that I was training with someone who could sing at ninety-eight.

About your desire to "sing out" and have a bigger/better voice . . . it strikes me that, in the world of cabaret, a huge voice is not necessarily required. And here you are, the "Crown Prince of Cabaret." Do you think you would have had a different career had you had a bigger voice? Do you think a larger voice would have served you well in cabaret?

Interesting idea. No, not particularly, because in my view cabaret is a word-based medium.

Do you mean lyric driven?

Lyric driven, absolutely. I love words. I am great admirer of the practitioners of brilliant wordplay, and that's what drew me to these songs.
I grew up listening to my mother playing the songs on the piano (not
singing). Then later, I heard singers on recordings and on the radio.
The first male singer I ever heard was Bing Crosby. So, I knew about
"easy-going" singing, but then I also knew about Mario Lanza. Now, I
didn't know so much about opera, but I knew that he had this thrilling, exciting voice. I had succumbed to the power of a high note. And
I thought, *Well, that's over there in another country and I never will
achieve that.* ♪

*I think there are many generations of people who are glad that you
didn't!*

[*laughing*] Really? Well then, maybe I'd be one of a thousand people
who could sing a high B♭, and not really be me, right? Is that what you're
saying?

*What you have is such a gift—and so unique—even in the world of
cabaret, the ability to communicate the lyric uniquely, and intimately.
You do sing very well, and you play for yourself. It's the triple threat of
cabaret. So, I'm very glad that you didn't "succumb" to the high notes.*

[*laughing*] Okay . . . well. Yes, I understand.

I wonder if it would be different had you discovered your "bigger" voice.

Yes, it would have been different. It would have been a different career.
But fortunately, the cabaret world is lyric driven.

*Fortunately for the cabaret world, you're lyric driven. Changing the
subject, you also teach master classes . . .*

Yes. Now, I don't have single "how to" to teach people (a technique for)
singing. But I do coach them performance-wise. It allows me to express
myself. I will tell you I've thought about this. I'm writing up my own
experiences as a teacher in my book.

When is your book going to be published?

Who knows? I keep resisting it. But today I did think of something to include. The first time that I ever thought I could sing a love song, which for me is closer to "singing" than doing funny numbers, because you usually must hold a note or two. I was coaching at the time. I was coaching this man and I remember the song. The music was right in front of me, and I was so eager to get that music off the page and into his ears. So, I sang it for him, and I really gave it my all. And he said, "Oh, you should sing that song." And I said, "Oh no. No, I don't sing love songs." And he said, "Well, you should. I thought it was terrific." So that night, I tried singing it. And people didn't laugh at me. They were pleased and moved after I sang it. You may remember this song. It was a song called "If."

Oh, yes.

[*singing*] "If a picture paints a thousand words . . ." That was the first ballad I ever sang in public. It's a very simple, sweet love song. I was shocked at what happened. I mean, the room didn't go to a hushed silence, but it was quiet enough so at least they heard me. Now, I'm not one to overdramatize the event. But I really liked expressing my feelings about romance. That was the beginning, because these songs . . . well, as I say in my show, "If we all waited for happy love songs, we would have a much smaller number of tunes to do." People sing because they're sad or they're regretful or they're remorseful . . . a lot of times anyway. So, I thought, *Gee, could I do that? Could I? Do they really want to hear about me and my love affair?* Because I'd personalized the song instantly, something I learned the first time I heard Mabel Mercer. A friend who was a year older than I and had already moved to New York said, "You have to come up, the Metropolitan Opera is closing. You must come up. It's the last week." So, I drove up from Washington and I got to see . . .

The old Met?

Yes, the old Met, I saw Zinka Milanov and Richard Tucker doing Andrea Chénier. That was fabulous. And then he said, "You have to go and hear this woman named Mabel Mercer." Well, she changed my life.

She changed a lot of people's lives on a nightly basis.

[*laughter*] You're absolutely right. Well said. She was at the Downstairs at the Upstairs, which was one of the last clubs on West Fifty-Sixth Street. This woman came out looking a little unusual, you know . . . she wasn't Dinah Shore or Doris Day. She came out and sat in her chair and . . . (every time I tell this story, I well up). She started singing "Try to Remember." And I started welling up with tears, as I am doing now. And I thought *What is that? What's* that? Nobody had ever done that to me before. I maybe had cried in a movie once or twice. But no one had ever given me that experience . . . being five feet away from someone singing and them making me cry. I started getting very emotional, as I am now recalling it. That was an earth-shattering and pivotal moment.

A transformative experience.

Right then I understood that someone could excite people with something other than high notes. That's what I wanted . . . I wanted to move people. I wanted excitement, I wanted love, I wanted attention. . . . Now I can do that with the piano, but I knew that the voice was a more immediate connection to another person. That's what I wanted. And when I experienced it . . . wow! I didn't have a "five-year plan" on how to get there, but I knew I wanted to get there.

Mabel Mercer exemplifies what we come to understand as a cabaret performance technique: a very intimate, person-to-person . . .

The key is intimacy.

Is that how you would define a cabaret technique or style?

These days in America? I was trying to think about this because I'm asked that a lot. Let me form my thoughts. . . . "An intimate style of singing or intimate singing experience based on verbal communication."

And "verbal" meaning?

Word communicating, lyric communicating, communication through lyrics . . . which sets it apart from jazz in a very distinct way. Of course, cabaret is more demanding of the audience than jazz. In jazz, there is no demanding of the audience to go on a journey. The other night, I felt they (the audience) were with me on some journey . . . that I was guiding them through. Now, the experience of a brilliant jazz singer is thrilling and exciting, but it's not the same experience.

Jazz seems more music driven . . . more about the arrangement, harmonies, and the rifts.

Sometimes you get these extraordinary, stellar performers that do both. Sometimes we get a Nina Simone who will break your heart or a Carmen McRae who swings her ass off and can get at the deepest part of that lyric. There are some that can swing and also show themselves. But not many. Now, there are many young singers around today who seem to blend their abilities and their singing. I had a young girl come talk to me the other day, as well as sing for me. She is a graduate of LaGuardia (High School of Performing Arts), and I had seen her in their production of *The Sound of Music*. They do terrific productions—very "top end." And she was lovely in *The Sound of Music*. But she spent four years at a performing arts high school, and nobody told her to open her eyes! [*laughter*]

Yes, and communicate with us.

Yes. Which again adheres to my favorite topic: Is there communication with the audience?

Well, I think that's why cabaret is an "old soul" art form . . .

Absolutely.

You need to have life experience. You need to be comfortable in communicating yourself to others.

I sat there, as she was singing some song from her book, and there were more melismas than I had ever heard in my life. Afterward I said, "I am very impressed, but now I want you to stand there—with your hands at your side—and then open your eyes, look at me, and sing that song again." And God bless her, she did it! It was very touching. She said, "Gee, they never talked to me about that."

This goes very directly to the point of a cabaret performance technique—not gesticulating, not having a lot of melismas, or displaying vocal pyro-techniques—but rather communicating the lyric and placing the voice, everything, in service of the lyric.

Yes, everything is in service of the lyric.

I know you agree with that.

I absolutely do.

Is there anything else that you would say is part of a cabaret perfor-mance technique? Specifically, how does it compare to music theater? You sang some Sondheim when I saw you last week. You didn't sing it the way they would do it in the show.

I didn't.

You didn't sing it in a music theater fashion. You sang . . .

No, I sang the words.

That's right. So, tell me about that. Tell me about singing a song origi-nally written for a musical but singing it with the appropriate cabaret performance technique. How is that different?

I sang a song the other day that was . . . may I use the *L* word? A "legit" song. It was the Robert Goulet song from *The Happy Time*, "I Don't Remember You."

That was beautiful. You did a beautiful job with that.

Well, thank you. That's Maria (Zhorella). I wouldn't have had that F♯ if she hadn't taught me how to connect everything. I can get away with singing that song, but that's about as "legit" as I get.

A singer in music theater might sing that same song and hit that same F♯, and very often we would see that singer present with the lyric for the first beat of that note but then dissolve into "tech head," worried about the technique of how to "hold" that note.

Yes, that's right. Because that's what they spent a lot of money learning how to do.

Right, but (and I'll say it, because you won't) you are in the lyric of that note for its entire duration. Your emotion carries the note for its full length.

I don't see how else you could do that. I thought that when you were up there, if the note is on the word [*singing*] "remember," then that's the expression of my emotion on that note. Isn't that what the big opera singers do?

Well, I would say in elite performance, yes, emotion carries the day. The voice doesn't "hold" a note—your emotional vehicle "carries" the note.

That's right.

But that's on a very elite level. And that does not happen often. No, held notes tend to dissolve into a technical awareness of "what I'm doing," rather than a continued lyric connection.

I remember distinctly Barbara Cook, whom I adored. Now there was someone who had a phenomenal voice! And she had clarity on the top. She didn't have to change those vowels—it wasn't, "I love yaw." She did it all. I toured with her in the seventies as a matter of fact. She did a big series of master classes, often at Lincoln Center. And part of the mandate was to get students from Juilliard. She never got students from the cabaret world who could have profited from her. So, she had to spend half an hour telling these students not to sing. So maybe that's what I would do too, if I were to coach. The key thing is not to oversing. Mable didn't have a microphone. But it was a very small room, so you could hear her voice. It would be wonderful if I could communicate what I must communicate and not use a microphone. I have also worked with lavalier microphones that were successful (many of them are not), but I love the feeling of not having anything between me and the audience. Nothing to hinder the communication aspect. Then I can also turn around, gesture, and do all that.

As a coach and a teacher of this style, when you are with a voice that is prone to oversing a Great American Songbook standard, what do you say? How do you get them to pare down?

By the time we've done what I like to do—analyze the words and give the lyric a bit of a context—I usually find that they're not happy just "singing" anymore.

Isn't that interesting . . . it changes their relationship to the song?

Suppose they're singing a Lorenz Hart lyric, like "My Funny Valentine." I'll ask, "What does 'stay' mean? 'Stay little valentine, stay.' Why does he say 'stay' twice?" By the time we've done that whole exercise, we've *real*-ized the entire sentence to sing; for example, let's take "If Ever I Would Leave You" from *Camelot*. I want them to say the words but only emphasize it *one* word at a time. So, it's "*IF* ever I would leave you . . ." And then, "If *EVER* I would leave you," and so on. That's called "*REAL-izing*" what it means to you. "*If—Ever—I—Would—Leave—You*?" By the time we've done all of that, they are intrigued and want to continue doing that. They will leave "long-note land."

Well then, isn't that a cabaret performance technique?

Oh, that's interesting . . . I suppose so. Well, it's not a revolutionary, world-shaking thing. But I have found it to be very important. After we've gone through all of that, they become a "cabaret singer" as it were, because they can sing the "words." We get what they're doing, and what they're doing doesn't require a huge voice. It's a different kind of singing.

Other styles are certainly valid and entertaining. I mean, I really enjoy jazz singers. I don't expect them to reveal themselves. I'm not taking an emotional journey with them. I'm hearing their extraordinary vocalizations and all that. And I think it's fantastic! And they bring, you know, a positive and engaging personality. Anita O'Day was one of the greatest singers I ever heard. In her last concert, she went and stood by the piano and sang a ballad, but not without her own unique melismas. And I was very moved by it. It was a bit of Anita. I got a little bit of her. She had this very long and strained life with drugs and all that, but usually you never heard that. What you heard was her going through her brilliant paces. I was very moved by that, realizing that everybody has stories. But by the same token, not everybody feels compelled to share them. I do. I'm word based because I acquired that taste by doing it. But that is less important to other people. When I perform in other cities, people will ask, "Cabaret . . . what is that? We don't do cabaret. We do jazz." I'm going this weekend to Florida to sing in a jazz club in Delray Beach. They're not going to hear swinging. I'll sing what I sing, and they'll hear Édith Piaf! ♪

The Great American Songbook is a staple of cabaret repertoire. Why do you think that is so? Also, regarding the Great American Songbook, is it defined by a date, a certain style, or a certain set of composers? And lastly, how do you feel about the inclusion of newer songs into the Great American Songbook? Is the Great American Songbook expanding, or is it confined to that specific era and repertoire?

I must say, to my quiet chagrin, that when I go and hear performers (unless they're a performer of a certain age), I don't hear any Cole Porter songs. People aren't singing the composers that I think represent the songbook. They're doing something else. I don't know what they're doing.

The basics of it: the "Old Testament" would be twenties, thirties, and forties with all the composers that we know and love—the hallowed hall of fame. Then, perhaps the "New Testament" would be after that—later Broadway songs that the kids have in their books that could work in a cabaret setting. When I coach a singer who wants to do a cabaret (no matter what era or type of song), I do the same thing that I always do: start with the lyric. If the lyric is strong, I can "gussy-up" the music. But the lyric must be strong. It doesn't have to be traditional. It doesn't have to rhyme or observe the same prosodic rules as the classic songs—it just must mean something.

So then, you would not consider a certain tone quality to be part of the cabaret performance style? If someone is singing in a more popular tone quality, that's okay?

Yes, of course. Otherwise, I think I would be limiting my enjoyment, because I don't think a particular tone quality is required. What is required is to be truthful. You cannot lie, in your singing . . . or be mendacious, if you're five feet away from someone.

And that's the whole basis of an intimate cabaret performance technique. You can tell if someone's lying in a second.

You can. You absolutely can.

You see it wash over their eyes. "Nope, you're not in it."

Yes, you can tell immediately.

That's why I think cabaret is difficult. I think it's one of the hardest performances to give. And yet, many people do not think that it is difficult to do, because they think that it's just singing music theater pieces in recital. They don't understand the difference or what one is really supposed to be doing in cabaret.

It's the investigation of the word. Investigation and personalization. I will never be Don Quixote. But if I sing that song, the truth of it must be *my* truth. And that's what I work on. . . . So yes, that's very important. I'll never forget—and bear with me, since this is a story I love telling— traveling with Julie Wilson. She was extraordinary, strong, and nothing but the words. Every word adds something . . . *every word.* Once I went to hear her, and she sang "My Old Flame" and immediately I was where she was. I asked her, "Julie, where did you get that?" And she said, "Every time I begin to sing that song, I think of that son-of-a-bitch that tossed me out of his car."

22

THE COUNTESS OF CROSSOVER

An Interview with Karen Mason

Karen Mason's illustrious career has included performances on and off Broadway, on television, and on recordings. Theatrescene.net writes that She "has few peers when it comes to ripping the roof off with her amazing voice that knows no bounds!" Mason, a thirteen-time MAC Award winner, received the MAC Award for Major Female Artist for six consecutive years, and recently received the 2019 MAC Lifetime Achievement Award. Her highly acclaimed recordings include her newest single, "It's about Time." She is the winner of the 2006 Nightlife Award for Major Female Vocalist and has also won three Bistro Awards. Mason has headlined at Carnegie Hall, Lincoln Center, Feinstein's at the Regency, Rainbow & Stars, the Algonquin Hotel, Arci's Place, the Supper Club, and the Ballroom in New York; the Cinegrill and the UCLA/ASCAP Concert Series in Los Angeles; the Plush Room in San Francisco; Davenport's in Chicago; and the Kennedy Center in Washington, D.C. She has shared concert stages with Michael Feinstein, Jerry Herman, Chita Rivera, Luciano Pavarotti, Rosemary Clooney, Liza Minnelli, and John Kander and Fred Ebb, among others. Mason has given concerts in the United Kingdom, Sweden, Brazil, Scotland, and Japan. She has also been featured with the Long Beach Symphony Orchestra with Michael Berkowitz, the Philly Pops with Peter Nero,

Figure 22.1. Karen Mason. *Photo by Bill Westmoreland.*

the New York Pops with Skitch Henderson, the Oklahoma City Philharmonic with Joel Levine, the Chicagoland Pops (in their premier concert), the Indianapolis Philharmonic, and the St. Louis Symphony Orchestra with John McDaniel. We are grateful that she took the time out of her busy schedule to chat with us about her career and the art of cabaret. ♪

Thank you, Karen, for sharing your time and expertise with us. There are not many elite professionals who have been equally embraced by both the cabaret and Broadway industries. There are cabaret singers who flirt with Broadway and Broadway stars who do an occasional cabaret show. But you have the unique perspective of having headlined in intimate cabaret rooms and starred in big Broadway musicals throughout your career. You have received accolades and awards in both of these genres. And in both styles of performance, you are an example of professionalism and authenticity.

Well, thank you. When I started out, I wanted to be a music theater performer. I didn't know anything about cabaret or nightclubs or solo performance. I just wanted to have my name on a marquee on Broadway. I worked at this restaurant in Chicago that had singing waiters and waitresses and met a gentleman there who wanted similar things in his career, only he was a composer and pianist. We started working together and developing an act, and opportunities would drop in our laps.

This was your longtime collaborator Brian Lasser?

Yes. He was an MD (music director) and a composer. But at that time he was working as the music director for a place called Lawrence of Oregano, an Italian restaurant. Isn't that a great name? We started working together, and we had a real affinity for each other . . . a real comfort. Working with him I felt like I had found where I was supposed to be. He became my mentor. He knew stuff I didn't know—a lot! I was happy there. We got hired to do certain shows in Chicago and private parties, including New Year's Eve at a restaurant called the Other Side. ♪

What year was this?

1976. We did New Year's Eve and I sang every depressing song I knew. [*laughter*] "Happy New Year!" From that moment on, we worked a lot in Chicago. When you're doing three shows a night four or five nights a week, you learn how to get people to pay attention to you. You learn what works and what doesn't. It was a fabulous training ground for us. We were figuring out who we were—together as a musical team—and figuring out who we were as people and artists.

We moved to New York in 1978 or 1979. We had been doing concerts in Chicago and selling them out, and it was time for us to go one way or the other: either New York or Los Angeles. Both of us wanted to be in New York because of our theater background, and Brian wanted to write shows. So, we moved to New York and started working. It was right at the time when Erv Raible and Rob Hoskins had purchased the Duplex down in Greenwich Village—the first Duplex on the other side of Seventh Avenue—and they gave us every Saturday for as long as we would like. Of course, we made absolutely no money. I think our cover charge was five dollars or something. And sometimes we had *no* people in the audience or *four* people in the audience, and sometimes we were sold out. But the club owners always supported us and said, "We know you're building." They were building too. We were given a chance to grow and learn. Those luxuries are not around so much these days.

At the same time, I was auditioning for a lot of stuff, and I got cast in my first Broadway show called *Play Me a Country Song*. During that time, Brian also had a couple of shows that were produced. The first one was called *The Matinee Kids*. Liz Callaway played either the younger me or, as she likes to say, I played the older her. [*laughs*] During that time, I got offered the role of the torch singer in *Torch Song Trilogy* when it moved from off-Broadway to Broadway. However, *Play Me a Country Song*—which, by the way, closed on opening night—wouldn't let me out of my contract. So I missed that opportunity. However, Harvey (Fierstein) did lovingly let me do Susan Edwards's vacations.

Brian and I were always going back and forth between cabaret and Broadway. Cabaret was a way to keep my chops up *and* to work with somebody I loved. At that time, we were just working on songs. He'd say, "Oh, hey, this is a song that I think you'll really love." He'd write the arrangement, I'd learn it, and we'd throw it in that night. We had enough repertoire to choose from, so we'd throw in a new eleven o'clock number or a new ballad. It wasn't so much about having a structure to the show at that time. . . . It was very much about us.

It was about Karen Mason.

And Brian Lasser. We just kept going, and we always respected the opportunities, both the ones that came to us individually and the ones that came to us together.

Would you say that with cabaret you are creating *the art and in music theater you're* pursuing *the art, perhaps in a quest to* get *something else . . . the job?*

Yes! Absolutely. The difference is this: When you do cabaret, you're producing yourself. You are the writer, the producer, and the star. It's all you. In theater you're a hired gun. And yes, it's someone else's perception of what the show is, and hopefully you can find your way through that other vision.

I've always said that what helps me *and* hinders me is that I have a strong sense of who I am on the stage. Sure, I have panic moments like everybody else, but for the most part, I feel confident walking out on a cabaret stage. And that's helped me in theater—to hold onto that strong sense of myself. A lot of times directors are either intrigued with that or it turns them off. Honestly, I like working with the ones that are intrigued by it, especially as I get older, because I am usually cast as a character who has to come in hot and take the stage. I really do feel that all my cabaret experience—all of the really bad shows and really bad jokes and horrible arrangements *and* all the good ones—are why I have that confidence and know who I am.

I can imagine that being a cabaret performer singing three shows a night, every night for years also makes your audition experience quite different as well. You're singing all the time. A lot of young singers don't have that experience.

So much of their experience now is about the voice as a separate entity as opposed to a way to express yourself. The voice is disembodied from emotions, especially on television shows like *The Voice* or *American Idol*. Every time somebody hits a high note the entire audience stands. I'm here to tell you this: that's not interesting. What *is* interesting to me is having that connection—that emotional connection—between my voice and my spirit, my voice and my heart. That was always how I wanted to use my voice. It wasn't just something used to impress people. Rather, that's how I could express myself best—through my voice.

When people say that singers are not actors, that's not true because it's the same method of telling a story. You're just using somebody else's meter. That has always been one of my greatest challenges, going from being as comfortable as I am in music—where it just feels natural to me to express myself in three and a half minutes—to expressing myself without that structure while acting. In music, I know what I want to say, I know how I want to say it, and I'm very comfortable after decades of experience. But it took me a long time to get there. Having that sense of freedom and comfort with a monologue—and setting up my own meter—was scary at first.

I think one of the reasons people feel that singers are not actors may be that the training of singing tends to treat the voice as a separate entity, something that needs to be trained, reined in, enhanced, or in some way adjusted. Young singers don't receive enough connective instruction— connecting their voice to their emotions and allowing that emotion to affect the use of the voice, good or bad. The technical voice teacher wants the best sound all times, but sometimes the best sound might not be the right sound for the character. The right sound is the best sound, but that may not be the prettiest sound.

I love the way that's phrased. For me, going to a voice lesson is about learning how to be in command of your voice, so you can be in command of your voice and then let it go. Tell me a story with it. What do you want to express? I was doing a little review called "Hey, Love!" And Richard Maltby said to me, "You know, always the best advice you can give a singer, or an actor? 'Start from zero.' This is the beginning of the thought. It's not [*in a melodramatic voice*] "You must prepare." Yes, the preparation is going on, but that must happen before you show up in front of an audience and are telling them a story. You "start at zero." The thought just hits you. What are you feeling and thinking? How can you tell me about that experience?

You've sung "As If We Never Said Goodbye," both on Broadway and in cabaret. How are those two performances different, given the venue and genre?

In a Broadway house or in a big theater, you can get carried away with all the other stuff around you. It's almost easier because you have a lot of external stimuli: the huge orchestra, lights, costumes, all the other actors around you, and so forth. When you're in a cabaret and you have a room of a hundred people—or four, depending upon the night—staring at you, there must be a moment where it's a personal statement. You need to be more specific and more personal than you have ever been in your life about what that song means to you. That's the energy you need to have. There is always a moment where I think about something that is very, very personal.

Could you use that same personal moment when you're onstage as Norma Desmond?

It depends on what I need that day. Like I said, the external stuff sometimes does it. She's got her own story . . . and the fabulous costumes. It's like you're there.

In other words, as an actress, you've been living that story throughout the night.

Right. You're living in that story. But on the cabaret stage, it's just me and a piano. I love the addition of a band, but to me the cleanest moments take place when it is just me and a piano.

I think it was Erv Raible who said (and I'm paraphrasing), "Cabaret doesn't produce performers—cabaret produces stars." Cabaret is an excellent training ground for authenticity, for truth in the moment. Untruthfulness doesn't fly on a cabaret stage.

Oh, heck no. Even if you're doing a character, it must be honest. It must be real.

Training for a career and life in cabaret seems extremely beneficial for having a career in theater. But I'm not so sure if it works the other way around.

I agree.

There are a lot of Broadway performers, stars, who have attempted cabaret but have not really succeeded at it. Why do you think that is?

I once had a wonderful actor say to me, "I like losing myself in a character. . . . I don't want to do cabaret where I have to be myself." I think that's the part that's missing for a lot of people who go from theater to cabaret. They *think* they know who they are as a performer, but when they're onstage it's really someone else they're trying to be. It's that whole *authenticity* thing.

They've never actually been themselves onstage.

That's right. You can do an hour of character songs, but that in-between part—where people get to see *you*—it's naked. And if it doesn't work, it's even more naked, because it's both naked and a failure. [*both laugh*] People think that cabaret is going to be this easy-peasy thing to do, like "I'll just show up and sing some tunes." That couldn't be further from the truth. Sure, you can sell out once or twice . . .

You could do a friends and family show and have great success once or twice . . .

Yes! Right. *Bon Chance!*

But building an audience and being a cabaret professional, that's a different thing.

A very different thing.

You opened the room at Don't Tell Mama. I believe it was you and . . .

Nancy LaMott. Yes.

Now that's a piece of history. How did that come to be? What was that opening experience like?

It was a very big deal because so many other clubs had closed: Les Mouches, Brothers & Sisters, Downstairs at the Upstairs, Upstairs at the Downstairs, Reno Sweeney's. . . . That was the end of a golden age. So,

Figure 22.2. Karen Mason standing next to the opening night poster at Don't Tell Mama. *Photo by Stephen Mosher.*

to open a brand-new club that was this beautiful was an honor. Nancy and I were both very different but were "known" as singers who were working a lot. We alternated nights. She would take late shows one night and then the early show the next night. The poster is hysterical. Both of us with this curly 1980s hair. She was a diminutive little thing, and I . . . was not.

The space was shiny and new. And people were excited about it. Barbara Cook was there. Lots of theater and film stars were there. It was exciting. It was a new venue, and it was going to be a new time for cabaret. The man who booked us was named Bruce Hopkins.

I knew Bruce! I worked with him in La Gran Scena for years.

Did you? Oh, my God. I loved Bruce. And I loved La Gran Scena. I have to say that was such a brilliant, brilliant thing.

It really was. Ira (Siff) was brilliant. Bruce was brilliant. And that entire company, which sustained for over twenty years touring around the world . . . all of that started with cabaret at the Ballroom.

Wow.

Meanwhile, back at Don't Tell Mama . . .

Right. That first night I was introduced as Karen Akers. "Ladies and Gentlemen, Don't Tell Mama's is proud to present . . . Karen Akers." [*Mason laughs*] This has happened to me so many times—it's either Karen Akers or Karen Morrow. Anyway, that night we did our opening number. Brian (Lasser) had done an arrangement of "Something's Coming" for the club's opening. It's still one of my favorite arrangements of his. I have no idea what was in the rest of the show. I tried to find the set list, but I wasn't particularly organized at that time, so I don't have it. ♪

Did you know back then that the room would become so legendary?

No. I was so young. I never thought about that kind of stuff. I just thought we were lucky to have a gig. I wasn't thinking about the room or the history of it. Probably I was thinking, *How can this lead me to the next job, which will (of course) make me a star.* You know, that delusion that happens when you're that age.

You also teach master classes. I've observed you teaching a master class for Lennie Watts's Singnasium. Do you do that often?

I do. I'd like to do it more. I really enjoy it.

When working with young singers who have just graduated from college, have you noticed a commonality in their training? Do you perceive anything universally missing in their understanding of vocal performance?

Yes, but I'm not sure that it *can* be taught in college. It's that connection—really knowing who you are and the "why" of it all. I think that happens later on. In college you're just learning the techniques. I don't think you can put it all together for yourself until you're not in that situation anymore. In college you think you know things, but what you don't have yet is the connection to "why"—why you're doing what you're doing. It's really knowing the "why" and being comfortable with it. The reasons we sing are always so personal. College kids don't have that capability yet. And then there are all the lies we tell ourselves and all the pressure that we put on ourselves. When I teach cabaret to these kids, I love being able to say, "Okay, now, you can just *tell* us. You can be an *actor* now. You can be a storyteller. You can be *you* as a storyteller. You don't have to be a character."

There's no course of study in institutional theater or music programs on how to perform authentically as yourself. You can study a technique of voice or how to become a character. You can study the "realness" of Stanislavski and method acting, and so forth, but ultimately, that is still within the given untrue circumstance of the play or musical. There's no course of study on how to authentically be you onstage.

I think that's what cabaret does. And honestly, when I did *Sunset Boulevard*, that was the thing that saved me. It was the fact that, through my years of growing up in cabaret, I knew who I was, or at least, I knew I was still on the journey of knowing who I was.

What the best advice you've gotten from a teacher?

I still study with Bill Schuman, and he's always on my case: "Let go of the voice and just tell the story. Just tell me the story." Always remember that it's about communication. The reason you sing—the "why"—is to communicate.

The "why"—not the "how"—to sing.

That's right. The "how" is very important, but then let go of that. It's a means to an end, but the end is communication, and that's the reason to do it—not just for the vocal gymnastics of hitting that high F. The *reason* you might need to sing that note is because of the story and what you want to say. Honestly, I think it would be valuable to have a cabaret-type curriculum or class in universities. I know that Lennie (Watts) is doing something with Marymount. It's invaluable to give young students the sense of "letting go of it" and knowing what it feels like to have a room of people staring at you. You don't have costumes and lights. It's just you and a piano.

One of the most moving experiences I've ever had was *not* with somebody who had a killer voice. Do you remember Hearts and Voices?[1]

Yes, I do.

We would go into hospitals. Chris Denny put a show together for the patients and asked if I would sing. I said, "Of course, I will do anything I can do." It was me and Austin Pendleton and Chris. Austin Pendleton was the original Motel Kamzoil in *Fiddler (on the Roof)*. He's an amazing actor and director and writer. The man can do anything. Anyway, he's got this "eccentric" voice and he got up and sang. Now, mind you, I was working my ass off for this. I was being as perky as I could possibly be and trying to "entertain the troops" and distract them from what was going on in their lives. Meanwhile, he got up and sang "Somewhere" (from *West Side Story*) with this craggy voice, and it was so moving and so stunning. . . . I will never forget it. There wasn't a dry eye. It was so quiet, and everyone was just there with him because he was *talking*— talking to us on pitch . . . not singing or talking *at* us. He was telling of a dream. And from that moment on, I thought, *Oh, wow. It's lovely to have a beautiful voice, but* that's *the meat of it.* That's *the reason to do it.* You can make someone—if only for a second—dream, and feel outside of what's going on within them, and feel like they can share the crap in their lives because someone else gets it. I will never forget that. I've used that image in my head for the longest time. Don't show me your big high notes. I don't care. Make me feel something. Make me feel like I'm not alone. Start at zero and tell me a story. Tell me a dream. Tell me something you're sharing with me. It always sounds slightly pretentious . . . until you see it in action. ♪

NOTE

1. Hearts and Voices was a program started in the 1980s in response to the AIDS epidemic. Broadway singers would perform for patients in hospital AIDS wards.

㉓

THE PRINCESS OF BIRDLAND

An Interview with Natalie Douglas

Natalie Douglas is a two-time Bistro Award winner, an eleven-time MAC Award winner, a BroadwayWorld Cabaret Award winner, and recipient of the Donald F. Smith Award and Margaret Whiting Award given by the Mabel Mercer Foundation. She has been described as "a true force of nature" and "in a league of her own" by Clive Davis of the *Times* for her London appearances, and she is one of the most celebrated and honored cabaret artists working today. Affectionately known as the "Princess of Birdland," her portrait hangs on the legendary jazz club's "Wall of Fame." Since 2016 she has performed at Birdland in a series of different shows featuring tributes to Nina Simone, Lena Horne, Nat King Cole, Sammy Davis Jr., Stevie Nicks, Stevie Wonder, Dame Shirley Bassey, Barbra Streisand, and Dolly Parton. She has also performed in shows with themes as diverse as café society, the music of the 1970s and 1980s, songs of various civil rights movements, and gospel-influenced jazz and blues. Douglas's third album, *Human Heart*, was released at Birdland in March 2016, and her first two albums, *To Nina . . . Live at Birdland* and *Not That Different*, are available on iTunes, Amazon, Spotify, and GooglePlay. She also appears on *Fine and Dandy* for PS Classics and *Broadway by the Year: 1940* on Bayview Records. Her music is often featured on NPR, Sirius XM Radio, and

Figure 23.1. Natalie Douglas.
Photo by Bill Westmoreland.

BBC Radio London. Douglas is also an esteemed cabaret performance coach, conducting master classes and workshops for the Manhattan Association of Cabarets. She also specializes in diversity workshops for public and private schools. She is a Phi Beta Kappa graduate of the University of Southern California (magna cum laude) with an undergraduate degree in psychology and certificates in theater and women's studies. She also holds a master's degree in psychology from the University of California, Los Angeles (UCLA). We had the opportunity to speak with Natalie Douglas after one of her sold-out performances at Birdland. ♪

Natalie, thank you so much for sharing your time and expertise with us. How and when did you decide to become a "cabaret singer"?

When I was about four years old and my parents took me to see the Count Basie Orchestra. We went to see them every year when they came to Los Angeles, but this time (that I remember) I was four. The first act was the orchestra playing all the instrumental hits, so people were dancing and enjoying the evening. The second act began with the singer Joe Williams. I was very aware of the moment that the intermission ended and the second act started because now there was only one man onstage. The orchestra was behind the curtain. That brilliant, gorgeous, gifted, and [*sighs*] luminous man stepped in front of the curtain and began to sing "Something to Live For," and the entire auditorium froze. No one moved or breathed. It was the most glorious sound, and I looked at my mother and said, "*That*, I want to do *that*. How do I do *that*?" She thought I was kidding, so she ignored me. But right then my journey began. ♪

My parents had the most fantastic and eclectic record collection. They had everything, and they loved every kind of music. I grew up listening to Ray Charles, Dolly Parton, George Jones, Ramsey Lewis, Maria Callas, and Doris Day, among many others. The Gisele MacKenzie album was one of my favorites. We went to see a lot of live performances. In addition to the Count Basie Orchestra, we would also go to hear Nancy Wilson and the Mills Brothers, and my mother's favorite opera was *Madame Butterfly*, so we would see that once a year as well. And Saturday mornings I participated in the Young Peoples' Classical program at the Dorothy Chandler Pavilion. ♪

One day my mother came home from work, and I was probably pestering her with a million questions, and she told me that she would teach me a song and then I could go rehearse in my room. If I learned it, then I could come back and perform it for both of my parents. The song was "You'll Never Know." I went to my room and worked it out. I came up with an arrangement and even a little tag. I don't know where I got it. I must have heard it on albums, and I thought, *That's how you do that.*

Prior to my Linda Ronstadt show in the summer of 2017, I read her book and she talked about learning this harmony with her brothers and sisters. They were older, and they put her up on a table (or something) so that her mouth was higher, and they harmonized together. And she talks about being so little that she didn't have a lot of words for everything but thinking, *Yup. I'm a singer. That's what I do. I'm a singer!* When I read that I thought, *Yes! I know that moment.* As soon as I began to sing, I knew that *Oh, I'm a singer.* I didn't think of it as a career, but I knew that was who I was.

When I decided what I wanted my creative outlet to be, it was acting. Singing was just the thing I did on weekends with friends and their bands. I was in Los Angeles, singing regularly, kind of getting paid for it—not quite, but almost. There was a steakhouse in Westwood, and this guy had the gig singing and playing the guitar. Someone requested "Blue Bayou," and he said, "I can play it, but I don't know the words," and I said "I do—if you can play it in C." He responded, "Sure." I sang and afterward the manager came over and said, "If you want to come work on his night, I can't pay you, but I'll feed you." I was sixteen when I went to college, nineteen went I went to grad school, so you know, smart but no money. I was excited to be doing those kinds of things, but not really seeing the path to cabaret or nightclub—or singing—for a living.

In New York, however, it seemed possible, so I decided to move here. I wasn't really introduced to cabaret by that title until I came to the city, which was in the mid- to late 1980s; I met some people in a piano bar who took me to see Sidney Myer, who booked my first cabaret show at Don't Tell Mama.

Wow.

And Karen Mason was my second cabaret show! Karen Mason at Mama's. And when I saw cabaret, I realized it was a present-day experience much like the live records that I loved. *Sammy Davis Jr. in Vegas, Lena Horne at the Plaza* . . . those albums that I listened to: nightclub singing . . . supper club singing. The thing that I thought was gone actually existed in this new form. I mean it's not a new form, but we call it something different now. And I suddenly thought, *I could do this . . . maybe.* ♪

Several people have suggested this book shouldn't even be called So You Want to Sing Cabaret *and instead should be* So You Want to Sing Nightclub, *fearing that the word "cabaret" might have negative associations. How do you define cabaret?*

I define cabaret as *the place*. The place where we do this, the size of the rooms, the fact that they are usually intimate. But also—and more important—I think what makes it cabaret is the conversation. There is an interaction between the performer and the audience that has elements of spontaneity in it like a conversation does. I've done my Nina Simone show probably seven hundred times, and the songs are set. But each time I perform, the show is never the same, and that's because it's like a conversation you're having with the audience. I may be telling a story, but *each time* I tell that story it's not the same exact story. I am having a conversation with you right now that is different than the conversation I had with the last person I told the story to. So, I think cabaret has that element of a conversation. It's "of the moment." ♪

Do you think that there is a specific cabaret performance technique that a performer should learn?

My personal taste is for a cabaret performer who understands that— whether you're a scripted performer or not—in terms of your patter, you are *talking* to an audience. It is a *dialogue*. When you're onstage you're not alone. The audience is your scene partner; they just don't have any lines. And if we're onstage together and you don't have any lines, I don't pretend you don't exist. If we're having a conversation, but the bulk of it is mine, you don't *disappear*. We're still together. You have an inner life, and I have an inner life. And that same thing is true with your audience. They're not a mirror. They don't just come there to reflect back to you how awesome you are. I don't enjoy, for the most part, performers who are in a box, giving the exact same performance they would give whether it's to seniors or twelve-year-olds. If the room was on fire, they wouldn't know. They press "play" and go.

As for performing in cabaret, is there a definitive way to perform in that space that is different than other vocal genres?

In this art form the sound of your voice isn't always the most important thing. There are cabaret artists who are exceptional, and yet their voices are not the most glorious instruments. When that is the case, I think it is because that performer is so good at making a connection with the audience that we are utterly captivated by the story they tell and not listening for perfect notes. We're experiencing this tale. However, I am not a fan of "Oh, it doesn't matter how you sound." I personally think that it *is* as much about music as it is about lyrics. The lyric matters, but the music is part of it.

In terms of any negatives attached to the word, that's just a product of the economic shift that started around the 1970s. There was a time when you went to see a show at the Oak Room and you knew (because it was the Oak Room) that you'd see a certain caliber of performer. So maybe you hadn't heard of Diahann Carroll because she was some new ingenue. You don't know who she is; you don't know what she sounds like. But you knew that you could spend that money to go and do that because there was just a certain level of performer who showed up there. It also wasn't a week's salary for you to do that, and so nightlife had an appeal and draw that wasn't *just* the name of the performer. A performer could *build* her name. But in the 1950s and 1960s that started to have competition from television, and the fact that people moved out to the suburbs. ♪

When people are living in cities, their favorite places (where they go to eat or to listen to music, theater, etc.) are all within walking distance or a short cab ride away You can do a bunch of things in one night: have dinner, meet people for drinks and then go see a late show, and so forth. That's viable. But when you're in the suburbs, once you get home you're not coming back unless it's a special occasion like an anniversary or because you've spent a lot of money on a theater ticket. You don't do that routinely. So, when that migration began to happen, the clubs had a much harder time filling the rooms. The economic model didn't work, and it became, "If anyone can fill this room, they can book this night." And as far as the club was concerned, that was something they absolutely had to do. And I don't think there's anything wrong with that. But there is a difference between people who do this for a living and people who do it as a hobby. If I have never been to a cabaret before, do I want to spend money for parking and dinner, and then pay a $20 to $65 cover and a $25 minimum to see someone who has a lot of heart and warmth but is not really a singer and hasn't yet figured out how to sing for people they don't know? Because you know, when we start this, we almost always have an audience of people who know and love us and want to be supportive. One can be misled thinking *that's* your audience, but you can't make living at that. You need to have strangers come and see you. You need to figure out how to sing to the strangers. How do you reach people who don't already know you, who aren't predisposed to love you? If I'm that person from the suburbs, and I come in and all these people know you, but I don't, then I'm sitting there thinking, *I don't get these jokes, I don't know what's happening. She seems nice, but I don't really get her.* Am I really going to walk away thinking, *Well, that was worth $250. Let's do it again!*

You've built a career in a cabaret over the past thirty years, crossing over from friends and family to building up an audience that does not know you and even developing a fan base. You clearly understand the business of cabaret. How does a young singer who is preparing for this kind of performance make that transition?

I think part of that transition—from doing shows for friends and family to doing shows that strangers will enjoy—is figuring out where that line is, riding it carefully, and figuring out the balance. Cabaret is personal— it must be about you. People who enjoy cabaret want to know something about you. But it cannot be so much about you that we stop caring. We are not here for you. You are here for us.

I know when people come to see the Nina Simone show (or the Elvis show or the Sammy Davis Jr. show), some—luckily enough—have come to see me. But some people don't know me at all. They've come to hear Sammy Davis Jr. songs or stories about Sammy because they are huge fans of *his*. And some people are brought by those people and don't even know who Sammy Davis Jr. is! I have to craft a show that's entertaining for *all* of those people. I don't want anyone in my audience thinking, *Oh, this part is for the insiders. I'll check out for this.* So, I find some deep cuts that hopefully the superfans will get excited about, but there are also people who only have a glancing acquaintance with the artist's work and they want to hear the hits. People come to the Nat King Cole show and want to hear "Unforgettable." I think it's important to honor your audience; they come from different places and have different expectations. I don't think that means you have to meet every single expectation because that becomes filling out a checklist and ceases to be our craft. But I do think it's important to understand your audience and where they are coming from.

When I created the Dolly Parton show, I knew I would have to sing "I Will Always Love You" even though a lot of people's associate the song with Whitney Houston. I had to honor the fact that Dolly wrote it but did not sing it like Whitney. How do you create a moment that honors both of those things, and what story do you tell so that it makes sense? And how do I make the performance entertaining for everybody?

I think part of what can also help make that transition from friends and family to a wider demographic is helping your audience to hear these songs in new way or find songs that they may not know. I think we have to find a way to make listening to this music more captivating. I like all kinds of music, but I do not pretend that the modern pop I enjoy listening to is deep. Some of my favorite pop singers don't really say a single consonant. I have no idea what they're saying. And if that is how someone is accustomed to listening to music, you cannot expect that person to walk into a room and fall in love with cabaret easily.

You sing in many different styles. Is that something you could always do? Did you learn that through any sort of vocal training?

My mother taught me to sing. She would teach me songs by singing them to me and then have me repeat them after her. I started playing piano when I was around four or five years old and then began playing the harp when I was about eight. But in my youth, I never took a voice lesson. I didn't have formal vocal instruction until college.

Did you study vocal performance?

No. My undergraduate degree was a self-created major that combined psychology, theater, and women's studies. My graduate degree is in psychology with a concentration in theater.

You have performed in both music theater and cabaret. When singing the same song in a theater context or a cabaret context—how is that different?

I think the biggest difference is that quite often in a role you are singing to someone in the scene, and the reason for singing this song comes from the circumstances of the play. In cabaret we create the circumstance, and it can be anything. One of the things that I like to do is sing songs that I would never sing in music theater. For instance, "Lonely House" from *Street Scene* is not sung by a woman, nor is it sung by a person of color. But the first time I heard it I instantly knew that the lyricist was black even before I knew it was Langston Hughes. The poetry is so clearly written from a black experience and perspective. And when I first put it in the show, I thought of it very much as a moment in time. It feels very postwar to me, and specifically a black woman in that time, so I'm not singing it as the character within the show. I use imagery to put myself in the time and place, so my particular vision for "Lonely House" is that I see me (the character that I created for this moment) standing in my apartment looking through the blinds into the street, and the street is wet and the light shines down and I'm waiting for him—knowing that he's probably not coming, but waiting. As soon as I have that picture of my mind—with everything I've created in my head—it's there. Every word of the song is connected to this life that I've created. The words mean something specific to me.

It sounds to me like you just have described a cabaret performance technique?

Oh, I guess so! That's what I do. [*laughs*] I know different people have different ways of making it happen, but for me it's like every song is a little movie, and I am someone in it.

It's your movie.

Yes, I've created it. And it tells the story I want to tell. And I do believe that you can take a song and bend it a bit. The circumstance and even the gender don't have to line up with the song's original intent. You've heard me talk about Bojangles. Well, Jerry Jeff Walker did not write that song about Bill "Bojangles" Robinson. But clearly, when black artists recorded it, that is who they were referencing and what they were thinking. That song got shifted from its composer's original intent. But I don't think it bends the song to the breaking point. There are some songs, however, that are not as pliable. Songs are not endlessly mutable. There are parameters. I've had students come to me with ideas, bringing in a song and saying, "But I want to do this with it," which could mean rewriting it a little or just infusing the story they bring to it. And sometimes I will say, "Well, I think that song does not handle the weight of your story. There is a better song for that story. Let's find that better song."

Do you have a vocal warm-up routine?

The first time I ever had any kind of vocal issue, I went for a note and there was a crack that had never happened before. I panicked. I said to my husband, "I guess this is aging and I'm losing it. Maybe I should learn to type." And God bless my brilliant and beautiful husband. He said, "Don't be ridiculous. Go to the doctor and find out what's going on." So

I did. And luckily for me, I found the best ENT in New York, Dr. Peak Woo. I love him. He checked me out and said, "Oh, acid reflux, you'll be fine." He pointed me in the direction of Linda Carroll. She gave me my first real warm-up and warm-down that I have used for the last ten years of singing and traveling—and singing and traveling with a cold! Singing with a cold isn't that hard. It's tiring, but I can do it. My problems happen as the cold is going away and the cough starts. *That's* when I start having trouble. Linda is the one who gave me all the techniques for that and the things that help, including my steamer. She changed my life. Between the two of them, I am singing better than I did in my twenties. So yes, warm-up/warm-down; I believe in it wholeheartedly. I try never to open my mouth to sing without warming up first, even to the point that I sometimes beg off those moments when somebody says, "Oh, come on, why don't you sing with me?" Because I know I have not warmed up that day, that's why. I believe in this. I think it's smart.

As a cabaret singer, are there any certain vocal techniques or exercises that you find especially helpful?

I think lip trills are great because it's nearly impossible to hurt yourself. It is a gentle way to just get things moving a little bit. And they are the perfect warm-down. I have different warm-ups for different needs. But the lip trills and breathing exercises are really helpful.

Do you travel with your own humidifier?

I do. I have a little humidifier that sits by the bed, and I also have a My-PurMist cordless that I really love. It uses cartridges with sterile water; you don't have to clean it the way that you have to with others. You can take the cartridges on the plane because they are under three ounces, so they'll fit in your carry-on bag.

As someone who teaches independently in this field and works with young singers who have largely come from a more formal education of vocal performance—either classical or music theater—what have you noticed about what's not being taught to undergrads? When students graduate, what are they still missing?

Figure 23.2. Natalie Douglas teaching a young singer. *Photo by Sadie Foster.*

I think so much of the time—and rightfully so in programs and conservatory—we are learning about ourselves. And we need to because *we* are the instrument. But I think it can make us so inwardly focused that we forget that once the performance is happening, that's *not* the time to think, "Oh, that F wasn't exactly how I wanted it." That's not where your head should be. That's for rehearsal. I think we can get so obsessed with the *perfect* intonation and the *perfect* vowel or the *perfect* support, and I wish there were a little more room for some intuitive work.

I personally am a big believer in letting who you are and your identity influence your work and perspective, particularly in cabaret. I also think that's true for artists in all fields. Nina Simone said, "The artist has a responsibility to society—to talk about what's going on, to fight, and to be an activist if that is necessary." In cabaret, there's even more room because *this is you*. What do *you* have to say?

If you were in a room full of technical voice teachers, what would you ask them to spend more time on, and what would you ask them to spend less time on?

I would hope that teachers encourage students of color to listen to and embrace this music because so much of the time the image in our head is pretty white ladies in gowns singing Great American Songbook. But in fact, this music doesn't exist without black and brown people. It belongs to all of us.

I'm glad you brought this up. Marilyn Lester, of the ASA, also mentions the great contributions to the songbook by composers like Duke Ellington and Fats Waller . . .

Yes, and not just the composers but also performers like Florence Mills and Adelaide Hall. We know and rightly revere Lena Horne, but she wasn't operating in a vacuum. Billie Holiday was brilliant, but when she died it wasn't the end of the black chanteuse. I recently saw an interview with someone talking about his favorite cabaret performers, and everyone that he mentioned from the past was black—Bobby Short, Eartha Kitt . . . every name. But every name that he mentioned from the present was white and very "downtown Joe's Pub." And I thought, *So, do you think black people stopped singing this music?* And what does that say about where we're going? It would be great if a cross-cultural appreciation for this music could be taught.

Between the composers and performers of the "Black American Songbook" there is so much material for students of color to authentically sing.

Yes. And I don't know how many more blonde sopranos need to sing "Summertime." There is other material. I judged a competition a few years ago, and this beautiful young man came in with a very hipster way about him. His two song choices were "Swing Low Sweet Chariot" and "Go Down Moses." And this was a white kid with a stunning voice—that bass-baritone richness that we don't get to hear that often. But I had no idea what the story was.

What his personal point of view was?

Right. He was singing the songs beautifully, but he wasn't singing them like he grew up singing them in a black church. So what story was he telling? This was the kind of competition where they just walked in the room, gave us their number, sang the two songs, and walked out again. I had no opportunity to find out what it meant to him. I would bet that his teacher, who assigned him those songs or helped him with those choices, didn't even think of that.

Possibly they were picked simply because they were bass-baritone songs that worked well in his range?

They sounded great in his voice, sure. But "Ol' Man River" is about something specific, even though it wasn't written by black people. If you sing it and you're not black, that's fine. But then I do need to know what it's about for *you*.

Let me ask you the other side of the coin then. How would it be for a white singer to sing Duke Ellington?

Please do! I don't mean to say that white people can't sing these songs. I wouldn't have been perplexed at all if I knew what story the hipster was telling.

His performance didn't give you a point of view?

Know what you're singing about! When I approach a Harry Warren tune, I want to know what was happening in his life when he wrote it. Is this during a happy period of a romance or an unhappy period? I think the Irving Berlin songs from his depressions are breathtakingly beautiful—even more so because he struggled to find the beauty. He was sure there wasn't any left. He threw away "How Deep Is the Ocean" and "Say It Isn't So," because he thought they were terrible. *He threw them away!* His copyist (because Berlin didn't write his own songs down) pulled them out of the trash and sent them to the publisher.

It sounds as if you are equally concerned with the "why" as much as the "how."

At least twice—if not twelve times in a show—I am going to tell you what was happening when this song was written. There's a Roberta

Flack recording (that's really hard to find) of her singing "Oh Freedom" a cappella—the old "negro spiritual" (as we call it). It was recorded in the Gate of No Return, a cave where captured Africans were held before they were packed onto ships and sent to America. In 1973, Roberta Flack, Tina Turner, James Brown, and other black performers went to Africa. It was an anniversary of African independence. They had this huge concert, and on that occasion she sang "Oh Freedom" in those caves, and it is one of the most beautiful things you will ever hear. And knowing where she was standing when she sang it takes it to a whole other level. That's worth knowing. I would love technical teachers to get as excited about that aspect of the material.

In cabaret many types of music are performed and generally with a contemporary use of voice. For the most part, it's not meant to be a classical sound. When someone begins to sing with an overtly classical sound that is absolutely not appropriate to the song, do you address that?

I try to. In cabaret the kind of singing we do is, for the most part, conversational. And so that is what's appropriate for the material.

Can we define "conversational"? That does not mean a limited range but rather through one's entire range the voice still sounds like the singer is "talking" without engaging a lofted classical resonance.

Right. It is not that kind of sound. I don't think the range should be limited to the conversational range of the normal speaking voice. It just shouldn't go into that opera place. And it is rare, I think. I know only a few singers—and by the way, you are one of them—who are truly able to have gorgeous classical placement and also sing a pop tune, a country tune, a folk tone, or a show tune in that conversational place.

Well, thank you.

No, it's very rare. It's not an easy thing to do, and I am aware of that. So, in a class when that happens, when the sound doesn't match the song, I don't want to make that singer feel outmatched. But I do try to address the concept. It's not about completely shifting your technique and relearning how to sing as much as it is about just thinking about it differently, which is something people don't always allow themselves to do. Sometimes the classical training sort of beats it out of you. Not literally, but you know what I mean. Just the permission to make sounds differently is a big deal.

Is that something you'd ask of voice teachers—to give singers permission to make different sounds?

Yes, because there are so many different kinds of resonance. There are so many different kinds of production and placement and support. If you shift any one of those things, you can make all kinds of different sounds.

Last February, I was in Grand Cayman for the Arts Festival. It was my second year teaching a master class there with KT Sullivan and the Mabel Mercer Foundation. On the first day, I found myself talking about "making sound" because we had a couple of students in a row who were really, really quiet singers. And I said, "You know what, I don't care if you make mistakes. There's nothing wrong with that. That doesn't make you a loser. If you hit a wrong note, that's fine. The only time you are losing is when you are hiding." I hadn't planned to say that, but I thought, *That's actually true.* It's okay to make the wrong choice. It's okay to make a choice that's less successful. But if you are hiding, that's the only choice that's not ever going to benefit you. And it's hard to do, this thing that we are learning and teaching and doing to ourselves; it's insane and difficult. "Be who you are *fully*, out in front of strangers, and we'll judge you. And sing the right notes and the right words. OK . . . go!" If we think about it too much we would start screaming and never stop. It's this incredibly difficult thing.

I guess I would hope that teachers who are exceedingly good at technique would also teach the song in terms of the gestalt of the thing. Because technique is important, please Jesus! But there's an *entire* performance to talk about. And technique only gets us focused on *us*.

. . . When we shouldn't be focused on us.

Yes, because we're already focused on that. We're actors. We don't know any other way.

Every day of the year there are new songs being written that could very well become part of the Great American Songbook. Do you think that there is a criteria for a new song to be considered part of a new *Great American Songbook?*

Yes and no. Some of the newer songs will endure. But there are some new songs that are written very much in the Great American Songbook mold. They are lovely "of the moment" contemporary songs that harken back to the golden age, but I don't know that we'll be singing those songs in seventy years.

And why is that?

Because I think some of those songs are written with more nostalgia than real human emotion. The reason the songs that we are nostalgic about now have lasted is because the writers were not writing from an "Oh, remember back in the good old days" perspective. They were writing about what they were feeling in the moment—now.

They were writing about their experience.

Yes. Larry Hart wrote about what he was feeling, what he thought, what broke his heart, and what made him happy (briefly). And he did it so cleverly. He wasn't trying to "bring back" something. Some of the newer material is written as sort of a thumb in the eye to modern pop music, and that's not the point of music. If you don't like Ariana Grande (and you're allowed to *not* like her), fine. But your work can't be about your disdain for her either. Your work must be about something *you* love. If you don't like something, great. Don't sing that. But then, what are *you* creating? It can't just be an "antidote" to that other thing. I think that it must be about something you do like and not a reaction to something you don't like. If people are standing in rooms all over the world singing your songs, then those words must resonate with all those people. The lyrics won't resonate if it's a generic thought like *Isn't love wonderful?* Well . . . duh! What else do you have to say? Quite honestly, *Isn't love wonderful?* doesn't *really* resonate with many people. Yes, it is, but doesn't love also make you sick to your stomach? And doesn't it give you a headache? And doesn't it break your heart? You hear someone sing about *that*, and it takes you to a place in your life. It could be right now. It could be what you hope for in the future. It could be what just happened. Those are real feelings. You hear someone singing "Isn't the world a happy place?" and you think, *Yeah, sometimes.* There are no stakes involved in that.

Great American Songbook songs, whichever era they are from, have "skin in the game." *Somebody* has *something* on the line in that song, even if it's just a happy little tune like "Sunny Side of the Street," which is not super complicated in terms of its emotions but is still not one dimensional either. There are levels. When I teach a song like that, I talk about finding the place where the music gives you a clue that maybe there's a shadow around the corner—or maybe you are coming from a shadow. Find the place in a happy song that isn't happy. Find the place in an unhappy song that is happy. If the song is about heartbreak, find a place where it is funny. *That's* what life is, and *that's* what gets all of our juices going, both as actors and as humans.

THE FUTURE OF CABARET

TRAINING TOMORROW'S SINGERS

Interviews with Lina Koutrakos, Corinna Sowers-Adler,
Lennie Watts, John McDaniel, Tim Schall,
and Wendy Lane Bailey

To date, there are no university programs that train singers exclusively for a solo career in popular American song or Great American Songbook, and certainly no institutional programs that teach the business and craft of cabaret. Recordings of great singers have preserved the common performance practices that are unique to this art form. However, without historical context or understanding the art and craft of this genre—which is still largely passed down in a generational legacy from singer to singer—a new performer of cabaret may believe their job is simply to imitate the performances they have admired. Nothing could be further from the truth. Cabaret is ever evolving and ever changing. The one constant throughout the genre's history is the intimacy and authenticity with which a singer must perform. Authenticity and imitation are antithetical. Therefore, serious study of both the history and performance practices of cabaret is required.

To that end, there are a handful of small private training programs available in cabaret. However, it is predominantly the private teacher and performance coach who are on the front lines of this educational battle, ensuring the art and craft of cabaret survives for tomorrow's singers. In this chapter, we spoke with some of the industry's leading teachers about their work.

LINA KOUTRAKOS

Lina Koutrakos is the artistic director and teacher of the Performance Connection series of advanced workshops for aspiring cabaret singers. Over her thirty-year career, she has garnering rave reviews and won multiple MAC awards as both a singer and director, including the Petite Piaf award in Paris. Koutrakos teaches workshops with multiple singers in one room, bridging the gap between performer and audience, giving the performer access to both instruction and audience connection. She developed various Performance Connection workshops that concentrate on the singer's individuality and authenticity in the art and craft of cabaret performance.

Performance Connection has grown to include an ongoing advanced performers workshop in New York City, an annual, three-day Midwest Cabaret Conference in Chicago each July, the Gateway Conference in St. Louis in January, and a weeklong workshop on the island of Myko-

Figure 24.1. Lina Koutrakos teaching Wendy Kaufman Harper. *Photo by Rick Jensen.*

nos, Greece, every September. Koutrakos has been called a "walking master class" and has taught master classes and workshops in Santa Fe, Las Vegas, Boston, Los Angeles, and Washington, D.C. She is one of the most respected teachers in the field of cabaret pedagogy, which she has—along with a few esteemed colleagues—helped to create. We had the opportunity to speak with Koutrakos about her career as both a teacher and a singer. ♪

Lina, thank you so much for sharing your expertise with us. You are a multi-award-winning performer and director in cabaret, but today let's talk about your teaching. Can you describe your curriculum and how you implement it?

I don't think I ever sat down with a piece of paper—even a metaphoric piece of paper—and figured out what my "curriculum" was going to be. A million years ago I was a waitress and singer in the cabaret rooms, and at the same time, I was performing with a rock band in clubs in New York City. In both situations, I had the opportunity to watch and learn. There were usually three shows a night, sometimes four. Seeing all those cabaret shows while working, the singer in me would watch and think, *Why does that work?* Just when I understood why something worked, somebody completely different—who thrilled me as much as the other person—would come and break those rules and I would have to go back to square one, and again think, *Now, why did that work for them?* So, the bottom line is—and I'm going to overuse this word like crazy—it's all about "authenticity." Cabaret is personal and individual. The curriculum is dictated by each performer, at their level and with the sum of their parts—not just their voice. I try to help them focus on what they are sending out to make sure that nothing between that microphone and singer—or that soul and brain—gets lost in translation on its way to the front table, whether they are in a club or the back of an auditorium. *That's* my curriculum, to honor each person's authentic self.

When you work with a new singer and they're "singing" their heart out, how do you get them to shift their perception regarding what they should concentrate on. Are there specific exercises or "ways in" for that person?

The conversation starts with my asking them, "What are you thinking about?" Or I'll ask a specific question. For example, if somebody sings the song "I Remember" (from Sondheim's *Evening Primrose*), they will begin with these words: I remember sky. It was blue as ink. And I will ask, "Where?" And if they ask, "Where what?" then I know where I have to start. "Where was the sky blue as ink?" If they say, "In the sky," I say no. "Where for *you*? How old were you? Where did you live? What season was it? What day was it? Why were you looking up?" Just the idea of getting someone to stop and have a new thought about the way they sing a song and suddenly connect to a lyric—it's fabulous to watch. And it's amazing how many singers don't know to do that.

How would you define lyric connection in cabaret as opposed to music theater?

In music theater, I still have to—*Lina* still has to—play the character within the play. But with cabaret, it's *all you*. But you must be careful not to stand there in song and do some sort of fragile therapy session in front of people. Do I want you to pull your guts out and pour your heart out to me, really? No! Not if I feel like I must take care of you while I'm in the audience watching. But do I want to hear from you and nobody else but you? Yes, and that's a fine line.

There are a few young singers in cabaret, but the majority are older. It seems you have to have had your heart broken a few times and/or have had life experience in order to relate to the lyric of the song.

I was twenty-five years old when I received one of my first reviews in *Variety*. I can't quote it exactly, but it said something like "She's got some voice" and "She's somebody to keep your eye on." And at the very end it said, "As for her foray into songs like 'Cry Me a River' and 'My Man,' Koutrakos has not yet lived enough to understand what these songs are really about." Back then, at twenty-five years old, I would have fought him tooth and nail, but now I think to myself, *Yup, he was he right.* [*laughs*] So yes, it's easier to sing cabaret when you have lived a life. Recently, somebody got up and sang "Lush Life," and as it started and she sang "I used to visit all . . ." I said, "No, no, no. You're under thirty. No!" Technically, she did a good job, but emotionally she didn't have a clue. Yet another time I was directing somebody in her early thirties, and she wanted to sing the same song ("Lush Life") and I said, "No, it's not age appropriate. You can't." She asked, "Can I try?" She sang it, and I said, "OK, I was wrong. *You* can do it." It made me realize that "age" is not always chronological.

Why was she able to sing it?

She had a reference point, something to relate to. I'm kind of a "method acting" singing teacher. I haven't done it yet, but I would love to take ten singers that I love in the cabaret industry and have a three-hour workshop in which they all sing "I Remember" with no arrangement changes. It would be fascinating to see what each of them would do (subtextually) to connect to their own unique sensory memories, feelings, and ideas. I would love to see how that song could change ten different times with nothing besides the individual's life experiences informing it.

Connecting to the lyric is somehow different, more important, in cabaret. Why is that?

It's clearer, I think. Like I said, for twenty-five years I was very well known in the downtown rock 'n' roll scene in this city, and at the same time I was winning MAC awards for best female vocalist. I think the reason that I was taking center stage as a young woman with a rock band was because of my cabaret training. I was bringing more than just a powerful voice. I don't think people in the rock genre had any idea what the "it" factor was. But the "it" factor, I believe, is the sum of your parts, making this connection. When I first saw Bruce Springsteen live I thought, *He's almost doing it.* And now, all these years later, my perception was validated because he actually did do it on Broadway.

You're not the only person who's mentioned Bruce Springsteen and how authentic his performance was.

I was calling him a cabaret singer twenty years ago. He even vamps underneath the stories that he tells before he sings a song, even with the full E Street Band in Giants Stadium. In contrast, the lack of that kind of storytelling drives me crazy. When I watch *The Voice* and *American Idol*, after a while, my ears stop listening to all the vocal pyrotechnics. I like them. I tip my hat, but I also tune out. There is too much riffing and jumping around for my taste. Even if that's the genre, so much of the focus and the energy, the nucleus and core of the song, gets dissipated and becomes lost. The core of a song (the lyric) must inform the rest of it—the riffs and how and where to move, and so forth—but not vice versa. Start small and still. Start with the lyric. You may not keep still once you get cooking, but that's where you have to start.

My first director was Bruce Hopkins, and I often hear myself saying things that he said. The idea that you could dissipate the energy and focus onstage by "oversinging" a song or moving around too much—that's all Bruce. One day during a rehearsal he asked me, "What are you doing with your hands and your arms?" I said, "Well, I'm singing this from the point of view of a little kid. I'm kind of nervous in the backyard." He said, "Well it looks to me like you're going to take flight. You're distracting me. So, just stand still. You are dissipating the *real* energy of the song." I did what he said, and in doing so I discovered so much more about the song. For that performance I got a review from Roy Sander, and I remember this quote well: "Lina Koutrakos exudes more energy standing still than most performers who bound about the stage." That is a huge compliment, and I owe it all to Bruce Hopkins. As a performer, you should never defuse the core energy before it can really be used and channeled. That's such an important thing to remember. Otherwise, you run the risk of taking it to silly places and having it not translate the way you might want it to.

Translate?

So many things you *think* are working onstage might not be. If that is occurring, then your idea isn't *translating* in execution. You can only work on your own to a certain point; then you need to have that third eye watching the performance and making sure that what you are doing is translating well to your audience. Having both a director and a teacher is very important. I have done cabaret shows for thirty years and teach this art form full time. I know what I'm doing at this point.

And still—even now—when I'm ready, I bring in a director. That third eye is indispensable because I need to be sure that I am translating the way I intend to.

I was with a director for my cabaret show *Torch*, which consisted entirely of torch songs, a lot of which are from the Great American Songbook. I was singing "It Had to Be You," and the arrangement was deathly slow. In my version the lyric was not interpreted in a happy way, so this was deliberately not a happy arrangement. I brought in director Mark Waldrop, who at the time was directing Bette Midler's show. (I saw that show and thought, *Wow, he's good*), and after I sang it he said, "What is your point of view on this song?" and I said, "Well, this situation has left me numb." And he said, "Well, you're doing a really good job because all that translated to me is numbness, and it doesn't work." I would never have known that on my own.

Do you think it's possible that the interaction with the audience can change the way you sing a song?

Absolutely. That's what makes cabaret different. It's a very different experience than singing in a musical. In a show you're basically on a track, and you're going to tell that same story every night no matter what. But in cabaret, your story could change due to reaction from the audience. Of course, you must prepare your narrative in your head . . .

Your subtext?

Right. You must have a narrative—a beginning, a middle, and an end—even when you are talking to your audience. You must be anchored in personal truth. Then, if your "scene partner" is the people in the audience, and one of them doesn't make eye contact with you or spills a drink or smiles back at you—something as silly as that—it can change the story a little bit. Anything like that can change the molecules in the room. And we are *all* in the room. We don't have a fourth wall. We are in that room for the hour, and we are all standing on that stage with you. However, I would not suggest getting up there and letting that take you over. I believe that kind of singing in the moment is for more seasoned performers.

So, the singer has their narrative and subtext, and there are certain things they "plan" to do. And then there are those things that just happen that—depending on your experience level—you can acknowledge in the room and let it affect you for that phrase or that moment.

That's the ultimate example of "singing in the moment." It happens when all the elements of that live moment come together and you're experiencing all of them at once. And we, the audience, get to follow your lead. We might not know exactly what it is or who you're singing about, but we are still sharing the moment with you and having our own thoughts and feelings. If I'm singing about my first boyfriend, David, I bet a million bucks you're *not* going to think of *my* first boyfriend David, but if I do my job well and I remember *my* David, then you're probably going to remember *your* Jimmy.

In one section of our book we've detailed some of the different preparation techniques in cabaret, and we specifically talk about using subtext and the "singing in the moment" phenomenon.

Phenomenon, I like that.

It's certainly an advanced technique. It's something that we want to have happen in cabaret. That kind of energy and interaction in the room that is completely different than any other vocal performance genre. It doesn't happen in jazz or music theater, and it certainly doesn't happen in classical music.

You don't even do it in rock 'n' roll because there's so much happening onstage. Cabaret is an art form that is strongly associated with a venue that is intimate and small. It's not a theater. It's not an auditorium. Cabaret is "picture framed" for something that is physically small, which creates the intimacy for which it's known. There are some exceptions, of course. Bette Midler, for instance, did a show with an orchestra at Madison Square Garden. But she did a cabaret show! Her performance was so intimate with the audience that after a while the size of the venue didn't matter. And as I said earlier, I saw Bruce Springsteen do it with the E Street Band in Giants Stadium.

So, then the defining characteristic of cabaret itself is not the venue but rather this extremely intimate performance technique?

Yes, that's exactly right. I go back to my buzzword: I don't think you can be intimate without being *authentic*. Therefore, I strive *not* to teach students how to be intimate but to give them permission to be their authentic selves and strip away all the techniques and nonsense that they learned imitating others. Only then can they be their own authentic selves. It's a performance style, but the style is not only vocal. The performance must be informed by *you*. If everything—your lyrics, your story, your vocals, and so forth—is *not* informed by you, then we have strayed from the path of cabaret.

Truthfully, developing this kind of authenticity onstage is good for everyone. I don't care if you're a rock singer. I don't care if you're out there in the theater world auditioning to play other characters, even if you want to sing with a jazz trio, there's still something to learn from cabaret. A lot of jazz people come to me, and as good as they are and as much as I love that sound, they become background music very quickly and you think, "How does a voice and a style like that slip into the background?" Any singer of popular genres will benefit themselves greatly by learning about cabaret performance technique.

Music theater actors also do a lot of personal subtext work. They fulfill their personalized subtext. They have internal work going on, but the lights and costumes and settings bestowed on the stage—and on that character—obliterate our ability to see their personalized internal work. We can't help but see everything within the context of the play.

Yes, I guess that's true. But do you want to know something? (And this is my own personal opinion.) When Karen Mason was understudying Glenn Close in *Sunset Boulevard* and she walked out onstage and sang, "I don't know why I'm frightened," it was different. Something "popped." It was different because she was actually telling *her* truth. That night, I saw Norma Desmond. I did not see Karen Mason. I had to check myself and ask, "Did I lose my breath because it's so magnificent to see Karen walking out like that on a Broadway stage? Or did I lose my breath because that actress, that woman, that cabaret singer, and that character just did all of that at the same time?" Donna Murphy is another one. I love watching her in a cabaret room.

Most of the books in this series are aimed at younger singers. However, not everyone has a stable of university kids or young professional wannabees. There are thousands (if not millions) of voice teachers in this country and around the world who have rosters of older singers. There's an entire singing community of "second chance" people out there who've had a career in one thing and then have come back to singing, and this is the kind of repertoire, this is the kind of work that they need to be doing.

You are absolutely right. I was sitting in Chicago with KT Sullivan last year. She was my guest teacher. We were sitting in the dark watching a show, and an older woman from Boston got up and sang an old standard. She had an okay voice, but not a great voice. However, she sang her song and KT said (to herself as much as to me), "*That* is why we need these older people in this genre." She sang her entire life in three minutes, and everyone in that audience's breath was taken away . . . and 90 percent of them had no idea why.

We do have to get those "twentysomethings" interested in cabaret as well. There's no shame in being twenty-five years old. And the sound that you can make at twenty-five is often wonderful. But cabaret singing must always be coupled with *a life*. I mean, if you're singing about how upset you felt when the arm of your Barbie doll got ripped off and you *mean* it, I'll listen to you. It's about being in touch with what you really feel. If she doesn't tell me she's singing about a Barbie doll, who am I to judge her feelings?

There was a beautiful young singer who came to take a workshop with me in St. Louis. She was already working professionally and sang one of the songs from her traveling Carole King show called *It's Too Late*. After she sang, I asked, "What are you singing about?" and she said, "What?" The idea was so foreign to her. Now jump ahead two years later; she's performed at Carnegie Hall with KT. She's working her butt off and has already done her two shows here in New York. She sings Jason Robert Brown's "Another Life" from *The Bridges of Madison County*, and I have never believed anybody more than I believe this twenty-year-old gorgeous blonde girl who didn't have a clue what she was singing about two years ago. She recently said to me, "Oh my God! You opened the door for me and showed me what singing really is. And to think, I could have just sung with this voice for the rest of my life and never felt this. Thank you."

Is there a methodology for teaching cabaret performance technique? Everyone is learning and "getting there" in their own way; I realize that. But is there a first priority in the methodology that you teach?

Yes, absolutely. The first thing to do is to take away everybody's places to hide, their bad habits. You need to be stripped naked. What does your authentic voice sound like? Not just your singing voice, your soul voice, you heart voice, even the little voice in your head. Who the hell are you? What we *must* do first is take things away, and it's scary as hell to stand there without everything that's worked for us in the past. I have repeatedly said to people, "I promise, I will give this all back to you. Just have the courage to stand there without any of it, without your loud or long notes, without your killer high note, just for a minute. We've got to clean all that stuff away." So, you must leave all your tricks (even the good ones), your habits good and bad, and your "go-to" places. You must leave all that aside. That's step one. Be naked.

Deconstruction?

Deconstruction, yes. Then you start with the lyric. We're working with the understanding that you can sing, so *don't sing* right off the bat. You'll get everything—your singing, phrasing, and vocal tricks—back at the end of the process, and then you can decide what you want to take with you. You will definitely take some of it, but you're not going to take all of it. And some of that "stuff" you may put in different places than before. Stripping away the tricks immediately makes you more human. If this humanity makes you cry, bring it on. The truth is, if you cry in front of a group of people that you don't know, we're on the way to something *real* a hell of lot quicker. Do I want you to sit there and weep about your childhood the entire time we work? No. But if your journey doesn't start from some place that is real, a little unpretty, and a whole lot human, I don't think you're going to get where you need to go. I'm going to put you on your feet "entertainment ready," but it's all going to be from some place authentic, and you've got to know where that place is. So, deconstruction. Yes. That would be the word.

I think a lot of voice teachers would say the same thing. With a new student they're deconstructing old habits, deconstructing compensatory tensions.

And sometimes it's even harder with the older, more established people. We all have our own bag of tricks. I have all those "places" that I go, and they work for me. But I also have to use my head and always need to go back to square one.

And square one is?

The lyric, of course . . . the story as told through the lyric. If you're going to sing "I Remember," the first thing you have to sing (and pay attention to) is the word "I." So, you're informed from the get-go. This is a song about me . . . "I"! You haven't even said the second word yet. Talk about deconstructing!

You teach in many different cities. Is the experience of teaching and/or working outside of New York very different?

Yes, I do a lot of work with people in different cities. Many of their issues stem from the fact that they don't have a plethora of musical arrangers who can facilitate this art form and help them be as authentic as they want to be. In many cases, their pianist can't arrange the song the way the singer feels it.

Some pianists don't even know that is part of the job.

Exactly. I teach these singers the tools they need to work with [whomever] they have in their cities. I teach them how to find a pianist—for not only cabaret but also music theater and jazz—in their towns in Iowa, Illinois, New Mexico, and so forth, and figure out if he or she (the pianist) is someone who's equipped to deal with "feeling" the song the way the singer wants to interpret it. The singer needs to be able to hand the pianist a piece of music that looks *nothing* like how they "feel" it and say, "This is what it should feel like." Or share a recording of a similar arrangement that inspired them in the first place. Start from there and then ask, "Do you want to play with me?" And by "play" I mean, "Do you want to get in the sandbox and create?" A lot of these jazz players and theater people say, "Yeah, let's try that." And they too get better and better at starting from the lyric and telling a story along with you. I try to help people help themselves so that they don't have to go to the expense of flying in the "top guns" from New York. Alternatively, they can fly up to New York to work with me and an arranger for a solid weekend, lay down a bunch of arrangements, and then take them back and teach them to the pianist.

That happens even in vocal coaching. People come to New York because they feel they can't get the education they are looking for where they live.

And you must equip them in a way that you don't have to equip someone else who lives here. They have fewer resources, so you must give the out-of-towners a completely different tool kit.

So that they can self-maintain.

Yes, and when they can come back in six months to adjust it, you take some of those old tools out and put some new tools in. It's a different process.

Most young performers who have just completed their undergraduate work come to New York to realize their dream of being onstage. They want to be in music theater or even be an opera singer, and once they're here they discover the world of cabaret. And they find that some (if not all) of the training they have had really has to be (as you've said) deconstructed. What they have learned is not completely applicable in cabaret. In fact, it's a totally different thing. These young singers then spend another year or two, at considerable expense, learning what's expected of them in this genre. How can we circumvent that? What is it they need to know before they come to New York?

As we have discussed, number one is *the lyric*. We keep coming back to it, but cabaret is really about storytelling. The melody and the harmony and the vocal sound are *part* of telling that story, but if you don't know what personal story you're telling—your story, not the story of the song in the show—then it's a no-go. All the other musical information will color the story, but the lyric has to come first, and I don't see how that advice can't be anything but beneficial for *anybody* who sings *anything*. That, I cannot stress enough. I am so disappointed that I was never taught a cabaret performance technique in my schooling. I knew about it instinctively because of the people I admired as a child, but I never (ever) was taught this, and it was never even brought up. Had I been, wow, my world would have been different! I work with people in their thirties or forties who are working onstage for a living, and suddenly, they have tears streaming down their face because they've gotten in touch with their authentic selves for the first time. They are telling their own story through the lyric, and when that happens the sound of that beautiful voice touches us in a completely different way. My God, it changes the molecules in the room! I think that I continue teaching so that I can keep watching that happen.

* * *

CORINNA SOWERS-ADLER

Corinna Sowers-Adler is artistic director at NiCori Studios and Productions in Bloomfield, New Jersey. She made her solo New York cabaret debut in 2010 at the Laurie Beechman Theatre with *Stories: A Cabaret*. Since then, Sowers-Adler has produced and performed her own cabaret shows in New York City at venues such as the Triad Theatre, the Duplex, Feinstein's at Loews Regency, the Metropolitan Room, Feinstein's/54 Below, the Green Room 42, and the Appel Room/Jazz at Lincoln Center, where she debuted the concert series *Music over Manhattan: Something Beautiful*. She made her Lincoln Center debut as a featured singer in the Mabel Mercer Foundation's 24th Annual Cabaret Convention and has appeared several times at the convention

Figure 24.2. Corinna Sowers-Adler. *Photo by Matthew Wolf.*

since then. In 2011, Sowers-Adler began the monthly series *Music at the Mansion*, which was nominated for a 2012 MAC award. With her husband, Nicholas Adler, she created and produced the series *Cabaret on the Hudson* at the Irvington Town Hall Theater in Irvington, New York. NiCori Studios and Productions is dedicated to bringing vocal arts education—including the Great American Songbook and its performance opportunities—to future generations of young singers. Through this organization, the "NiCori Presents" initiative produces cabaret shows with its arts partners across the United States. We reached out to Sowers-Adler for her perspective on singing and teaching young people. ♪

Corinna, thank you for sharing your expertise with us. When/how did you first decide to become a cabaret singer?

I have always loved performing in intimate venues and singing directly to the audience, but I didn't know at first that cabaret was the name of my preferred way of performing. I had my first "aha" moment about twelve years ago when I attended the opening night of the Mabel Mercer Foundation's Annual Cabaret Convention. I came away from that night realizing, *Oh, that's me! That's what I do.*

Was cabaret singing always your main career path?

I come from a music theater background, but I fell in love with the art of cabaret early on. In retrospect, when I was cast in musicals, I often had roles that broke the fourth wall and had a more direct connection to the audience than traditional music theater roles. I loved singing and talking directly to the audience.

You are known for being able to sing in many different styles, including the Great American Songbook, contemporary music theater, and even opera and art song. Was this something you could always do?

The technique I studied and teach allows a singer to sing many styles of music while maintaining a healthy vocal instrument. Being a singer is like being an athlete. You need to have a practice regimen that strengthens your muscles and stamina so that you can achieve peak performance. I find it fascinating to manipulate vowels and change resonance strategies to create the style I need for each piece I take on. And as a teacher, I love to help others discover how to do that as well.

You mention that you "manipulate vowels and change resonance strategies to create the style." Can you tell us more about the technique you use and teach.

I combine the techniques that E. Herbert-Caesari speaks of in his book *The Voice of the Mind* with my acting work to continue the idea that singing is an extension of natural speech. In other words, the voice responds to the emotion and emphasis behind a phrase. Diction is different depending on the point of view and subtext of the character's objective and the archetypes of the character you are singing. For example, the tone is brighter if I approach the text from the archetype of a child versus a mature woman. In terms of changing musical style, the vowel choices and diction vary in different styles of song. For example, if I want the song to have a more "legitimate" or "classical" sound, then I will use the purest form of the vowel sounds—such as those used in Italian singing—even if I am singing in English. However, if I want the sound to be brassier and belty, which is often necessary in a Broadway song, I will sing a variation of the vowel that positions the resonance in a more forward position. A classical /a/ becomes more of an /æ/.

How would you define cabaret?

For me, cabaret is a musical conversation between the singer and the audience. It is taking a song that has a personal connection to the singer and discovering what aspects of it resonate with the human condition and emotions we all feel. The song is connected to the singer, but the singer must find a way to translate their personal experience to everyone else and make it universal. The audience may not have the same experience or connection to the story in the song as the singer, but—if done well—the audience will connect the performer's delivery of the lyric to their own story.

As both a voice teacher and singer, how important is vocal technique to the cabaret artist? And are there vocal techniques and/or other skills that are essential to the cabaret singer that may not be part of the traditional "classical" vocal performance curriculum?

I think the marriage of proper vocal technique and good storytelling is what we should all strive for. However, vocal abilities vary. It is each singer's responsibility to work on their instrument and hone it to the best of their ability. That being said, telling the story is the most important element of cabaret. Storytelling can, unfortunately, be overlooked in classical singing as most of the emphasis is placed on the technical aspects of playing the vocal instrument. Part of the reason I didn't choose to be in the classical world is because I so desired to be able to tell stories in an authentic way that people could relate to regardless of their musical tastes. On the flip side of that, I often feel that cabaret singers would do well to work on their vocal instruments and focus more on refining technique. In the end, it is all about balance and working on all aspects of your singing, both technical and emotional.

What other training did you need (or have you gotten) since your formal education in order to have an artistically successful career in cabaret?

I continued my vocal studies and have taken acting classes. Truthfully, seeing as many cabaret shows as possible—some very well crafted and others not as much—has been the best education. Also, working with music directors like Alex Rybeck has pushed me in new directions as a performer. Our rehearsal process was very much like a class for me. It was truly a growing experience, and one for which I will be forever grateful.

As a voice teacher and performance coach in cabaret, you work specifically with teenagers and young performers.

Yes, my husband Nick and I run NiCori Studios and Productions, which is dedicated to educating both young amateurs and professional performing artists alike.

In today's pop/rock world, how have you managed to engage young students with songs from the Great American Songbook?

I think the key to engaging my students with the Great American Songbook is to simply introduce them to it! Many young people today have never been exposed to these wonderful songs. So, that's the first step. I will often ask a student what they want to put into the world . . . what do they want to say about where they are, what the state of the world is, and what they are feeling or thinking about during this time of their lives. I then match a song to that feeling from their experience or perspective. They typically have a connection to what the lyric is saying first, and then they connect to the music of the piece through the lyric. I am also a great believer in mixing new with old. Parallel themes can be found in some of today's music if you look hard enough. Then it becomes about finding the connection and the sentiment of the song from today and linking it to a song from the past. This allows us to see how far we've come or how we all seem to struggle with—and find joy in—many of the same themes across time, genres, and cultures.

Do you think cabaret is restricted to the Great American Songbook, or are there new songs being written that would work well in a cabaret performance?

I really believe that any song, if it is well sung and executed—and directly connected to the singer's story or theme—is appropriate for cabaret performance. There are some shows, of course, that celebrate more traditional music from the American Songbook, and there is a place for that as well. I love crossing lines of genre and style in the same show. If the song fits your voice and serves the theme of your show, then in my opinion it's fair game. I think the Great American Songbook is ever evolving and continues to expand.

Where do you see, or hope to see, cabaret singing in twenty years, fifty years?

I hope to see an even greater appreciation for live performance. As the world gets more and more entrenched in technology, I think we are going to need to find ways to truly connect that don't involve social media and screens. I think people will long for that kind of human connection more and more. The art of cabaret could be a source for this. I see this appreciation in my own students who have fallen in love with the storytelling and the magic of live performance. They still love their technology, but they have found ways to connect through their singing and performances that are more rewarding than the amount of "likes" they get on Instagram. I think those of us in the world of cabaret need to find ways to foster this and use technology to our advantage. It is another example of the balance of old and new and how it can be tooled for growth and preservation. This is what keeps art alive.

* * *

LENNIE WATTS

In addition to being an award-winning singer and president of the Manhattan Association of Cabarets (MAC), Lennie Watts is the artistic director of Singnasium in New York City. As part of his interview in chapter 19, we spoke to him about teaching and Singnasium. Those comments have been placed into this chapter for continuity. For Watts's complete biography, please see chapter 19. ♪

Lennie, tell us about Singnasium, how and why you developed the program.

It was fortuitous. I had been teaching privately for over twenty-five years and was thinking about how to expand my program. Two MAC

Figure 24.3. Lennie Watts teaching Richard Becker. *Photo by Rob Sutton.*

board members came to me separately to talk about possibilities for expansion and that they would like to help and get involved. I had ideas about how to expand and who the teachers would be, so we put together a mission statement. We wanted to create a safe place in the industry for people of all levels to learn and explore their passion and a venue for them to create and sing. This is how Singnasium got started, and we are thrilled with how it has succeeded.

Is it a school? What is the time frame of the semester?

Yes, it is a school. Currently we're running several classes a week with an array of teachers, including me. We have two semesters, and each semester is divided into two parts. The fall semester goes from September to the end of the calendar year, and the winter-spring semester goes from mid-January through April, although sometimes we end in early May. This second semester is usually divided into two eight-week sessions with a week off in between. Then, over the summer we run two six-week classes and do a "jazz boot camp" with Gabrielle Stravelli, as well as an "arrangement boot camp" that I teach. We are still looking to add a class on recording and another music theater class or a series of workshops with Broadway professionals. We're also going to start a mentorship program and offer résumé/headshot assistance. There are a lot of new things on the horizon. We're now running year-round!

How many classes are currently offered?

We currently run anywhere from eight to ten classes, including the Arrangement Experience, CabLab, the CabLab Master Series, Swing Time (a jazz class), Rock 'n' Roll, a group voice class, a musicianship class, and a "zen" singing class. We are also adding new courses each semester.

How do you find your participants? And are all classes performance based?

Right now, most of our advertising is by word of mouth, and most of the classes sell out quickly. I have been doing this for many years, and I have a lot of regulars. However, we're also getting a lot of new faces. We do advertise on Facebook and send e-blasts to our big mailing list. We just published a few interviews, which drove a lot of people to the website. And, no, not all the classes are performance based. Some, for example, work on musicianship or song study.

On average, how many participants are in each class?

We keep the classes small. We only take six to eight participants in the performance classes to afford them enough time "onstage." The nonperformance classes like musicianship allow for more participants, but we only take ten people or so.

How important are programs like this?

Very important. I feel very proud of the fact that we're starting to en-hance not only the cabaret industry but also the performance commu-nity at large. The students and participants in class are all supportive and have become each other's cohorts. We're getting ready to organize the "Singnasium Outreach" program through which the students will utilize what they have learned in class to entertain people at senior centers and hospices. I am also looking to do outreach at different schools. All of these endeavors are very important. I wish something like this had existed when I was starting out.

Do you have any plans for Singnasium to travel?

Yes, we are starting a "Singnasium on the Road" program. There are people in different cities where I have done workshops who are helping to secure funding so that we can come to their cities to offer classes.

Are you available to be a guest teacher should someone want you to come to their school?

Absolutely! We're already looking into this. I am most willing to go into schools of any level to offer cabaret instruction and workshops.

* * *

JOHN MCDANIEL

The Eugene O'Neill Theater Center Cabaret and Performance Confer-ence is the grandfather of all cabaret training programs. Affectionately referred to as "Camp Cabaret," the Cabaret Symposium (as it was originally called) was conceived by Ellie Ellsworth and Betsy White, with Margaret Whiting serving as artistic director. Held in Waterford, Connecticut, at the Eugene O'Neill Theater Center, the Cabaret and Performance Conference was among the first programs to require a rig-orous and formal audition process. Being chosen to participate is itself

Figure 24.4. John McDaniel.
Photo by Steve Ullathorne.

an honor. The original program ran from 1989 to 2001 and was reinstated as an annual summer program beginning in 2006. The conference seeks to "push the envelope" of cabaret performance by reexamining, redefining, and revitalizing the cabaret art form for the twenty-first century by broadly defining cabaret as *"any* kind of live performance in an intimate space that often breaks the fourth wall." The conference also brings in some of the biggest names in cabaret who perform and provide valuable development and performance training for up-and-coming cabaret performers. Recent conference artists include Judy Kuhn, Tonya Pinkins, Norm Lewis, Molly Pope, Melissa Manchester, Karen Mason, Christina Bianco, Joyce Breach, Brad Simmons, Matt Baker, Eric Yves Garcia, Mark Hartman, Brian Nash, Natalie Douglas, the Skivvies, Nick Adams, Shirley Jones, Jim Caruso, Billy Stritch, Mimi Hines, Susie Mosher, Betty Buckley, and Tommy Tune. We contacted John McDaniel, the current artistic director of the program, to get his perspective on cabaret and learn more about the program, its history, and what it offers aspiring cabaret artists. ♪

John, thank you so much for taking the time to share your knowledge and expertise with us. What do you think makes cabaret performance so different than other vocal performance genres?

Cabaret is a broad and encompassing term, but most of all it tends to boil down to storytelling. How can performers engage an audience in the moment with their stories? How can they strip everything down to just what is needed and not overdecorate each moment? How can they frame the song or story with the right "feel" and with a perfect musical arrangement made especially for this particular moment and specific storytelling on this particular night?

Is there a cabaret performance technique? And if so, can you describe it or its intended result?

I think it has to do with finding the simple heart of the matter without muddying it up with too many false moves or old habits. Connecting honestly with a lyric—and an audience—is not as easy as it sounds.

What is the hallmark of a great cabaret performance?

Thinking back, I can remember nights at different cabaret clubs where I was really stunned and moved by some of the greats who dazzled their audience just by being themselves and revealing unique bits of who they are. Learning to do this takes time, and you learn it through trial and error. We have a motto at the O'Neill that serves us well: risk, fail, and risk again.

Tell us about the history of the O'Neill Cabaret Conference.

The Cabaret Symposium at the Eugene O'Neill Theater Center, as it was originally called, was created in 1989 by Betsy White and Ellie Ellsworth. That version of the conference ran until 2001, at which point it was disbanded. It was resurrected in 2006 under its current name, the Cabaret and Performance Conference. I was brought on as artistic director in 2013, and each year I look forward to these two beautiful weeks in August like a kid looks forward to Christmas.

Who is your faculty?

I bring in several master teachers and top music directors every summer. My core team includes Barb Jungr, Mark Hartman, Tracy Stark, and Lennie Watts, among others. The seaside campus buzzes with daily classes and ten nights of professional performances. Each artist who comes to do one of the nightly shows will work with our students the next morning. Those artists have included Tommy Tune, Melissa Manchester, Betty Buckley, Natalie Douglas—the list goes on and on. The students benefit from these sessions immensely.

Can you describe the curriculum?

We work for ten days with one well-deserved day off. We hit the ground running with daily morning and afternoon classes as well as nightly performances in the pub, which run late into the evening. It is a rigorous course of study, but incredibly immersive and often life changing.

Do you have an audition process, and if so, how do prospective participants apply?

The "cabaret fellows" are chosen each year through an online application process. There is a questionnaire, and applicants must also submit a video audition. Each year we look for a select group of people who will most benefit from our program; we strive for a balance of age and gender. And each year it's amazing to watch six strangers come together and invariably bond like a family.

What is your vision for cabaret at the O'Neill, its future?

I would like to find more ways to become increasingly inclusive. Cabaret is so much more than people think. It is certainly more than a middle-aged woman in a red dress singing in the crook of a piano. I encourage people of all ethnic backgrounds to apply. I want to stretch the medium and continue to include spoken word and other more varied programs. Humans have been storytelling since the dawn of time, and our program seeks to nurture this very specific art form.

What do you feel is the most important thing for a young singer to work on when performing in cabaret?

I don't want to see vocal technique or even think about *how* it's happening when someone steps up to bat. Of course, you must have technique. You must breathe properly and so forth. But I'm not a fan of being able to spot someone working to engage their voice. Know the song and story that you are telling. Know it well and let everything else go. It must appear to honestly come from you, your very soul, as though you are saying it to us for the very first time. Let us see *you*. Just tell the story.

* * *

TIM SCHALL

Tim Schall is the producer of the St. Louis Cabaret Conference. Under Schall's guidance, the St. Louis Cabaret Conference has developed into one of the top cabaret performance training programs in the country with an award-winning guest faculty that attracts more than thirty singers each year from across the nation. Additionally, he has taught numerous advanced performance classes and directed

Figure 24.5. Tim Schall. *Photo by Elizabeth Wiseman.*

more than thirty full-length cabaret shows and showcases for various singers, including Tony nominee Lara Teeter's New York cabaret debut at Feinstein's/54 Below. Schall has served as adjunct faculty at Webster University teaching the cabaret styles performance class in the university's Conservatory of Theatre Arts. Schall is also executive director of the Cabaret Project of St. Louis, a nonprofit organization with a mission to support, develop, and sustain the art of cabaret. He has been called "a consummate cabaret performer" by *Cabaret Scenes* magazine. He has performed his solo shows across the United States in small clubs and large concert halls. We asked Schall a few questions during his appearance at the thirtieth annual New York Cabaret Convention. ♪

Tim, thank you so much for the work you do at the St. Louis Cabaret Conference. Tell us about your faculty.

We have six to eight full-time faculty each year and three to four guest faculty. Teachers have included Christine Ebersole, Faith Prince, Jason Robert Brown, the legendary Marilyn Maye, singer/songwriter Ann Hampton Callaway, eminent New York cabaret performer Jeff Harnar, and Peisha McPhee, one of the top vocal coaches in Los Angeles. The faculty also includes some of the finest music directors/pianists in the field such as Billy Stritch, Tedd Firth, Alex Rybeck, Christopher Denny, and Michael Orland. Teachers come from a variety of backgrounds—Broadway, nightclubs, jazz, and so forth—but what they have in common is an understanding of how to perform in a way that connects singer to audience.

Can you describe the program and its curriculum?

The program attracts students from all over the country and even internationally. It is produced by the Cabaret Project of St. Louis. The conference spans nine days and offers three distinct learning tracks: a five-day introductory track, a seven-day "next step" track, and a nine-day professional track. We are proud to offer one of the strongest faculties in the nation, and each faculty member is committed to a student's personal growth. Students receive personalized mentoring and individual attention. We have an industry panel of professionals as well as breakout sessions on social media marketing. One evening there is a performance of St. Louis Cabaret Conference faculty. At the end of the program there is a performance showcase for the students.

Can you describe the different program tracks for us?

The five-day introductory track includes: in-depth song coaching in a master class setting; text analysis and lyric exploration; sessions on collaboration with music directors; coaching on microphone technique, vocal technique, and musicianship; and developing a personal relationship with your material and the audience. The seven-day "next step" track includes all those courses plus sessions on putting together a show and working with a director, marketing your show, creating arrangements, performing in clubs, and self-producing. The nine-day professional track includes mentoring from the entire conference faculty through daily master classes; an evening showcase in which each singer performs a fully directed and arranged four-song set; individualized feedback on your performance; sessions on developing the right marketing materials, including maintaining a website and social media presence; and a conference-wise industry panel forum. Students in the professional track also receive demo reel footage of their showcase for private use. For all participants we offer breakout sessions on the business of cabaret, self-promotion, and marketing, and sessions on creating patter and directing.

Do you have an audition process, and if so, how do prospective participants apply?

All interested singers must submit one or two videos of themselves singing, plus a résumé and references. Requirements vary per track of study.

What is your vision for the St. Louis Conference, its future?

It is my goal for the St. Louis Cabaret Conference to continue to be a proud leader in song performance training in the United States. Our conference mentors the next generation of professionals and creates a place for industry ideas and networking.

What is the most important thing for a young singer to work on when starting out in cabaret?

There are many important things that a singer new to this needs to work on. But since you asked for just one, I have to say the following: dig deep into the lyric of the song and the emotion of the song and the intention of the song, but don't do it for you—*do it for the audience*. Be drawn to the training that encourages and values you. Be open to critical feedback and learn from those you trust. But also give yourself room to make mistakes. Most important, keep doing it. You'll get better and better!

* * *

WENDY LANE BAILEY

Figure 24.6.   Wendy Lane Bailey.
Photo by Bill Westmoreland.

Although no longer in existence, we felt it necessary to place in the historical record the International Cabaret Conference at Yale University (2003–2013), which was conceived by its artistic director, the late Erv Raible, with Wendy Lane Bailey serving as associate director. As a performer, Bailey has earned critical praise for her versatility and sophistication. She has appeared as a guest artist on multiple recordings, including those of pop legend Lesley Gore and Broadway's Susan Egan. She received her training at the American Academy of Dramatic Arts, HB Studio, and the Eugene O'Neill Theater Center. Offstage, Bailey is a creative advocate for artists. While living in Washington, D.C., she founded a regional networking organization for musicians, and for five years she was the associate director of the Cabaret Conference at Yale University. She is the recipient of a 2007 Bistro Award for outstanding achievement and was nominated for a Washington Area Music Association Award (WAMMY). She served on the board of Pioneer Productions and through that company produced, directed, and appeared in several theater pieces. She is currently developing a solo theater piece with music titled *Hot Coffee, Mississippi* in collaboration with Michele Brourman and Gretchen Cryer. In addition to her work as a performer, she teaches and consults privately for singers of all genres. We were grateful for the opportunity to speak with Bailey about the history and mission of the International Cabaret Conference at Yale University, as well as its possible reemergence. ♪

Wendy, thanks so much for your insights on this historically important training opportunity. Can you please describe the Yale program? How long did it run, and when did it end?

The International Cabaret Conference at Yale was created for up-and-coming cabaret artists of all types, ages, and backgrounds. We brought together a renowned faculty of singers, actors, composers, musicians, directors, and designers each summer for ten days, and these individuals taught intensive master classes in all aspects of cabaret performance. During that time, students and teachers lived, ate, and performed on Yale's historic campus. In addition to daily classes, the faculty offered concerts so that the students could see them in action. The public was also invited to these events. The finale of the conference was always a performance by the students. The conference ran from 2003 until 2013, the year when founder Erv Raible passed away.

Are you planning to bring it back?

There has been much interest in reviving the program during the intervening years, and we are hoping to bring it back in a revised form soon.

How did the Yale conference come about?

When the symposium at the Eugene O'Neill Theater Center folded in 2001, there was a great deal of interest on the part of the faculty and staff in having a program that focused solely on the art of cabaret. Erv had a personal contact at Yale and thought that it would be an excellent location for such an event. Erv, Sally Mayes, and I put together some thoughts on what we thought such a program should look like. Erv took that vision to his contact at the university along with Carol Hall, who was also instrumental in getting the conference off the ground.

How did you find participants? What was the criteria for selection?

Participation was by audition only. We started by going to cities with solid cabaret communities and organizations that supported those communities. Our first year that list included New York, Boston, Washington, D.C., Los Angeles, Chicago, and Minneapolis. The cabaret performers and organizations in those cities helped us by spreading the word about the auditions. In many cases they went directly to performers they felt would be a good fit for us. We also accepted video auditions for anyone who was unable to attend in person. As time went on, some of our students went back and started their own organizations, gathering groups of like-minded performers. Many of those artists wanted to take part in the program, and we were able to add those places to our audition tour. We asked them to prepare two songs with a little patter in between so that we could get a sense of who they were as solo performers. We evaluated them on their performance ability, their résumés, and their stated goals. We wanted people who were serious about the art form and committed to honing their skills.

What did you teach?

When I began working with Erv, my job was to handle all the administrative duties. I handled the day-to-day operations, set up and ran auditions, worked with our faculty and the Yale staff, and dealt with any issues that occurred. However, as time went on I began to team teach the image consulting class with Broadway costume designer Fred Voelpel. We covered all of the visual elements of a performance and also talked about marketing materials and how to create a consistent image for marketing purposes. We wanted our students to feel confident stepping onto the stage, and part of that was helping them find ways to express themselves through their choice of performance wardrobe.

Who else was on faculty?

We had many wonderful faculty members over the years including Sally Mayes, Faith Prince, Lina Koutrakos, Heather MacRae, Jason Graae, Amanda McBroom, Pamela Myers, Steve Hayes, Carol Hall, Julie Wilson, Rita Gardner, Pam Tate, Laurel Masse, Fred Voelpel, Sharon McNight, Marilyn Lovell Matz, and George Hall. Our music directors included Tex Arnold, Rick Jensen, Michele Brourman, Michael Orland, Mark Cherry, Paul Trueblood, Alex Rybeck, Shelly Markham, Mark Burnell, Ron Abel, Patrick Brady, and Jeff Klitz. We also had guest lecturers like ASCAP's Michael Kerker, critics John Hoglund and David Finkle, and technical director Matt Berman.

Describe the curriculum and a typical day for a participant in your program.

The curriculum was extensive, covering performance technique; working with musicians, directors, and technical directors; visual image and arrangements; publicity and promotion; writing patter; and putting together a show. Students were divided into small groups that circulated among three-person teaching teams. This gave them several opportunities a day to perform and work with our instructors. A typical day would start with the students going to class with their small group. Then there would be lunch, a consultant talk, and another round of small group classes followed by dinner. What happened after dinner would depend on the day. Some evenings there were more small group sessions. On others there would be a consultant talk, a special class, or rehearsals for their finale performance. On the weekends there would be concerts. During the final days of the conference, students had the opportunity to book individual sessions with faculty members.

What is your biggest takeaway from working with the students at the International Cabaret Conference at Yale University?

I think the most exciting thing about the program was watching artists from so many different backgrounds and genres come together and form connections. Our faculty was excellent, and undoubtedly our students learned a lot from them, but they learned just as much from watching and being with each other. Witnessing them form connections and community because of their mutual love of a shared art form was a wonderful thing. We never had a group that wasn't unfailingly supportive of one another. They became their classmates' biggest fans.

How important are programs like this for up-and-coming cabaret singers?

I think they are enormously important. Aspiring cabaret singers need safe places where they can take risks. That's how they discover who they are. They need to know that they aren't alone and that they are part of an industry. They also need to be exposed to as diverse a community of performers as possible to continue growing. The opportunity to learn from accomplished artists is invaluable. The Yale program provided all of that and more. I am enormously proud to have been a part of it.

* * *

FINAL THOUGHTS

The teachers and programs included here are among the best in the industry. However, they are by no means the only programs or teachers working with students to develop a greater awareness and understanding of a true cabaret performance technique. The work is daunting. The repertoire includes songs from *every* genre of music, which must be reexamined through the artistic prism of cabaret, with a personal connection to text, devoid of character or show conceits, and with universal appeal for a wide audience.

The idea of reinterpreting a song, of *creating* an arrangement that is unique to each performer and provides a new relationship for the song to its audience, is an idea unique to cabaret. Except for jazz, there is no other manner of vocal performance that *requires* the singer to reimagine the song so specifically. This, however, has always been a hallmark of great artistic performance within the genre. Arrangements made specifically for Frank Sinatra, Judy Garland, Tony Bennett, and a host of other great performers during cabaret's "golden age" still rank among the best ever heard or performed. The idea that those arrangements *belong* to those performers and that *new* arrangements are not only possible but also *required* in order to continue the authentic performance of this music is, for many, a new and even controversial idea. Without this idea, however, without this commitment to intimately performing and reimagining the popular American song repertoire, cabaret can quickly descend into an imitation of itself.

It has been said many times within these pages that cabaret is a lyric-driven art form. Additionally, it must be noted that cabaret is a musically creative art, not a *re-creative* art. Just as much attention is paid to the musical arrangement and the singer's personal connection to it as is the specificity of the singer's lyric connection. Only through the diligent efforts of cabaret performance teachers and programs like these will this creative art form, which strives to breathe new life into a familiar song repertoire, survive for future generations.

25

SPANNING THE GENERATIONS

Interviews with Joie Bianco, Mark William,
Josephine Sanges, and Sally Darling

Cabaret has multigenerational appeal. The intimate connection of lyric, emotion, and music transcends age and musical tastes. Passing down the musical legacy, traditions, and common performance practice of cabaret and the Great American Songbook to Generations Y and Z is certainly one way to secure the future of this art form. However, one cannot discount the increasing number of Generation Xers, baby boomers, and even older members of the Silent Generation currently entering the study and performance of cabaret.[1] As established in previous chapters, both cabaret and the Great American Songbook have no age limit and no physical type, which is precisely what makes them perfect for vocal study at any age.

Voice studios are rarely comprised solely of singers from Generations Y and Z. Most studios, especially independent studios, have a generous helping of Generation Xers and baby boomers; some may even have a few singers from the Silent Generation. Where and what should these students sing? Unless they are auditioning on an elite level, they may be looking for a vocal/artistic outlet with a long-term goal. Crafting a cabaret show could be just the right project for both their vocal and their artistic needs.

The following interviews are with representatives from each of the four cohorts listed in the first paragraph of this chapter. All began to work in cabaret only within the past two to five years or have received major recognition within this brief period. They include a young woman who debuted at age fifteen, a young man in his twenties, a liturgical choir singer and director who is a baby boomer, and an octogenarian woman who won the Bistro Award in 2017. These singers represent the demographic of students who are also studying in voice studios across the country and who will—each in their own way and with the right mentoring and guidance—secure the future of cabaret. As teachers our task is to simply expose these singers to this vast and engaging repertoire and support their desire to sing and perform cabaret.[2]

GENERATION Z: JOSEPHINE (JOIE) BIANCO

Figure 25.1. Joie Bianco. Photo by Alina Reznik.

In her first-ever competition at the 2015 MetroStar Talent Challenge, Joie Bianco was an audience favorite and wowed the judges, finishing seventh out of sixty contestants. She was also a finalist in the Michael Feinstein Songbook Academy competition (see chapter 6). Bianco made her Mabel Mercer Foundation Cabaret Convention debut (see chapter 19) at the age of fifteen, only five years after she started singing. In 2017, she returned to the Metropolitan Room to celebrate her seventeenth birthday in her first solo show. She is also the protégé of the legendary cabaret and nightclub singer Marilyn Maye. At her debut Cabaret Convention appearance in 2015, Stephen Holden of the *New York Times* called Bianco "the most impressive among newcomers." When singing the song "People" from *Funny Girl*, the very young Bianco "reached deeply into the feelings within the lyric and music and the result was intense sensitivity. Her talent was especially impressive—a highlight of the night." ♪

Joie, thanks so much for sharing your experiences with us. And what wonderful experiences you've had, with a quote from the New York Times *at age fifteen! Tell us your story. As a teenager, what first attracted you the Great American Songbook and jazz standards?*

I was introduced to the Great American Songbook by my parents. As I got older, I preferred listening and singing that style of music. I listened to the songbook, show tunes, and rhythm and blues. One artist I loved to listen to was Liza Minnelli.

*Did you think "cabaret" was the movie (*Cabaret*) with Liza Minnelli?*

At first, to be very honest, I had no clue what I was getting myself into. My mom signed me up for the MetroStar Talent Challenge in 2015 with me having no clue as to what to expect. I did the competition for exposure and to get performing time under my belt. I didn't expect it to turn into my main creative outlet and possibly my career.

What do you feel makes cabaret singing different than other styles of vocal performance?

I learned that cabaret's most important aspect is storytelling. I am still learning how to incorporate stylistic choices while still being an authentic performer. What I have observed through watching cabaret shows is that most of the time artists in cabaret will sacrifice the opportunity to show off their voice and range for the sake of truthful storytelling. Another difference is that cabaret allows other genres of music to be showcased. It's not uncommon to go to a cabaret show and hear a big, belty music theater song immediately followed by a folk ballad. This is what surprised me the most about cabaret.

How do you see your future in cabaret?

Ideally, I'd like to be a full-time performer and songwriter.

Are you planning on recording an album?

I do plan on recording in the future. But for now, I have some performances on YouTube under "Joie Bianco Sings" and I have demo recordings from 2018 on Soundcloud. ♪

As one of Marilyn Maye's protégés, what have you learned from working with one of cabaret's most esteemed performers? How has she inspired you?

Marilyn taught me about the importance of phrasing and lyric interpretation. This has inspired me to continue working toward being an authentic performer. I also learned that the real "star" of the show isn't the performer but rather the audience itself.

When you are not singing American Songbook standards in cabaret, what kind of music are you singing?

Jazz, R&B, blues, classical, and some pop.

Do you want a career in this kind of singing, or do you have other goals, on- or offstage?

Right now, I am going to college. My major is jazz vocal performance and I am thinking about pursuing a graduate degree in it as well. I would like to pick up a double major in speech-language pathology and/or possibly nutrition.

Best of luck in school. I am sure that whatever you decide to do, you will be a great success!

* * *

GENERATION Y: MARK WILLIAM

Both critics and audiences alike are over the moon for Mark William. Theater Pizzazz said, "Mark William is the epitome of panache, adding his own brand of pizzazz. Whatever that 'it' is, he's got IT!" *Times Square Chronicles* called him "the newest star rising in the heavens of cabaret and musical theatre." Tony Award–winning lyricist Lynn Ahrens calls

Figure 25.2. Mark William. *Photo by Jeremy Daniel.*

him "Baby Sinatra," and John Lloyd Young, the original Tony Award–winning Frankie Valli in *Jersey Boys*, says he is "Golden Age Hollywood Reborn." William was named one of the top ten cabaret acts of 2018 by both Theater Pizzazz and *Times Square Chronicles* and rang in 2019 headlining the New Year's Eve show at the famed McKittrick Hotel. He has appeared around the world in such shows as *My Fair Lady*, *Mary Poppins*, *Mame* with Leslie Uggams, and *Jerry's Girls* with Susan Anton.

Mark, thank you for representing Generation Y. What age did you first start performing?

My first solo was singing "Jesus Loves Me" in church when I was five, but I was performing even before that. My mom is a pianist, so music and performance were a part of everyday life.

As a millennial, what first attracted you to singing cabaret and this kind of music?

I first fell in love with Broadway and show tunes, which in the golden age crossed over to become the popular music we now call the Great

American Songbook. In high school and college, I began to realize that I had an affinity for performing this type of song, so I embraced it. I think cabaret is truly a universal genre because, no matter your age, these songs can reach you emotionally . . . if you let them.

What did you think "cabaret" was prior to entering this field?

Before diving into it myself I thought of cabaret in terms that I was familiar with and made sense to me. Basically, I thought of a show as a professional recital.

Really? So how did you learn about what it is truly?

I am a big believer in learning by observing and by experience. Since moving to New York, I have tried to see as many cabaret shows and performances as possible, and I have done my best to take in and utilize the skills and ideas that I experience firsthand. After that, I just try things out on my own. Although I didn't make my New York cabaret debut until November of 2018, I had been preparing for that night for a long time.

In your opinion, how does cabaret differ from other musical styles?

I think cabaret gives you a freedom that no other genre allows. You can sing in any style you choose and even mix up styles within a single show. That freedom is very cool to play with. Beyond the vocal style, what makes cabaret unique is what takes place between the songs, and what takes place between the performer and audience. Figuring out how each song relates to one another, how the songs relate to you, and how you can share that with an audience is a daunting but rewarding task. Communication with the audience is key. In cabaret you are literally only a few feet away from your audience, so it's a very personal art form. The audience is an essential aspect of each individual performance. That kind of intimacy doesn't really exist anywhere else.

What surprised you most about this genre?

The biggest surprise for me has been how much my audiences have embraced me as a performer. From the average attendee to cabaret mainstays like Sidney Myer all the way to Broadway stars like Chita Rivera and John Lloyd Young, everyone has been incredibly supportive and complimentary. To have that kind of love behind me really gives me the courage to be myself and take risks.

Where did you first hear the music you are currently singing?

Some was through my parents and grandparents. Other songs I discovered as I became more and more of a Broadway nerd. The Peter Allen repertoire came to me via my management team, and I immediately felt an attraction to his songs. I also was a big fan of *Smash*. So, I really learned a wide range of sources over the course of many years.

Who are some of your favorite singers?

Well, the guy who really taught me the style first and foremost is the one and only Frank Sinatra. Without him I probably wouldn't be doing this. Since falling in love with cabaret, I've become a big fan of Steve Lawrence, Peter Allen, Nat King Cole, and Shirley Bassey. I enjoy contemporary music as well, but when I think of great singers, I'm always drawn back in time.

Where would you like your singing career to be in five or ten years?

I think cabaret will be a staple of my career that I will always come back to. I love performing in many genres, so I hope to have a varied career that involves film, television, and theater, but cabaret will always be part of what I do. As I said earlier, that intimate dialogue with an audience is just something you can't get anywhere else.

Knowing what you know now, how can we introduce more people in your generation to this style of singing?

I think the firsthand experience of seeing a live performance is essential. If younger people haven't experienced the thrill of an intimate cabaret show, then they have no idea what they're missing. Recordings are great, but there's no real substitute for actually seeing a live performance.

* * *

GENERATION X/BABY BOOMER: JOSEPHINE SANGES

Figure 25.3. Josephine Sanges.
Photo by Bill Westmoreland.

Josephine Sanges spent the first part of her musical career as the director of her church choir, where she served as a "leader of song." In 2014, her musical life changed overnight when she entered the world of cabaret. Like Joie Bianco, she also entered the MetroStar Talent Challenge competition, where she was the first runner-up. Sanges was quickly met with success and recognition as her star steadily ascended. She received the 2017 ASA Margaret Whiting Award, the 2018 MAC La-Mott Friedman Award, and the 2019 MAC Award for Female Vocalist. She has appeared at many of the major clubs and cabarets in New York, most notably Carnegie Hall, Rose Hall at Lincoln Center, and Town Hall. ♪

Josephine, thank you for sharing your experiences with us. What first attracted you to singing cabaret?

I grew up listening to the standards: my mother's record collection of Judy Garland, Johnny Mathis, Perry Como, and her one Broadway show recording, *Oklahoma!*

What did you think cabaret was back then?

I had no idea cabaret existed! I only knew it to be the title of a Broadway show and a movie that Liza Minnelli starred in.

How would you describe cabaret now? How it is different than other styles of vocal performance?

Live performance in a small room is the most difficult kind of performing there is. When I started out in cabaret, I remember being grateful
that the bright lights prevented me from seeing the faces of the people
in the audience. But as time went on, I've learned that when I am really
enveloped in the lyrics, when I'm putting myself and my own life experience into the song, then there is less room for the voice of insecurity
to take over.

What surprised you the most about singing cabaret?

I'm still amazed at the generous sense of camaraderie that exists here in
the cabaret industry and community. I am so moved by how supportive
people are toward one another in a field that you might otherwise expect
to be competitive. I have found that I have an extended family in cabaret. People that understand the drive to artistically create and perform
in a way that family and friends can sometimes fail to grasp. We are a
quite an extraordinary breed!

*You came to cabaret rather late in life, previously working as a church
choral singer and choir director. How did you discover cabaret?*

My friend and music director, John M. Cook, introduced me to cabaret.
John and I met through a mutual friend and church musician. I needed
an organist to play our Sunday evening mass. John lived close to the
parish and ended up doing that for about a year or so. As we got to
know each other better, I told him that I had always wanted to record
an album of religious music so that "my grandkids would someday know
that I could sing." He agreed to help me with the project and suggested
material that, while still faith inspired, was much more interesting than
the standard church hymns I had on my list. He arranged a jazz/gospel-
influenced "Amazing Grace" for me that was, let's just say, anything but
standard. We enjoyed our collaboration so much that we decided to
work on—and later record—songs from the American Songbook.
     John has a natural flair for writing jazz-inflected arrangements, and
he challenged me to try scatting for the first time. We called that album *Color Me Blue*. After recording that album, John asked if I'd ever
thought of doing my own show, and he told me about the Duplex, Don't

Tell Mama, and the Metropolitan Room. John had played some of those rooms years earlier. I was totally astonished that you could book your own show in the city! I always thought you had to be asked, but—much to my surprise—it was as easy as that!

How has your formal vocal training helped you to transition into this genre? How did you come to your new jazzy-standard style of singing? Did you study jazz?

I never studied jazz. I don't have formal music training other than taking private voice lessons early on. The best vocal training I got was from listening to "the greats" and from being in choirs. The fact that I work as a church musician means that I sing regularly—almost daily. So, I don't really have time to get "rusty." However, singing in a choir trains you to "stick to the music" because in choral music it's so important that voices blend and combine to sing as one. For example, holding a note out for exactly four beats, sounding the final consonant on the first beat of the next measure . . . all that formality is almost counterintuitive to solo singing. In choral singing individual voices should *never* stand out. In church singing you act as a leader of song, never as a performer or soloist. And as a director, I've always been sensitive to the choir, allowing them to have their shining moments rather than taking an opportunity to sing a solo myself. This thinking most definitely had to be undone if I was to be a successful cabaret singer, and I still struggle with this.

You came onto the scene and in quick fashion received major reviews, won several awards, and are now playing high-profile gigs. To what do you attribute this? And what do you feel you still need to work on to achieve an even higher level of success in this genre?

I have been very fortunate to work with John. His experience, intuitiveness, and extraordinary musical abilities have inspired me to continue growing as an artist. His contribution to any success I have had is immeasurable. Since making my debut almost five years ago, I've watched and studied other performers and have come to realize the importance of digging into the lyrics in ways I hadn't thought of before. In a sense, I've used this time as my "college education" in cabaret performance, learning not only about performing but also about publicity, networking, and using social media. I would like to become more comfortable speaking to an audience. "Setting up" the song in a way that is personal can sometimes be a challenge for me. I am still learning to trust and be at peace with my own instincts. Trusting the process . . . that's a big one.

What would you like to do, or continue to do, in this field?

I'd love to be able to perform in larger venues, expand my audience, and not struggle so much to fill a room. I hope to find representation, if that still exists. I love recording albums, and I'd like to find ways to do that without breaking the bank. Really, I just want to be able to do more of what I've already been doing.

You have three solo albums . . . where can our readers hear your beautiful work?

Yes, they are *In Endless Song*, *Color Me Blue*, and our MAC award-winning album *Finding Beauty: Celebrating the Music of Ann Hampton Callaway*. They are available on Apple Music, CD Baby, and Spotify. ♪

* * *

THE SILENT GENERATION: SALLY DARLING

Sally Darling, our octogenarian representative, is anything but "silent." On stage she has run the gamut, with everything from comedy to drama to farce. Darling has narrated more than 250 books, most famously Harper Lee's *To Kill a Mockingbird*. She has also directed theatrical productions from Shakespeare to Tennessee Williams, has staged operas, has dubbed films, and is currently directing cabaret shows . . . all while still performing. The many shows she has acted in and directed include Molière's *Actor from Vienna*, *The Drunkard* (musically directed by Barry Manilow), *The Tronzini Ristorante Murders*, Gilbert and Sullivan productions with LOOM (Light Opera of Manhattan), and lots of children's theater. Darling made her professional acting debut as

Figure 25.4. Sally Darling. Photo by Bill Westmoreland.

Anna in *The King and I* in Garrison, New York, and joined the Actors' Equity Association as the leading lady in *The Three Cuckolds*, a commedia dell'arte show. Her cabaret career acknowledgments include the 2016 MAC Hanson Award and the 2017 Bistro Award for the Best Tribute Show. She was also a MAC Award nominee for Best Female Singer in 2017, 2018, and 2019. ♪

Sally, thank you so much for sharing your wisdom with us. First off, how long have you been performing?

My first performance was in grade school. Either fifth or sixth grade I believe.

What kind of music were you first attracted to?

Songs from what is now referred to as the Great American Songbook are actually the songs I grew up with! I was a child during that era.

What did you think cabaret was back then, and what was your biggest surprise so far about this genre?

Cabaret? I had no idea what it was! What has surprised me is how comfortable cabaret has made me onstage.

Has your previous performance style changed with this new genre?

My background was theater and music theater. I loved the protection of the fourth wall and the distance it gave between the audience and me, and I have had to work hard to dismiss it. What sets cabaret apart is the intimacy. The audience is so much closer than in theater; you connect with the audience in a much more personal way.

How did you learn to dismiss the fourth wall and acquire the intimacy that cabaret requires? Did you take classes or just go to shows and study the genre?

I had to drop the training I had and make my performance style more personal. The fourth wall is something I learned to drop on my own after several people told me I was holding back and seemed distant.

How did you come to learn that cabaret even existed?

I was singing with Paul Trueblood, who is now my music director, just for the joy of it after a twenty-two-year period of not singing. One day he said that I had enough songs for a program and encouraged me to do a show. I was stunned. That possibility had never entered my mind.

Your Noël Coward show Totally Noël *was such a piece of history that it should be in the library! How did this award-winning show come about? Did you feel a pull toward Coward's body of work?*

When I began working with Paul Trueblood, it was natural to sing songs from the revues I had created and directed. The first three were comprised of Noël Coward and Cole Porter songs. I think I was the first to combine these two particular songwriters. I love their wit, their intelligence, and their ability to write simple, direct ballads.

What's next for the amazing Sally Darling?

A new show: *And Kurt Weill Begat Kander and Ebb!*

Do you have any advice for other singers of your generation who may want to try cabaret for the first time?

We can offer years of living and lots of experience. In cabaret, it is important to know what your talents are and be secure within them, and that comes with age. After that, it's just a matter doing your homework and getting onstage and delivering. You can do it.

* * *

FINAL THOUGHTS

The future of cabaret is in the hands of all generations. Securing that future, however, is in the hands of voice teachers and vocal performance coaches across the country and around the globe. As mentioned in earlier parts of this book, to date there are only a handful of training programs specializing in cabaret performance. In universities, the golden age of music theater is—for the most part—passed over as an early vocal requirement for undergraduates. However, most singers who come from a music theater background do not fully understand the history of this music and the contribution it has made to the development of later vocal styles. Would there have been an Ethel Merman without Irving Berlin, a Mary Martin without Richard Rodgers and Oscar Hammerstein, or a Frank Sinatra or Ella Fitzgerald without Cole Porter? We may never know the answer to those questions. What we do know, however—what we do have—is a legacy of great music and a performance style that must be taught and performed on stages large and small. Welcome to the cabaret!

NOTES

1. *Merriam-Webster* defines these generation cohorts as follows: Generation Z refers to people born in the late 1990s and early 2000s; Generation Y, a.k.a. Millennials, refers to people born roughly between 1980 and the mid-1990s; Generation X refers to people born in the 1960s and 1970s; baby boomers are the people born in the United States following the end of World War II, usually considered to be the years 1946 to 1964; and the Silent Generation refers to people who were born between 1925 and 1945.

2. An interesting note: All four of these singers were completely unaware of what cabaret was until they started singing the repertoire.

GLOSSARY

action. An element of the lyric connection process in cabaret. An "action" is stated as a one-word verb (flattering, encouraging, etc.). It is what you are "doing" to the *who* you are talking or singing to, in order to overcome the *why* and get the *what* of the "five Ws." The action is not a state of being (happy, sad, etc.). It must be expressed as a verb. Also known in acting training as a "tactic."

American Songbook. See *Great American Songbook*.

American Songbook Association (ASA). The American Songbook Association is a nonprofit arts and education organization dedicated to stimulating and promoting public interest in the legacy of the Great American Songbook and the unique art form of cabaret. The ASA also publishes *Cabaret Scenes* magazine, the only print magazine in the world with a focus on the art form of cabaret.

American Standards. See *Great American Songbook*.

artist tribute show. A cabaret show that pays tribute to a specific vocalist and thus contains only songs associated with that artist.

ASA. American Songbook Association.

authentic training. Exercises designed to develop the range and color of the authentic voice. Exercises and repertoire place the singer's voice into the musical environment of the chosen genre and allow the singer's use of voice to grow out of their recognizable speaking voice.

Authentic training for singers is distinct from the training offered by most universities and many private voice studios, where the primary focus of vocal training is the development of the voice as its own entity or instrument, using guidelines first set forth in the seventeenth and eighteenth centuries. Authentic training is directed toward the professional development of singers within their chosen genre (most notably CCM). Exercises may be more word or consonant based; scales using different resonance strategies will be practiced on both "open" and "closed" vowels; and articulation (and disarticulation), communication, and expression may be addressed as "whole body" endeavors, integrating the use of voice with both movement and storytelling.

authentic voice. The voice with which one speaks. It is the sound by which one is immediately recognized. It is not a manufactured sound or a sound solely used within the genre of music being sung; for example, most opera singers don't speak the way they sing. The singing voice in cabaret must be recognizable as, and grow out of, the speaking voice. It can have substantial range into and above the passaggio. However, the authentic voice remains unmistakably recognizable as an outgrowth of the speaking voice.

baby boomer. The generation of people born in the United States following the end of World War II, usually considered to be the years 1946 to 1964, and the Silent Generation refers to people who were born between 1925 and 1945.

ballad. A slow (or downtempo) song.

Bistro Awards. Annual cabaret awards established by Bob Harrington in 1985 in his "Bistro Bits" column in the weekly trade newspaper *Backstage* under the longtime editorship of Sherry Eaker. Award recipients are selected by the Bistro Awards committee. The award is meant to recognize, encourage, and nurture cabaret and jazz artists and is the oldest award of its kind in the industry.

cabaret. Used to describe both a venue and a performance practice. As a venue, the word "cabaret" describes an intimate space where performer and audience are in close proximity. The cabaret club may also serve food or drink. As a performance practice, the word "cabaret" describes an intimate and personal connection to song lyric and an authentic communication with the audience.

café chantant. A café where singers or musicians entertain the patrons.

café concert. A café offering a program of light music.

CCM. Contemporary commercial music.

classical singer. A category of singer in cabaret. This singer maintains a classical vocal technique or tone (or both), which—depending on the song—can be inappropriate and can be detrimental to both the emotional connection and the distinguishability of the lyric. The classical singer often oversings the lyric and performs with a strong fourth wall convention. This singer can provide a wonderful entertainment but is not using an authentic cabaret performance technique.

composer/lyricist show. A cabaret show in which all of the songs are selected from the canon of a particular composer or lyricist. The patter often tells the story of the composer's or lyricist's life and can reveal interesting anecdotes about that individual.

concept. The kind of show you would like to create. Your concept answers the question, *What is it that you want to say, and how do you want to say it?* Once this is established, then you are ready to choose songs, write your patter, and tell your story.

contemporary commercial music (CCM). The term used for all styles of vocal music that exist outside the genre of Western classical singing. The term CCM was coined by Jeannette LoVetri as a more positive alternative to its pejorative predecessor, "nonclassical."

cover. (1) A term, mostly used in theater and opera, that refers to the understudy of a major role. (2) The cover of a song is the replication of another singer's performance. Covers of songs are distinct from singular interpretations, or reinterpretations, which are preferred in cabaret performance.

director. A person used/hired as the objective eye who coaches the performer and may oversee all aspects of a cabaret show. The director is part of a team that also includes the music director, technical director, and performer.

eleven o'clock number. In cabaret, a song that ties the theme together in a big showstopping way. It is usually programmed toward the end of a cabaret show, perhaps number eleven or twelve of a fourteen-song set.

Eugene O'Neill Theater Center Cabaret and Performance Conference. Known as the grandfather of all cabaret training programs, and affectionately referred to as "Camp Cabaret," the Cabaret Symposium (as it was originally called) was first conceived by Ellie Ellsworth and Betsy White, with Margaret Whiting serving as artistic director. The original program ran from 1989 to 2001, and was then reinstated as an annual summer program beginning in 2006 with John McDaniel as artistic director.

feel. The quality of song in terms of its style, tempo, and mood. On one hand, it identifies the genre or type of song being sung (e.g., up-tempo, ballad, Latin-feel, jazz, waltz, or pop), but "feel" can also refer to the emotional "color" of a song (e.g., dark, peppy, happy, blue, hopeful, funny).

five Ws. An element of the lyric connection process in cabaret. Within the lyric personalization, "five Ws" must be defined. These are as follows: *Who* are you talking to? *What* do you want from them? *Why* don't they give it to you right away? *Where* are you? *When* is this conversation taking place? The answers to these questions must be considered from *your* perspective, devoid of any other character's needs. The five Ws help to establish your own personal point of view within each song.

floor show. A series of acts presented at a nightclub or restaurant.

fourth wall. An imaginary wall that seemingly separates performers from their audience and prevents them from directly addressing any member of the audience. The opening of a modern stage proscenium is considered to be a "fourth wall." This convention is absolutely not used in a cabaret performance technique, where performers are expected to make contact with the audience individually and as a group.

gallows humor. Black comedy or dark humor.

Generation X. Refers to people born in the 1960s and 1970s.

Generation Y. Refers to people born roughly between 1980 and the mid-1990s. Also called *millennials*.

Generation Z. Refers to people born in the late 1990s and early 2000s.

Great American Songbook. The canon of the most important and influential American popular songs and jazz standards, mostly dating from the first half of the twentieth century. The Great American Songbook includes the most popular and enduring songs from the 1920s to the 1950s, most of which were created for Broadway theater, Hollywood musicals, and Tin Pan Alley. The Great American

Songbook contains works by George Gershwin, Cole Porter, Irving Berlin, Jerome Kern, Harold Arlen, Johnny Mercer, Richard Rodgers, and many others. These songs are sometimes called "American Standards."

International Cabaret Conference at Yale University. A training program for up-and-coming cabaret artists of all types, ages, and backgrounds that took place on Yale's historic campus. The conference ran from 2003 until 2013, the year that founder Erv Raible passed away.

intro. (1) The opening number of a cabaret show. (2) Sometimes refers to the opening sequence of patter, or scripted remarks. (3) The opening measures of a song before the vocal line begins; also frequently called the *verse*.

jazz singer. A category of singer in cabaret. This singer has a keen sense of the music, its rhythmic cadence and harmonic structure. He or she may also strive to "fit into the band" as one of the instruments and not necessarily be the "front sound." The use of voice can be gentle and is often quite musical. The lyric may or may not come forward as the primary element of the performance. Emotional connection is often tied to the musical arrangement and its use of suspended chords and blue notes, as well as other stylistic characteristics of jazz. Sometimes, there is even use of technical vocal pyrotechnics—scat singing, melismata, and so forth—that are not necessarily lyric driven. The jazz singer's performance is often mistaken for cabaret because of its intimate nature. Some "jazzys" can, and sometimes do, perform with a cabaret performance technique—at least on some songs. But for the most part, the musical arrangements in jazz lend themselves to improvisation of both melody and harmony, and possibly a complete stylistic retreatment of the song itself, which may also "overplay" the lyric. This singer can provide a wonderful entertainment but is not using an authentic cabaret performance technique.

Kabarett. The German version of cabaret that flourished in the opening decades of the twentieth century. Kabarett often featured political satire and gallows humor.

lounge lizard. A tongue-in-cheek pejorative term for someone who performs in a Las Vegas–type hotel lounge that "affects" the worst stereotypes of intimate venue performance, similar to the personality traits of Bill Murray's *Saturday Night Live* character "Nick" or Nora Dunn and Jan Hooks's SNL's "Sweeney Sisters." Today the term more commonly refers to an unctuous man who hangs around lounges trying to pick up rich women.

lounge singer. Someone who typically sings in a Las Vegas–type hotel lounge. Lounge singing is distinct from cabaret in that the lounge act is often considered background music, whereas the cabaret show demands both attention and sophistication from its audience. This singer can provide a wonderful entertainment but is not using an authentic cabaret performance technique.

lyric. The words of a song.

lyric connection. The ability to interpret and personalize the lyric of a song, devoid of artifice. Authentic lyric connection is perhaps, more than any other aspect of performance, the hallmark of a great cabaret artist.

Mabel Mercer Awards. Annual cabaret awards sponsored by the Mabel Mercer Foundation. The foundation bestows three awards per year: the Mabel Mercer Award for lifetime achievement; the Donald F. Smith Award, given to a singer who best exemplifies the qualities that founder Donald F. Smith admired most; and the Julie Wilson Award, recognizing an outstanding young performer who shows great potential for carrying on the tradition of legendary songstress Julie Wilson. In recent years, they have also given out awards to promising high school–age performers. The awards ceremony takes place at the New York Cabaret Convention at Jazz at Lincoln Center.

Mabel Mercer Foundation. An organization established in 1985 to preserve and advance both the classic popular song and the performance and education of American cabaret. The foundation provides outreach to students across the country via workshops, seminars, competitions, concert tickets, and scholarships. The organization also remains the central source of information for artists, presenters, promoters, and the general public about Mabel Mercer, the quintessential cabaret performer of the mid-nineteenth century, and the art form she exemplified. The foundation sponsors live performances throughout the year, by both new and established cabaret artists, including the annual New York Cabaret Convention at Jazz at Lincoln Center.

MAC. Manhattan Association of Cabarets.

MAC Awards. Annual cabaret awards given by the Manhattan Association of Cabarets.

Manhattan Association of Cabarets (MAC). An association founded in 1983 primarily as an organization for cabaret owners, managers, and booking agents. The organization opened its enrollment to performers in 1985. MAC's first president was Curt Davis who, upon his death, was succeeded by founding member Erv Raible, co-owner of several New York piano bars and cabarets. Other past presidents include Jamie deRoy, Michael Estwanick, Barry Levitt, Judy Barnett, Scott Barbarino, and Ricky Ritzel. The current president is Lennie Watts, who began his appointment in 2009. MAC strives to advance the education, art, and business of cabaret entertainment.

medium tempo. A medium-paced song that falls between a ballad and an up-tempo song.

melisma. A group of notes or tones sung on one syllable and often sung as embellishments. The plural form of melisma is melismata.

millennials. See *Generation Y.*

moonlighting. Holding down a second job in addition to a regular job.

music director. The instrumentalist/arranger who collaborates with the singer to create a show. The music director has overall responsibility for the music produced by the other musicians. Some music directors also create arrangements specific to the singer's interpretation of the song and can even serve as a musical/vocal coach during the rehearsal process. The music director is part of a team that also includes the director, the technical director, and the performer.

nightclub singer. A category of singer in cabaret. The distinction between a nightclub and a cabaret singer can be confusing in that they share repertoire and (very often) venues. In addition, the nightclub singer may employ a cabaret performance technique in one or more of their songs. However, the nightclub singer's main objective is far different from that of the true cabaret artist. In the words of cabaret critic Roy Sander, "The objective of a nightclub [singer] is to entertain the audience. Not necessarily to move them, to enlighten them, or to make them think. There is generally less attention paid to lyric connection in favor of a presentational approach. Arrangements, even for ballads, may be larger and slicker," requiring multiple instruments. While this kind of singing and performance style can produce a wonderful show, it doesn't necessarily require the attention or sophistication of the listener.

objective. In lyric connection, identifies what the storyteller wants or desires.

obstacle. In lyric connection, the challenge that the storyteller must overcome to satisfy their wants or desires.

outro. (1) The closing number of a cabaret show. (2) Sometimes refers to the closing sequence of patter, or scripted remarks. (3) The closing measures of a song, after the vocal line ends.

oversinging. Occurs when the singing voice, or the technique of singing, draws attention to itself as opposed to serving the lyric. Oversinging the lyric should always be avoided in cabaret.

paid gig contract. Contractual agreement in which the club or venue pays the performer a flat fee. In this scenario, at any level, it is the responsibility of the headlining artist to pay the music director and band out of the total fee received.

pansy show. A show whose star projects a weak or effeminate (homosexual) man or boy. This term is dated and is now considered to be offensive.

patter. The script of a cabaret show, usually written by the performer with input from his or her director.

percentage split contract. A contractual agreement in which the singer takes a certain percentage of the show's intake. This "split" can range from 20 to 40 percent of the cover charge taken by the club. For example, a $1,000 night (a $20 cover charge with fifty audience members) with a 60/40 percentage split would mean that 60 percent ($600) would go to the artist and 40 percent ($400) would go to the club. The "percentage split" contract is a relatively recent development in the world of cabaret.

personal story show. In cabaret, a show that places the focus on the performer and his or her life. In a personal story show, performers might choose to talk about how (or why) they became a singer or reveal personal struggles that they overcame. In this type of show the personal story should also have a universal appeal or message.

pop singer. In cabaret, a category of singer who sings contemporary pop/rock songs with a "higher, louder, longer" vocal approach. Range and decibel are often stretched to the singer's limit, and notes are held "straighter" with minimal or no perceived use of vibrato. Lyric connection is almost always oversung and often (quite literally) "beat" to death with a constant rhythm that does not allow for variance of thought or emotion. Rather than observing a fourth wall, the pop singer conversely runs to the other extreme and performs as if he or she were singing in a giant stadium with little regard for the size of the audience, thereby obliterating any sense of intimacy. The pop singer is a relatively new species of singer in the world of cabaret, an outgrowth of not only the popularity of modern music but also Broadway's recent acceptance of and reliance on this vocal style. This singer can provide a wonderful entertainment but is not using an authentic cabaret performance technique.

Prohibition. A nationwide constitutional ban on the production, importation, transportation, and sale of alcoholic beverages that was in effect in the United States from 1920 to 1933. Prohibition inspired the emergence of speakeasies, as well as the resurgence of Parisian cabaret.

protest song. A song usually written and performed to express disapproval.

revue. A production consisting typically of brief, loosely connected, and often satirical skits, songs, and dances.

saloon show. (1) A set of twelve to fourteen songs, not connected by theme or patter, but whose individual interpretation is so authentic and compelling that each one stands on its own, which in and of itself becomes the connecting theme of the performance. (2) A show that happens in a bar, tavern, or taproom that is first and foremost a place to drink as opposed to a legitimate cabaret venue.

saloon singer. (1) A singer who specializes in the saloon show format. Sylvia Syms preferred to be thought of as a saloon singer because she treated everything she sang as an authentic personal communication; in her words, "When you perform it's a one-to-one love affair with the people out there. That's how it has to be." Frank Sinatra was also referred to as one of the great saloon singers of his era. (2) Sometimes used to a describe a singer who performs in a nightclub, bar, or an establishment where alcohol is served. See *saloon show*.

showcard. A physical postcard that is distributed to advertise a show.

singer guarantee contract. A contractual agreement in which the singer guarantees the club a certain amount of patronage or a minimum dollar value. For example, a venue may offer a "prix fixe" dinner for a certain amount (e.g., $60) as well as a cover charge (e.g., $40) for the show, which goes to the artist. In this scenario the club requires the artist to guarantee a certain number of patrons at the full price of $100. This is a new development in the world of cabaret contracts, mostly occurring in the higher-end supper clubs.

singsong. A verse with marked and regular rhythm and rhyme. Singsong also refers to a voice delivery that is marked by a narrow range or monotonous pattern of pitch.

speakeasy. A place where alcoholic beverages are illegally sold. Speakeasies were primarily active during the prohibition era.

St. Louis Cabaret Conference. Produced by the nonprofit organization called the Cabaret Project of St. Louis, the conference spans nine days and offers three distinct learning tracks: a five-day introductory track, a seven-day "next step" track, and a nine-day professional track featuring small class sizes and a showcase evening. Tim Schall is the artistic director and producer as well as a faculty member.

subtext. An element of lyric connection. Refers to the thoughts the singer is thinking while he or she is singing the lyric. Subtext is additional information that is not exactly what the lyric is stating. For example, a simple phrase like "thank you" can be said with tears in one's eyes as a genuine expression of love and gratitude or be muttered under one's breath, sarcastically, to dismiss the person or change the subject. Subtext, therefore, colors the spoken or sung text with emotion and relevance. Short for "subconscious text."

supper club. Any live music club that operates as a fully functioning restaurant (versus just bar or snack food being offered) and that offers the experience of having a formal dinner before or during the show. Supper clubs are typically more intimate and more sophisticated than nightclubs.

tag. The practice of repeating the ultimate or penultimate phrase (or part of the phrase) of music, sometimes with a key change, for emphasis of the lyric or musical ending. A tag repeats the phrase once, whereas a triple tag repeats the phrase three times.

team. In cabaret, this refers to the director and music director but can also include the band members and, depending on how involved he or she is, the technical director.

theater singer. In cabaret, a category of singer who sings primarily with a theatrical sensibility and therefore a strong sense of the fourth wall. He or she does not sing *to* the audience but rather *at* the audience and always as the character of the show from which the song originates. This type of singer may be a strong actor, but only insofar as the portrayal of the character within the show. The theater singer does not reveal his or her authentic self. This singer can provide a wonderful entertainment but is not using an authentic cabaret performance technique.

theme show. A type of show centered on a specific topic. This can include such topics as one's job, love life, marriage, politics, or a personal story.

thirty-two-bar song form. The standard American popular song form used during the golden era of song (from approximately 1926 to 1950). The basic structure of thirty-two-bar song form is simple: AABA, with eight bars of music devoted to each section. While the lyric of a thirty-two-bar song usually has four distinct lines, the third line (sung to the "B" music) often reveals a different mood, impregnating the returning "A" section of the final eight bars with greater wisdom or meaning. Songs cast in thirty-two-bar song form (and variants of it) comprised the majority of standards in the music theater and jazz repertories during the 1920s, 1930s, and 1940s. Most of the songs from Tin Pan Alley and the Great American Songbook are in thirty-two-bar song form. Jazz, cabaret, and music theater specialists still perform this repertoire with regularity, and many contemporary composers in these genres continue to be influenced by this song form.

Tin Pan Alley. The nickname commonly given to the American sheet music industry of the early twentieth century. The Tin Pan Alley era spanned from the 1880s through the 1950s, when the phonograph and LP records finally replaced live music at the piano as the principal form of home entertainment. "Tin Pan Alley" can also be used to describe the style of songs that came out of the industry. A Tin Pan

Alley song is formulaic, usually in thirty-two-bar song form with an introductory verse. The later years of Tin Pan Alley are closely related to the Great American Songbook.

trio. Three instrumentalists who play together as a group or who accompany a singer in a cabaret show; in the latter case, the instruments are most typically piano, bass, and percussion.

triple tag. See *tag*.

up-tempo. A fast song.

vaudeville. A type of stage entertainment consisting of many short, unrelated, and unconnected presentations by performers displaying a wide array of skills, most of which were unrelated to music. While variety shows were taking place in many parts of the United States, vaudeville proper is usually thought of as a New York City genre that peaked during the period between 1880 and 1920. Especially the province of various immigrant communities, specific types of vaudeville are often clarified with the addition of a preceding "ethnic" adjective: Jewish vaudeville, Italian vaudeville, Irish vaudeville, and so forth. In addition to songs, featured entertainments also included instrumental numbers, comic routines, magic tricks, lectures, monologues, dancing, acrobatic feats, and circus-like animal tricks. Almost any creative stage presentation was fair game and included under the genre.

verse. An introduction to a song. Verses often precede the thirty-two-bar songs found in the Great American Songbook. Sometimes called an "intro" in cabaret culture. In more contemporary songs, the term is also used to distinguish the nonrepeating stanzas of a song from the chorus or refrain.

Yiddish cabaret. A specific theater-type club/venue where all performances are performed in Yiddish with predominately Jewish humor and themes.

INDEX

MAC resources for, 267, 300; open mic performances role in, 267–68; PR professionals help in, 274–78; scheduling factors for, in publications, 277; showcards design and considerations for, 261–68, *262, 263, 264, 265*; social media role in, 260, 261, 270–73, 278

Donald F. Smith Award, 227, 340, 412

donations, 258

Don't Tell Mama, xxxiv, 3, 65; Mason and LaMott opening night show at, *335*, 335–37; stars beginning at, 67–69, 343

Douglas, Natalie: Birdland tribute shows by, 166, 340; on business of cabaret, 345–46; cabaret defined by, 343–44; cabaret introduction for, 342–43; career and accolades for, 340–41; on conversation and spontaneity with audience, 343–44; early musical inspirations for, 341–42; on Great American Songbook, racial diversity in, 350–52; on Great American Songbook criteria, 355–56; on historical context of lyrics, 352–53; on lyrical depth, 355–56; lyric personalization approach of, 347–48; master class offerings and approach of, 341, 354; on music theater contrasted with cabaret, 347–48; on song interpretation, 348; vocal and performance training offerings and approach of, 341, 349–51, *350*, 353–54; on vocal health tips, 349; vocal training experience for, 347; vocal warm-ups and cooldowns for, 348–49; on voice and lyric connection balance, 344; on voice exercises, 349

Drescher, Fran, 68, 92

drugs, 155–56

Duke Ellington Center for the Arts (DECFA), 269, 280, 283

Duplex Cabaret Room, 3, 16, 24–25, *25*, 33, 330

eating disorders, 141

Ebb, Fred, xxxvii, 38, 43n2

economics: evolution of cabaret, 33–34, 35, 301, 344–45; offsetting costs and, 258. *See also* budget

educational and outreach programs: AIDS, 300, 338–39, 339n1; at festivals, 269; in future of cabaret, role of, 359, 405; Great American Songbook, 77, 81, 82–83, 286, 291, 393; MAC, 297, 299–300, 341; Oak Room, 31–32; options, 359; Singnasium, 337, 377–78, 380. *See also* master classes and workshops; vocal and performance training

Eighty-Eights, 3, 29, 32–33

Eleven Executioners (Elf Scharfrichter), 12

eleven o'clock number: definition of, 169, 409; music theater approach to, 49

Elf Scharfrichter (Eleven Executioners), 12

Ellington, Duke, 286, 352; as Great American Songbook notable, 281–82, 283, 351; interpretations of, 281–82; music categories resistance from, 282. *See also* Duke Ellington Center for the Arts

Ellington, Mercedes, 283

Ellsworth, Ellie, 380, 382, 410

encores, 169–70

epiglottis, 130

equalization (EQ): about, 198; graphic, 201, *201*; for live performance, 200; opinions on use of, 201; parametric, 198, *199*, 200, *200*; shelf, 198, *199*

ABOUT THE AUTHORS AND CONTRIBUTORS

David Sabella is internationally recognized as a master teacher in music theater and contemporary commercial music voice techniques. He served as a two-term president of the New York Singing Teachers' Association (NYSTA) and as an executive director of the Broadway Theatre Project. He has also served on the music theater voice faculties at Montclair State University and Fordham University, as well as NYU's Tisch School of the Arts, CAP21 Studio, the New School's Mannes Prep precollege program, Purchase College, and SUNY at New Paltz. Additionally, Sabella has been a faculty member and workshop presenter at the Voice Foundation's annual symposium and has conducted master classes, faculty training workshops, and music theater pedagogy seminars throughout the contiguous United States, Alaska, and South America. Sabella is a member of the National Association of Teachers of Singing (NATS) and presented a master class titled "Beyond Belt: Acoustics and Mechanics of the Contemporary Commercial Belt" at the 2012 NATS National Conference in Orlando. He has been awarded NYSTA's Distinguished Voice Professional Certificate and is known as a singing voice specialist, working in tandem with several New York physicians and speech-language pathologists who specialize in care of the professional voice. Sabella was featured in *So You Want to Sing CCM* as one of twelve international pedagogues to have put forth a modern vocal technique for teaching contemporary commercial music. Sabella is the owner and editor in chief of CabaretHotspot.com, an online magazine and educational resource dedicated to the art and craft of cabaret and small-venue performance. He is also a reviewer for BistroAwards.com.

As a performer, Sabella has enjoyed a long and varied career. In 1996 he originated the starring role of "Mary Sunshine" in the 1996 revival of *Chicago* with Bebe Neuwirth, Ann Reinking, and Joel Grey. Sabella also worked on the developmental workshops of Kander and Ebb's last collaboration, *The Visit* (with Angela Lansbury and Chita Rivera), for which John Kander wrote the role of Luis Perch specifically for him. Off-Broadway, Sabella has performed leading roles in many productions including *The Phillie Trilogy* (Winner—Outstanding Lead Actor in a Play, Fresh Fruit Festival 2017); *Jules* (on the life of Julian Eltinge); *Kiss and Make Up* (New York International Fringe Festival); *The Green Room* (HBO Productions); *Hexed in the City, Foxy, Watch Your Step, So Long 174th Street* (Musicals Tonight!), and *O'Henry's Lovers* (New York Musical Theater Festival). As a voiceover artist, Sabella has worked on several network television cartoon series, including *Peter Pan and the Pirates* for FOX and *Teacher's Pet* for Disney.

As a countertenor in classical music, Sabella was named a winner in several prestigious competitions, including the Luciano Pavarotti International Voice Competition and the New York Oratorio Society Competition at Carnegie Hall. He was also named a finalist in the Metropolitan Opera Eastern Regional Auditions. He has appeared in many operas across the United States and Europe, including the title role of *Giulio Cesare* (Virginia Opera, available on Koch International Label), *L'incoronazione di Poppea* (Utah Opera), and *Die Fledermaus* (Lincoln Center). He has appeared numerous times at both Carnegie Hall and Lincoln Center as a principal soloist in such works as Bach's *Mass in B Minor*, Handel's *Messiah*, and Peter Schickele's comical *Three Bargain-Counter Tenors*. He has toured internationally with the now legendary La Gran Scena Opera Company. ♪

Sue Matsuki is the recipient of the first Julie Wilson Award, given by the Mabel Mercer Foundation in 2004, and was personally chosen to receive this award by Julie Wilson herself. She is also a three-time MAC Award winner: 2002 for Female Jazz/Pop/R&B Vocalist; 2006 for Jazz

Duo/Special Productions for *Ten Years in the Making* with her music director Gregory Toroian; and 2008 for Specialty Song with "One Stop Shopping" (Matsuki/Toroian/Page). Additional MAC nominations include a 2002 nomination for Best Female Recording for *A New Take*; a 2004 nomination for Duo/Group (with Marcus Simeone); nominations in 2007 and 2010 for Female Vocalist; and in 2008, 2011, and 2012 for Duo/Group (with Edd Clark).

Matsuki is a thirty-five-year veteran cabaret/jazz singer and has played in many legendary jazz clubs, including the Village Gate, Birdland, the Iridium, and Sweet Rhythm. She has also performed in virtually every New York City cabaret room, including Feinstein's/54 Below, Feinstein's at the Regency, Birdland Theater, the Algonquin, the Metropolitan Room, the Laurie Beechman Theatre, Town Hall, Arci's Place, Don't Tell Mama, Eighty Eight's, Judy's, Danny's, Jan Wallman's, the Duplex, the Triad, Caroline's Comedy Club, Helen's Hideaway Room, and Broadway Baby. In addition to these prominent clubs, Matsuki has toured nationally and appeared in numerous jazz and cabaret clubs throughout the contiguous United States and Alaska. Matsuki has recorded two albums: *A New Take* and *Sue and Edd's Fabulous Christmas* (with Edd Clark). She can also be heard on Christine Lavin's album *Christmas Angel* and on *A New York Holiday*.

Matsuki is a managing coeditor, reviewer, and a columnist ("Sue's Views") for CabaretHotspot.com, an online entertainment and educational resource for cabaret and small-venue performance. She has also written for Cabaret Hotline Online and NiteLife Exchange. Matsuki is highly regarded as a teacher of cabaret and has presented workshops and seminars for the Manhattan Association of Cabarets (MAC), the Ridgefield Theater Barn, the University of Connecticut, and the Canadian School of Performing Arts. She has served on the board of directors for both MAC and the Salon. She is honored to have been asked to coauthor *So You Want to Sing Cabaret.* ♪

* * *

Matthew Edwards is associate professor of voice and voice pedagogy at Shenandoah Conservatory and artistic director of the CCM Voice Pedagogy Institute. His current and former students have performed on and off-Broadway as well as on national and international tours and on major motion picture soundtracks and have appeared on Billboard music charts. Edwards is the author of *So You Want to Sing Rock 'n' Roll* and has contributed chapters to *Manual of Singing Voice Rehabilitation, The Vocal Athlete, Get the Callback,* and *A Dictionary for the Modern Singer.* He has authored articles for the *Journal of Singing,* the *Journal of Voice, American Music Teacher, VOICEPrints,* and *Southern Theatre.* Edwards regularly presents workshops on functional training for the CCM singer at conferences and universities throughout the United States. ♪

Wendy LeBorgne is a voice pathologist, speaker, author, and master class clinician. She actively presents nationally and internationally on the professional voice and is the clinical director of two successful private practice voice centers: the ProVoice Center in Cincinnati and BBIVAR in Dayton. LeBorgne holds an adjunct professorship at University of Cincinnati College Conservatory of Music as a voice consultant, where she also teaches voice pedagogy and wellness courses. She completed a BFA in musical theater from Shenandoah Conservatory and her graduate and doctoral degrees from the University of Cincinnati. Original peer-reviewed research has been published in multiple journals, and she is a contributing author to several voice textbooks. Most recently, she coauthored *The Vocal Athlete* textbook and workbook with Marci Rosenberg. Her patients and private students can currently be found on radio, television, film, cruise ships, Broadway, off-Broadway, national tours, commercial music tours, and opera stages around the world. ♪

Scott McCoy is a noted author, singer, conductor, and pianist with extensive performance experience in concert and opera. He is professor of voice and pedagogy, director of the Swank Voice Laboratory, and director of the interdisciplinary program in singing health at Ohio State University. His voice science and pedagogy textbook, *Your Voice: An Inside View,* is used extensively by colleges and universities throughout the United States and abroad. McCoy is the associate editor of the *Journal of Singing* for voice pedagogy and is a past president of NATS. He also served NATS as vice president for workshops, program chair for the 2006 and 2008 national conferences, chair of the voice science advisory committee, and as a master teacher for the intern program. Deeply committed to teacher education, McCoy is a founding faculty member in the NYSTA Professional Development Program (PDP), teaching classes in voice anatomy, physiology, acoustics, and voice analysis. He is a member of the distinguished American Academy of Teachers of Singing (AATS). ♪

Erv Raible was the cofounder and first president of the Manhattan Association of Cabarets (MAC), the first cabaret trade organization of its kind. He was also the executive director of Cabaret and Concert Artists International and was the executive/artistic director of the International Cabaret Conference at Yale University from 2003 to 2013. Raible was a New York–based cabaret coach, director, publicist, consultant, and talent representative. In a career that spanned more than forty years, Raible produced and directed cabaret internationally and presented more than four thousand artists, many of whom many went on to achieve recognition and stardom on Broadway and television. Over the course of his career, he received numerous awards as a director and was an avid historian and beloved teacher within the genre of cabaret.

Roy Sander is the cabaret industry's most ardent fan and esteemed critic. A fixture on the New York cabaret scene—and known simply as the "Chairman of the Board"—he is one of the industry's most prolific writers, having penned reviews, articles, and columns on the craft of cabaret for more than forty years. His most notable position was an eleven-year stint at *Backstage*, covering cabarets/clubs as well as Broadway and off-Broadway theater through reviews, commentary, and articles. Sander has reviewed cabaret and theater via the *New York Theater Review* on PBS, WLIM radio, and Citysearch.com, during which time he was a voting member of the Drama Desk. He has written columns of advice and commentary for the Manhattan Association of Cabarets (MAC) and has participated in numerous panel discussions on various aspects of cabaret performance and the cabaret scene. Sander was chairman of the judges for the MetroStar Talent Challenge at the Metropolitan Room during the ten years of the contest's existence. He has coached a number of cabaret performers privately, and he has twice appeared as a guest instructor at the London School of Musical Theatre.

He has received two Bistro Awards in recognition of his contributions to cabaret. Sander is currently chairman of the advisory board of MAC and review editor of BistroAwards.com, where he writes reviews and commentary, serves as a member of the awards committee, and is associate producer of the annual awards ceremony.